Also by Deepak Nayyar
INDIA'S EXPORTS AND EXPORT POLICIES IN THE 1960s

ECONOMIC RELATIONS BETWEEN SOCIALIST COUNTRIES AND THE THIRD WORLD

Edited by

DEEPAK NAYYAR

University of Sussex

LANDMARK STUDIES
Allanheld, Osmun/Universe Books
Montclair and New York

ALLANHELD, OSMUN AND CO. PUBLISHERS, INC.
Montclair, New Jersey

First Published in England in 1977 by
THE MACMILLAN PRESS LTD

Published in the United States of America in 1978
by Allanheld, Osmun and Co., 19 Brunswick Road,
Montclair, N.J. 07042, and by Universe Books,
381 Park Avenue South, New York, N.Y. 10016
Distribution: Universe Books

Library of Congress Cataloging in Publication Data
Economic relations between socialist countries and the
    Third World.
    "LandMark Studies."
    1. Underdeveloped areas — Foreign economic
relations — Case studies.   2. Communist countries —
Foreign economic relations — Case studies.   I. Nayyar, Deepak.
HF1413.E25   338.91'172'401717   77-84409
ISBN 0-87663-824-8

Printed in Great Britain

To
P.G., A.M. and P.P.S.

Contents

Preface

For many years, research scholars interested in problems of development and underdevelopment have regarded it as fashionable to study the interaction between rich and poor countries in the world economy. At the same time, an increasing number of studies in international economics have sought to examine how the communist countries relate themselves to the world capitalist system. Surprising as it may seem, economists have paid scant attention to the relationship between the rich communist countries and the poor nations of the world. It is hoped that the present book, which brings together a collection of essays around this theme, will fill a gap in the literature.

The first essay, by Deepak Nayyar, serves as an introduction to the volume. It begins by outlining the dimensions of the relationship, as reflected in trade turnover and aid flows, between socialist countries and the Third World. It goes on to examine the implications of these economic ties for the poor countries, analyses the conditions under which they might derive significant benefits from them, and discusses the interest of the communist countries in establishing such widespread economic interaction with the underdeveloped capitalist world. Given the wide range of countries and the diversity of their experience, the paper does not even attempt to draw together the conclusions of the other essays. Instead, it seeks to explore the principal issues arising from economic relations between the socialist bloc and the LDCs, as well as identifying some of the themes that emerge from the book.

Manfred Bienefeld's paper on Tanzania starts with the premise that trade does not necessarily benefit all trading partners and that, in the real world, gains from trade are often unequally distributed. In this situation, economic relations with the socialist countries present a unique opportunity if trade ceases to be a mere exchange of commodities and becomes an element of planned economic integration. He argues that the scope for such gains is limited by the fact that Tanzania is essentially a capitalist economy, leading to the conclusion that Tanzania's trade with the socialist countries, except for trade with China, is merely an exchange of commodities. Although this exchange is on terms which are as good as, and sometimes better than those obtained from the capitalist world, trade with the European socialist countries has not given rise to any *special* gains for Tanzania.

On the continent of Africa, the socialist countries have had the closest ties with Egypt. Robert Mabro outlines the development of Egypt's economic relations with the USSR and Eastern Europe, and places it in its historical context. He finds that economic ideology within Egypt has not played a significant role, and that political factors arising out of a desire to assert national independence, the quest for national security and changes in the international balance of power were the most important determinants of the relationship. In this environment, close links with the socialist countries became an integral part of Egypt's international economic relations. Throughout the 1950s and 1960s, the countries of the socialist bloc were Egypt's major trading partners as well as the most important source of economic assistance and military supplies. All these transactions were conducted through bilateral agreements. Robert Mabro shows that, under such agreements, export and import prices related to world prices, often with a premium in favour of Egypt. In addition, he argues that trade was linked to generous credit facilities which were of enormous advantage to Egypt. Although this bilateral relationship had its problems, he points out that Egypt did not always have the option of engaging in multilateral trade or receiving aid from diverse sources. Given the limited nature of the options available, the author concludes that Egypt did well out of the relationship.

Although Egypt and Tanzania have received much of the attention in the literature on the subject, other countries in Africa have also had economic ties with the socialist world. In Chapter 4, Christopher Stevens examines the interesting case of West Africa. He examines the USSR's economic relations with Ghana and Nigeria during the period 1960–72. Ghana was one of the first black African states to attempt an economic and political entente with the USSR, but its close neighbour, Nigeria, was much more reserved about establishing relations with the communist bloc. Between them, these two countries illustrate the problems and possibilities of Soviet aid and trade. A study of their experience suggests that there is a threshold to successful economic collaboration with the USSR: a certain commitment is required on both sides before sporadic commercial contacts mature into a fuller relationship. The author finds that trade with the USSR offered distinct possibilities of benefit to West Africa, but that Soviet aid was problematic.

The scene then moves across to Asia. In Chapter 5, Deepak Nayyar tries to evaluate the gains that accrued to India from its trade with the socialist countries. Unlike the case of Tanzania, there was a genuine element of bilateralism in this relationship. Economic interaction occurred in a framework of trade agreements, the distinct feature of which was that payments for all transactions were made in rupees. Bilateral rupee trade, which increased most rapidly after 1960, not only provided India with imports that were essential for its development programme, but was also responsible for 40 per cent of the growth in India's total exports during the period under review. What is more, nearly 80 per cent of the goods sold to the socialist countries were a *net* addition to India's exports, insofar as it would have been rather difficult to sell them elsewhere. Given that the terms of trade under bilateral agreements were, on balance, probably favourable to India, the conclusion is that India derived substantial benefits from its trade with the socialist world.

Pramit Chaudhuri's essay on East European aid to India completes the picture, and is also a useful case study of the economic and technical assistance offered by the socialist countries to the Third World. It is shown that the European socialist countries were a significant, though not dominant, source of aid to India. The author finds that easy generalisations about the terms of Eastern bloc aid to India, in comparison with aid from other sources, are not possible. Among other things, this is because aid is only a part of the wider economic relationship with the socialist countries. The conclusion arrived at is that the main usefulness of the East European countries as a source of aid has been in their willingness to give aid for public sector projects and in improving India's bargaining power *vis-à-vis* other donors.

The political element in the relationship between socialist countries and the Third World is brought out most clearly by Akbar Noman's paper on Pakistan. He distinguishes four phases in the development of Pakistan's economic relations with the socialist bloc; in each, trade and aid followed the swings of the political pendulum. Strained political relations led to a sharp contraction in trade and vice-versa. Interestingly enough, these changes had little to do with internal political developments in Pakistan. They were much more the product of developments on the international political scene – in particular, on the Indian sub-continent. Nevertheless, there was a marked expansion in trade during the 1960s, largely through the mechanism of bilateral agreements. Noman finds that Pakistani exports to the socialist countries diversified considerably less than exports to the rest of the world, but the terms of trade were more favourable. Pakistan also received aid from the USSR, Eastern Europe and China on quite favourable terms.

The remaining essays in the volume depart from the country-study approach. Chapter 8 explores various aspects of the relationship between the Soviet Union and the Third World countries in the sphere of the oil industry. Biplab Dasgupta begins with an historical account of the growth of the Soviet oil industry and its ownership pattern, leading up to a discussion of the 'Soviet oil export offensive' in the 1960s. It is argued that the entry of Soviet oil into the world market had extremely important implications for the less developed countries. Its initial impact was to undermine the world parity pricing system and thereby weaken the grip of the seven multinational corporations that dominated the international oil industry from exploration through refining and transport to marketing. This improved the bargaining position of the poor oil-consuming countries *vis-à-vis* the major oil companies. Paradoxically enough, it also strengthened the hand of the oil-producing countries in the Middle East, and was one of the important factors responsible for the emergence of OPEC as a powerful force in the political economy of world oil.

In the last chapter, Suzanne Paine examines China's economic relations with the Third World. As a first step, the essay reviews the evidence on the magnitude, direction, composition and terms of Chinese trade with the non-socialist LDCs and surveys the corresponding evidence on Chinese aid. The principles according to which the Chinese claim to manage their policies *vis-à-vis* the African, Asian and Latin American countries are compared with actual experience. But the author also formulates alternative criteria for an evaluation of Chinese policies and of their impact on LDCs. It is argued that Chinese aid compares most favourably with aid from other sources — both Western capitalist countries and the socialist countries of Eastern Europe — as does the aid-cum-trade package. Trade *per se* with the non-socialist LDCs, however, is shown to be more problematic. While it might have been qualitatively different from trade with the Western world, it differed only in degree from trade with the Soviet Union and Eastern Europe.

The issues outlined here, and discussed in the following pages, are obviously crucial. However, there are many questions that remain unanswered. For instance, in what manner, and to what extent, did the experience of the less developed socialist countries differ from that of the countries discussed in the book? Is a new international division of labour possible when, for all practical purposes, the poor countries are an integral part of the world capitalist economy? If not, what is the future of the relationship between the socialist countries and the Third World? Is it likely to be governed largely by developments on the international political scene? Answers to these questions can only emerge from further research.

Some of the essays in this book were first published as part of a special issue of *World Development,* Vol. 3 No. 5, May 1975. Of these, Chapters 5 and 8 are reprinted in unchanged form, whereas Chapters 2, 3, 6 and 7 are revised versions of the earlier papers. Chapters 1, 4 and 9 have been written specially for this volume. I am grateful to all the contributors for their co-operation in the preparation of the manuscript. I would, in particular, like to thank the publishers of *World Development,* Pergamon Press, for release of the copyright and for their kind permission to use material from the journal.

February 1977   DEEPAK NAYYAR

Notes on Contributors

MANFRED BIENEFELD is a Fellow at the Institute of Development Studies, Sussex. He is the author of *Working Hours in British Industry: An Economic History* (Weidenfeld & Nicolson, 1972). He has also written a number of papers in the development context concerning urbanisation, wages, employment, trades unions and capital accumulation. He has a special interest in Tanzania where he spent four years working at the University of Dar es Salaam.

PRAMIT CHAUDHURI is Reader in Economics at the University of Sussex. He has edited a book of *Readings in Indian Agricultural Development* and is part-author of *Aspects of Indian Economic Development* (George Allen & Unwin, 1972). He has recently completed a book on *The Indian Economy: Development and Poverty.*

BIPLAB DASGUPTA is a Fellow at the Institute of Development Studies, Sussex. He is the author of *Oil Industry in India: Some Economic Aspects* (Frank Cass, 1971) and co-author of *Patterns and Trends in Indian Politics* (Allied Publishers, 1976). He has also edited a book on *Village Studies in the Third World.* His current research interests include agricultural and rural development.

ROBERT MABRO is Senior Research Officer in Economics of the Middle East and Fellow of St Antony's College, Oxford. He has a special research interest in Egypt where he worked as a civil engineer for some years. He is the author of *The Egyptian Economy: 1952–1972* (Oxford University Press, 1974) and co-author of *Industrialisation in Egypt* (Oxford University Press, 1976).

DEEPAK NAYYAR is Lecturer in Economics at the University of Sussex. He is the author of *India's Exports and Export Policies in the 1960s* (Cambridge University Press, 1976). His present research interests include the international aspects of development and underdevelopment. He has written some papers on issues related to this subject.

AKBAR NOMAN is a Staff Economist at the International Monetary Fund, Washington. Much of his research has been on problems of economic development, with special reference to Pakistan.

SUZANNE PAINE is a Fellow of Clare College and Lecturer in the Faculty of Economics at Cambridge. Her previous work includes publications on development in Japan and the Middle East and a book on *Exporting Workers:*

the Turkish Case (Cambridge University Press, 1974). Since she visited China in 1973, she has been working mainly on aspects of development in Asian economies, especially China and India.

CHRISTOPHER STEVENS is a Research Officer at the Overseas Development Institute, London. He is the author of *The Soviet Union and Black Africa* (Macmillan, 1976) and several articles on economic and political relations between the USSR and Africa. In the past, he has worked as an economist in Botswana and as a tutor at the University of Ghana.

1 Economic Relations Between Socialist Countries and the Third World: An Introduction

DEEPAK NAYYAR

The literature on development economics abounds with studies of the relations between rich and poor countries. More often than not, however, these studies focus attention on the western capitalist countries and their economic relations with the less developed nations of the world. In fact, the most controversial issues raised by economists, when considering the international aspects of development and underdevelopment, have been discussed in this context. These issues range from questions about aid, private foreign investment and transfer of technology to debates about the terms of trade between countries. All such problem areas have been subjected to a considerable amount of research. Strangely enough, very little attention has been directed towards examining the relationship between the rich communist countries and the poorer nations, which for want of a better phrase, I shall refer to as the Third World.

In recent years, the economic ties between the socialist countries and the Third World have become quite strong. Indeed, in the world of today, they represent an important part of the development strategy for several poor countries. It is hardly surprising that the developed socialist countries of Eastern Europe, including the USSR, should have attempted to assist the less developed socialist countries such as Cuba, Mongolia, North Korea and North Vietnam. Much less predictable is that the socialist countries have sought to assist the development process in the poor capitalist countries, through economic and technical assistance. But that is not all. The past two decades have also witnessed a phenomenal growth in trade between the socialist bloc – USSR and Eastern Europe – on the one hand, and the less developed capitalist countries on the other.[1] This occurrence is rather interesting for two reasons. In the first place, such trade is one of the most dynamic components of world commerce. Secondly, and in my view more important, it suggests a strengthening of economic ties between two sets of countries with entirely different political and economic systems. It would clearly be worthwhile to examine the nature of this relationship, and its implications for the poor countries. Yet, in terms of research this is a relatively unexplored area. The economic aspects of relations between the socialist countries and these less developed capitalist economies is, therefore, the theme of this essay.

1

As a starting point, it is necessary to outline the dimensions of the relationship. The first section, which is devoted to that task, sets out the orders of magnitude as well as the trends in trade and aid. Section II examines the implications of these economic ties for the poor countries and attempts to determine the conditions under which they might derive significant benefits. The interest of the socialist countries, in establishing such widespread economic interaction with the underdeveloped capitalist world, is explored in section III. The final section of the chapter seeks to provide an overall evaluation and comment upon the political economy of the relationship.

I. Dimensions of the Relationship

Over the last fifteen years, the European socialist countries have established economic relations with a very large number of countries in the Third World. A significant proportion of these ties has been developed since the late 1950s, when several newly independent nations emerged from the colonial era in Asia and Africa. There is no doubt that the relationship between the two groups of countries strengthened considerably in subsequent years. That is borne out by available evidence.

Table 1.1 outlines the trends in trade between the European socialist countries and the less developed capitalist countries over the past two decades. Trade expansion was indeed remarkable. From 1952 until 1968, the turnover of trade virtually doubled every four years. The growth did slow down thereafter but, in absolute terms, the increase was substantial. Given the orders of magnitude, it is not surprising that this trade accounted for an increasing share of the total trade for both groups of countries. Between 1960 and 1970, the share of the developing countries in Soviet and East European exports rose from 8·1 per cent to 14·8 per cent while in imports it increased from 8·8 to 11·1 per cent.[2] Over the same period, the share of the socialist countries in exports of the developing world increased from 4 to 5·7 per cent while their share in imports rose from 3·6 to 7·8 per cent.[3] Available evidence suggests that such trade expansion has not continued in the last few years, even though relative shares have been maintained at the levels attained in 1970.[4]

It is interesting that East European trade with the less developed socialist countries increased at a much slower rate than trade with the less developed capitalist countries. To some extent, of course, this occurrence is explicable. The former group comprises a very small number of countries, including China. After the Sino-Soviet rift, there was a sharp contraction in trade between the USSR and China which is reflected in the much lower turnover during the 1960s.

It should also be pointed out that socialist bloc trade has been evenly distributed across the three continents of the underdeveloped world. Over the last decade or so, Asia accounted for 40 per cent of the trade turnover while Africa and Latin America accounted for 30 per cent each.[5] Within these

TABLE 1.1 TRADE BETWEEN THE SOCIALIST COUNTRIES OF
EASTERN EUROPE[a] AND THE THIRD WORLD (IN US $ MILLION)
AT CURRENT PRICES

	1952	*1956*	*1960*	*1964*	*1968*	*1972*
Less developed Capitalist Countries[b]						
Exports to: [d]	175	470	880	2100	3070	5080
Imports from:	215	405	950	1520	1940	2820
Trade Turnover:	390	875	1830	3630	5010	7900
Less developed Socialist Countries[c]						
Exports to: [d]	860	1213	1767	1122	1717	2180
Imports from:	610	1130	1722	1010	863	1160
Trade Turnover:	1470	2343	3489	2132	2580	3340

Source: United Nations, *Yearbook of International Trade Statistics,* several issues.
Notes: (a) Albania, Bulgaria, Czechoslovakia, East Germany, Hungary, Poland, Rumania and the USSR.
(b) Corresponds to the UN category of developing market economies.
(c) China, Cuba, Mongolia, North Korea and North Vietnam.
(d) These figures are based on exports of the less developed capitalist/socialist countries to the socialist countries of Eastern Europe. Although this method may not be entirely accurate, it does provide a reasonable approximation.

continents, however, trade as well as economic relations have been directed towards a limited number of nations. The major trading partners of the socialist countries in the Third World have been: Argentina and Brazil in Latin America; Algeria, Egypt, Ghana, Sudan and Tanzania in Africa; Afghanistan, India, Iran, Iraq, Malaysia, Pakistan and Sri Lanka in Asia.[6] Taken together, these countries were responsible for a little more than 70 per cent of socialist trade with the Third World, during the decade which ended in 1970. Among them, India and Egypt were overwhelmingly important.

The economic assistance extended by the socialist world to the poor capitalist countries has also been concentrated in a similar manner. If anything, the aid has been directed towards even fewer nations. Over the period 1954–1972, the fifteen principal recipients of aid, listed in Table 1.2, accounted for 83 per cent of the total funds committed by the socialist countries to the underdeveloped capitalist world; Egypt and India alone received 29 per cent of the total.[7] The USSR was the principal donor responsible for 52 per cent of all the commitments, while the East European countries contributed another 32 per cent.[8] The rest is accounted for by

TABLE 1.2 ECONOMIC ASSISTANCE FROM THE SOCIALIST
BLOC TO THIRD WORLD COUNTRIES: 1954–72 (GROSS
COMMITMENTS IN US $ MILLION)

Egypt	2327	Indonesia	794	Sudan	283
India	1830	Brazil	726	Tanzania	280
Iran	1401	Pakistan	638	Sri Lanka	218
Iraq	965	Syria	587	Chile	202
Algeria	907	Afghanistan	576	Argentina	174

Source: United Nations, *Statistical Yearbook 1973*, p. 715.
Note: The data in this Table include Chinese aid but, among the
countries listed above, only Pakistan, Tanzania and Sri Lanka
received substantive aid from China.

Chinese aid which has become significant only in recent years and has been
extended largely to African countries south of the Sahara.

Trends over time are difficult to establish because statistical information
is limited. All the same, it is fairly certain that the increase in aid did not match
the trade expansion.[9] In absolute terms, of course, socialist aid is not very
large particularly when compared with the total foreign aid received by the
Third World. However, the fact that it has been concentrated in a small
number of countries means that it might well be quantitatively significant in
those countries. Soviet aid to Egypt is an obvious example.[10] Whether poor
countries derived any benefits from such economic assistance is a question
that will be discussed later in the paper.

The remarkable growth in economic cooperation between the socialist
countries and the Third World has taken place largely in a framework of
bilateral agreements. Economic aid, development credits, technical assistance,
offers of scientific cooperation and trade are all incorporated into long-term
agreements negotiated with individual governments. In fact, bilateralism is an
integral part of the overall system of economic relations between the communist countries and the less developed world. Although this framework is somewhat different from the usual *modus operandi* of international trade and
commerce, it is to be expected that socialist economies would want to plan
their economic relations with the rest of the world, as a part of the process of
planned production.

The principal features of such an arrangement between a socialist country
and a poor capitalist country are as follows:[11] (i) The agreement specifies the
objectives of economic cooperation for both partners and attempts to set out
planned needs as accurately as possible. (ii) Trade balances outstanding at the
end of each period are settled in exports and imports of mutually agreed
products or in inconvertible currency. (iii) The socialist partner pledges to
provide economic assistance in the form of capital equipment, technology,
know-how, etc. Aid as well as debt repayments are automatically converted
into trade flows; credits extended to the poor country, for instance, can be

repaid in the inconvertible domestic currency, traditional exports or the output of aid-financed projects. (iv) As far as possible, all transactions are carried out in terms of world prices, except that bilateral agreements seek to eliminate short-term fluctuations.

This is a typical, but by no means universal example. In a few cases, trade, along with the other transactions, is conducted in terms of hard convertible currencies. If that is so, trade with the socialist countries is no different from the usual international exchange of commodities as far as the poor country is concerned. Special advantages, or disadvantages, might arise only if the relationship has a bilateral character. Hence the following discussion is based on the most prevalent form of cooperation between the rich socialist and the poor capitalist countries.

In assessing the economic relationship between the socialist nations and the Third World, I shall focus attention on trade and, to some extent, aid. This does not mean that other aspects of the relationship are not important. Indeed they are. It is just that, in the economic sphere, trade is the principal medium of interaction between the two groups of countries.

II. The Implications for Poor Countries

For the poor capitalist economies, the benefits of bilateral trade with the socialist countries seem fairly obvious.[12] First, in the absence of this trade, economic assistance in the form of development credits may not have been extended by the centrally planned economies of Eastern Europe. Second, given the extreme shortage of foreign exchange in most of these countries, the introduction of bilateralism added to import capacity, at the same time underwriting an expansion in exports. This is particularly significant in view of the problems faced by underdeveloped countries attempting to promote export growth. What is more, the existence of the special payments arrangements reduced the burden of debt servicing in so far as repayments could be made in exports, domestic currency or the output of aid-financed projects, instead of scarce convertible foreign currencies. It should be remembered that repayments still involve domestic resource costs. Thus the debt servicing burden is reduced, and the capacity to import increased, only if there is an exportable surplus in the country. Without such a surplus, increased exports to the socialist world could well be at the expense of domestic consumption.

Although the benefits appear to be quite straightforward, any measurement or quantification poses a problem. It is clear that an expansion of trade *per se* is no index of the gain accruing to poor countries. After all, it is perfectly possible that a part of the increase in exports to bilateral agreement markets is illusory, in as much as it represents a diversion of exportable commodities from other traditional markets. Alternatively, the prices received for exports may not be favourable. Even if they are, the real benefit of bilateral trade would also depend upon the choice of imports offered by the socialist countries and the import prices charged. In principle, therefore, an evaluation of the gains from trade must be based on some assessment of: (i) the *net* increase in exports, (ii) the composition of imports, and (iii) the terms of trade obtained.

This kind of conventional analysis is necessary in order to say something about the distribution of gains from trade between communist countries and the Third World. A complete evaluation of trade with the socialist countries, however, must go beyond the apparent net gains or losses arising from an international exchange of commodities, and examine the impact of trade on development. It must also consider how the gains from trade are distributed inside a poor country, for gains accrue not so much to countries as entities as to groups or classes *within* countries. The traditional view of trade as an engine of economic growth is considerably discredited, particularly in the context of poor capitalist countries. In fact, economists of radical persuasion have argued the opposite, suggesting that trade between unequal partners might be responsible for the perpetuation of underdevelopment and the widening gap between rich and poor countries.

In a very elementary sense, of course, there are gains to be derived from trade if imports of a commodity are cheaper than production at home in terms of domestic resources used. The real world is far more complex. In a poor country, the import of commodities, technology or capital from abroad might inhibit local capitalist development, discourage indigenous technical progress, introduce demand patterns inappropriate for the level of income in the economy and, perhaps, worsen income distribution. Similarly, export specialisation in a narrow range of commodities might freeze the economy into a structure of production and pattern of trade which evolved during the colonial era. It would involve too much of a digression to embark on a discussion of these issues here.[13] Suffice it to say that increased trade in itself is not desirable. While some benefits might arise out of commodity exchange across national boundaries, trade should also assist a poor country in harnessing its productive resources so as to alter the structure of production and to set in motion the forces of development. Thus one important question is whether or not international trade places a poor country on the road to independent development. The other fundamental issue is who gains from such trade within the underdeveloped countries.

The implications of trade between the poor capitalist countries and the socialist economies of Eastern Europe must, therefore, be examined at two levels. To begin with, it is necessary to consider the simple gains from trade which accrue to countries in the aggregate. The following discussion tends to focus attention on this aspect of the problem. The subsequent analysis of the broader issues arising from trade with the socialist world is relatively brief although, in my view, it is more important.

A. *The Gains from Trade*

It was established earlier that the benefits derived from trade with the socialist countries depend upon the net increase in exports, the composition of imports and the terms of trade obtained. I shall examine each of these factors with reference to the experience of Third World countries.

There are two reasons why the net export growth in trade between the socialist bloc and the underdeveloped world may be less than the apparent increase. In the first place, it is possible that a poor capitalist country meets a part of its commitment under bilateral agreements by diverting exports from convertible currency markets to the new trading partners. Now, as long as there is no constraint on increasing the domestic production of exportables, the question of diversion does not arise. However, supply conditions might be such that domestic production cannot be stepped up adequately to meet all increases in demand. Secondly, socialist countries might re-export goods imported under special agreements to the rest of the world. They may do so for the following reasons. Many of them suffer from foreign exchange shortages, and the resale of products imported from poor capitalist countries through bilateral arrangements might be one way of obtaining convertible currencies. Alternatively, it is possible that on account of commitments written into trade agreements they end up importing goods for which there is little demand; such products might then be dumped on the world market, again for the purpose of obtaining foreign exchange.

What is the likelihood of implicit diversion and of re-export? The former is an empirical question about which generalizations are rather difficult. However, research on India's trade with the socialist countries has shown that a very large proportion of exports under bilateral trade constituted a net growth in exports.[14] The second question is more susceptible to analysis. While there have no doubt been instances of re-export by the socialist countries, this occurrence could not have been all that widespread. The argument is quite straightforward. It is well known that a large number of traditional commodity exports from the Third World face near saturated markets and rather low income elasticities of demand in the metropolitan countries. In such cases, the socialist countries provide welcome new markets; there is obviously little room for re-exports on a significant scale. It is also most unlikely that the communist countries could have resold manufactured goods imported from the Third World in western capitalist countries for the simple reason that, in such goods, product differentiation, brand names and quality are rather important, and exporting involves marketing expenses in the form of advertising costs, etc. As a matter of fact, poor countries themselves have found it rather difficult to increase their exports of manufactures, so that socialist economies are unlikely to have fared better with the same goods.

A priori reasoning of the kind set out above can always be challenged on the basis of empirical evidence from individual countries, but that is a problem with most generalised hypothesis. Apropos this issue, however, an important point still needs to be made. To the extent that there is an implicit diversion of exportables, trade with the socialist countries obviously does not lead to a net gain, but it should be stressed that it does not necessarily constitute a loss.

That would happen only if the terms of trade actually worsen on account of bilateral trade. All the same, there are economists who argue that a premium attaches to convertible foreign exchange earned, so that even at equivalent terms of trade any diversion of exports constitutes a cost. On the contrary, it is possible to argue that the uncertainty and risk of convertible currency markets is largely eliminated in bilateral trade markets owing to the contractual nature of long term agreements, thereby yielding a benefit.

A characteristic feature of trade between the socialist countries and the Third World is that transactions are frequently carried out in terms of inconvertible currencies. Given that export earnings from such trade can only be used to finance imports of goods and services from the USSR and Eastern Europe, the composition of imports is clearly of considerable importance. The point at issue is whether a poor capitalist country's imports under bilateral agreements are high priority items necessary for its development programme or are they low priority goods which it is forced to buy in order to use up the trade surplus in its favour. Of course, the price and quality competitiveness of these imports is equally important.

An examination of international trade statistics reveals that machinery and transport equipment account for nearly half of the poor capitalist countries' imports from the socialist world, while intermediate goods such as base metals, chemicals, fertilizers and petroleum products constitute a very large proportion of the remainder. During the early 1970s, these manufactures accounted for approximately 80 per cent of exports from the European socialist countries to the Third World.[15] There is no doubt that capital goods and intermediate products are essential to the industrialisation programme in poor countries, and not low priority goods which they were forced to import. Of course it is possible to argue that such imports could, alternatively, have been obtained in the world market. Indeed they could, but not with the same ease because most poor capitalist countries suffer from acute shortages of convertible foreign exchange. Thus, buying on the world market may not have been a feasible option for many of them.

The pattern of trade is obviously relevant to our analysis but it cannot be considered in isolation from the terms of trade. Under bilateral agreements, the terms of trade are directly dependent on prices received for exports and prices paid for imports. Therefore, in order to compare the terms of trade obtained from the socialist countries with those obtained from the rest of the world, price comparisons are unavoidable. It need hardly be stressed that prices of traded goods are notoriously difficult to compare because of quality variations which are present, not only in manufactured goods, but also in apparently homogenous primary commodities. Nevertheless, to the extent that it is possible to indulge in price comparisons, evidence available from Egypt, Ghana, India, Pakistan and Tanzania suggests that socialist countries offered terms which were sometimes better and, at any rate, no worse than those offered by the rest of the world.[16]

If one thinks about this statement, it stands to reason. After all, socialist bloc trade with the capitalist economies is carried out on a commercial basis. State trading corporations from Eastern Europe and the USSR conduct transactions with local capitalists or traders in the Third World;[17] there is no reason why individual exporters should sell for less than prices obtainable elsewhere or individual importers should pay more than the going price. If anything, it is likely that socialist countries attempting to establish trade relations with poor capitalist economies have to offer small premiums in order to break into long established market channels.

The existence of the socialist bloc as an alternative outlet for exports might offer two special advantages to the poor countries. Trade with the socialist countries might improve the terms of trade *vis-à-vis* the rest of the world and it might create greater export stability. Both these points need some elaboration. The first is best explained through an example. Suppose a poor capitalist country exports a primary commodity and is an important supplier in the world market. Let us also assume that there are no close substitutes, that the short-term supply elasticities in competing countries are low and that the demand is price inelastic. Incidentally, these conditions are quite common in the world market for some commodities. Now, if the socialist countries buy a significant proportion of the poor country's exportable output of the commodity, their entry into the market might push up prices and thereby improve the terms of trade for the exporter. Empirical investigation is obviously necessary but Egyptian cotton, Brazilian coffee, Ghanaian cocoa and Indian tea or cashew nuts are possible examples where this might have happened.[18]

There remains the question of stability. Fluctuations in the level of prices and of demand are a common feature of world commodity markets and an inherent characteristic of capitalist systems. Underdeveloped countries dependent on the export of one or a few commodities are therefore particularly vulnerable. In such cases, economic relations with the socialist bloc could give rise to significant benefits not only because centrally planned economies are less prone to fluctuations in the level of economic activity, but also because they offer the possibility of long-term contractual agreements. A superficial examination of trade statistics may show a considerable amount of variability in the volume of exports even to the socialist countries. This is because poor capitalist countries tend to use socialist markets as outlets in bad years and in periods when they find it difficult to sell elsewhere. Therefore, conclusions about the stability or instability of bilateral agreement markets should not be drawn from looking at data on exports to the socialist countries in isolation. It is important to see whether trade with the socialist countries makes for greater export stability on the whole.

B. *Wider Implications of Trade with the Socialist World*
The discussion so far has concentrated attention on questions of international commodity exchange, which provides only a partial view of the problem because trade also influences production relations within an economy. Hence it is necessary to consider the effects of trade with the socialist countries on

the structure of production and on income distribution in the poor capitalist economies.

The international division of labour between metropolitan and peripheral countries took shape in the colonial era when the world economy was dominated by imperialist powers. Under such conditions, the needs of capitalist development in the western world were paramount while all developments in the colonies were subordinate to these needs. Apart from a few modifications, this division of labour has continued in the post-independence years. Trade with the western capitalist countries has tended to reinforce the historically determined patterns of production and trade in the Third World. Does trade with the socialist countries offer an opportunity to change the situation? If so, poor capitalist economies are likely to derive substantial benefits from their economic relations with the socialist world. Within these economies, of course, the distribution of benefits might be rather unequal. As we shall see later, that is what did happen.

It was pointed out earlier that a very large proportion of Third World imports from the rich communist countries comprise capital goods and intermediate products, both of which should stimulate industrial production. The impact of these imports on the pattern of production and therefore trade, is obviously quite crucial. Such imports are financed either through exports by the poor countries or through economic assistance offered by the centrally planned economies of Eastern Europe. In a poor capitalist economy, the composition of imports financed by exports depends largely on internal factors. The socialist world can exercise some influence only in the case of aid-financed imports.

There is no doubt that the principal objective of socialist aid to the Third World has been to develop a modern industrial sector in the underdeveloped economies and to harness the productive resources available. The investments have, in fact, been concentrated in (i) the development of natural resources such as coal and oil, (ii) the setting up of infra-structural projects, for example, dams, power stations, transport and communication networks, and (iii) the building of industrial complexes for the production of steel, base metals and chemicals.[19] The credits extended for these purposes have usually been for a period of 10 to 15 years at interest rates ranging from two to three per cent. A characteristic feature of socialist aid has been the debt servicing mechanism which enables poor countries to make repayments in traditional exports or in the output of aid-financed projects. A potential advantage of this arrangement is that, over a period of time, a poor capitalist country can reduce its dependence on external finance.[20] Socialist aid, like aid from other sources, is frequently tied to the country of origin and to a particular project. Some would argue that this imposes costs on recipients in the Third World and reduces the real resource transfer. However, it must be remembered that repayments are also tied and do not have to be paid in convertible currencies. Therefore, aid and trade cannot be treated as separate issues. The value of development credits extended by the socialist countries depends on the overall terms of trade obtained and not on the prices of aid-financed imports alone.

Economic relations with the socialist countries potentially offer a wide range of possibilities. The important question is whether or not trade as well as other economic ties with the socialist world, in fact, place a poor capitalist economy on the road to self-reliant development. If that is the case, it must be reflected in changes both in the structure of production and in the pattern of trade. As such, it is necessary to look at the actual experience of Third World countries. Available evidence suggests that these changes did not occur to any significant extent; and I shall return to this issue a little later.

III. The Interests of the Socialist Countries

It is now apparent why the poor capitalist countries of Africa, Asia and Latin America might have sought to establish economic ties with the rich communist countries of Eastern Europe. But what interest did the socialist world have in developing such extensive economic relations? In my view, as far as the socialist countries are concerned, there are two sets of objectives which may have prompted the relationship with the underdeveloped capitalist world: those which tie in with their own economic interests and those which relate to the needs of poor countries. Before discussing the outcome, it is worth spelling out each of these objectives briefly.

The last fifteen years have witnessed a considerable amount of change in the attitude of the COMECON countries towards trade with the outside world and interaction with the world capitalist system. In the early years of socialist transition, foreign trade was assigned a minimal role but, of late, it has become an increasingly explicit and prominent factor in their strategy of growth. This change in the basic economic philosophy has meant that the plans of all Eastern European countries assign trade and the international division of labour an important role in shaping the domestic economy. The expansion of economic relations with the poor capitalist countries should, therefore, be seen in its broader context. But there are other, more positive, reasons which stem from the economic interests of communist countries. Trade with the poor world offers the European socialist countries an opportunity to import goods which are either too expensive to produce at home or cannot be produced at all. Under bilateral arrangements, such imports are then financed through exports so that there is no need to part with scarce convertible currencies. Although one cannot be certain, it is extremely unlikely that socialist countries would have increased their trade with the less developed countries to the extent they did, in the absence of special payments arrangements which eliminated the use of convertible currencies in trade.

The second set of objectives relating to the needs of poor countries are the ones which are overtly stressed by the USSR and Eastern Europe. While pursuing their own economic interests, the socialist countries also want to establish stable economic as well as political relations with the newly independent nations of the Third World. The latter objective is summed up well in the following passage:

> ... the world socialist system actively facilitates consolidation of the principles of sovereignty and equality, mutual benefit and friendship among nations in international economic relations. Expansion of economic cooperation of socialist states with Asian, African and Latin American countries, based on these principles, is an important factor promoting the independent economic and political progress of young national states.[21]

Given the history of exploitation by the western capitalist countries, the communist countries tend to stress the equality of trading partners and express the desire to develop a new type of division of labour. The stated intention is to eliminate backwardness and assist in the development of a dynamic, modern sector in poor capitalist countries. It is hoped that this would ultimately raise the living standards of the poor in the Third World.

To what extent have these objectives been realised? Consider first, the interests of the socialist countries. In principle, it may be possible to meet all the import requirements from the world market but, in practice, most COMECON countries suffer from a scarcity of foreign exchange. Given the limited access to convertible currencies, the underdeveloped countries are a useful source of imports and also an obvious market outlet for exports. Thus the socialist countries have sold machinery, transport equipment and other manufactured goods to the poor world in exchange for primary products and industrial raw materials. Until as late as 1970, more than 75 per cent of East European exports to the less developed capitalist economies were constituted by manufactured goods, whereas primary products and raw materials accounted for more than 70 per cent of Third World exports to the socialist bloc.[22] Of course, such traditional patterns of trade can neither transform the structure of production in poor countries nor make for a new international division of labour. It need hardly be stressed that diversification in the pattern of trade is an imperative first step towards those ends.

Table 1.3 outlines the trend in exports of manufactures from the underdeveloped capitalist economies to the socialist countries of Eastern Europe, including the USSR. There is no doubt that manufactured exports increased rapidly during the 1960s and early 1970s, both in absolute and in relative terms. However, even as late as 1973, manufactured goods accounted for about one-sixth of total exports from the poor capitalist world to the European socialist countries. In this diversification, India and Egypt fared better than other Third World countries, and, by 1972, more than 40 per cent of their total exports to the socialist bloc were manufactured goods.[23]

Admittedly, patterns of production and trade which have evolved in the poor countries over a long period of time could not have been changed overnight. However, in the past decade or so, the diversification in the pattern of trade, with the possible exception of India and Egypt, has not been very significant. The transition to the so-called international socialist division of

TABLE 1.3 EXPORTS OF MANUFACTURES[a] FROM POOR
CAPITALIST ECONOMIES[b] TO THE EUROPEAN SOCIALIST
COUNTRIES (IN US $ MILLION) AT CURRENT PRICES

Product Group	1962	1966	1969	1970	1971	1972	1973
Textiles	83	152	165	215	220	300	285
Miscellaneous Manufactures (c)	15	64	159	166	211	226	317
Chemicals	17	45	44	41	43	40	55
Machinery and Transport Equipment	1	4	5	5	10	22	22
TOTAL above	116	265	373	427	484	588	679
Manufactured exports as a percentage of total exports	5·0	11·0	16·9	15·4	18·1	19·9	16·8

Sources: The data for 1962 and 1966 are taken from UNCTAD, *Trade in
Manufactures of Developing Countries, 1972 Review,* New York,
1974, p. 33. The figures for the period 1969–73 have been
calculated from the UN *Monthly Bulletin of Statistics,* July 1975,
pp. xxiv–xxxix.

Notes: (a)   SITC Sections 5 to 8 less division 68.
     (b)   Corresponds to the UN category of developing market economies
except for 1962 and 1966 because the UNCTAD classification
includes Cuba and Israel in the category of developing countries.
     (c)   SITC Sections 6 and 8, excluding textiles and non-ferrous metals.

labour clearly calls for a more determined effort towards diversification.

The socialist countries also attempted to assist poor capitalist economies in
building up a modern industrial sector and in eliminating backwardness. There
is no question about the efforts made towards the former; we have already
seen that the bulk of socialist aid was channelled into the development of
natural resources, infra-structural projects and basic industries. For political as
well as economic reasons such assistance may not have been available from the
metropolitan countries.[24]

It is interesting that almost all the aid from socialist countries was concentrated in the public sector of Third World economies. This was, in fact, an
explicit element of policy on the part of East European countries, prompted
by a belief that, in underdeveloped countries, the State sector is the most
capable of mobilizing resources if the objective is to eliminate backwardness
and, ultimately, alleviate poverty. Here is the fundamental mistake which
reflects an inadequate understanding of the class character of the State in poor

nations. While socialist countries propagated and supported State capitalism as the most desirable path to development for the Third World, the State in these countries continued to protect the interests of the privileged classes. It is now widely accepted that the principal beneficiaries of State capitalism in the underdeveloped world have been capitalists in the private sector and not the majority of the people. Under such circumstances, the economic benefits derived from trade with the socialist countries are unlikely to have filtered down and accrued to the poor. On the contrary, it is likely that the benefits were appropriated by local capitalists and traders. While it might be tempting to do so, this occurrence cannot be blamed on socialist trade and aid because it was the outcome of factors internal to the polity of Third World countries.

IV. Towards a Political Economy

The fundamental points to emerge from the discussion so far can be restated as follows. For the poor capitalist economies, the distribution of gains from trade with the socialist world was probably as favourable — if not more so — as that in the case of trade with the Western capitalist countries. The socialist countries of Eastern Europe also derived significant benefits from their trade and economic relations with the African, Asian and Latin American nations. Contrary to pronounced objectives, however, trade with the socialist countries has not led to a radical transformation in the patterns of production and trade in the Third World, or to a new international division of labour.

To focus attention on the economic aspects alone, as I have done so far, is to ignore the important politics of the relationship. Formulating a political economy of the interaction between these two groups of countries is no doubt essential, but it is a complex task. The following paragraphs only contribute some thoughts towards it.

The underdeveloped capitalist countries promoted their relationship with the communist world for a variety of reasons. Interestingly enough, economic ideology or political developments within the poor countries exercised relatively little influence. International political developments were far more important. In the early stages of the post-colonial era, several Third World countries sought to exploit cold war rivalries and use relations with the socialist bloc to accelerate the process of decolonization and assert their national economic independence. Later, it became a method of improving their bargaining position *vis-à-vis* the western capitalist countries. In fact, the existence of the communist countries on the international scene did add to the bargaining strength of poor nations. This may have been because the socialist countries were an alternative source of technology, imports or finance and an alternative outlet for the traditional exports of third world countries. Close ties with the communist countries were also valuable for internal political reasons; they enhanced the 'socialist' image of governments which made almost no effort to alleviate poverty but made a great deal of political capital out of the so-called public-sector-oriented strategies of development.

The socialist countries, on their part, also attempted to cultivate relations with the poor capitalist nations. In crude political terms, it might be argued that this was motivated by a desire to extend spheres of influence. This factor was no doubt very important but there were other reasons as well. The communist countries did consistently support the struggle against colonialism and imperialism in Africa, Asia and Latin America. In this context, nationalist movements were always regarded as a progressive force by the socialist world. However, it is important to remember that nationalist movements were frequently led by the elite, which did not obviously set these countries on the road to socialism. For that reason, among others, the struggle between capitalism and socialism continues in many Third World countries. The attitude of the European socialist countries to this conflict is interesting. They regard the concentration of resources in the hands of the State – a characteristic feature of East European aid – as ' . . . a vital means of counteracting foreign monopoly capital and the sections of the local bourgeoisie oriented towards co-operation with these monopolies. Where the public sector is absent or small, the economic development of the new States is usually unstable and becomes dependent on private capitalist elements.'[25] Paradoxically enough, strengthening the hands of State capitalism may not have been in the interests of the poor in Third World countries; on the contrary, it probably consolidated the position of the ruling elite. Given the economic and political system in these countries, the outcome was almost inevitable. Yet, to put the problem in perspective, the socialist countries could have done little to alter the politics in poor nations and their presence on the international scene probably did give rise to some advantages for the underdeveloped world.

Notes

[1] In the last few years, there has also been a rapid expansion in trade between China and the poor capitalist countries. Although China's relationship with the African, Asian and Latin American nations does raise several interesting issues, it is not discussed in this chapter. Instead, I shall focus attention on the richer socialist countries. For a discussion of China's economic ties with the Third World, see Suzanne Paine, Chapter 9.

[2] Cf. *Statistical Review of Trade between Countries having different Social and Economic Systems*, UNCTAD Secretariat, TD/B/410, Geneva, 23 August 1972, p. 6. It should be pointed out that the UNCTAD classification of developing countries also includes Cuba and Yugoslavia. As such, it does not correspond exactly with the category of less developed capitalist countries in Table 1.1. From our point of view, therefore, these figures may be slight overestimates but they are still a perfectly reasonable index of the changes in relative shares.

[3] Ibid, p. 8.

[4] During the period 1971–3, developing countries absorbed 14·7 per cent of exports from the European socialist countries and were responsible for 10·6 per cent of their imports; calculated from UNCTAD Secretariat document No. TD/B/499/Supp.1/Add.1, Geneva, 22 July, 1974, p. 1.

[5] The percentage share of the three continents in the socialist bloc's trade with the developing world was as follows:

	1960	1965	1970	1972
Africa	30·2	27·3	30·7	30·0
Asia	43·3	40·5	37·7	41·8
Latin America	26·5	32·2	31·6	28·2

Source: UNCTAD Secretariat, calculated from document No. TD/B/505/Supp.1
          Annex, p. 1

It should be noted that the relatively high share of Latin America is attributable to trade with Cuba, which is included in the above statistics as part of the Latin American continent.

[6] Cf. *Trade Relations among Countries having different Social and Economic Systems*, Report by the UNCTAD Secretariat, TD/112, Geneva 20 January 1972, and V. Vassilev, *Policy in the Soviet Bloc on Aid to Developing Countries*, OECD Development Centre, Paris, 1969. It should be mentioned that trade with Indonesia was important in the Sukarno years, as also with Chile during the Allende regime.

[7] During 1954–72, the total bilateral aid commitments made by the socialist bloc to the poor capitalist countries were $14,405 million; see UN *Statistical Yearbook 1973*, p. 715.

[8] Calculated from ibid.

[9] UN statistics reveal the following trend in bilateral aid commitments (in millions of dollars) by the centrally planned economies to the poor capitalist countries:

	1954–60	1961–5	1966–70	1971–2
Africa	933	1735	1566	1240
Asia	2096	1539	2951	1179
Latin America	111	285	394	582
Total	3140	3559	4911	3001

[10] See Robert Mabro, Chapter 3.

[11] For a detailed discussion, see a study prepared for UNCTAD by the Moscow Institute of Economics of the World Socialist System, *Innovations in the Practice of Trade and Economic Co-operation between the Socialist Countries of Eastern Europe and the Developing Countries*, TD/B/238/Rev.1, New York, 1970, pp. 8–11.

[12] The following discussion draws upon the analytical framework of the author's essay on India's trade with the socialist countries; see Chapter 5.

[13] For an analysis of some related issues, see Manfred Bienefeld, Chapter 2.

[14] See Chapter 5, where it is estimated that less than 15 per cent of India's exports to the European socialist countries were diverted from other markets.

[15] Calculated from UN *Monthly Bulletin of Statistics*; several issues containing data on exports of centrally planned economies.

[16] For evidence on Egypt, pp. 68–70; on Ghana, pp. 85–7, 91; on India, pp. 130–5; and on Tanzania, pp. 43–5 of this volume. Similar evidence on Pakistan's trade with the socialist world can be found in M. Kidron, *Pakistan's Trade with Eastern Bloc Countries*, New York, 1972, pp. 47–54.

[17] Very few underdeveloped countries have State trading agencies, and even where these exist the bulk of the foreign trade is carried on by private firms and individuals.

[18] For supporting evidence in the case of Ghanaian Cocoa, see Christopher Stevens, Chapter 4.

[19] For a detailed discussion, see *Innovations in the Practice of Trade and Economic Co-operation between the Socialist Countries of Eastern Europe and the Developing Countries*, op. cit., pp. 5–8.

[20] Aid from the Western capitalist world provides a marked contrast, as gross inflows are often maintained only to service past debts.

[21] *Fundamental Principles of the International Socialist Division of Labour*, Moscow, 1963, pp. 8–9.

[22] Cf. *Statistical Review of Trade between Countries having different Social and Economic Systems*, UNCTAD Secretariat, TD/B/410, Geneva, 23 August 1972, p. 9.

[23] India's manufactured exports to the socialist countries of Eastern Europe increased from $31 million in 1962 to $268 million in 1972 (see Chapter 5) while Egypt's exports of manufactures to the socialist bloc rose from $62 million in 1965 to $172 million in 1972, see UNCTAD, *Trade in Manufactures of Developing Countries, 1972* and *1973 Reviews*.

[24] Cf. Robert Mabro, Chapter 3 and Pramit Chaudhuri, Chapter 6.

[25] S. Skachkov, 'Economic Co-operation of the USSR with Developing Countries' *Social Sciences*, No. 3, 1974, USSR Academy of Sciences, Moscow, p. 10.

2 Special Gains from Trade with Socialist Countries: The Case of Tanzania

MANFRED BIENEFELD

Small countries must trade. Technologically backward countries must trade. Hence small technologically backward countries are doubly and critically dependent on trade. The reasons for this are well-known and often deemed obvious. A small country cannot produce all of its requirements as the complexity of its economy grows, and a technologically backward country has much to gain by obtaining access to more advanced technology. Unfortunately, like most simple truths this one needs qualification, and this paper will explore these qualifications in the light of the experience of one small, technologically backward country, Tanzania.

I. The Gains from Trade

There is no question that there are benefits derived from trade when, given demand, a country obtains a commodity for a lesser net expenditure of resources through trade than would have been true had the commodity been produced by itself. Those who advocate free trade point to this eloquent fact; then add that the trade of which they speak is entered into voluntarily by the trading partners; and conclude that hence, quite irrespective of who appropriates the larger part of the total net gain from trade, each partner derives some benefit from it. The logic of this argument is impeccable. The very existence of trade becomes proof of its mutual benefit, though even the sharing of benefits is regulated fairly so long as all equivalent factors of production have identical prices. At this point, trade becomes merely exchange which happens to cross at least one border post.

Under these circumstances, an analysis of trade which seeks to assess the significance of current levels or patterns is narrowed down to a discussion of various kinds of imperfections in factor or product markets, for example of the structural conditions of production and exchange.

This argument does, however, critically depend upon the implicit assumption of full employment. It also ignores so-called market imperfections, but these may at times be so extensive and so systematic as to distort very significantly the final result of the process. What are the major structural impediments to the free working of the market and of comparative advantage? More particularly, in the context of these impediments, what are the potential advantages or disadvantages involved in trade between a country like Tanzania and socialist countries?

As has been suggested, in the absence of such impediments the principle of comparative advantage would lead to the establishment of an international division of labour and the associated trade would yield large net benefits to the participants. Furthermore, if the conditions of perfect competition were met then technical conditions of production and transport would determine the degree and pattern of specialisation, given the location of raw materials and of markets. However, perfect competition does not prevail in the real world and this raises the possibility that the gains from trade between specific partners may be arbitrarily distributed. Moreover, there may be costs to be set against these gains, and for some trading partners the net effect may be negative.

The distribution of gains has been much discussed. It centres on the terms of trade and is ultimately determined by the ability of the capital or labour of one trading partner to command a relative higher real profit or wage rate. It is generally agreed that this is plausible only when resources are not perfectly mobile, and when they are not widely dispersed in location and ownership. However, it is generally argued that while such distortion may reduce the net benefits of trade to certain participants, it will generally not transform them into losses. It is hence seen not as an argument against trade, but rather as one for better, or more equitable, terms and for the assurance of free resource movement.

These sanguine conclusions are unfortunately not justified, since there are very plausible circumstances in which trade occurs in ways which involve costs that outweigh the benefits for certain participants. What are these circumstances?[2]

The first and most obvious case is that of colonial trade which does not involve two independent trading partners. Relaxation of the condition that trade is voluntary removes the presumption that trade implies mutual benefit. Furthermore, under these conditions the discipline of the market cannot be invoked and the resulting terms of trade must be considered arbitrary. The 'trade' for gold by the Spaniards in Latin America, and the 'trade' for slaves by Britain and others in Africa were illustrations of this pattern.

However, apart from this obvious case, in all other instances the principle of voluntary trade is also modified to a greater or lesser degree. The fact is that the more narrowly specialised an economy (and especially a small economy) becomes, the more meaningless the concept of opportunity cost becomes. The alternative cost of producing a particular commodity at home hence loses all meaning. At the same time the option of finding substitutes for particular products disappears when the number of such traded products increases and when technical options are narrowed by the increased international integration of production. In this way it is possible to become locked into a certain pattern of production and trade so that even if the terms of trade deteriorate dramatically it is not possible to shift in the short or medium term to a different pattern of production or trade because capital equipment, infrastructure, expertise, and market access are all too specialised. Under such circumstances salvation always appears to lie in a further extension of present activities and this merely raises the spectre of still further adverse shifts in the terms of trade. To say that countries in such a position trade voluntarily is to caricature their situation.

The matter is complicated further because it is generally not countries who trade, and the fact that private entities trade raises all of the familiar questions of private versus public benefits. When the private bodies trading are foreign operators, or local residents with an eye on retirement or movement abroad, then additional problems are raised involving differences between the real and ostensible terms of trade. These problems include the whole transfer pricing controversy, as well as the debate concerning the net effect of externalities and of the relationship between private and social benefits and costs. Certainly there is little justification for simply relying on micro-rationality to produce an optimum pattern of specialisation.

Apart from the expatriation of surplus effected through transfer pricing, there is the problem of the artificial creation of demand for certain imports which displace local products and exert further pressure on the balance of payments and hence on the terms of trade. This points to the general issue of the unequal access to markets which pervades such free trade relations in general.

Most significant, however, is the problem of short-term versus long-term benefits. When Professor Wiles, in his interesting and iconoclastic work *Communist International Economics,*[3] announces rather militantly to an unidentified but apparently misguided host of radicals, that in trade 'we must behave as micro-rationally as possible' he does so with the apparently casual *caveat* that this is true 'once the macro-economic proportions are fixed'. But surely that is to nullify the criticism implied. The concern that is felt on this score is felt precisely because there is deemed to be a connection between these 'macro-economic proportions' and the micro-rationality of bodies involved in trade. In this way the micro requirements of the moment always take precedence over the macro possibilities of the future, and the insistent demands of the balance of payments are among the most compelling constraints. At one and the same time they divert resources into exports at an accelerated rate when terms of trade worsen, and they contribute to that worsening by increasing the competition for markets and for foreign capital which becomes progressively more crucial to balancing the external account.

The fact is that trade ought to assist in the mobilisation of resources generally and any evaluation of volumes and patterns of trade must look beyond the simple net gains or losses incurred in particular commodity exchanges. Rather, it is necessary to assess the consequences of particular types and degrees of specialisation on the broader need to mobilise resources and to set in motion the cumulative development of skills and of technology.

With regard to exports it is tempting to say merely that one should export those commodities in which foreign exchange earnings are highest per 'unit of resource' used in production. Even if one had an unambiguous measure of a 'unit of resource' one could not simply apply this rule, for it is a fact that commodity X may be the most efficient converter (of resources into foreign exchange) and yet it may be unwise to stress production of this commodity: because it provides little or no stimulus to the development of skill or encouragement for innovation; because it depletes a non-renewable resource with extensive potential linkage effects before the economy is in a position to take advantage of these; because its income elasticity is low or its markets are volatile; or finally because the commodity in question can at present be produced only through foreign capital so that the net social benefit, and especially the net effect on the balance of payments, are much less than the gross figures would suggest.

All of this does not mean that countries must export manufactured goods — or primary products — or any other specific type of commodity for that matter. It means rather that an optimal export strategy cannot be defined without specification of the time-horizon considered, or without explicit consideration of the way in which production of certain export commodities links with other productive activities — both present and future. It means also that the types of commodities one should aim to export will change over time for any one country. For the analyst it means that generalisation is a perilous matter.

The expenditure of resources to produce exports is justifiable only through the imports this makes available. These must therefore be chosen so as to confer the greatest possible benefit on the economy in question, and when one considers benefits from a social and a long-run perspective, simply insisting on micro-rationality will not suffice here either. Here it is again necessary to ensure that the impact of imported goods reinforces the general strategy for the mobilisation of resources, if such a strategy exists.

As has been argued elsewhere for foreign investment,[4] so with trade, it is necessary that its net effect be to stimulate the mobilisation of local resources, or in other words that it be complementary to this process. When imports destroy local producers, choke off local initiative and technical development, or bend demand patterns in their favour through heavy advertising, then it is not sufficient merely to point out that the importers are more efficient (micro-rationality!), without calculating the cost of the transition, asking what happens to the resources so 'liberated', or dealing with the effect on the existing processes through which skills, techniques and production were developing.

Probably the most telling point in this list concerns the employment of resources. To assume that international specialisation on the basis of comparative advantage can be conceived as operating across all capitalist economies and all commodities, is to posit a truly staggering degree of flexibility. The fact that some writers lament the absence of such flexibility is praiseworthy,[5] but it does not help make it any more likely or plausible. In reality it is often the case that for individual small or medium sized underdeveloped economies, absolute advantage takes precedence over its comparative variant. This occurs because the capacity constraints, which must be reached if the developed trading partner is to be forced into the either-or choice which will lead him to abandon production of goods in which he has the smallest absolute advantage, are not often operative. Developed countries struggle to maintain full employment of resources and attempt (at least) to regulate the costs imposed by major shifts in their industrial structures — not just for political or welfarist reasons but also because such disruption tends to impair the vital confidence of the investor. Under these circumstances it is little wonder that comparative advantage has proved a rather lame horse for poor countries — except, of course, when these countries start exporting goods in effect being sold by giant international producers to themselves or to one another. These organisations can make relatively effective use of the principle of comparative advantage, but their fees for this service are not negligible, and the scope of such developments is always limited by the global considerations of these organisations.

In this brief introduction to questions of gains from trade it remains only to deal with the problem of instability. A heavy reliance on trade ties a nation to its balance of payments and makes its economy critically dependent on the imports involved. Such simple dependence is sometimes said to be of no significance since it applies to everyone, but surely the point is that it does not apply to everyone in the same way or to the same extent. It is the more serious: the more of total domestic production is geared to exports; the more one is a price taker in the markets in which one sells; the more inelastic one's demand for the major imports purchased; and finally, the more one's trading partners influence domestic policies in undesirable ways. The greater one's dependence, the more seriously one is exposed to the effects of fluctuations in international markets, and this instability is likely to be greater if trade is concentrated in a very small number of commodities (the risk spreading principle); if it is concentrated on trade with a small number of partners (though countries with closely linked economic fortunes should be counted as one partner); and if it is concentrated in markets which are volatile, either because supply or demand are unstable, or because the price determining free market — for a relatively homogeneous commodity with a large global volume of trade — handles only a small proportion of that total.[6] These are of course the main reaons why primary exports were for so long viewed as liabilities, not because of any qualities inherent in these commodities.

For small relatively specialised economies such instability is debilitating and disruptive. Such economies have little flexibility and hence cannot easily turn to substitute products or to home production, and limited resources make it doubly difficult to cover the dramatic fall in revenues which such fluctuations impose from time to time. The adjustments in the internal economy which such fluctuations impose are ultimately most costly of all. Heavy investment in certain areas of production is condemned to scrap when markets collapse, only to cry out for renewal when they revive; infrastructure, developed to service certain types of production is suddenly under-used; and activities dependent on imports have to be curtailed. Gains from trade based on average terms of trade have to be adjusted for these costs.

II. Trade with Socialist Countries

This brief statement concerning the gains from trade in general, provides a basis for discussing the particular problems and possibilities of trade with socialist countries under three headings: the terms of trade, the pattern of trade, and the stability of trade. Unfortunately expectations in this regard depend on whether the trading nation is itself a socialist country. Indeed the particular interest in Tanzania's trade with socialist countries stems from its own socialist aspirations and tendencies.

When socialist countries trade with capitalist trading partners it is to be expected that they should behave in a competitive manner, taking advantage of their size and any bargaining advantages they may have. This means that for standardised commodities they will trade on terms which are close to those current in the free markets, since better terms are not generally available[7] and worse terms need not be accepted. It is not surprising, therefore, that most of this trade should be carried on at international market prices, though only for relatively homogeneous primary commodities are such prices easy to establish. For manufactured goods this is often more difficult, and for intermediate goods it is most difficult of all, since for each commodity there are often as many markets as there are producers.

There are therefore no *a priori* grounds to expect the terms of trade between socialist countries and capitalist countries to be either better or worse than they are in trade between capitalist trading partners. Just as these latter terms are not uniform so the terms of socialist country trade may deviate, being slightly better for countries with extensive trade ties, providing substantial markets and representing a significant source of imports (as with preferential tariffs and trading bloc arrangements generally), or for countries whom one wishes to support for long term economic or political reasons.

As for the terms of trade between two socialist countries, these must be assessed from a broad perspective since in such a case trade becomes more than the exchange of commodities. It becomes one facet of the integration of planned markets and production capacities. While such exchange is also in-fluenced by economic constraints, these are much broader and more flexible when long range planning is involved. Hence within these limits explicit political considerations play an important role in the fixing of terms.

It is therefore the degree to which there is an attempt at the integration of economies which determines whether one might expect significantly different patterns of trade to emerge. There is little reason why a poor capitalist country's trade with socialist countries should differ from its trade with other trading partners: especially when such trade is carried out in hard currency, much of which ultimately accrues to rich country interests. Furthermore, so long as the purchase of commodities occurs independently of the sale of other commodities, a market determined pattern is all but inevitable.

On the other hand, when such trade is of a strict bilateral nature and is carried out on the basis of an accounting currency it is relatively insulated from international exchange generally and this raises the possibility that one, or both, partners purchase commodities which are more expensive than they need to be. This in turn raises the possibility of a greater diversification of exports than would otherwise have been possible. Although in the context of micro rationality this represents diversification at the expense of the efficiency available under ideal circumstances, it has been pointed out already that ideal circumstances do not exist outside such bilateral pacts, and these in any case do not differ in principle from other types of trading bloc arrangements. Furthermore, such short run inefficiency may well be the basis for long-run efficiency — as in the familiar infant industry arguments — though under unfavourable circumstances it may also be an encouragement to permanent inefficiency.

It is important to remember that non-optimality is defined in relation to an ideal, not in relation to the actual world. Since in the real world the logically impeccable principle of comparative advantage fails to be effected because the vested interests involved in established patterns of production are not generally forced to make way for products having a comparative advantage, a small economy integrated into the free market, whose access to markets is impeded in this way, will generally suffer from the inability to employ many of its resources in some form of export production. Worse still, employment of these resources to meet domestic needs will also be hampered by its free market orientation. Under such circumstances, additional markets obtained through bilateral agreements will normally represent a substantial net benefit.

The implication of this discussion is that significant long term changes in market-determined patterns or terms of trade are to be expected only if the poor country trading with the socialist bloc is itself socialist. In this case one might expect some diversification of trade; if only because the principles of comparative advantage have a better chance of implementation when national planners discuss balanced multilateral trade in the context of their respective draft economic plans. Here long term gains can be aimed at, while the short term costs of transition can be minimised by planning for gradual transitions.

Of course, this too is an ideal picture, and the real world is in this case also troubled by the rigidities of vested interests, but the requirement that trade must be balanced bilaterally represents a powerful lever to move these obstacles. In addition, the fact that under such circumstances trade is inte-grated into national plans, means that the failure to pursue the principle of comparative advantage to its fullest extent has a much lesser inhibiting effect on the local mobilisation of resources, if only because those branches which have not specialised according to the principle will not be exposed to competition on the rather more one-sided principle of absolute advantage.

The third aspect of trade concerns the instability of prices or of levels of demand, or both. In this area there are clear and unequivocal advantages to be gained from trade with socialist countries because these economies tend to be less volatile and because their long planning perspectives together with their centralised purchasing agencies, make long term contracts a real possibility. The benefits of such stability to economies operating on precariously narrow margins and reserves, need no further emphasis. Against this it is sometimes argued that the socialist countries may manipulate such deals to earn hard currency by reselling the purchased commodities on the world market, but this argument is a red herring. Whether or not such re-selling imposes a cost on the less developed economy can be established only through a comparison of the price paid for commodities purchased under long-term agreements, with the average price of commodities on the free market. If this comparison is favourable there is little merit to a complaint that occasionally, as world prices rise, these long term trade prices are unfavourable — whatever the purchaser decides to do with the commodities purchased.

It is a fact that the instability of trade is seen as one of the major liabilities of heavy dependence on it. Tanzania's efforts have been directed at the diversification of trade — both in terms of commodities sold and trading partners — in an effort to minimise the risks involved. Indeed it is in the context of these efforts that trade with the socialist bloc has been encouraged.

In his frontal attack on fallacies about trade structure Professor Wiles makes great sport of his discovery that efficiency is efficiency is efficiency, and that conformity to the principles of comparative advantage will get one all three. 'Defiance of the price mechanism', he concludes (as if the perfect market existed after all) is therefore not justified for any reason, except strangely and significantly in a general way to diversify exports, without paying attention to any of the other reasons usually advanced. But for all of the bravado of the argument and Wiles' put-down of those who have not seen the light, that seemingly small concession gives the game away. If diversification is an argument that 'has intellectual content', then all of those other reasons, so disdainfully rejected — capital or labour intensity, primary *versus* manufactured goods, consumption *versus* investment goods — come into their own again because diversification is considered a sensible aim on account of its risk reducing effect. But surely it is obvious that the risks of trading in different types of markets are not all the same, so that anyone who considers diversifying his trade must consider the type of markets he should aim to move into and cannot, by definition, rely on the market to make these choices.

III. Tanzania's Foreign Trade

It has been pointed out that Tanzania's economy is heavily oriented towards foreign trade. Table 2.1 shows the extent of this involvement, while at the same time giving a clear indication of a gradual and substantial reduction in the proportion of monetary GDP devoted to exports since independence. While domestic exports amounted to very nearly half of total monetary GDP in the year prior to independence, by 1971 this proportion had fallen to 28 per cent, though the recent upward jump in commodity prices is likely to have raised this proportion marginally. In any event the trend is unambiguous and clear.

This trend reflects the increased mobilisation of domestic resources since independence. Certainly the persistent visible trade surpluses which existed prior to independence and which persisted until 1967, were an indication of the extent to which the colonial administration was unwilling and/or incapable of using the funds so painfully earned through exports. Much of this surplus was nullified by deficits in invisibles (insurance, banking, freight, and remittances) and the remainder was in effect lent to the UK through the Currency Board. The I.B.R.D. pointed out in 1960 that 'in effect the territories have foreign exchange reserves more than sufficient to meet any call on them' and recognised that these funds were 'taken away from the alternative use of productive investment within the territory',[8] though it did not of course conclude from this that Tanzania should establish its own central bank to administer its own reserves.

That this situation would change was recognised in the First Five Year Plan which pointed out that 'the expansion of internal demand [will] lead to a rising level of imports − and tend to divert resources from export industries to those catering for the domestic market'.[9] Unfortunately, although such a diversion of resources is certainly possible, it is not easy to substantiate. In fact it is only in the case of cotton and of meat products (not a major export commodity), that it is at all plausible to suggest that commodities otherwise destined for export were locally consumed on a significant scale. Other more indirect effects involving the diversion of investment resources inhibiting the production of exports, are not easy to establish, though it is clear that for three major exports − sisal, coffee, pyrethrum − this is unlikely to have been significant since the market constraint was the effective constraint, while in the case of diamonds such diversion was never an issue, the constraint being the supply itself.

The performance in terms of export expansion has been relatively poor, with some major setbacks in specific markets. The cumulative rate of growth of the value of external domestic exports (outside the East African Community) has been about 4·7 per cent per annum if one uses current prices and the years 1960 and 1973 as end points. However this growth has been far from smooth. The rate of growth for the period 1960−71 was only just over 3·4 per cent per annum, and with the averages for 1960−2 and 1971−3 as the end points, a growth rate of slightly over 4 per cent per annum emerges. Furthermore, this growth in export earnings must be seen against a background of highly unstable prices and a general increase in price levels.

TABLE 2.1 TANZANIA: DOMESTIC EXPORTS AND MONETARY
GDP, 1960—73 (IN Shs MILLION)

Year	Domestic external exports[a]	Domestic exports to EAC[b]	Total domestic exports	Monetary GDP[c]	Exports as % of monetary GDP
1960	1086·5	46·5	1133·0	2277	49·8
1961	965·3	44·7	1010·0	n.a.	
1962	1018·5	47·8	1066·3	n.a.	
1963	1262·2	68·5	1330·7	3345	39·8
1964	1395·1	102·6	1497·7	3824	39·2
1965	1245·8	118·3	1364·1	3845	35·5
1966	1570·9	93·0	1663·9	4464	37·3
1967	1540·7	80·8	1621·5	4688	34·6
1968	1525·8	90·9	1616·7	4991	32·4
1969	1514·5	103·9	1618·4	5335	30·3
1970	1579·3	147·5	1726·8	5834	29·6
1971	1556·4	196·6	1753·0	6178	28·4
1972	1786·9	133·1	1920·0	n.a.	
1973	2005·0	170·2	2175·2	n.a.	

(a) These figures are taken from East African Customs & Excise *Annual Trade Reports*. They attempt to minimise the distortion introduced by the incorporation of Zanzibar into the statistics from 1968. Hence for 1960—67 figures exports to Zanzibar have been excluded (on the grounds that after that date they constitute internal trade), and for 1968—73 the figures for cloves have been excluded. This still leaves some upward bias in the 1968—73 figures due to other Zanzibar exports now being included in the figures.

(b) Figures from East African Customs & Excise, *Annual Trade Reports*.

(c) This is Monetary GDP at factor cost. The figures come from: 1960 — *Development Plan for Tanganyika 1961/2—1963/4*. 1962 and 1963 — *Tanzania Second Five Year Plan for Economic and Social Development*, Volume I, p. 208. 1964 to 1970 — *National Accounts of Tanzania, 1964 to 1970*, C.B.S., Dar es Salaam, 1972.

This very sluggish growth in export receipts was undoubtedly accompanied by steady increases in import prices, with the result that the purchasing power of Tanzanian exports remained virtually static for the period 1960—5,[10] and certainly grew much less quickly than the modest 4 per cent per annum by which earnings at current prices increased over the entire period. It is not possible to quantify this relation more accurately at this stage since the computation of import price indices is a most difficult exercise in view of the great variability in composition and quality of imports. Certainly one may discount the beneficial effect of the upward spurt in primary commodity prices in 1972—73 because this also included the costly oil price increase and was followed by substantial increases in the prices of manufactured imports. On balance there is little doubt that the terms of trade worsened significantly for Tanzania between 1960 and 1973. As for the instability of prices and

demand, the extent of this problem can be gathered from the fact that over
the period 1964—73 receipts from the exports of the three most important
export commodities — cotton, coffee, and sisal — suffered variations of more
than 33⅓ per cent *in consecutive years* on six separate occasions. Year to year
fluctuations in total foreign exchange earnings from commodity trade were
naturally less pronounced, but even they ranged from a drop of 11 per cent to
an increase of 26 per cent over the previous year. Little wonder that a 1964
study of trade prospects concluded that 'in this sector any estimates, however
careful, are very liable to be quite far from the mark, particularly as regards
performance in any particular year'.[11] Under such conditions planning becomes very difficult indeed and dependence takes on a very real meaning.

This difficulty has meant that from its earliest days the Tanzanian policy
towards exports has been to expand and to diversify. The record on expansion has been given; the record on diversification is somewhat more
encouraging.

Diversification is important both in the sense of increasing the range of
commodities and of trading partners. The record on diversification of commodities appeared quite favourable until 1971. Until then it was possible to
speak of a falling trend in the proportion of total export earnings derived
from the three most important export commodities — coffee, cotton and
sisal. Since that time this trend has been reversed and by 1973 these three
commodities again accounted for 52 per cent of total export earnings —
compared with 58 per cent in 1960.

Closer examination of these figures reveals that the falling trend during
1960—71, was very closely related to the collapse of the sisal market. Hence
the proportion of total exports generated by coffee and cotton did not
diminish, and the trend of export earnings generated by cotton, coffee and
cashews has been a rising one over the period, with the proportion of total
export earnings derived from these three crops approaching the level achieved
by coffee, cotton and sisal in 1960. In any event, the issue of diversification
raises the question of diversification into what? Clearly if such a policy is to
have a significant impact it must involve diversification into relatively unrelated markets. Contrary to some simplistic views this does not simply mean
markets for processed goods. Indeed, if the purpose is to reduce short-term
variability, it may be better to add a primary export like cashew nuts to sisal
exports, than to 'diversify' into sisal twine and rope. Nevertheless there may
be some presumption in favour of seeking markets for manufactured goods
since these are generally easier to separate from competing markets through
product differentiation. This makes them easier to control and therefore less
volatile.

Unfortunately the complexity of the question is compounded when one
considers it from a longer run perspective, since then it is necessary to consider
external effects on the development of skills and technology, as well as the
potential ability of an economy to satisfy its own demand. The first point is
familiar, though no less important for that; the second ought to be more

TABLE 2.2 TANZANIA: MAJOR UNPROCESSED COMMODITY EXPORTS (OUTSIDE EAC), 1960–73 (IN Shs MILLION)

	1960	1961	1962	1963	1964	1965	1966	1967	1968	1969	1970	1971	1972	1973
Coffee	146·5	135·2	131·5	136·7	220·9	171·6	302·5	238·6	265·1	257·1	312·2	227·4	383·0	495·3
Cotton	176·3	135·9	147·8	214·3	197·6	244·2	349·9	251·4	282·9	234·7	247·2	244·8	336·4	333·1
Sisal	308·8	280·6	314·7	453·4	437·3	285·6	234·7	200·9	158·7	159·6	178·8	133·8	144·8	221·6
Cashews	42·5	36·1	46·7	40·5	65·8	82·5	100·1	92·2	101·6	118·9	115·2	119·6	150·3	141·3
Diamonds	93·1	115·2	108·5	99·0	135·6	142·3	180·0	222·9	135·4	177·5	161·0	208·8	87·6	170·2
Oil—Seeds	68·5	43·0	39·9	67·0	53·6	44·4	42·7	38·8	52·9	41·5	36·1	40·2	38·0*	48·0
Tobacco	1·8	1·6	1·6	1·4	0·7	9·6	16·1	33·5	39·6	35·3	44·8	43·1	49·0	55·5
Tea	23·0	26·7	32·2	30·9	30·3	28·8	43·7	42·0	44·9	48·3	42·2	48·9	53·8	54·2
Hides & skins	36·7	35·2	29·8	33·4	25·6	30·3	42·9	29·0	31·5	35·6	27·3	26·8	41·6	46·6
Other	189·1	155·4	165·0	188·1	228·8	206·8	257·6	391·4	412·0	405·9	413·8	463·8	505·7	439·1
Total (exc. Zanzibar & cloves)	1086·5	965·3	1018·5	1262·2	1395·1	1245·8	1570·9	1540·7	1525·8	1514·5	1579·3	1556·4	1786·9	2005·0
Proportion of total exports made up by each commodity (%)														
Coffee	13·5	14·0	12·9	10·8	15·8	13·8	19·3	15·5	17·4	17·0	19·8	14·6	21·4	24·7
Cotton	16·2	14·1	14·5	17·0	14·2	19·6	22·3	16·3	18·5	15·5	15·7	15·7	18·8	16·6
Sisal	28·4	29·1	30·9	35·9	31·3	22·9	14·9	13·0	10·4	10·5	11·3	8·6	8·1	11·1
Cashews	3·9	3·7	4·6	3·2	4·7	6·6	6·4	6·0	6·7	7·9	7·3	7·7	8·4	7·0
Diamonds	8·6	11·9	10·7	7·8	9·7	11·4	11·5	14·5	8·9	11·7	10·2	13·4	4·9	8·5
Oil—Seeds, tobacco, tea & hides	12·0	11·1	10·2	10·4	7·9	9·1	9·2	9·3	11·1	10·6	9·5	10·2	10·1	10·2
Other	17·4	16·1	16·2	14·9	16·4	16·6	16·4	25·4	27·0	26·8	26·2	29·8	28·3	21·9
Total	100·0	100·0	100·0	100·0	100·0	100·0	100·0	100·0	100·0	100·0	100·0	100·0	100·0	100·0
% for cotton, coffee & sisal	58·1	57·2	58·3	63·7	61·3	56·3	56·5	44·8	46·3	43·0	46·8	38·9	48·3	52·4
% for cotton, coffee & cashews.	33·6	31·8	32·0	31·0	34·7	40·0	48·0	37·8	42·6	40·4	42·8	38·0	48·6	48·3

*estimated

Source: East African Customs & Excise, *Annual Trade Reports*.

widely acknowledged especially by those like Professor Wiles, who recognise that 'political preconceptions dominate and should dominate all theories of international trade'.[12] The fact is that trade engenders rivalries and that international markets are unstable, so that it is necessary for an economy to consider the flexibility of its productive structures. Extremely specialised economies are likely to be less flexible and hence more dependent.

It still does not follow that therefore diversification into manufactures is necessarily always advisable. Long-term gains have to be weighed against possible short-term losses. The production of primary commodities is not necessarily technically less demanding or stimulating, and the terms and conditions under which manufacturing takes place (foreign subsidiaries) may nullify most of the potential benefits derived from such diversification into manufacturing. In short, there are no good or bad exports *per se*, and certainly 'manufactured' and 'primary' are not proxies for either. Rather for any economy at any one time, the question of the optimal export strategy has to be dealt with in its complexity. It is no more amenable to simple dicta about exporting manufactures, than to magical resolution by the 'invisible' hands of commodity dealers and their clients.

Whatever Tanzania's optimal strategy may be, it is a fact that it has aimed at diversification into manufactured exports. However in the event, its external exports for 1973 reflect a pattern which gives little indication of any fundamental restructuring of the economy, nor even of far-reaching risk-reducing diversification. 83 per cent of export earnings still accrued from the sale of raw materials processed only so far as is necessary for shipment; the remainder consisted of exports processed beyond this minimal point.

On the basis of 1973 figures, raw material exports can be grouped into: major commodities (coffee, cotton, sisal, cashews, diamonds); moderately important commodities (tobacco, oil-seeds, tea, hides and skins); and minor commodities. In 1973, the 'major commodities' group accounted for 81·8 per cent of all primary exports, and for 68 per cent of total exports. Corresponding figures for 1960 were 76·5 per cent and 70 per cent respectively.

The 'moderately important' group of commodities earned 12·3 per cent of primary commodity export revenues and 10·2 per cent of all export revenue in 1973. Again the corresponding figures for 1960 — 12·6 per cent and 11·5 per cent — are very similar, especially since the comparison is between commodity groups based on the 1973 pattern. It would be closer still if one merely looked at the ten most important foreign exchange earning commodities in each year.

Table 2.4 looks at exports in this way and suggests that diversification of exports by commodity has not proceeded very far. The lists of the ten most important primary commodity exports are almost identical for 1960 and 1973, only that gold and lead have been replaced by tobacco and vegetables. It is arguable that this substitution was unfavourable from a risk-avoiding perspective since gold and lead are not weather dependent, and since their markets are relatively unrelated to the markets for the other major exports,

TABLE 2.3 TANZANIA: EXTERNAL EXPORTS
(OUTSIDE EAC) BY COMMODITIES 1960 AND 1973
(IN Shs MILLION)

| | 1960 | | 1973 | |
	Raw	*Processed*	*Raw*	*Processed*
Cashews	42·5	—	141·2	33·3
Coffee	145·7	0·8	495·2	0·4
Cotton	176·5	—	333·1	0·2
Sisal	308·8	—	221·6	73·1
Tobacco	1·8	—	55·5	0·7
Oil/oil—seeds	64·6	14·1	48·2	46·7
Tea	23·0	—	54·2	—
Wattle	0·5	6·6	1·2	15·7
Pyrethrum	—	—	0·2	17·4
Hides & skins	36·7	—	46·6	1·2
Diamonds/ precious stones	93·1	—	173·8	—
Gold	24·6	—	—	—
Vegetables	15·5	3·5	24·8	—
Animals/meat	4·8	39·3	21·4	18·2
Fish	2·7	—	3·8	—
Spices	0·1	—	15·8	—
Timber/paper/ printing	0·3	13·0	1·7	7·5
Cereals	17·8	9·8	9·2	8·6
Petroleum	—	—	—	87·9
Carvings/ jewellery	—	0·1	—	6·7
Other veg.	11·8	1·3	13·2	4·8
Other animal	3·1	0·3	1·5	—
Other mineral	27·8	3·3	7·0	8·4
Total	1001·8	92·1	1669·3	331·4
% of Total	91·6	8·4	83·4	16·6

Source: East African Customs & Excise, *Annual Trade Reports.*

concentrated as these are in food and textiles.

Even though the share of total export earnings derived from processed goods has doubled between 1960 and 1973, going from 8·4 to 16·6 per cent, the ten most important raw material exports still earn 79 per cent of total export incomes in 1973, compared with 85 per cent in 1960. This is a substantial proportionate reduction, but its effect on possible trade instability is substantially reduced because many of the 'processing' activities are aimed at markets which are very closely related to the original raw material markets — cashew kernels instead of nuts; sisal twine instead of fibre; oil instead of

TABLE 2.4 TANZANIA: THE TEN MAJOR COMMODITY EXPORTS, 1960 AND 1973 (IN Shs MILLION)

	1960				1973		
Rank in 1973	Ten Major Export Commodities	Exported Raw	Exported Raw or Processed	Rank	Ten Major Export Commodities	Exported Raw	Exported Raw or Processed
3	Sisal	308·8	308·8	1	Coffee	495·2	495·6
2	Cotton	176·5	176·5	2	Cotton	333·1	333·3
1	Coffee	145·7	146·5	3	Sisal	221·6	294·7
4	Diamonds	93·1	93·1	4	Diamonds	173·8	173·8
8	Oil—Seeds	64·6	78·7	5	Cashews	141·2	174·5
5	Cashews	42·5	42·5	6	Tobacco	55·5	56·2
9	Hides & skins	36·7	36·7	7	Tea	54·2	54·2
	Gold	24·6	24·6	8	Oil—Seeds	48·2	94·9
7	Tea	23·0	23·0	9	Hides & skins	46·6	47·8
	Lead	21·5	21·5	10	Vegetables	24·8	24·8
	Total Ten Commodities	937·0	951·9			1594·2	1749·8
	% of Raw material exports	93·5				95·5	
	% of Total external exports	85·4	88·8			79·4	87·2

Source: East African Customs & Excise, *Annual Trade Reports*.

oil-seeds — and the share of total export earnings based directly on the ten major raw materials and closely tied to the markets for those materials has in fact shown a marginal increase, from 86·8 per cent to 87·2 per cent. In the same way the proportion of total export earnings based directly on the cotton, coffee and sisal markets is 57 per cent in 1973 when sisal twine sales are included. This compares with the 58 per cent share of these three commodities in 1960. It should be noted that such an argument does not deny that the extension into processing activities is a significant development, but in terms of the diversification of commodity trade to reduce the risks of international market fluctuation, little seems to have been achieved.

The significance of the modest changes indicated is further reduced if one considers *net*, rather than *gross* foreign exchange receipts. More than a quarter of all foreign exchange received from the sale of processed goods came from the sale of petroleum products, but these were based on imported inputs, machinery and skills, and there was foreign participation in the equity capital of the producing firm. If all of these factors were considered for all of the processing industries their real contribution to foreign exchange earnings would be far less than the 16·6 per cent indicated above, and would probably lie below ten per cent.

By contrast, Tanzania has had considerable success in diversifying its geographical export markets. Whereas in 1960 it sent 32 per cent of its external exports to the UK, 27·6 per cent to the countries now in the EEC (excluding the UK) and altogether 80·7 per cent to the developed countries, this had changed significantly by 1973, when 21 per cent of such exports went to the UK, 19·6 per cent to the rest of the EEC, and only 62·4 per cent to the rich countries generally.

The biggest change between 1960 and 1973 was the reduction in the value of exports going to the EEC (the Nine) from 60 to 41 per cent. Half of the vacuum left by this decline was filled by the socialist countries, with the rest going in approximately equal proportions to other African countries and the Far East (excluding Japan).

This diversification was of particular significance because it involved new markets some of which were not very closely related to the original export centres, and hence not fully subject to the same fluctuations. It is in this respect that the trade with the socialist bloc is of particular significance.

Figure 2.1 shows the volume of export earnings received from each of the six major trading blocs. It shows quite clearly that generalisation of any trend is risky. Exports to the UK increased for the period 1960–7 and then fell during 1967–73; EEC (excluding UK) markets declined steadily until 1971, but this was dramatically reversed in 1971–3; exports to the Far East (excluding Japan) showed the most consistent development, increasing steadily and rapidly over the whole period 1961–73; exports to North America were stagnant over the 1961–7 period and then embarked on a rapid climb until 1973; markets in the rest of Africa were quite stagnant up to 1965, then expanded rapidly (with the opening of the Tan-Zam oil pipe-

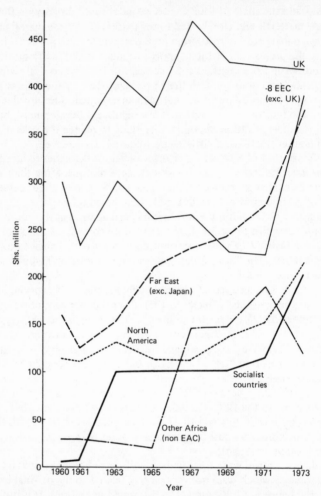

FIGURE 2.1: *Tanzania: Exports to selected trading blocs, 1960–73*

line) only to reverse themselves during 1971–3; finally the socialist countries' markets were opened in 1963 but throughout the period 1963–9 they remained on a plateau, only to increase rapidly during the 1969–73 period.

When one looks at trade with individual nations this diversification is still evident, though one cannot fail to be impressed by the degree of continuity. Of the top ten national export markets in 1960, eight are still among the top ten in 1973, and the ninth and tenth have only slipped to twelfth and fourteenth place. These same ten countries bought 87 per cent of all exports in 1960, 75 per cent in 1965 and a still substantial 68 per cent in 1973. The

TABLE 2.5 TANZANIA: EXTERNAL* EXPORTS BY DESTINATION AREA 1960–73

	1960	1961	1963	1965	1967	1969	1971	1973
			(Shs MILLION)					
UK	347·7	347·9	413·3	379·3	470·4	427·8	423·5	420·3
EEC (Eight excl. UK)	299·7	232·9	301·8	262·5	266·7	228·0	225·3	393·4
Far East (excl. Japan)	159·7	125·9	155·6	211·7	231·7	244·8	279·0	378·6
North America	114·2	111·1	134·2	114·4	114·0	138·1	154·3	216·7
Socialist countries	5·6	7·4	100·6	101·1	101·7	103·7	117·2	204·2
Africa (excl. EAC)	29·5	29·9	25·9	21·4	147·3	149·7	191·5	122·3
Japan	60·0	44·6	37·8	33·5	67·0	80·4	45·3	87·9
Europe (non EEC)	16·4	15·8	23·8	36·6	44·4	41·2	44·3	87·1
Australasia	35·9	28·3	50·4	34·0	24·7	27·3	29·9	46·4
Middle East	12·2	14·9	11·7	42·9	53·4	42·8	29·7	28·1
Other	5·8	6·7	6·8	8·1	14·2	11·3	10·7	15·2
Ships' stores	0·1	–	0·2	0·3	5·1	2·6	5·8	4·8
Total (excl. Zanzibar and cloves)	1086·5	965·3	1262·2	1236·1	1540·7	1514·5	1556·4	2005·0
Zanzibar	10·5	7·7	8·9	9·7	12·9	–	–	–
Cloves	–	–	–	–	–	152·3	179·0	233·3
Total External Exports	1097·1	973·0	1271·1	1245·8	1553·6	1666·8	1735·4	2238·3
			(Percentages)					
UK	32·0	36·0	32·7	30·7	30·5	28·2	27·2	21·0
EEC (Eight excl. UK)	27·6	24·1	23·9	21·2	17·3	15·1	14·5	19·6
Far East (excl. Japan)	14·7	13·0	12·3	17·1	15·0	16·2	17·9	18·9
North America	10·5	11·5	10·6	9·3	7·4	9·1	9·9	10·8
Socialist countries	0·5	0·8	8·0	8·2	6·6	6·8	7·5	10·2
Africa (excl. EAC)	2·7	3·1	2·1	1·7	9·6	9·9	12·3	6·1
Japan	5·5	4·6	3·0	2·7	4·3	5·3	2·9	4·4
Europe (non EEC)	1·5	1·6	1·9	3·0	2·9	2·7	2·8	4·3
Australasia	3·3	2·9	4·0	2·8	1·6	1·8	1·9	2·3
Middle East	1·1	1·5	0·9	3·5	3·5	2·8	1·9	1·4
Other (inc. Ships stores)	0·5	0·7	0·6	0·7	1·3	0·9	1·1	1·0
TOTAL	100·0	100·0	100·0	100·0	100·0	100·0	100·0	100·0

Source: East African Customs & Excise, *Annual Trade Reports*.
*External means excluding East African Community trade.

major new export markets to emerge during this period were China and Zambia, with Sweden and Yugoslavia rising to moderate importance.

What is possibly of greater significance is the fact that the top ten export markets bought 87 per cent of exports in 1960, but only 72 per cent in 1973. In other words there was genuine diversification in the sense of a significantly larger share of total exports being sold to markets which were individually unimportant — that is each accounting for less than two per cent of total exports. Unfortunately this success in diversifying export markets has some potential drawbacks. For example, it has been argued that concentration of trade provides more leverage and hence a chance of better terms.[13] While this sword quite clearly has two edges, this is a general point to which the discussion will return.

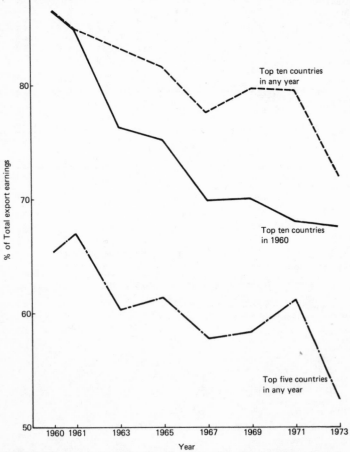

FIGURE 2.2: *Tanzania: proportion of export earnings derived from the major markets, 1960–73*

TABLE 2.6 TANZANIA: RANKING ORDER OF MAJOR EXPORT MARKETS, 1960–73

	1960	*1961*	*1963*	*1965*	*1967*	*1969*	*1971*	*1973*
UK	1	1	1	1	1	1	1	1
USA	2	2	4	6	6	3	4	2
Germany	3	3	2	3	5	8	7	3
India	4	6	7	4	4	2	2	4
Netherlands	5	5	6	7	8	9	8	9
Japan	6	7	10	10	7	6	9	7
Hong Kong	7	4	3	2	3	5	5	5
Belgium	8	8	9	8	(11)	(11)	(12)	10
Australia	9	10	(12)	(12)	(16)	(18)	(14)	(14)
Italy	10	9	(11)	(11)	10	10	10	(12)
China			5	5	9	7	6	6
Canada			8	9				
Zambia					2	4	3	8

Proportion of Total Exports Earnings Received from:
(Percentages)

The 10 countries most important in 1960	86·5	84·9	76·3	75·2	69·9	70·3	68·0	67·6
The 5 top countries in each year	65·4	67·0	60·3	61·4	57·7	58·4	61·1	52·4
The 10 top countries in each year	86·5	84·9	80·1	81·6	77·6	79·7	79·5	72·0

Source: East African Customs & Excise, *Annual Trade Reports*.

This brief sketch of the development of Tanzania's exports has shown that since independence Tanzania has sought to expand and diversify its export earnings. Expansion has been modest in current value terms, and even less in terms of purchasing power; diversification of the products sold has not been very significant, though diversification of national export markets has been considerable.

Over this same period the growth of imports has been very much more rapid so that the early substantial balance-of-trade surpluses have turned (since 1968) to dramatic deficits which became devastating in the years 1972–4 when food and fuel bills shot up as inflation coincided with poor harvests. These increases were only partially offset by gains in export earnings due to improved prices (see Table 2.7).

To the picture so far presented it is necessary to add the trade within the East African Community. Here Tanzanian exports expanded rapidly between

1961 and 1965 (165 per cent increase), then fell back in 1965—66, rose again to a peak in 1971 and then retrenched once more. Overall this represented a healthy if erratic increase which meant that by 1973 exports to the EAC partners were equal to 8.5 per cent of external exports (excluding cloves) compared to only 4·3 per cent in 1960. Imports increased in a rather similar pattern, reaching a peak in 1965, then suffering a slight recession only to grow again from 1968 onwards. The annual trade deficit lay between Shs 167 million and Shs 235 million over the entire period 1961—73, with the sole exception of 1971 when it dipped to Shs 114 million.

TABLE 2.7 TANZANIA: BALANCE OF
TRADE WITH EAST AFRICAN COMMUNITY
AND WITH THE REST OF THE WORLD
(IN Shs MILLION)

	EAC	Rest of World	Total trade balance
1960	−137·2	+375·7	+238·5
1961	−167·4	+218·5	+ 50·9
1962	−185·9	+275·2	+ 79·3
1963	−178·7	+494·4	+315·7
1964	−211·4	+548·8	+337·4
1965	−215·2	+280·6	+ 65·4
1966	−235·1	+407·2	+172·1
1967	−195·5	+286·4	+ 90·9
1968	−211·0	+ 95·1	−115·9
1969	−187·3	+269·7	+ 82·4
1970	−163·9	−234·9	−398·8
1971	−114·6	−622·2	−736·8
1972	−198·4	−454·1	−652·5
1973	−169·1	−722·9	−892·0

Source: East African Customs & Excise, *Annual Trade Reports*.

The most noteworthy feature of Tanzania's exports to the rest of the community was the relative importance of manufactured goods, with a substantial volume of textiles, processed foods, furniture and metal products among the total.

IV. Tanzania's Trade with Socialist Countries

It is against this backdrop that an assessment of Tanzania's trade with socialist countries needs to be made. The basic changes in the total volume of that trade have been discussed earlier. Trade was negligible until 1963; then it grew quickly to Shs 100–120 million. There it remained until 1969 when it resumed its growth reaching the Shs 200 million mark in 1973. In this discussion it is essential to remember that the trade in question was carried out in convertible currency, and was not subject to iterative bilateral balancing. When the export figures are disaggregated their apparent stability emerges as the outcome of the averaging of a number of highly unstable individual series, and since there is no evidence that such trade as there was, was coordinated in any way it seems necessary to conclude that this stability was largely fortuitous.

The instability in question manifests itself at every level. Table 2.8 shows the annual value of exports sold to each socialist trading partner, and indicates clearly that the trade between Tanzania and the socialist bloc has not in fact benefited from those potential gains in stability described earlier. Indeed there is a reverse side to this coin which applies to countries exporting to the socialist countries, whose exports are not of great importance to the importing economy and whose trade is not subject to long term trade agreements or to the need for short-term bilateral trade equalisation, an arrangement which would ensure that reduced purchases would soon jeopardise reciprocal export markets. Such non-integrated trading partners of the socialist economies will find themselves trading in the margin of the planned economy which serves as the buffer zone required to absorb the stresses and strains of deviations from the Plan. It goes without saying that both demand and supply in this margin are highly unstable so that trade based on it is also doomed to instability.

Such instability as appears in Table 2.8 may of course have a variety of causes including price and crop yield variations. It is therefore instructive to look at the pattern in terms of quantities of commodities shipped and to do this for commodities for which the effective constraint is an insufficiency of markets — namely coffee and sisal. Table 2.9 confirms the pattern of instability rather dramatically. It shows the quantities of coffee and of sisal exported to socialist countries over the period 1960–73. With the sole exception of the sale of sisal to Czechoslovakia between 1963 and 1970, all of the markets are extremely erratic. Indeed, there were eighty-one year to year changes in export volumes and in less than a quarter of these was the change less than plus or minus 50 per cent. Nor was this extraordinary result due to sustained rapid growth, since fully half of the year to year changes recorded were in a downward direction.

It is clear that Tanzania's trade with the socialist bloc has not been significantly more stable than its trade with other areas. However, there are some indications that the fluctuations in the volume of exports to socialist countries had a slight tendency to be counter-cyclical. Hence an analysis of annual changes in the quantities of cotton, coffee and sisal exported to socialist and non-socialist markets revealed that in twenty out of thirty cases the movement was in opposite directions — for sisal it behaved like this in every year between 1962 and 1970, for coffee in every year between 1966 and 1970 and for cotton in eight out of ten years between 1961 and 1971. Even if

TABLE 2.8 TANZANIA: VALUE OF EXPORTS TO SOCIALIST COUNTRIES, 1960–73 (IN Shs MILLION)

	1960	1961	1962	1963	1964	1965	1966	1967	1968	1969	1970	1971	1972	1973
China	5·3	–	–	74·3	46·4	86·3	67·8	55·1	54·9	77·8	58·7	84·1	135·5	98·2
GDR	–	–	–	–	–	0·1	8·9	6·5	3·7	3·0	8·1	8·7	8·4	26·7
Poland	–	–	–	3·7	16·3	5·6	17·7	20·5	7·9	10·1	8·4	9·5	8·0	8·1
USSR	–	–	–	1·4	6·5	5·5	11·3	3·0	10·5	19·6	9·0	4·4	9·8	23·7
Czechoslovakia	–	0·3	2·3	3·6	2·4	1·8	2·2	1·6	4·8	2·6	5·7	1·9	0·1	1·9
Hungary	–	–	–	2·1	0·6	–	2·2	11·6	0·3	–	–	–	–	0·1
Romania	–	6·7	–	–	–	–	1·3	–	0·2	–	–	–	5·2	–
Bulgaria	–	–	–	–	–	–	–	–	–	–	–	–	–	0·2
COMECON	–	7·0	2·3	10·7	25·8	13·0	43·6	43·3	27·4	35·3	31·2	24·6	31·4	59·9
Yugoslavia	0·3	0·4	0·2	15·6	4·3	1·9	6·8	3·3	7·3	9·5	23·5	8·5	7·5	46·1
North Korea	–	–	–	–	–	–	–	–	–	0·7	–	–	–	–
Total soc. countries	5·6	7·4	2·5	100·6	76·4	101·1	118·3	101·7	89·6	123·3	113·4	117·2	174·3	204·2

Source: East African Customs & Excise, *Annual Trade Reports*.

TABLE 2.9 TANZANIA: QUANTITIES OF ARABICA COFFEE AND SISAL FIBRE EXPORTED TO THE SOCIALIST COUNTRIES 1960–73

Arabica coffee (Quintals)

	USSR	Poland	GDR	Czechoslovakia	Hungary	Yugoslavia	China	Other	Total
1960	—	—	—	—	—	—	—	—	—
1961	—	—	—	—	—	—	—	—	—
1962	—	—	—	—	—	—	—	—	—
1963	—	2,740	—	—	—	3,048	—	—	5,788
1964	4,557	10,996	—	—	—	1,785	—	—	17,338
1965	1,818	641	—	—	—	—	—	—	2,459
1966	1,818	18,846	9,877	907	907	517	—	—	32,872
1967	—	17,718	7,913	454	3,802	—	—	—	29,887
1968	4,633	—	1,689	3,812	533	7,225	2,727	663	21,282
1969	13,763	7,346	1,845	—	—	8,085	—	—	31,039
1970	10,499	853	6,589	5,248	—	9,999	—	—	33,188
1971	—	—	3,206	2,000	—	4,874	—	—	10,080
1972	n.a.	n.a.	n.a.	n.a.	n.a.	n.a.	n.a.	n.a.	n.a.
1973	29,670	—	17,617	—	—	18,492	—	—	65,779

Sisal fibre (Metric Tonnes)

	USSR	Poland	GDR	Czechoslovakia	Hungary	Yugoslavia	China	Other	Total
1960	—	—	—	—	—	157	1,179	—	1,336
1961	—	—	—	—	—	—	—	—	—
1962	—	146	—	1,448	—	143	1,290	—	1,591
1963	9	865	—	1,440	—	2,035	5,313	—	4,920
1964	624	488	51	1,175	—	584	3,508	—	8,561
1965	2,569	1,057	317	1,161	—	573	7,096	—	8,350
1966	7,533	1,292	—	1,030	—	66	3,048	—	17,099
1967	2,407	—	406	979	—	3,499	5,207	—	11,225
1968	5,722	943	—	1,266	—	2,190	5,501	—	15,797
1969	7,442	640	300	1,365	—	2,880	4,471	—	18,392
1970	2,890	900	950	1,284	—	4,049	2,511	15	13,909
1971	4,810	305	—	198	—	4,044	—	—	12,821
1972	n.a.	n.a.	n.a.	n.a.	—	n.a.	n.a.	n.a.	n.a.
1973	2,568	50	742	495	—	6,922	—	—	10,777

Source: East African Customs & Excise, *Annual Trade Reports*.

this is of no further significance it illustrates the advantages of export diversification into markets which are not entirely interdependent.

So far the discussion has been largely in relation to the cotton, coffee and
sisal markets. The question of how significant these commodities are in the
trade with socialist countries raises the related question of the impact of that
trade on the pattern of trade, and particularly on the pattern of exports.

TABLE 2.10 TANZANIA: PROPORTION OF EXPORTS TO SOCIALIST
COUNTRIES REPRESENTED BY SALES OF RAW COTTON, COFFEE
AND SISAL 1960—73
(Percentages)

	USSR	Poland	GDR	Czecho-slovakia	Yugoslavia	China	All socialist countries
1960	–	–	–	–	100	98	96
1961	–	–	–	42	–	–	93
1962	–	–	–	100	100	–	100
1963	2	69	–	95	95	100	95
1964	83	70	–	100	76	100	90
1965	100	69	100	97	45	92	90
1966	100	81	96	91	96	96	93
1967	94	70	100	96	97	96	91
1968	99	40	47	81	99	99	90
1969	99	41	43	57	98	99	91
1970	99	25	75	92	99	90	87
1971	98	4	38	82	88	93	80
1972	n.a.	n.a.	n.a.	n.a.	n.a.	n.a.	n.a.
1973	100	1	73	100	92	89	85

Source: East African Customs & Excise, *Annual Trade Reports.* Exports of cloves and
coconut oil were excluded from the figures from 1968 so as to exclude the effect of
the inclusion of Zanzibar exports from that date onwards. The quantities excluded from
the total export figures were in Shs million: 1968 – 8·4; 1969 – 9·1; 1970 – 17·4;
1971 – 8·7; 1973 – 0·5.

The evidence on this point is clear and unambiguous. Trade with the socialist
countries has strongly reinforced the old colonial specialisation in cotton,
coffee and sisal. It has been shown that these three commodities earned
roughly between 40 and 60 per cent of total export earnings in each year
since independence. By contrast, until 1969, these three commodities
accounted for between 90 and 100 per cent of export earnings from socialist
countries. Since 1970 this proportion has fallen, but only to remain at
between 80 and 90 per cent.

Even this recent modest reduction in the dependence on these three
commodities has no broader significance and does not indicate that markets
for 'new' commodities or especially for manufactured goods have been

opened. Rather it stems from a relative expansion of the sale of wattle bark products, of oil-seeds and of sisal twine. The latter seems to be the only connection between efforts to add more value to Tanzania's primary exports, and the trade with socialist countries. Even this one connection is modest enough with sisal twine exports amounting to three per cent of exports to these countries in 1971, and nil in 1973. Meanwhile, since 1969, Poland has begun buying quantities of wattle bark, thus undermining the development of the local industry producing wattle extract which had developed relatively early and had almost come to process all of the local bark produced.

Whatever the optimal pattern of export diversification may be for Tanzania it is clear that trade with the socialist countries is not making any special contribution to the process of achieving it.

Finally there is the question of the terms of trade. In this instance this can be considered only in respect of prices received for homogeneous commodity exports, since a comparison of important values is not possible with available data (if indeed it is ever possible).

The record on prices shows that for cotton and sisal the socialist countries have consistently paid a premium over and above the prices paid by non-socialist buyers, a premium averaging 4—5 per cent for cotton and about 11 per cent for sisal. For coffee the record is more erratic which is no doubt related to the significant influence exercised by quota agreements in that market. Nevertheless in the market for Arabica coffee, prices paid by socialist and non-socialist buyers fluctuated about the same trend, with divergences roughly cancelling each other out. Only for Robusta coffee was the price paid by the socialist countries consistently below the average price paid by other buyers, with an average differential of eight per cent. This is a reflection of the fact that the socialist countries have generally bought non-quota coffee.

The evidence so far suggests that Tanzania's trade with the socialist bloc has been of no particular significance in terms of its impact on the stability of trade, the patterns of trade or the terms of trade, although it should be pointed out that this conclusion is reached without any attempt to value or assess the imports received from the socialist countries in return. Most of these imports were manufactured goods ranging from household buckets to heavy machinery, although in a very few years large quantities of refined sugar were imported. Since the purchase of these imports was not directly tied to the sale of exports one can argue that there was no special reason to believe that imports purchased were not reasonable value for money, though there may well have been cases where such an assumption was not warranted.

By way of explaining the findings presented in this paper it is necessary to focus on the fact that Tanzania is not a socialist country, does not have a planned economy and until recently did not effectively control the expenditure of foreign exchange. Furthermore, one of its major planks of foreign policy, consisted of the firm and repeated assertion that it was beholden to no one, and that it did not intend to become aligned with any power bloc. Such a stance clearly had its advantages, but it also meant that Tanzania could not

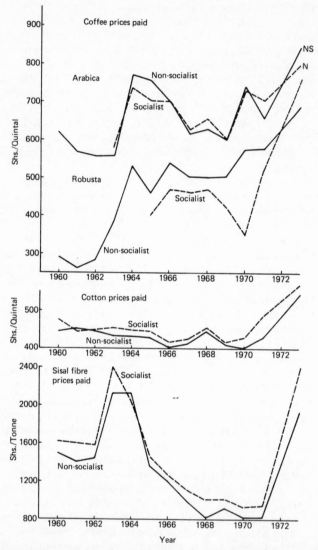

FIGURE 2.3: *Tanzania: average price received for major export commodities 1960–73*

hope to obtain the potential benefits of integrating its economy with the planned economies of the socialist bloc, even if the latter had been interested in such integration in the short term. While such integration has potential benefits it also demands certain things as prerequisites; namely the introduction of planning and a commitment to the other economies involved.

TABLE 2.11 TANZANIA: AVERAGE EXPORT PRICES RECEIVED FOR MAJOR
COMMODITIES 1960–73

	Cotton (Shs/Quintal)				Sisal fibre (Shs/Metric Tonne)		
	Non-socialist	Socialist	Relative* prices		Non-socialist	Socialist	Relative* prices
'60	446·5	478·2	1·07	1960	1501	1625	1·08
'61	451·0	446·8	·99	1961	1409	–	–
'62	446·7	–	–	1962	1448	1583	1·09
'63	432·9	455·1	1·05	1963	2138	2402	1·12
'64	434·6	449·8	1·04	1964	2137	2049	·96
'65	429·6	447·3	1·04	1965	1368	1478	1·08
'66	403·8	418·1	1·04	1966	1207	1271	1·05
'67	410·9	427·4	1·04	1967	997	1111	1·11
'68	448·9	456·6	1·02	1968	834	1018	1·22
'69	412·4	417·7	1·01	1969	929	1028	1·11
'70	402·6	431·5	1·07	1970	830	943	1·14
'71	433·1	490·0	1·13	1971	825	957	1·16
'72	n.a.	n.a.	n.a.	1972	n.a.	n.a.	n.a.
'73	548·5	572·3	1·05	1973	1950	2414	1·24

	Arabica coffee (Shs/Quintal)				Robusta coffee (Shs/Quintal)		
	Non-socialist	Socialist	Relative* prices		Non-socialist	Socialist	Relative* prices
'60	620·4	–	–	1960	292·6	–	–
'61	568·6	–	–	1961	264·0	–	–
'62	563·0	–	–	1962	285·5	–	–
'63	565·0	581·6	1·10	1963	388·7	–	–
'64	772·4	737·7	·96	1964	534·5	–	–
'65	755·8	705·2	·93	1965	460·5	404·4	·88
'66	700·1	703·4	1·01	1966	542·0	470·1	·87
'67	618·4	626·9	1·01	1967	506·8	463·3	·91
'68	633·0	659·0	1·04	1968	504·9	471·8	·93
'69	603·1	606·4	1·01	1969	506·5	423·0	·84
'70	744·5	727·7	·98	1970	575·4	353·3	·61
'71	660·8	707·8	1·07	1971	579·5	520·6	·90
'72	n.a.	n.a.	n.a.	1972	n.a.	n.a.	n.a.
'73	848·9	800·9	·94	1973	692·8	762·8	1·10

Source: East African Customs & Excise, *Annual Trade Reports*.
Relative prices are Socialist ÷ Non-socialist prices.

When Cuba's trade with the USA was abruptly halted and it had to find other markets in which to sell its exports and from which to buy its imports, it was said that 'to do so with the socialist countries meant planning'. Moreover, this connection between planning and trade was very direct and continuous, so that later when the planning process was rudely interrupted by the 'Bay of Pigs' it had to be quickly resumed 'with an increased sense of urgency' because 'preliminary versions of the plan were needed – to serve as the basis for trade negotiations with the other socialist countries'.[14] It is questionable whether Tanzania even today has the ready capacity to plan in the manner required.

The question of why there was not closer integration with the socialist economies after independence must therefore be answered thus in the first instance: because the newly independent Government did not wish it; because the mass of the population did not demand it; because the administrative machinery could not cope with it; and because the socialist countries themselves were only remotely interested in it.

Without the real possibility of such integration there was no reason to expect trade with the socialist countries to be significantly different from trade with other countries. Indeed the potential for more stable relations could be expected to turn into its opposite so long as it could be said that in the socialist planning mechanisms 'exports of "very many goods" come out as a "resultant item" of the balances' and 'took the brunt of the adjustments made to deal with a deficit'.[15]

Furthermore, the current efforts of some countries in the European socialist bloc to achieve a much fuller integration with the high technology economies have advanced to the point where some are seriously considering '*gradually* to allow world-market impulses to act on the national economy, so that, parallel with economic development, also the national price proportion will approach those prevailing in the world market'.[16] While none of the COMECON economies have adopted such a strategy, which would of course mean the abandonment of any claim to being socialist, the movement by some of them in this direction is an indication of the difficulties which would be encountered by an economy which sought to be integrated into the socialist bloc precisely in order to avoid the consequences of international integration based on the world market. It is not surprising in view of Tanzania's own situation and in view of these trends that although general trade agreements were signed with a number of socialist countries in the 1960s these have never been used to establish specific bilateral arrangements except in the case of China. It follows that there have been no special clearing arrangements operating in accounting currencies, so that none of the difficulties concerning the identification of effective exchange rates generally associated with such arrangements arise in this case. The experience appears to bear out the analyst who wrote in 1966 from Tanzania that the 'socialist countries entered into these (payments agreements) during a phase when it was extremely difficult for them to obtain convertible currencies' and they suffered from 'shortages of important commodities'. However, even then it was said that 'neither of these considerations has so much force nowadays and it is possible that within a few years they may seek to withdraw from payments agreements and aim at more unilateral (though less plannable) arrangements'.[17]

In general, developments in the European socialist countries may make it less likely that a less developed economy could derive special advantages from integration with these economies. In any case, for a less developed capitalist country integration is out of the question and, at best, an underdeveloped economy could use this trade to obtain some additional markets. In such trade the socialist countries would naturally operate from the principle that 'it is understood that cooperation with capitalist and other countries must serve the common goal, that is, reinforce the economic power of the socialist community'. A paper to a recent COMECON conference has described one way in which this is perceived.

> The socialist countries purchase modern installations and technological know-how in the West . . . . But the shortage of certain raw and other materials can still be felt in the socialist market. The development of economic relations with capitalist market and primarily with developing countries makes it possible to meet a substantial part of the demands of the socialist countries for fuels, raw materials and foodstuffs.

At the same time the commodities being sold to pay for the Western imports are not deemed 'satisfactory' because 'raw materials dominate the composition of exports to this (capitalist) market' (93–94 per cent) and this is thought to be 'largely due to the discriminatory measures by the West against exports of finished products'.[18] It is not surprising that from such a perspective a pattern of trade has developed which has involved the export of primary commodities from countries like Tanzania and in return their import of manufactured goods. In other words a pattern which is similar to that of trade with the developed capitalist countries.

It is true that within UNCTAD, some of the socialist countries have pressed for the abolition of tariffs on manufactured exports from the developing countries, but unfortunately these recommendations have often been accompanied by a demand for reciprocal tariff concessions.[19] Such a demand for free trade is hardly a revolutionary step forward for the less developed countries. On the other hand some efforts have been made to encourage more diversified exports from the developing countries, so that it was reported that

> while the (GDR's) imports in the fifties and sixties were made up largely of the traditional raw materials which dominated the exports of Afro-Asian and Latin American countries, in the last few years a significant increase in the proportion of semi-manufactured and manufactured goods has been registered, reflecting the progress these countries have made in industrialisation and the development of manufacturing industry.[20]

This description of the earlier period confirms the basic pattern found in the Tanzanian case. The progress which it describes for more recent years is a welcome indication of change but it had not been reflected in Tanzania's trade by 1973, nor does it represent a terribly hopeful development in that the change is presented as being simply the result of the modest changes which have occurred in the economies of these countries.

Finally one can reiterate the fact that since trade with less developed countries is often trade with multinationals, there would be good reason for the socialist bloc to be cautious about the way in which it made special conditions available. In the end the point to be stressed is that the important potential gains to be obtained through trade with the socialist bloc can only be obtained by planned economies. Even for these the road from long term trade agreements to economic integration is a long and arduous one.

At this stage, a specific word about Tanzania's trade with China, which accounts for more than half of its exports to socialist countries in most years, is necessary. Of course, the preceding description and discussion has included the Chinese figures and the general conclusions of that discussion apply to this particular case. Thus the trade with China was rather unstable (in terms of exports purchased); conformed to the same patterns, i.e. primary produce exports and manufactured imports, and involved the payment of a small premium on primary commodity exports from Tanzania. What is significant about this trade is its enormous imbalance. Although other trade balances also fluctuated widely, the size of the trade deficit with China was truly staggering – i.e. in 1973 imports of Shs 701 million against exports of Shs 98 million.

The explanation of this extraordinary pattern lies in the connection between this trade and the major aid projects in which China is involved. At present this means the Tan–Zam Railway project which is financed by a long term interest-free loan with money for local costs being raised through the importation and sale of Chinese goods. With the railway project nearing completion a major iron and steel complex may be financed in a similar manner. The economic significance of these arrangements lies in the fact of 'tied aid' which raises well known difficulties of assessing the real terms of such credits – although the very favourable basic terms of the credits involved leave a considerable margin before the terms would actually become relatively unfavourable.

The broader issue that is raised is the issue of the political pressures which can be exerted through trade, that is, through the control of export markets or supplies of imports. Such potential for influence naturally increases the more unequal are the trading partners. Hence if exports from X to Y represent a high proportion of the total exports of X, but a tiny fraction of the total imports of Y, and vice versa for the trade flows in the other direction, then X is clearly exposed to considerable pressure from Y. Such influence will tend to be used once it is in existence, but the issue is whether the influence thus exerted is a positive or a negative force for development.

TABLE 2.12 TANZANIA: BALANCE OF EXTERNAL TRADE WITH SOCIALIST COUNTRIES AND WITH ALL COUNTRIES, 1960–73

	1960	1961	1962	1963	1964	1965	1966	1967	1968	1969	1970	1971	1972	1973
Bulgaria	–	B*	–	B*	-0·3	-0·5	-0·8	-0·2	-0·2	-0·3	-0·2	B*	n.a.	+0·2
Czechoslovakia	-3·9	-2·9	-0·9	-1·3	-2·4	-4·0	-6·4	-5·8	-5·1	-7·0	-1·5	-9·8	n.a.	-7·1
GDR	-0·1	-0·1	-0·1	-0·9	-1·8	-2·3	+3·3	+2·5	-1·8	-6·3	-1·9	+2·1	n.a.	+14·6
Hungary	-0·4	-0·7	-0·6	+0·9	-1·8	-2·1	-1·0	+9·0	-4·1	-3·9	-3·9	-1·5	n.a.	-5·4
Poland	-0·1	-0·1	-8·1	-1·2	+15·4	+2·0	+10·8	+17·1	-0·2	+6·9	-3·7	-7·8	n.a.	-31·6
Romania	–	+6·7	B*	-0·1	-0·1	-0·1	+1·1	B*	-0·2	-0·3	-0·6	-3·1	n.a.	-6·0
USSR	–	–	B*	+1·1	+5·0	+2·8	+7·9	+1·0	+4·2	+15·6	+0·8	+0·1	n.a.	+18·3
COMECON	-4·5	+3·0	-9·7	-3·4	+14·2	-4·2	+14·9	+23·5	-7·4	+4·7	-3·7	-20·1	n.a.	-16·9
China	+5·1	-0·1	-0·2	+72·4	+40·2	+51·4	-6·3	-6·9	-19·3	-1·6	-206·6	-516·9	n.a.	-602·7
N. Korea	–	–	–	–	–	–	–	–	–	+0·3	-0·7	-0·1	n.a.	-2·9
Yugoslavia	-0·7	-0·8	-1·2	+13·3	-2·5	-2·4	+2·7	-16·6	+3·3	+6·3	+20·8	+6·3	n.a.	+37·4
All Soc. Countries	-0·1	+2·1	-11·1	+82·3	+51·9	+44·7	+11·4	B*	-23·4	+9·7	-188·8	-530·8	n.a.	-585·1
All Countries	+375·7	+218·3	+275·2	+494·4	+548·8	+280·6	+407·2	+286·4	+95·1	+269·7	-234·9	-622·2	-454·1	-722·9
Outside EAC														

*B means that trade was in balance within + or – Shs 50,000
Source: East African Customs & Excise, *Annual Trade Reports*.

It does not suffice merely to minimise all outside influence ('non-alignment'), attractive as such a position is intellectually. What is necessary is to minimise perverse influences, but this requires a recognition or an assessment of what is perverse under present circumstances. It requires taking a position. Espousing 'socialism' but keeping all options open, which has been Tanzania's policy, may be the perfect recipe for 'falling between two stools': preventing one from taking advantage of the real, but distorted and ambiguous benefits of capitalist development, but also preventing one from espousing the equally real benefits derivable from a socialist international division of labour. Indeed it is conceivably that a true policy of non-alignment seeking to minimize the pressure from any one bloc or trading partner could lead to a set of pressures so diverse as to virtually paralyse actions on domestic economic policies and make it impossible to construct a fully coherent set of policies or planning procedures. Under such circumstances one stands condemned to remain a marginal trading partner of the socialist bloc with whom one trades from a short-term perspective and who uses the trade to smooth out deviation from internal plans; while also being a small protagonist in the 'free' international market, totally exposed to the violent fluctuations of demand, of prices and of capital flows, and subject to competitive pressures which make the mobilisation of local resources painfully difficult.

V. Conclusions

This paper has suggested that Tanzania has not derived any special benefits from its trade with socialist countries other than gaining access to some additional export markets. It has further argued that this was inevitable in view of Tanzania's unwillingness to make a commitment to socialist development. Such a commitment would require the abandonment of its central foreign policy plank of non-alignment.

Unfortunately, even if such a commitment were feasible it appears difficult to envisage Tanzania's integration into the socialist international division of labour since some of the European socialist economies appear anxious to integrate themselves into a global division of labour, and for Tanzania that would simply mean going to where it already is. Even where no such trend appears in the socialist economies the integration of two economies at relatively different levels of technical development presents major, if not insurmountable, obstacles.

So long as integration is ruled out, the socialist country markets appear merely as complements to the rest of the world market. While they do not appear to have any special significance *per se,* they do represent additional markets, they do offer terms of trade roughly comparable to those obtainable elsewhere, and they help to smooth out fluctuations in other markets, though in the Tanzanian case only because their fluctuations were counter-posed to those of the 'free' international market, and not because they were themselves more stable. In the meantime the most significant aspect of socialist country trade and especially of Chinese trade, may be the extent to which it has been connected with projects which are conducive to Central African economic integration – Zambia, Mozambique, Tanzania. This may be the most important dimension of the trade since that is the direction in which expansion, diversification and integration will find their real opportunities.

Notes

[1] Most recently by Arghiri Emmanuel in his eloquent treatise on *Unequal Exchange*, Monthly Review Press, London 1972.

[2] For an illuminating presentation of the Neo-Ricardian case showing that even in a two factor Ricardian world trade may lead to a reduction in the standard of living ('consumption') see L. Mainwaring 'A Neo-Ricardian Analysis of International Trade', *Kyklos*, Vol. 27 No. 3 1974.

[3] P. J. D. Wiles, *Communist International Economics*, Basil Blackwell, Oxford 1968.

[4] See for example the very interesting presentation of arguments along these lines in A. O. Hirschman *How to Divest in Latin America, and Why*, Princeton University, Essays in International Finance, No. 76, Princeton, 1969.

[5] A recent paper by Bhagwati has stressed the need for 'more effective compensatory policies to improve the domestic mobility of labour' in the rich countries if the international division of labour, based on comparative advantage, is to proceed. J. Bhagwati, 'Trade Policies for Development' in G. Ranis *The Gap between Rich and Poor Nations*, Macmillan, London, 1973.

[6] It has been estimated that less than 15 per cent of world sugar production, and less than half of world sugar exports pass through the free market. D. Boorstein, *The Economic Transformation of Cuba*, Modern Reader Paperbacks, New York and London, 1968, p. 188.

[7] If the socialist country in question is very large it can probably obtain some quantity discounts due to the size of the deals it is proposing. Some recent but unpublished work on early Soviet dealings with western economies by D. Yaffe would support this contention.

[8] I.B.R.D. *The Economic Development of Tanzania* John S. Hopkins, Baltimore, 1961, pp. 35 and 331–2.

[9] The United Republic of Tanganyika and Zanzibar *Tanganyika Five-Year Plan for Economic and Social Development*, 1st July, 1964–30th June 1969, Volume I: General Analysis, p. 97.

[10] J. F. Rweyemamu, *Underdevelopment and Industrialisation in Tanzania*, Oxford University Press, Nairobi, 1973, p. 43.

[11] B. V. Arkadie and P. Ndegwa, 'Future Trade, Balance of Payments and Aid Requirements of East Africa', E.D.R.P. Paper 31, Makere University, Kampala, Uganda, 1964.

[12] Wiles, op. cit., p. 7.

[13] M. J. Yaffey, 'Self-Reliance and Foreign Trade', *Uchumi*, Vol. 1, No. 1, Journal of the Economic Society of Tanzania, Dar es Salaam.

[14] D. Boorstein, op. cit., p. 158.

[15] J. M. Montias, *Central Planning in Poland,* Yale University Press, New Haven, 1962, p. 99.

[16] T. Kiss, *International Division of Labour in Open Economies With Special Regard to the CMEA,* Akademiai Kiado, Budapest, 1971, p. 251.

[17] M. J. Yaffey, 'Special Bilateral Payments Agreements (Clearing Agreements) Between Socialist and Non-socialist Countries', Economic Research Bureau Paper 66.0, University of Dar es Salaam, 1966, p. 9.

[18] B. M. Shastitko, and Y. S. Shiryaev, 'Inter-relations with Non-Socialist Markets' in T. Kiss (ed.) *The Market of Socialist Economic Integration: Selected Conference Papers,* Akademiai Kiado, Budapest 1973, pp. 160—2.

[19] Gottfried Freitag, 'Probleme der Entwicklungslander bei der Erweiterung des Exports von industriellen Halb-und Fertigwaren', *Asien Afrika Lateinamerik* Vol. 4, No. 3, 1976. p. 421. See also UNCTAD, TD/B/AC. 5/L 14; TD/B/378/ Add. 1; and TD/B/C. 5/SR 48.

[20] Gottfried Freitag, op. cit., p. 422.

3 Egypt's Economic Relations with the Socialist Countries

ROBERT MABRO

I. Introduction

The pattern of economic relations between Egypt and the rest of the world has been dominated since the mid-1950s by close and significant links with the Soviet Union and other Eastern European countries. These links involve trade, technical and financial aid, as well as arms supplies and other forms of military assistance. Soviet bloc countries have contributed to major development projects, mainly in industry and irrigation, by supplying a substantial part, or the whole of the 'package'. The High Dam at Aswan is the most notable, and now the most controversial example of close co-operation between Egypt and the Soviet Union in economic development.

In 1972, and more significantly after the October 1973 War, Egypt embarked on a new policy, the twin components of which have been a liberalisation of the domestic economic system and an overture towards the West. Determined attempts have been made to attract Western and Arab private investment, to diversify sources of arms supplies and to attract grants and loans from non-Communist countries and other aid donors. This trend may continue and lead to a new pattern of economic relations. The West, Japan and some developing countries could then displace the Soviet bloc from its privileged place in trade; Arab and other oil-producing countries such as Iran could become the main, if not the exclusive, sources of foreign capital and aid. We may be at the turning point between two eras with very different characteristics. The long period of close economic links with the Soviet bloc may well be drawing to an end; and the appraisal of these relations could then be regarded as an assessment of a self-contained chapter of Egypt's economic history. Yet, we may be in for some surprises: policy reversals are not impossible in the unstable Middle-Eastern world. Arab involvement in the Egyptian economy is likely to increase through an expansion of investment and aid flows and to become a permanent feature of development in the next ten or twenty years; but the very significant shift in the direction of trade from East to West, which many observers expect, may not take place. Egypt may have to revert to a closer political relationship with the Soviet Union, if the US fails to deliver either arms or peace. Egypt may find itself dependent for a long time on supplies of armaments from the Soviet Union and, for convenience, may pay part of the import bill within the old framework of bilateral trade agreements. It may also experience difficulties in penetrating export markets in new areas. Egyptian industry is not ready for this task, and may not be so for some time yet. The transformation of the economic structure which foreign investment, liberal trade policies and changes in the economic system are expected to bring about, is a slow process hindered by serious obstacles. The Soviet bloc could retain a dominant position as a trade partner for many years to come even if it is displaced in other areas — finance, grants, technical assistance — by new partners. The period over which the economic relations between Egypt and the communist countries are studied in this paper may not represent a closed chapter. Though firm predictions are impossible to make at this stage, we should not be unduly surprised if continuity prevailed in some significant form at least throughout the next five or ten years.

A fair assessment of past economic relationships between Egypt and the Soviet bloc cannot be easily arrived at. One familiar difficulty consists in the lack of data. Little is publicly known about the exact stipulations of trade agreements, the terms on which loans are secured and the arrangements governing military aid. The exact magnitude of financial flows is difficult to ascertain; and the trade statistics, though widely available, are not free from flaws and puzzles.

The choice of criteria for assessment poses other difficulties. In economics, costs and benefits are assessed relative to the best alternative available opportunities. The recognition of these opportunities may appear simple at first. The alternative to bilateral trade with the Soviet bloc is multilateral trade in the open world market, which does not exclude commercial transactions with the USSR and Eastern Europe; the alternative to unilateral dependence on Soviet aid and assistance is diversification of sources. The interesting question, however, is whether alternative opportunities were always feasible. If alternative opportunities are merely notional, fully available only in an ideal world free from constraints, political forces and impediments, assessments can be misleading. A comparison of an actual relationship with relationships that are either unattainable, or difficult to attain in a given historical situation, distorts the assessment. A balanced appraisal must also refer to the constrained opportunities available *hic et nunc*. The identification of these opportunities and a judgement on the reality and strength of constraints which limit the options is the difficult task. No wonder that many economists shy away and take refuge in notional comparisons. A correct judgement is difficult to formulate because historical situations involve many complex and interrelated elements. It is as easy to exaggerate the rigidity of constraints for example, as to dismiss their significance; and the economist will fall into either trap simply by ignoring this or that dimension of the historical context. There are technical difficulties too in all comparisons with a hypothetical situation. The characteristics of the alternative opportunity may not have remained unchanged if taken as an actual option. The price of Egyptian cotton on the world market at a given time would probably change if all Egyptian cotton sold to Soviet bloc countries was instead disposed of in that market. The reasons are that (a) the demand for Egyptian cotton is not perfectly elastic and (b) Soviet bloc and free world markets are not perfectly linked to one another.

A final difficulty arises in interpreting the scant literature on the subject. Economists, including the present author, are not entirely free of prejudices. The relations between a given country and the Soviet bloc are a topic rarely analysed with sufficient objectivity, for the reason that the issue elicits ideological and political sentiments. Some will be inclined to look more carefully at the costs rather than at the benefits; others will tend to exaggerate the benefits and minimise, to some extent, the costs. Changes in political mood have repercussions on the literature. The Aswan High Dam was differently appraised in Egyptian writings in the mid-1950s, than in the 1960s; and the tone has changed again. Yet, elements of positive knowledge about the defects and merits of the Dam have hardly changed throughout this period. The list of advantages and costs is the same, but the emphasis shifts from period to period. Great critical awareness is thus required in using available studies in this field.

The remainder of this paper is divided into two parts. In the first, the development of Egypt's relations with the Soviet bloc is described and put in its historical context. In the second part, an attempt is made to evaluate these trade and aid relations.

II. Origins and Development of Economic Relations with the Soviet Bloc[1]

Before the Second World War, Egypt traded mainly with the United Kingdom. This privileged relationship between an imperial power and a politically-dependent state—colony, protectorate or client — was characteristic of international trade during the colonial period. Though the share of the United Kingdom in Egyptian trade declined significantly in the 1930s, it remained large on the eve of the Second World War. In 1938, one-third of Egyptian exports were directed to, and slightly less than a quarter of total imports originated from, the United Kingdom. It was worth noting that at this time Egypt was engaged in commercial exchanges with most Eastern European countries. In 1938, Eastern Europe, including the USSR, accounted for some ten per cent of Egypt's exports and for a similar proportion of its imports. Trade links between Egypt and this set of countries long preceded the establishment of special relations in the second half of the 1950s. A number of economic factors favoured trade with Eastern Europe: proximity and complementary natural resources. Romania, for example, was a traditional source of timber exports, Poland of coal, Bulgaria of food products and Czechoslovakia of machinery. All of them imported cotton and other agricultural produce from Egypt.

Significant structural changes in foreign trade took place soon after the Second World War. The notable features were a drastic reduction in trade with the United Kingdom, whose share in Egyptian exports fell to as low as two to five per cent in the second half of the 1950s, an increase in Egyptian imports from the USA, which became a very significant source in the late 1950s and early 1960s, and a big increase in trade with the Soviet bloc and some developing countries. The changes involved more than a mere shift from the UK to the Soviet bloc.

Before 1956 economic factors were mainly responsible for this transformation in the pattern of foreign trade. During the immediate post-war years Egypt had a large pent-up demand for imports; she also held considerable sterling reserves in London, estimated at £E400 million. These assets were blocked because of the economic and financial difficulties experienced by Britain during the difficult reconstruction period. Egypt was also a member of the sterling area. Her foreign exchange earnings were deposited in the London pool, and though she was entitled, in principle, to draw on these deposits in the various currencies required for payments to her foreign suppliers, London restricted the amounts that could be drawn in dollars and other hard currencies. Egypt was thus accumulating sterling balances which she could not use to satisfy entirely her demand for imports because neither the UK nor Western Europe were in a position to supply the volume and the variety of goods required. At the same time she was unable to finance desired imports from the US and other countries which could have met her demand, because she could not easily acquire dollars. In July 1947, at the time of an abortive attempt by Britain to re-establish the convertibility of sterling, Egypt left the sterling area. The switch in the pattern of foreign trade from the traditional partnership with the UK has its origins in the events of this period. Egypt attempted then to diversify her external markets. The first bilateral trade agreements were entered into in 1948, well before the 1952 revolution – a fact which tends to be ignored by those who want to associate the bilateral deals with the ideology of the military régime. Indeed, significant trade took place with the USSR in 1948. In that year, the share of the USSR in Egyptian exports, hitherto negligible, rose to 8 per cent and the import proportion to 7 per cent. This early shift towards the Soviet bloc was immediately reversed by the Korean boom. Yet this feature of the trade pattern in 1948 could not be dismissed as an oddity. It reveals the natural tendency of a trading country to search for new partners when difficulties are experienced in traditional foreign markets. There was no ideoligical affinity between the political régime in Egypt in 1948 and the USSR. This historical precedent should warn against simplistic views about the ideological causes of later changes in Egypt's pattern of trade – the shifts that took place under Nasser.

After the Korean boom Egypt seems to have experienced difficulties once again in Western export markets. Demand for cotton and cotton yarn contracted, largely for cyclical reasons. Perceptions about future trends might also have been pessimistic. The long era of sustained growth which followed the post-war reconstruction and recovery in Europe and Japan, and which led to such an expansion of world trade in the past twenty-five years, was not foreseen in the early 1950s. At this time the prevailing philosophy about trade and developing countries was distinctly gloomy. Egypt also had specific worries. New competitors were emerging in the world market for long-staple cotton, and the development of textile production in developing countries seemed to presage a long-term decline of this industry in the UK and the West. Efforts were thus made in 1953 and 1954 to renew trade relationships with Eastern Europe in order to gain a foothold in countries where the potential expansion of markets had not yet been realised because of delays in post-war reconstruction and recovery. In 1954 Eastern Europe absorbed 10 per cent of Egypt's exports, the same proportion as in 1938. This share rose to 24 per cent in 1956. But this shift in the direction of trade did not involve the USSR at this time. The Soviet Union remained a minor trade partner in all the years, save 1948, that separated the Second World War from the Suez war. Changes in the geographical distribution of exports were not paralleled by identical changes in the composition of imports by source. Until 1956 the proportion of imports from Eastern Europe remained exceedingly small.

The switch to Eastern European markets and sources of supply, initiated at first by economic factors, soon received a new impetus from other forces. In September 1955 Nasser announced important purchases of arms from Czechoslovakia. He claimed that the West had placed unacceptable conditions – specifically Egypt's membership of the Baghdad Pact, which would have aligned the country with the USA and the UK in one of the two blocs engaged in the cold war – on his request for armaments. Egypt needed hardware for her army. Her vulnerability to an Israeli attack had just been demonstrated by military raids on her Eastern border, allegedly launched in retaliation for guerilla activity. Egypt was also trying to end the very long colonial episode by securing the complete and final evacuation of British forces from her territory. Having just signed the evacuation agreement, Nasser did not want to – and probably could not – open a new door to a possible return of foreign troops. The Czechoslovakian arms deal should be construed in this context. The two important political factors which dominate the interpretation of Egyptian history (political as well as economic) in the last thirty years, that is decolonisation and the Arab–Israeli conflict, explain this event. They continued to influence, and in some cases determine, the whole pattern of international relations throughout the 1950s and 1960s, even to the present day. And though the significance of the first factor – decolonisation – has recently diminished, that of the Arab–Israeli conflict, always considerable, further increased in 1967 and thereafter.

Recourse to the Eastern bloc for imports of strategic equipment, the only available option in the context just described, reinforced the earlier shift in the geographical composition of trade. The chain of reactions and events which followed the Czechoslovakian arms deal, in late 1955, both completed and perpetuated the structural transformation in Egypt's pattern of trade. The subsequent events run as follows. The USA and the UK reacted to the deal, and more fundamentally to Nasser's refusal to join the Baghdad Pact, by withdrawing their promise of financial assistance for the projected High Dam at Aswan. The IBRD offer of a loan for that project, conditional on the support of the two Western powers, was also withdrawn. Nasser retaliated by nationalising the Suez Canal in July 1956, an act which should be construed both as an immediate reaction to US and UK policy and as a fundamental act of decolonisation. The response to nationalisation was the Suez war, preceded and followed by a trade blockade imposed by Britain and France. These events completed the demise of the UK as a significant trade partner. They restricted further the market for Egyptian exports in Western Europe; they increased her dependence for armaments imports on the Soviet bloc; and they opened the door for a new economic relationship with the USSR, the only country now able and willing to assist Egypt in her development efforts which involved two major designs: the construction of the High Dam and an ambitious industrialisation programme. In a context of super power rivalry the USSR could not but step in.

Developments in international economic and political relationships in the second half of the 1950s and the first half of the 1960s involved more than a simple switch from Western Europe and towards the Soviet bloc: the USA also became involved. She had entered the scene just before the revolution, as an aid donor. Egypt became a beneficiary of American aid in 1952, as a result of an agreement signed in 1951. Until 1954 US aid almost exclusively took the form of technical assistance under Point Four. In 1955 and also in 1956 – that is, just after the withdrawal of the High Dam offer – US aid continued and included both financial grants and commodity supplies. Suez affected this relationship during the next two years – 1957 and 1958 – when the volume of US aid was reduced to a trickle. The great success of Nasser's policy, which drew maximum advantage from the cold war, was to secure a resumption of US aid in 1959, while the USSR was increasing her commitments towards Egypt. The US supplied mainly wheat and foodstuffs under Public Law 480 and the aid commitments, reflected in the US share in Egyptian imports, increased steadily betwen 1959 and 1962 when they reached a peak. US aid remained significant until the mid-1960s. The combination of USSR and US support (the latter being the more significant) in 1957–64 partly explains the high rates of economic growth achieved during this period. The growth performance of the Egyptian economy in the three decades spanning the period between the Second World War and the present day was at its best during these seven or eight years. But this economic growth, which was increasingly financed by aid – thus involving larger and larger deficits on the balance of payments, both in absolute terms and relative to GNP – became extremely vulnerable to the vagaries of foreign assistance.

The political factors mentioned before – post-colonial independence and the Arab—Israeli conflict — as well as other elements of foreign policy played again in the mid-1960s and led to the severance of economic relations with the US. Nasser had embarked earlier on the ill-fated Yemen war. This move, which was not universally condoned by the Egyptian leadership, is difficult to appraise. It was consistent with a fundamental objective of his policy — leadership in the Arab world through support for revolutionary movements. The policy paid dividends at first. It could be argued that neither the USSR nor the USA would have gone to the same lengths in their economic support for, and political flirtation with, Egypt if Nasser's influence had not extended beyond his country's borders. And the cold war helped. But a combination of factors and circumstances began to change US attitudes. In the 1960s the climate of international relations was no longer dominated in the same way by the cold war as in the previous decade. Nasser's actions and inter- ventions in the Arab world, culminating with the Yemen war, threatened the security of régimes friendly to the US. The Yemen was seen as a stage post of Egyptian ambitions in Saudi Arabia, where the US had considerable oil and political interests. A strong Egypt could become a serious threat to Israel; and the Democratic Administration was even more committed to the support of this country than its Republican predecessor. It is said that the US exerted pressure on Nasser, through the sanction of aid, for a withdrawal from the Yemen. This was viewed as being unacceptable interference with national sovereignty, almost an absolute value for a country which had regained its independence slowly, after so many difficulties and so recently. This inter- ference contrasted with the USSR's attitude at the time, being careful to emphasise the separation of aid from political conditions. The USSR's policy was not to press for immediate advantages, such as military bases, freedom of action for the Communist Party or support for friendly régimes in the Arab world. Relations were not always perfectly smooth, however, especially when Nasser suppressed the Egyptian communist parties or when Nasserite elements clashed with communists in Iraq. Yet the USSR seems to have refrained from threatening a reduction or a withdrawal of aid in dealing with these issues. Soviet policy was perhaps the building up of goodwill for the future. The US was either blunter or was perceived not to be making the same distinctions; the memories of the Dulles incident — the withdrawal of support for the High Dam — were still vivid and may have cast their shadow on these perceptions. The result was that US aid was drastically curtailed in 1965.

The economic consequences of the sudden decline in US assistance were severe. The substantial amounts of wheat and other foodstuffs received under PL480 (some £Egyptian220 million worth of commodities in 1962) had to be imported and paid for in foreign exchange. The current account deficit in the balance of payments, which had reached the equivalent of 7 per cent of GNP in 1964, could no longer be financed after the withdrawal of US aid, an action which also had inevitable repercussions on the willing- ness of other Western donors and lenders, as well as on multilateral agencies, to supply finance. The only way out in such a situation was to curtail both investment and consumption. As public consumption was expanding fast at the time, because of growing military requirements and because of the government's employment policy, the whole brunt of the reduction was taken by investment and private consumption. Both the rate of economic growth and the rate of improvement in private standards of living fell drastically. Subsequent strains on the economy arising from the 1967 Arab—Israeli war, its aftermath and a host of other factors hindered sustained recovery. Egypt has not yet emerged from the phase of low economic performance which she entered in 1964—5.

The US withdrawal ended the partnership which Egypt has succeeded in maintaining with the two superpowers and left her with the Soviet bloc alone. But the links with the USSR did not change very significantly, until the war of 1967, when Egypt found herself both defeated and deprived of military capability. Though Arab oil-producing countries stepped in with financial assistance to the tune of £100 million a year, the equivalent of the lost revenues from the Suez Canal, she still had to rely mainly on the Soviet Union for both military and economic aid. The issue was no longer one of armament supplies but one of sheer survival. The armed forces had to be completely reequipped and trained. The arms race entailed recourse to sophisticated weaponry; and the protection of Egyptian territory from outside aggression, during the interval necessary for restoring Egypt's military capability to a much advanced level, called for new forms of Soviet involvement. In such an emergency Nasser had little option but to offer naval and airport facilities to the Soviet Union and to ask them to man the more sophisticated weapons. Many observers concluded at the time that Egypt was losing, or had indeed lost, the independence which she had so jealously tried to preserve, sometimes at very high cost. This view underestimates Nasser's toughness in bargaining, his ability to circumscribe concessions and the strength of his attachment to initial objectives. It also misconstrues the nature of the relationship with the USSR, which never deteriorated into the dependent relationship of a satellite state. The ease with which President Sadat in 1972 asked the Soviet Union to withdraw most of her military personnel and the ease with which the superpower complied, reveal perhaps something of the true nature of the relationship.

To sum up: initial changes in the geographical pattern of Egypt's trade reflect the normal economic responses of a trading country experiencing difficulties in selling export goods in traditional foreign markets and in obtaining desired imports from her traditional suppliers. As the desired imports were armaments and strategic goods, the issues had an important political dimension. A chain of events and a complex of political factors combined to freeze changes in the trade pattern. Flexible economic responses to the evolving circumstances of world trade would have probably resulted in successive shifts from one set of export markets to another in a continual search for better opportunities. A number of historical precedents suggest that Egypt is capable of flexible response. But political factors impose rigidities or, more precisely, a logic of their own on the pattern of international economic relations. For more than twenty years Egypt had little option but to turn to the Soviet bloc for essential purchases of armaments. The option left is on the form of payment: foreign exchange or exports. If exports are supplied at world prices, the means of payment is indifferent. Gains or losses are involved if exports are delivered to the Soviet bloc on terms which diverge from ruling world prices. We shall approach this question in the next section. As we are concerned here with the causes of structural changes in trade, it will suffice to retain a simple point: the significance of arms purchases in determining the geographical pattern.

Aid, the second dimension of international economic relations, involves both economic and political factors. Politics partly motivate the donor. Aid-giving on a substantial scale is not without political leverage. In some circumstances, the recipient can benefit from the political motivations of competing donors. Egypt drew aid from both the Soviet bloc and the US for as long as political circumstances permitted. She succeeded in avoiding for a period exclusive dependence on a single source. When a clash of objectives — political independence versus economic gains — was rightly or wrongly perceived she severed the relationship with the US. Political factors provide the main explanation for most changes in the pattern of aid receipts by source. In 1973 the US re-entered the scene; and oil-producing countries, including Iran, emerged as significant donors. Once again, politics started playing a new role.

Finally, it is necessary to emphasise that the dominant political factors in these developments relate to national independence, national security, inter-Arab and international relations. Economic ideology, affinities to this or that type of economic system, did not determine behaviour. Egypt turned to the Soviet bloc for export markets and purchases of armaments when her economic system was still capitalist in essence and many years before the adoption of 'Arab socialism'. There are no indications that trade and aid relations with the Soviet bloc influenced significantly the transformation of Egypt's economic system from private enterprise to public ownership of the means of production in the modern sector. Ironically, US aid reached its peak in the years when the most drastic 'socialist' measures were introduced. Ties with the Soviet Union did not prevent Nasser from suppressing the Communist Party. The remarkable feature of the period studied here is the extent to which Egypt succeeded in preserving her domestic autonomy while caught in a system of external economic relations fraught with dangers of dependence.

III. Trade and Aid

A. *The share of the Soviet bloc in Egyptian trade*
The quantitative importance of Egyptian trade with the Soviet bloc may

be surmised from data presented in Table 3.1.

A few preliminary remarks are in order. Firstly, Egyptian trade data do not include imports of military equipment. Secondly, the treatment of imports financed by long-term credit or grants has not been consistent throughout the period. This is a major difficulty which we have been unable to resolve. It calls for great caution in the interpretation of the figures. Thirdly, there exist two sources of trade data in Egypt: Customs Administration and the Central Bank. The first records movements of goods at the port of exit or entry and the second bases its estimates on payment data. The UN data used here are originally derived from the Customs source. Discrepancies between the two sources are impossible to reconcile. We prefer customs figures because they are not interfered with in the same way as Central Bank data whose main purpose is to present an official picture of the balance of payments, on both current and capital accounts. These interferences, as Mead explained, can take a variety of forms: (a) imports financed by foreign credit, as well as the credits, are left out of the picture in order to understate foreign liabilities; (b) these imports are omitted and the offsetting exports undervalued, an unlikely adjustment which distorts the current account while giving a true picture of the capital account; (c) strategic imports are disguised under a different entry.[3] There is no doubt, however, that official estimates of the balance of payments cannot be trusted. The Customs data, of course, give no clue as to the balance-of-payments position, since they refer only to merchandise trade in non-strategic goods. But they are more accurate on the items covered than other sources. The absence of main interferences other than the explicit restriction on coverage helps in the interpretation of apparent balances of trade.

The main feature of Table 3.1 may be summarised as follows. As mentioned earlier, the Soviet bloc's share in Egyptian trade began to increase before the 1956 Suez war. The share in total merchandise trade rose indeed from 9 per cent in 1954 to 15 per cent in 1955, and to 23 per cent in 1956. This tendency accelerated in 1957 when the share rose to 36 per cent and then levelled off. Not surprisingly, variations in the proportion of trade with the Soviet bloc are associated with changes in political relations with the US and the West. During 1957–9, because of the trade blockade and the slackening of US aid, the Soviet Union's shares in both exports and imports were as high as 50 and 30 per cent respectively. Both fell during 1960–4, the share of imports more markedly than that of exports. During these years US aid was at its peak. The proportions rose again in the period 1965–72 when the US ceased to provide assistance and when Egypt's military requirements increased significantly. The export share reached a peak of 60 per cent in 1970–2, while the import proportion remained well below peak around 32 per cent. This interesting feature reveals something about the scale of arms purchase during the years of preparation for the 1973 war. Large increases in exports – or more accurately a widening in the apparent export–import gap – suggest increases in unrecorded imports of strategic goods. Data for

TABLE 3.1. SHARES OF THE SOVIET BLOC AND THE USSR IN EGYPTIAN TRADE, 1948–74 (PERCENTAGES)

Years	Exports			Imports		
	Share of Soviet bloc in exports	Share of USSR in exports	Share of USSR in exports to Soviet bloc	Share of Soviet bloc in imports	Share of USSR in imports	Share of USSR in imports from Soviet bloc
1948	13	8	61	11	7	64
1954	11	1	9	5	1	20
1956	28	4	14	12	4	33
1958	47	17	36	31	13	42
1959	51	18	35	30	13	43
1960	44	16	36	25	10	40
1961	45	15	33	25	11	44
1962	41	15	36	23	8	35
1963	45	19	42	20	5	25
1964	46	18	39	18	8	44
1965	53	21	39	23	9	39
1966	53	23	43	27	9	33
1967	50	25	50	42	21	50
1968	48	28	58	39	16	41
1969	52	53	63	31	13	42
1970	60	38	63	32	12	37
1971	61	40	65	33	14	42
1972	60	35	58	31	13	42
1973	52	33	63	25	7	29
1974	52	33	63	18	9	50

Source: IMF, *Direction of Trade.*

1973 indicate a decline in the Soviet share of Egyptian exports which could reflect either Egypt's pressing needs for free foreign exchange in a deteriorating economic situation or the beginning of a new phase in her relations with East and West.

The second feature of the table worth commenting upon is the increase of the USSR's share in Egyptian exports to the Soviet bloc beginning in 1963, and which became very significant in the years 1967–72. This again reflects the increased reliance on the USSR for military equipment. The USSR's share in imports from the Soviet area had not exhibited any particular trend. Apart from one or two odd years this share remained fairly stable at around 50 per cent. In other words, the geographical structure of Egypt's imports of non-strategic goods from the Eastern bloc (as revealed by the import data) did not change very much between 1957–72. But the structure of total imports, strategic and non-strategic, paradoxically revealed by movements in export shares, shifted very significantly after 1965 towards the USSR.

The third feature of trade with the Eastern bloc is the large and systematic divergence between imports and export shares. Table 3.2 provides data on the trade surplus in favour of Egypt in the export–import of non-strategic goods account.

TABLE 3.2. EGYPT'S
APPARENT BALANCE
OF TRADE WITH THE
SOVIET BLOC
(US$ MILLION)

1958	13·8
1959	44·5
1960	85·3
1961	42·4
1962	−2·0
1963	69·5
1964	72·5
1965	106·3
1966	34·9
1967	−47·8
1968	39·6
1969	196·2
1970	211·9
1971	190·2
1972	223·4
1973	359·4
1974	379·4
Total	2019·5

Source: IMF, *Direction of Trade.*

The apparent balance of trade with the Soviet bloc has always been in surplus except in 1962, when there was a negligible deficit, and in 1967, a very bad year of war and economic difficulties. This apparent surplus was very large in 1969—74. The accumulated total of seventeen years is US$2019·5 million. This apparent surplus provides a rough indication of payment in kind made by Egypt to the Soviet bloc over this period on account of strategic goods and purchases, and in servicing other developmental and trade debts. The indication is rough because Egypt may have been running small credits with one or two Eastern European countries and because she may have enjoyed genuine surpluses at times with some of them which had been partly settled in foreign exchange. There is little evidence, however, for such payments, and it seems legitimate to infer that Egypt's export surpluses to the Soviet bloc should be construed as payments rather than claims. If balance-of-payments accounts were to reveal the true picture, they would include imports of strategic goods on the debit side, and an offsetting item for those merchandise exports representing repayment of debt in kind.

B. *Form and content of trade*

Trade between Egypt and the Soviet bloc is conducted, of course, within a framework of bilateral agreements. The main drawback of bilateral trade is its lack of flexibility. Barter implies coincidence of wants. The use of money as a medium of exchange breaks this nexus which restricts the scope for choice and the ability to take maximum advantage of potential opportunities. Barter also limits the volume of exchange as desired transactions may be frustrated either by the lack of coincidence between wants or by the costs involved in the search for a suitable partner. However, the analogy about barter between individual traders on a domestic market and bilateral foreign trade between countries should not be pushed too far. When one of the trading partners is a very large economy with diverse wants and a varied output, the restrictions imposed by coincidence of wants may not be very severe. The restrictions are not so much on the volume of exchange. The USSR, for example, has a use for most of Egypt's exports and, in principle, can supply a large proportion of the import range. There is, however, a potential loss of welfare because the spectrum of goods offered by an economy, whatever its size, is narrower than the range available in the world at large. The analogy with strict barter between individuals is too extreme in yet another respect. Bilateral trade is not the only mode of exchange between Egypt and the rest of the world. The mixed structure of foreign trade (Egypt sells perhaps a third of her exports in the open market) provides some degree of freedom.

Gains and losses in bilateral trade (relative to multilateral trade) result from divergences between agreed and world market prices. Divergences may occur for a variety of reasons: lack of good information, differences in the bargaining skills of negotiating partners, monopoly or monopsony power, etc.

Price negotiations for bilateral trade agreements — and Egypt—Soviet trade is no exception — attempt to refer to world prices. This reference often makes theoretical sense but raises all sorts of practical difficulties. One may ask: is the reference valid if the world market for a commodity is imperfect, or, is there a single world price for any given product? It is possible to argue that the answer to the first question is generally yes. Reference to the world price is justified by the notion that it represents an actual alternative opportunity to the trading country; whether the world price is the *ideal* price or not is irrelevant in this context. But an important proviso is in order. If the trading country can influence the world price by sales or purchases, reference should be made instead to marginal revenues or marginal costs. The practical difficulties that would be met in such a case are almost insuperable. Egypt's cotton trade raises this particular issue. The world demand curve for long-staple cotton is not perfectly elastic. Reference to the world price of cotton in bilateral transactions between Egypt and a partner loses its meaning since Egyptian supplies are an important determinant of this world price. The opportunity cost to Egypt of selling cotton at the world price to the USSR, for example, depends on the nature of the alternative. Assume that Egypt enjoys some monopoly for long-staple cotton in both the Soviet and the rest-of-the-world markets and, further, that these two markets are completely iso-

TABLE 3.3. SHARE OF THE SOVIET BLOC
IN EGYPTIAN COTTON EXPORTS, 1951–70
(PERCENTAGES OF EXPORT VALUES)

	Share of Soviet bloc	*Share of USSR*
1951	12	—
1952	12	7
1953	19	3
1954	12	2
1955	23	5
1956	11	4
1957	55	21
1958	67	28
1959	69	30
1960	58	19
1961	69	24
1962	66	20
1963	66	29
1964	43	22
1965	64	29
1966	62	30
1967	68	24
1968	43	16
1969	49	27
1970	63	38

Source: Ministry of Planning, Egypt.

lated. In such a situation profit maximisation implies equalising marginal revenues in the two markets, not necessarily prices. Now assume that the Soviet and non-Soviet markets are not isolated; then the two demand curves for Egyptian cotton are additive. In the absence of bilateral agreements, Soviet countries would still buy Egyptian cotton. The alternative to the actual practice (sales on the open market which determine a price p taken as a reference for other sales to the Soviet bloc) would be sales for foreign exchange in a unified market. The price which maximizes Egypt's revenues in this alternative framework might be very different from p. Finally, assume that Soviet countries would not buy cotton outside bilateral agreements. Without them, Egypt would be left only with the non-Soviet market. Total demand for her cotton would be drastically reduced in this situation, involving a potential loss of revenue from cotton exports. The three 'alternative' situations examined here are based on extreme assumptions. They illustrate, however, two points. The opportunity costs of a course of action are difficult to determine when the alternatives involve many unknowns. What is certain, however, is that reference to the world price in bilateral trade for a commodity like long-staple cotton is not theoretically correct. This price, whatever the alternative, is likely to diverge from the opportunity cost (which could be either higher or lower). These comments do not yield a practical guide to behaviour. Whether the theoretical points are well understood or not by Egyptian and Soviet negotiators is an open question; what is almost certain is that they are left with no precise operational rules. Agreed prices are the outcome of a combination of factors – hunches, flair, bargaining strength, market judgement – which may be allowed to play within the framework of simple rules.

The answer to the second question, 'is there a single world price for a given commodity?', is usually no. At any given time the price of a commodity depends on the type of trade transaction. Statistical sources on prices offer different types of information: spot exchange quotations, reference prices published in trade journals, unit values derived from foreign trade statistics, contract prices in commercial agreements. The first makes economic sense, but as they reflect day-to-day conditions and fluctuate accordingly they are difficult to use as a reference for future transactions. The last seem more relevant to bilateral trade agreements, as they reflect price expectations during the period of the contract; unfortunately, they are seldom published. Further problems arise in respect of manufactured, especially capital, goods. The search for a unique world price (even a narrow range of prices) is usually vain for a variety of reasons: product differentiation; sales of capital goods in a technical package, involving sometimes construction and training; market segmentation; different quotations from firms with long order books and firms with spare capacity; and other similar factors.

The evaluation of prices in bilateral agreements between Egypt and the Soviet bloc, given these conceptual as well as statistical difficulties, is a disheartening task. The known facts are as follows. Most goods exported by

Egypt to the Soviet bloc are highly tradable. The Soviet share in goods like cotton, rice, onions, yarn and textiles is high. In 1973 the Soviet bloc absorbed 49 per cent of Egyptian rice exports, 50 per cent of onions, 71 per cent of cotton yarn, and 37 per cent of cotton textiles. Historical data on the Soviet share of the value of Egyptian cotton exports are presented in Table 3.4.[4] Reference to world prices is easier for Egypt's exports than for many of her imports which include machinery, producer goods and armaments.

TABLE 3.4. COTTON EXPORT PRICES TO THE SOVIET BLOC AND TO
THE FREE MARKET 1961–71
£E PER KANTAR

	Extra-long Cotton			Medium-long cotton		
Year	Soviet bloc	Free market	% Differential	Soviet bloc	Free market	% Differential
1961	19·4	18·3	6·0	16·6	16·4	1·2
1962	17·8	16·8	6·0	15·3	14·1	8·5
1963	20·2	18·5	8·4	17·1	15·9	7·5
1964	21·4	18·5	15·6	17·7	16·3	8·6
1965	24·9	21·9	13·7	20·3	18·2	11·5
1966	23·6	21·2	10·2	18·1	17·4	4·0
1967	23·6	20·3	16·2	18·1	15·9	13·8
1968	25·4	21·7	17·0	20·8	17·1	21·6
1969	30·1	25·0	20·4	23·5	19·0	23·7
1970	30·8	25·2	22·2	23·7	18·6	27·4
1971	31·0	25·0	24·0	23·4	17·9	30·7

Source: Egypt Price Planning Agency, *Memo No. 11, I. Cotton,* May 1972

For cotton, available data show that Egypt sells to the Soviet bloc at prices which are generally higher than unit values realised in the same year in open transactions. Table 3.4 indicates that the differential has steadily risen between 1961 and 1971 from 6 to 24 per cent for extra-long cotton. The price differential has also widened for lower quality cottons reaching a value of 30 per cent in 1971 but the behaviour of this latter series is more erratic. We have argued, however, that there is no certain way of assessing whether Egypt is better off under this system than under other alternatives. For other exports, such as rice, onions, yarn, etc. reference to a world price is valid because of the absence of monopolistic advantages. Here the evidence is that agreed prices tend to move up and down with the market, but the export price in bilateral trade carries a premium. Hansen and Nashashibi[5] presented some data on unit values of cotton textile exports which reveal very wide differentials between unit values of yarn and cloth exports to OECD countries and to Eastern Europe (see Table 3.5).

TABLE 3.5 UNIT VALUES OF COTTON TEXTILE
EXPORTS TO OECD COUNTRIES AND EASTERN
EUROPE. £E PER TON.

Year	Yarn		Cloth	
	OECD	*Eastern Europe*	*OECD*	*Eastern Europe*
1964	464.7	840·0	467·2	n.a.
1966	482·2	914·5	536·0	1018·0
1967	473·9	925·1	496·4	1110·0
1968	468·1	946·4	509·8	1015·0
1969	511·5	1014·9	530·2	1117·0
1970	542·6	1009·2	543·4	1130·0
1971	n.a.	1015·8	n.a.	n.a.

Source: B. Hansen and K. Nashashibi, *Foreign Trade Regimes and Economic Development: Egypt*, New York, 1975.

Part of these price differentials may be explained perhaps by quality differences on the assumption that the USSR supplements its own coarse yarn production with imports of fine yarn from Egypt. Yet a large part remains unexplained. Some have suggested that the premium is not genuine as it simply compensates for distortions in official parities between Egyptian pounds, roubles and hard currency. Others think that the premium on export prices is compensated for by over-pricing of imports. Let us turn now to that issue.

A study by Kardouche for UNCTAD suggests that Egypt obtained many primary commodities and intermediate goods from the Soviet bloc at advantageous prices.[6] Kardouche limited himself to a set of well-specified commodities for which like-to-like comparisons were possible. He found that agreed prices diverged from world prices by varying amounts and that the divergences were in Egypt's favour for the majority of items. This type of evidence is not very strong. It reveals, however, the absence of a systematic tendency to overprice goods sold to Egypt by Soviet bloc countries. The general impression one derives from these data is that world prices tend to be the norm in negotiations with some give and take. Divergences measured *ex post* reflect both bargaining and differences in the type of information available to the negotiator and to the student effecting a post-mortem on the statistics.

The moot question relates to the pricing of machinery and other capital equipment purchased by Egypt from the Soviet Union. The only evidence is hearsay. When Egyptian engineers and civil servants are interviewed on this topic they tend to give an unfavourable picture. But engineers always suffer from a technological bias. They naturally favour the best technology and their views about economic considerations should be treated with great caution. To them Soviet machinery may appear expensive partly because of a tendency to treat second-best equipment as worthless. That the quality

of Soviet equipment exported to developing countries does not compare
well with the best machinery available in the West seems to be supported
in many instances by engineering evidence. But Soviet prices are generally
lower; and whether the price differential is large enough to compensate for
inferior quality is an open question which I am unable to answer.

Bilateral trade may involve certain advantages when it leads to trade
creation. We mentioned earlier that Egypt initially turned to the Soviet bloc
when she experienced restrictions in traditional markets. But world economic conditions evolved in the late 1950s until the early 1970s in ways
which favoured trade expansion. Advantages from trade creation initially
offered by bilateral deals were perhaps of a temporary nature. The con-
tinuation of bilateral trade when opportunities for re-entering the world
market present themselves means that trade creation gives way to trade
diversion. Though the largest portion of Egypt's export basket to Soviet
countries consists of tradable goods, we cannot confidently assert that bilateral trade over twenty years can always be characterised as trade diversion.
Because of its very permanence the initial diversion closes options (opportunities that are not seized at the right time often cease to be real opportunities and a long absence from a market makes re-entry that much more
difficult); and with the passage of time the 'diverted' component of trade
may either shrink or in any case vary in size.

It is sometimes argued that bilateral agreements enable partners to exchange
manufactured goods which would be heavily discriminated against in open
markets because of inadequate quality or other defects. There is no evidence
of significant absorption by Soviet countries of Egyptian manufactured goods
which correspond to this description. True, Soviet bloc countries import some
leather goods (mainly shoes), some copper produces (mainly ornamental) and
refrigerators. But the amounts are small and the foreign exchange content of
certain items, such as refrigerators, is so high in relation to export prices that
one wonders whether Egypt does not end up by exporting negative value-
added. The significant purchaser of manufactured goods in the bilateral relationship is Egypt herself. There seems to be more trade creation for the
Soviet bloc than for the developing partners. There are known instances where
Eastern European countries and the USSR exported equipment and material
for which they had little alternative use.

The main advantage to Egypt of bilateral trade with the Soviet bloc arises
from the link with aid. The attraction of bilateral deals is not, as often alleged,
the simplistic notion that 'imports would be acquired without disbursements
of foreign exchange'. For exports, which complement the deal, are foreign
exchange. The attraction is that trade with the Soviet bloc, because it is
always associated with credit, enables the developing countries to run a
deficit, that is to import more than they can immediately pay for. This
facility is not always available on the very advantageous terms offered by the
USSR ($2\frac{1}{2}$–3 per cent interest, medium-term maturity), in the capitalist
world. For Egypt, which needs to import expensive armaments and whose

export capacity falls short of the level of imports necessary to achieve a modest five per cent rate of real economic growth, the credit element is of paramount importance. It is unlikely that the losses incurred by Egypt on other counts (restriction of choice or quality of the imported equipment) in its bilateral trade with the Soviet bloc have entirely cancelled this credit advantage.

C. *Aid*

Soviet aid to Egypt has two components: military and economic. Little is known about the first component except that it reached a very high level in the period 1967—73. Modern warfare is becoming incredibly expensive and both Egypt and Israel suffer for that reason from considerable foreign indebtedness. Neither could afford a fraction of their military expenditures without the financial backing of the super-powers. It is said that Egypt owes the socialist bloc countries some $6000—8000 million and the presumption is that 70 or 80 per cent of this sum represents military credit. Any conventional analysis of trade and economic relations is thrown off balance when due consideration is given to the military element, with all its significance. What room for choice is left to Egyptian policy-makers when they have to import arms on that scale mainly from a single supplier?

Economic assistance to Egypt began in 1958 as a result of an agreement signed with the USSR in 1957. The USSR offered 700 million roubles in soft loans for the financing of Egypt's First Industrial Plan. The terms conformed to normal Soviet practice. Credit was tied to imports of plant and equipment for the projects of the industrial plan. The USSR undertook to offer packages involving technical assistance in assessing, designing and executing projects, the supply of equipment and the training of Egyptian personnel. The rate of interest on loans was $2\frac{1}{2}$ per cent. No grant element was involved. The second aid agreement entered into in December 1958 related to the High Dam. The USSR pledged to help finance the first stage to the tune of 400 million roubles. In August 1960 they agreed to extend 900 million roubles for the second stage. Total commitments of economic aid from the USSR and the Eastern bloc to Egypt, in various periods, are estimated by the UN as shown in Table 3.6.

Disbursements lagged considerably at the beginning because of delays in implementing the High Dam and certain industrial projects. We think that by 1975 gross disbursements corresponded roughly to total commitments made by the end of 1972. But this is nothing more than a half-informed guess.

Data on Western and international agency aid to Egypt are not perfectly comparable with the figures available for Soviet bloc aid. During 1952—62 total Western commitments amounted to $1160 million compared with about $700 million (excluding military aid) from the Soviet bloc. The true totals are in fact much closer because credits for arms amounted to some

TABLE 3.6. SOVIET BLOC AID TO EGYPT
($ MILLION)

From 1954 to the year shown (cumulative)		Annual increments
1961	681	–
1962	711	30
1963	765	54
1964	1282	517
1965	1408	126
1966	1415	7
1967	1535	120
1968	1703	168
1969	1741	38
1970	1844	103
1971	2157	313
1972	2668	511
1973	2798	130
1974	3016	218

Source: United Nations, *Statistical Yearbooks.*

$400 to $500 million between 1954 and 1962. After 1962 net disbursements from the West were as follows:

	$ *million*
1963	204
1964	231
1965	119
1966	66
1967	27
1968	20
1969	–
1970	38
1971 and 1972 (average)	39
1972 to 1974 (average)	44

The withdrawal of US aid in the mid-1960s is readily detected in the series. Although strict comparisons are difficult to make, it seems that over the whole period Egypt has acquired more credit in economic aid alone from The Soviet Union than from the West. Total Soviet aid was probably four times larger than Western aid.

The terms under which aid has been extended differ markedly between the US and the USSR. US aid consisted mainly of foodstuffs under PL480, which involved a grant element and payment in counterpart funds. The US supplied little technical assistance and only small amounts of budgetary support. She was not generally involved in project aid and did not offer specific trade credit for imports of capital equipment and machinery. Western aid, other than the US, mainly took the form of loans at rates slightly lower than market rates. Western Germany participated in some industrial projects.

Soviet economic aid was mainly in the form of soft loans for capital goods imports and involved a considerable amount of project development. No aid was given in the form of consumer goods supplies, except on one occasion in the aftermath of the 1967 war. Soviet aid does not usually involve grants; it seems, however, that the USSR did agree to write off some part of Egypt's liabilities in the mid-1960s. On other occasions, she departed from normal policy and supplied some capital goods free of charge. It is also possible that military aid involved, at times, a grant element.

It is evident that US and USSR aid is complementary. Egypt needs to import food, capital goods and military equipment. If one donor chooses to supply, at concessionary terms, an item which the recipient country may import anyway, it releases resources which help to purchase another item. The similarity of US and USSR aid is in its being tied. Tied aid is not as advantageous to the recipient as untied credit facilities and, though generally attractive to the donor, it may sometimes involve certain hidden costs. Commodity aid can have drawbacks for the recipient if it encourages higher levels of consumption than could otherwise be afforded or if it reduces the incentive to develop agriculture. Despite fashionable views to the contrary, these costs are unlikely to cancel out all the benefits. In Egypt, commodity aid released foreign exchange, which served the development programme. Project aid to some extent restricts the recipient's choice of techniques, factor intensity and scale. The ultimate question, however, is whether the recipient country would be better off without it. Finally, the relative merits of grants and loans depend on the impact of grant receipts on developmental attitudes. Grants have obvious advantages to the recipient, though the puritan would argue that they encourage waste by concealing the true scarcity value of capital and that they may affect incentives to earn. There seems to be no case, on balance, for arguing the relative superiority of the Soviet or US type of aid. Egypt benefited to a large extent from both. She incurred significant economic losses when she severed relations with the USA. She has been too ambitious at times, borrowing for development purposes more than she could afford. But the crippling indebtedness which besets her now is largely the result of defence expenditures. Feasible reductions on other items of expenditures would have eased certain difficulties but not changed significantly the fundamental predicament.

A complete appraisal of Soviet aid to Egypt calls for detailed studies of the main projects built with Soviet assistance. This task cannot be undertaken here. A few comments must suffice.

The two main areas of Soviet project aid were industry and the High Dam. In the 1950s and 1960s Egypt followed a pattern of industrialisation which conformed to a prevalent philosophy in development economics. The strategy was import substitution helped by government intervention: protection, direct public investment and some forms of planning. This strategy leads to significant changes in industrial structure characterised by a decline in the share of consumer goods in favour of producer goods. Most Western economists have now lost their early enthusiasm for import substitution, which often entails misallocation of scarce resources and other inefficiencies. The tendency, when planners adopt an import-substitution strategy, is to attempt to produce domestically manufactured goods supplied from abroad. This is not always sensible. The better strategy is to select viable projects and to enlarge their markets by removing obstacles to exports.

Egypt had already embarked on an import-substitution strategy with an emphasis on producer goods, *before* Soviet involvement with economic aid. The erection of an iron and steel mill at Helwan began in 1954, the plant being supplied by a West German firm, Demag. The First Industrial Plan, which attracted the first Soviet programme of project aid in 1958 mainly incorporated work done by the Permanent Council of National Production (1953–7) independently of any direct Soviet influence. The USSR's main contributions to industry were in chemicals, petroleum, metals and engineering. It is fair to say that the shift in the manufacturing structure towards producer goods industries in the 1950s and early 1960s though initiated before the Soviet Union came on the scene was made easier and was perhaps accelerated by Soviet involvement.

Soviet influence on Egyptian industrialisation became predominant after 1967. The new iron and steel complex at Helwan is a Soviet project begun in 1967 and not yet completed. The project does not look economically sound and might represent a burden on Egypt's industrial structure in the future. But, to attribute the present problems and ills of Egyptian industry to the Soviet connection would fail to take account of a much wider set of factors and causes. These problems and ills, which unfortunately characterise the recent industrialisation of many lesser developed countries, are the product of bad planning, crude project selection, policy distortions, excessive trade pessimism and discrimination against exports, shortages of foreign exchange which create serious bottlenecks for industries dependent on imports of intermediate goods, bureaucratic inefficiencies, and the like. In Egypt an unfortunate conjunction of circumstances in the mid-1960s seriously aggravated the problems of industry: severe balance-of-payments problems hit the country at a time of major domestic upheaval, the displacement of private enterprise by the public sector. Around the same time the government committed itself to an employment policy which badly affected performance and productivity in industry.

The monumental symbol of Soviet aid in Egypt is the Aswan High Dam. What was hailed under Nasser as a great achievement in which the country took pride is now the object of controversy, second thoughts and recriminations. Disappointment with the visible benefits of the Dam, probably combined in some quarters with a political reaction against Nasser's legacy, explain this change of mood.

I have tried to appraise the High Dam in my book on the Egyptian economy.[7] A number of facts may help to put the issue in perspective. First, it is important to recall that a long-term water storage project was needed to complete the irrigation system, the life blood of Egyptian agriculture, developed in stages since the nineteenth century. Several schemes, including a High Dam in the Aswan region, were proposed and studied as early as in the 1920s. There is no doubt that the High Dam was, on balance, the most attractive scheme. It is also worth recalling that the High Dam is not a Soviet invention. The project was designed by a West German firm and was initially adopted by the IBRD, the US and the UK. Second, the technical aspects of the High Dam were studied and assessed by different teams of experts. The drawbacks and side-effects which are attracting so much attention now were all known and debated in the 1950s before the construction of the Dam. It was thought that the benefits would exceed these costs. Third, the nature of the High Dam as an *intermediate* project should be emphasised. The benefits of the Dam — mainly water and electricity — cannot be realised until the completion of a large number of complementary projects. Electricity is of no use until new industries are established. Land reclamation, irrigation and drainage projects are necessary to take advantage of the increased availability of water. Because many of these projects were delayed by the adverse economic circumstances in which Egypt found herself after the Dam itself was completed, the benefits are not yet realised. The costs and side-effects, however, have an immediate impact. Many of these effects can be eliminated by investments which were part of the initial package but which are also delayed. In short, judgements about the High Dam based on present advantages and defects are invalid simply because the Dam is part of an integrated package still incomplete. A valid judgement calls for a very detailed study of the costs and benefits of all the projects related to the High Dam. This a monumental task which nobody is attempting at present. The wise course, now, is to suspend judgement instead of indulging in premature controversies.

IV. Conclusion

I have attempted to place the development of Egypt's economic relations with the Soviet bloc in its historical context, in the belief that an understanding of the political and economic forces which influence policy decisions is essential to any appraisal. The assessment of these relations recognises (a) that multilateral trade in the open world market is generally preferable to bilateral transactions and (b) that access to a diversity of aid donors may be more attractive than an exclusive relationship with a single country or bloc. But great emphasis has been placed on the argument that Egypt did not always have the option of fully engaging in multilateral trade, nor did she always have access to diverse sources of aid. Nevertheless, she made successful attempts to use whatever room for manoeuvre she did enjoy — thus, the success between 1958 and 1965 in attracting both US and USSR aid and, in 1973, the swift response in the form of an overture towards the West to a change in the international environment. The analysis of bilateral trade with the Soviet bloc — though restricted in scope by insufficient availability of data — revealed known costs but also specific advantages in the form of special credit facilities. No evidence was found to support the view that Egypt was made to pay higher than world prices for her imports from the Soviet bloc, nor that she received less than world prices for her exports. It was argued, however, that reference to world prices is not always a valid rule. A short discussion on Soviet aid revealed both complementarities to and similarities with US aid. Tied aid has disadvantages but recipients have little choice in the matter; most donors have a clear preference for this form of assistance.

To speculate whether Egypt would have been better off had she been closely linked with the US and the West instead of the USSR is vain. Not that things could never be different from what they are. In this instance, however, too many circumstances, forces and constraints would have had to be different for the alternative to obtain. The main conclusion is that the present problems and difficulties of the Egyptian economy could not be solely attributed to past economic relations with the Soviet bloc, however defective these relations were. Egypt's main predicaments relate to different and more fundamental causes. She needed and still needs considerable external help. To open up to new sources, to look for improved terms, to develop beneficial relationships when opportunities present themselves, are all sensible policies. This is precisely what President Sadat is attempting now. To complain today, as many Egyptians do, about past relations which filled resource gaps which might have remained wide open otherwise, is, perhaps, unfair.

Notes

[1] The terms 'Soviet bloc' and 'socialist countries' are used interchangeably; they refer to the USSR, the Eastern European countries including Yugoslavia, and China.

[2] Robert Mabro, *The Egyptian Economy 1952–1972* (Oxford University Press, 1974), pp. 167–8.

[3] D. Mead, *Growth and Structural Change in the Egyptian Economy* (Homewood, Ill., 1967), p. 183.

[4] For the years 1970–75, data on the Soviet share in the *volume* of cotton exports are available. These are as follows (percentages measured from total volume of cotton exports in tons).

	1970/71	1971/72	1972/73	1973/74	1974/75
USSR share	32	30	27	24	45
Soviet bloc share	55	55	48	45	88

[5] See B. Hansen and K. Nashashibi, *Foreign Trade Regimes and Economic Development: Egypt*, New York, 1975, pp. 212–3.

[6] George K. Kardouche, *United Arab Republic: Case Study of Aid through Trade and Repayment of Debt in Goods or Local Currencies* (UNCTAD, 1968).

[7] Robert Mabro, *The Egyptian Economy, 1952–1972* (Oxford University Press, 1974).

4 Entente Commerciale: The Soviet Union and West Africa*

CHRISTOPHER STEVENS

I. Introduction

The Afro-Soviet *entente* is as much an economic as a political relationship. Although not yet substantial, commercial ties between the two continents are significant both because they are, in theory, mutually beneficial and because they provide scope for development from a few loose strands to a complex network of economic relations. Ghana was one of the first African countries to attempt to improve its economic links with the USSR and therefore illustrates better than most, the possibilities and pitfalls entailed in such an attempt. Its close neighbour Nigeria, was much more reserved in its dealings with the Soviet bloc and provides a valuable contrast which illustrates the gains and losses accruing to Ghana by virtue of its intimate contact with Russia. The potential of the USSR and the other centrally planned economies to provide a new market for the exports of less developed countries and to become an additional source of development assistance, is of particular interest at the present time when the Third World is groping towards a new international economic order.

This chapter considers the period 1960–72. To start with, it examines trade between the USSR on the one hand and Ghana and Nigeria on the other. As a next step it goes on to evaluate the aid relationship. The advantages and pitfalls associated with a rapid expansion of trade are well illustrated by Ghana's attempts to encourage the USSR to consume more cocoa. The Ghanaian objective was to use the USSR and other centrally planned economies as an additional market which would influence prices on the main market in the West. The difficulties it had to contend with in reaching that objective concerned the stability and price of Soviet purchases,

*The fieldwork for this research was undertaken in 1971–72 with the assistance of the Leverhulme Trust. The sections of this chapter dealing with Ghana and the Soviet Union are based on the author's article 'In Search of The Economic Kingdom: The Development of Economic Relations between Ghana and the USSR'. *The Journal of Developing Areas* (Illinois) Vol. 9, No 1, October 1974, pp. 3–26.

and the administration of bilateral barter agreements. This chapter attempts
to assess the extent to which the objective was attained by considering the
actual prices Ghana received for its exports and paid for its imports.

Just as Soviet trade was a supplement to Western commerce so Soviet aid
was an addition rather than an alternative to Western development assistance.
The attractions of Western and Soviet aid are compared at the nominal and
effective levels. Since Soviet aid has not been spectacularly successful in its
impact an attempt is made to assess the extent to which failure has been
due to inadequacies on the part of the donor or of the recipient.

II. Trade

The USSR, like the other centrally planned economies, prefers to trade on
the basis of bilateral agreements with each trading partner. Although some
trade does take place in the absence of such pacts, it is normally only
sporadic and at a low level. At the very least, the USSR likes to draft a
bilateral agreement that sets out the legal basis for trade, method of payment
and such like. Very often these agreements impose no obligations on either
side, but they do seem to assist the Soviet Union in its planning. Both
Ghana and Nigeria entered into bilateral pacts of this sort in 1960 and 1963
respectively. The Nigerian Government took the decision to enter into a
trade pact with the USSR at a time when domestic critics were attacking the
slow rate at which trade with Eastern Europe was growing, and claimed
that the mere existence of the agreement indicated a positive step to meet
this criticism[1]. However this was not correct; by itself such an agreement
has little effect on trade, as witnessed by the fact that Soviet–Nigerian trade
grew very slowly from $7 million in 1960 to $9 million in 1965[2]. The growth
of Soviet–Ghanaian trade was much more rapid, as brought out in Table 4.1.
In 1965, the peak year, the level of trade was five times the average annual
figure for the period 1955–59.

The difference in the Nigerian and Ghanaian growth rates for trade with
the USSR largely reflects a difference in the approach of the two governments. In Nigeria, before 1966, the Government was at best indifferent
towards increased trade with the socialist bloc and at worst hostile towards
it. There were allegations, for example, that the Government deliberately
blocked imports of Russian cement.[3] In Ghana, by contrast, a deliberate
decision was taken to increase such trade, and institutional changes were
introduced to give effect to this decision.

It is wise, however, to bear in mind that the trade of both countries with
the USSR has been small in relation to their total trade. Even in Ghana in
1965, the Soviet Union accounted for only 8 per cent, and Eastern Europe
as a whole for only 18 per cent, of Ghana's total trade. This is quite a high
proportion in comparison with other less developed countries, but is still

TABLE 4.1. VISIBLE TRADE BETWEEN GHANA AND THE USSR
1960—71 (IN US $ MILLION)

Year	World		USSR		USSR Trade as a percentage of World Trade	
	Imports from	Exports to	Imports from	Exports to	Imports	Exports
1960	363	343	2	20	0·6	5·8
1961	400	322	6	9	1·5	2·8
1962	334	313	5	11	1·5	3·5
1963	365	299	9	20	2·5	6·7
1964	341	318	17	17	5·0	5·3
1965	450	313	30	31	6·7	9·9
1966	363	207	20	25	5·5	12·0
1967	312	298	9	24	2·9	8·1
1968	311	328	7	11	2·3	3·4
1969	353	321	13	4	3·7	1·2
1970	411	451	16	41	3·9	9·1
1971	434	350	8	8	1·8	2·3

Sources: *Foreign Trade Statistics for Africa: Series A, Direction of Trade* (New York:
UN Economic Commission for Africa), nos 2—18 and *External Trade Statistics of
Ghana* (Accra: Central Bureau of Statistics, 1971) vol 21 no 12.

Note: Imports are c.i.f; exports are f.o.b.

small relative to Ghana's trade with the Western countries. The importance
of the USSR as a trade partner would have been greater than the small volume
of trade would suggest had it enabled Ghana to diversify her exports. However, Soviet trade did not assist diversification; while Ghana is heavily dependent upon a limited range of exports in general commercial relations, her
trade with the Soviet bloc is even more limited. In 1965, for example, 90
per cent of Ghana's total exports and 100 per cent of its exports to the
USSR and Eastern Europe constituted primary products and raw materials.[4]
Trade with the Eastern bloc has thus not been of major significance for
Ghana's economy, and this is as might be expected. Until the last decade,
practically all foreign transactions were with the West so that a tradition
of exporting to certain areas developed and with it has grown an expertise
for facilitating this trade.

It is precisely because Ghana's trade was oriented so strongly towards the
West that trade with the Soviet bloc could offer substantial benefits. Fluctuation in harvest size is a major problem for primary producers owing to
the low price elasticity of demand for their exports in traditional markets
and the consequent disastrous effect of a glut on prices. Any innovation
permitting primary producers to siphon part of an unusually large crop to a
new market and thus maintain prices to traditional buyers would be a real
boon. The development of markets in Eastern Europe promised to be just

such an innovation. It was hoped that when harvests were large the centrally planned economies would import sufficient quantities to stabilize prices on the free market.

A. *Exporting to the USSR: stability and prices*
It was this hope that prompted the Ghana government to try to increase sales of cocoa to Eastern Europe, and the Ghanaian experience provides valuable lessons for those who attempt something similar. The early 1960s was a rather distressing period for cocoa producers in general, and for Ghana in particular.[5] In contrast to the interwar years which had by and large been a buyers' market, the 1950s became a sellers' market in cocoa and prices rose. However, this good fortune carried within it the seeds of its own destruction: on the one hand cocoa production increased rapidly and, on the other, traditional buyers reduced their reliance on cocoa. As a result, the buyers' market reemerged during the 1960s and prices fell steadily — sometimes dramatically.

Discussion of a solution to the problems of cocoa centres on four main options: increase demand in traditional markets, control supply, develop new uses for cocoa, and develop new markets. The first of these options appears in may ways the simplest, but a major difficulty is that demand in the traditional markets — the high-income states of Western Europe and North America — suffers from both price and income inelasticity. Producers cannot, therefore, have any great confidence in attempts to increase demand in this area by holding down prices; only changes in taste can be expected to effect a major increase in consumption and this is by no means a simple task.

An attempt was made in the 1960s to improve Ghana's position by restricting output, but it was found wanting. In 1964, a Cocoa Producers Alliance (CPA) was formed by Nigeria, Ghana, Togo, Brazil, Ivory Coast, and Cameroun which attempted to set a minimum price below which members would not sell their cocoa. The CPA set this 'indicator price' for the 1964–5 season at 190 shillings per hundredweight and provided that if the price on the world market fell below this level for ten consecutive days, the members would withdraw and refuse to sell more cocoa until the world price once again equalled or exceeded the indicator price. In compliance with these regulations the CPA withdrew as sellers in mid-October 1964. Unfortunately, none of the producers was strong enough to withstand this loss of earnings, added to which the 1964–5 crop proved exceptionally large; some producers began to disregard the sales ban and consequently in February the 'cocoa hold-up' collapsed and prices plummeted.

Since producers could not afford to withdraw completely from the cocoa market, a variation on the same theme whereby some cocoa was siphoned off the market to be used in 'nonconventional' processes seemed more likely to succeed. These processes included the use of cocoa in the production of margarine, baking fat, and cocoa bread.[6] Unfortunately, to be used for the production of these foods, cocoa had to compete in price with other, much cheaper, raw materials, and even at a time when the price for conventional cocoa had slumped to 100 shillings per hundredweight it was more attractive than the 35 shillings per hundredweight which would be obtained by selling the beans to an oilseed crusher.[7]

The fourth method of increasing earnings by finding new markets met with more success. The Soviet Union and Eastern Europe represented the largest potential market capable of being tapped in the near future, and Ghana tried to develop it. In this she was successful, and the quantity of cocoa exported to the Soviet Union rose rapidly during the 1960s, reaching a peak in 1965 (see table 4.2). There is, of course, the problem whether the Soviet Union re-exported the cocoa on to the free market. If true, this would constitute an unfair practice, since not only would it defeat the whole object of the exercise for Ghana but, as trade between the two countries was organised for most of the time on a bilateral basis, it would deprive Ghana of much needed foreign exchange. The Ghana government was clearly worried that this might occur and several trade agreements concluded with the Soviet bloc specifically prohibited the resale of cocoa.

Unfortunately, it is difficult to make a definitive statement on this question. The only clear indication whether the Soviet Union re-exported cocoa beans is to be found by comparing the figures for imports and grindings of beans. Since the main concern here is with resale on the free market, trade among the centrally planned economies is acceptable. Table 4.3, therefore, gives the imports and grindings of the USSR and Eastern Europe (excluding Yugoslavia) for the period 1960–70. It shows that the shortfall of grindings in relation to imports was quite negligible and that the Soviet Union admitted to re-exporting cocoa bean only during 1960–2. For the remainder of the period it is likely that there were no Soviet re-exports since the difference between imports and grindings is well within the limit of reasonable stocks: during the 1960s the stocks of all consumers averaged around 30 per cent of grindings;[8] even in 1965, the shortfall of Soviet and Eastern European grindings over imports did not approach this figure.

The figures on grindings are not entirely reliable, however, and in any case this evidence does not rule out the possibility that the USSR processed the beans and exported cocoa butter. This practice would not be contrary to the letter of the trade agreement, and there have been accusations that it occurred. While it may have taken place, it seems improbable that it occurred on any large scale. Although cocoa butter is the most sought product of the cocoa bean, international trade in it is small since major consumers process their own beans. It would seem that in the early years of Ghana's independence the Soviet Union possessed only a small capacity to process cocoa and was reluctant to import; when Ghana pressed her to do so she agreed but may have resold beans onto the free market. During the 1960s, however, the USSR increased its capacity for grinding cocoa by over 300 per cent and there seems no reason to doubt that, in general it

TABLE 4.2. GHANA'S COCOA BEAN EXPORTS TO THE USSR, 1960—72

Year	Total cocoa bean exports	Cocoa bean exports to USSR	Total Soviet cocoa bean imports	Percentage exported to USSR (Col 2/Col 1)	Percentage imported from Ghana (Col 2/Col 3)	Value of Cocoa bean exports to USSR
		thousand long tons				US$ thousand
1960	303	34	57	11	60	20,361
1961	406	19	21	5	90	8,644
1962	423	25	48	6	52	12,152
1963	404	43	53	11	81	13,847
1964	382	33	65	9	51	11,707
1965	494	66	88	13	75	21,161
1966	391	55	56	14	98	16,896
1967	328	57	81	17	70	18,180
1968	329	28	107	9	26	10,853
1969	303	15	97	5	15	7,867
1970	396	47	98	12	48	40,040
1971	309	13	136	4	10	7,185
1972	n.a.	66	130	. .	51	40,214

Sources: *Ghana, Economic Survey* (Accra: Central Bureau of Statistics, 1963, 1969 and 1970), *1962*, table 2, *1968*, table 24; and *1969*, table 24; *External Trade Statistics of Ghana*, vol 20, no 12, and vol 21 no 12; *Vneshnyaya Torgovila SSSR: Statistichesky Sbornik 1918—1966*, (Moscow, 1967); and *Vneshnyaya Torgovila SSSR: Statistichesky Obzor* for 1968, 1970, and 1972 (Moscow, 1969, 1971 and 1973).

TABLE 4.3. TOTAL SOVIET AND EASTERN EUROPEAN IMPORTS
AND GRINDINGS OF COCOA BEANS, 1960–70
(IN THOUSANDS OF LONG TONS)

Year	Imports	Grindings	Imports minus grindings	Cumulative difference	Re-exports
1960	92	71	21	. .	8
1961	60	79	−19	2	5
1962	91	89	2	4	3
1963	106	106	0	4	0
1964	124	121	3	7	0
1965	156	134	22	29	0
1966	123	148	−25	4	0
1967	155	160	−5	−1	0
1968	190	176	14	13	0
1969	173	170	3	16	0
1970	172	188	−16	0	0

Sources: Gill and Duffus Ltd., *Cocoa Market Report*, no 241, and FAO, *World Cocoa Statistics* (Rome), vol, 14, no 3 and vol 9, no 3.

now has a bona fide interest in the crop. At the same time, the Soviet Union's intake of cocoa has on occasion exceeded the planned level of consumption of cocoa products, and some cocoa butter may have been re-exported.

The Soviet Union is now the second largest consumer of cocoa in the world, while Soyuzplodimport, the All-Union Foreign Trade Organisation responsible for importing it, is the world's largest single buyer. In 1966 the Soviet Union announced that it had placed a ten million dollar contract for the supply of a new chocolate and cocoa powder producing plant with an overseas firm; the new factory would have a daily capacity of 100 tons of goods packed and ready for sale.[9]

With the Soviet Union currently an important market for cocoa, there are two other questions which affect its attraction as a trading partner. Does it provide a stable market or, if unstable, does its instability offset or exaggerate instability in the free market? Further, is the price at which it purchases cocoa competitive with that offered by alternative purchasers? The question of stability is complicated because instability can result from the actions of either buyer or seller, and in analysing the Ghana–Soviet case much depends upon the time period chosen. Some early work suggested that the USSR provided an unstable market for cocoa.[10] More recent research, however, has questioned this and concluded that any instability can be attributed as much to Ghana's policy as to that of the USSR.[11] Since a potential advantage of trading with centrally planned economies is that prices on the free market may be stabilised, some instability may be an advantage. In 1962 the USSR contracted to increase its cocoa purchases to 60,000 tons in 1965; it reached this target a year early. Following the collapse of the Cocoa Producers

Alliance in February 1965, Ghana looked for alternative purchasers. She tried first to arrange a collateral deal, and on 7 April the Ghana Cocoa Marketing Co. announced to general amazement, that it had already sold its 1964/65 main crop. It later became known that the cocoa was in the hands of a European financial syndicate which had no use itself for cocoa but had agreed to find buyers. In this quest it was unsuccessful, and the Ghana government then turned to the USSR. In December 1965 the Soviet Union agreed to purchase 150,000 tons over 2 years and to increase its annual consumption to 118,000 tons by 1970. The deal was considered by the Ghana government, with some justice, to be the major factor responsible for the subsequent recovery of the free market.[12]

There remains the problem of prices. It has been alleged that the USSR was able to take advantage of Ghana's difficulties to obtain cocoa at unduly low prices. A comparison of the performance of Ghana and of Nigeria, where trade with the USSR has been more at arm's length, may at first sight confirm this charge. Table 4.4 deals with Ghanaian exports and shows the annual quantity purchased by the USSR and other buyers, the price paid, and the price per ton; it then shows the average unit price for the 11 year period. Table 4.5 gives the equivalent data for Nigeria. Direct comparisons between Soviet prices for cocoa from the two sources are not possible since Nigerian and Ghanaian cocoa are of different qualities. What may be done, however, is to compare the unit price paid by the USSR and all other consumers first for Ghanaian and then for Nigerian cocoa. Tables 4.4 and 4.5 suggest that the Nigerians struck better bargains with the Soviet Union than did the Ghanaians.

Yet this evidence is not conclusive. In the middle years of the decade, when Ghana's relations with the USSR were particularly close, Nigerian sales of cocoa to the Soviet Union were significantly smaller than Ghana's both in absolute terms and as a proportion of total cocoa exports. There is evidence that during this period the Soviet Union only purchased from Nigeria as a last resort and it is therefore reasonable to expect higher prices. What seems to have happened during this difficult period is that, in 1965, the USSR offered to pay Ghana more than the prevailing world market price for its cocoa (a figure of £172 per ton has been quoted), but that this price was below the level to which world prices rose later. The USSR would not negotiate a new price although it did permit deliveries to be extended over three years instead of the original two. The Soviet Union has thus laid itself open to the charge of only purchasing cocoa when it could do so at a low price. In 1965 it is clear that it did do this, but it did so with the consent of the Ghana government in order to restrict supply and so boost prices on the free market.

From the figures in Table 4.4 it would appear that the Soviet price tends to lag behind free market price, perhaps because it is based on the preceding year's free market price. Thus during periods of falling prices (as in 1960—7), the USSR has tended to pay above the free market rate, with the situation being reversed when there is a rising price trend.

TABLE 4.4. AVERAGE UNIT VALUE OF GHANAIAN COCOA BEAN EXPORTS TO USSR AND OTHER CONSUMERS, 1960–70

Year	Quantity exported to USSR	Quantity exported to all other consumers	Value of exports to USSR	Value of exports to all other consumers	Value per ton of exports to USSR	Value per ton of exports to all other consumers
	1000 long tons		NC: thousand		New Cedis	New Cedis
1960	34	269	14,544	116,256	428	432
1961	19	387	6,174	132,450	325	342
1962	25	398	8,680	125,366	347	315
1963	43	361	14,130	121,406	329	337
1964	33	349	11,946	124,530	362	356
1965	66	428	21,593	114,883	327	268
1966	55	336	17,241	85,816	313	255
1967	57	271	18,551	112,119	325(340)[a]	414(332)[a]
1968	28	301	11,074	174,526	395	582
1969	15	288	8,028	210,539	535	731
1970	48	349	40,863	259,535	851(409)[b]	744(422)[b]
Total	423	3,737	172,824	1,577,426	. . . .	. . . . .

Sources: Ghana, *Economic Survey 1962*, Table 2; *1968*, Table 24; and *1969*, Table 24, and *External Trade Statistics of Ghana*, vol. 20 No. 12.

Notes: a Average value per ton, 1960–67.
b Average value per ton, 1960–70.

TABLE 4.5. AVERAGE UNIT VALUE OF NIGERIAN COCOA BEAN EXPORTS TO USSR AND OTHER CONSUMERS, 1964–70

Year	Quantity exported to USSR	Quantity exported to all other consumers	Value of exports to USSR	Value of exports to all other consumers	Value per ton of exports to USSR	Value per ton of exports to all other consumers
	1000 long ton		US $: thousand		US $	
1964	8	192	4,431	107,848	538	560
1965	11	248	6,204	113,330	557	456
1966	–	193	–	79,129	–	409
1967	16	684	11,164	141,962	700	208
1968	21	187	15,153	129,722	720	690
1969	24	147	21,767	125,519	907	829
1970	24	169	24,561	161,765	1,041(744)[a]	952(616)[a]

Source: UN Economic Commission for Africa *Foreign Trade Statistics Series B*, Nos. 9, 11, 13, 16, 17; *Nigeria Trade Summary* December 1969 & 1970.

Notes: Cols 1–4 are rounded, cols 5 & 6 are calculated from figures before rounding.
[a] Average value per ton 1964–1970.

B. *Importing from the USSR: payment and quality*

Since 1961, the USSR's trade with Ghana has been conducted on the basis of a bilateral trade and payments agreement. Such agreements take one step further in planning trade than do the loose bilateral agreements signed by Ghana and Nigeria in 1960 and 1963 respectively. The agreement between Ghana and the Soviet Union concluded on 4 August 1960 was based on principles similar to those of GATT.[13] All payments were to be either in Ghanaian pounds (which were then convertible) or other freely convertible currency. The following year, however, Ghana chose to replace this agreement with a bilateral payments pact and to develop similar arrangements with the other Eastern European countries. Under these agreements the contracting parties make a list of the commodities available for trade and agree each year on the quantities and values to be exchanged. The aim is that there should be an equal exchange so that no transfer of money need occur. However, payments agreements normally provide a certain flexibility so that either side may accumulate limited export or import surpluses for short periods.

The conversion of the Ghana government to bilateral payments marked a distinct change in policy from 1958 when proposals had been received but not accepted for bilateral pacts with Czechoslovakia, East Germany, and Poland. Although in June of that year Ghana had signed her first bilateral trade pact with Israel, and followed this in February 1959 by an agreement with the UAR, it was not until 1961 that the government made a major policy decision in favour of bilateralism. Between May 1961 and January 1962, fifteen bilateral payments agreements were signed, ten of them with the centrally planned economies, and a special section was created in the Bank of Ghana's Foreign Department to deal with the new arrangements.

Bilateral trade holds several potential advantages for a developing country, one of which is that it need not involve the use of scarce foreign exchange. The 1961 payments agreement with the USSR provided that all payments should normally be effected in Ghanaian pounds, which were by then nonconvertible. This was thought by the Ghana government to be a valuable feature of the agreement. An alternative method of conserving foreign exchange is to use import restrictions (these were also introduced), but as the Ghana *Economic Survey* for 1961 pointed out, 'The problem is not to reduce external trade but rather to encourage a greater exchange of commodities in order to promote economic development . . . . Bilateral trade agreements have therefore been signed with this object partly in view'.[14] The gains were largely illusory. Since Ghana was exporting to her bilateral partners goods which would otherwise have been sold for convertible currency on the free market, perhaps at lower prices, the savings in foreign exchange expenditure brought about by bilateralism were offset by a decrease in convertible foreign exchange earnings.[15]

Two rather more important advantages of bilateralism may be cited. For a country like Ghana which is heavily reliant on the unstable cocoa market

TABLE 4.6. COMMODITY IMPORTS BY GHANA FROM USSR,
1962 and 1970

SITC Classification	1962		1970	
	US$ thousand	%	US$ thousand	%
0 Food	338	7	5,904	37
1 Beverages and Tobacco	10	...	4	...
2 Crude materials (inedible)	0	0	0	0
3 Mineral fuels	19	...	8,917	57
4 Animal and vegetable oil and fats	0	0	0	0
5 Chemicals	226	4	4	...
6 Manufactured goods	2,625	51	678	4
7 Machinery and transport equipment	1,834	36	204	1
8 Miscellaneous manufactured items	68	1	13	...
9 Miscellaneous transactions	0	0	28	...
Total	5,120		15,752	

Source: *Foreign Trade Statistics for Africa: Series B, Trade by Commodity*
(New York) UN Economic Commission for Africa, 1962 and 1970.
Notes: Imports are c.i.f.; percentages do not total 100 due to rounding
... Negligible.

to provide the wherewithal for purchasing imports, it permits a certain amount of planning. In addition, it may be used as a source of aid: the payments agreement with the USSR provided that either side might accumulate an import or export surplus of four million Ghanaian pounds before remedial action needed to be taken.[16] Since this balance was payable in non-convertible Ghanaian pounds, the arrangement allowed Ghana to import up to four million Ghanaian pounds worth of Soviet goods on terms which amounted to an interest-free loan which did not need to be redeemed until the payments agreement expired; if the agreement was renewed on a regular basis, it amounted to a free gift. Similar, but less generous arrangements were made with the other Eastern European countries. Consequently import licenses were issued in such a fashion as to 'alter the country's pattern of trade, more specifically in favour of those countries with which Ghana has trade and payments agreements'.[17]

However, in order to take full advantage of either the planning or the aid aspects of bilateralism, a country needs an efficient planning mechanism. The early years of bilateral trade between Ghana and the USSR far from showing the former extract aid from the latter, witnessed the reverse — Ghana ran an export surplus. At least a part of this was due to the inefficiency of Soviet exporters who generally lacked finesse in their techniques and were unprepared to alter them to suit the Ghanaians. Two complaints were that consignments arrived unintelligibly labelled (or not labelled at all) and delivery dates were not kept.[18] The centrally planned economies have also been accused of sending goods which were inappropriate to the Ghanaian market and this may be correct. It is true that the USSR attempted to persuade Ghana to accept large quantities of equipment and that Soviet machinery has not fared well in tropical conditions. In the early years of the decade, most of Ghana's imports from the USSR were in SITC categories 6 and 7, as may be seen from the schedule attached to the 1961 trade agreement listing the goods available for trading. However, this was largely due to imports of machinery in connection with Soviet aid projects, and the composition of Ghanaian imports soon changed. The current arrangement is for Ghana to import mainly fuel.

An associated problem is that of prices: even if both sides have goods which the other desires, bilateralism will function smoothly only if the prices at which they are offered are mutually acceptable. The principle stated in numerous trade agreements between Ghana and the USSR is that the prices of goods should conform to world market prices, 'that is the prices on the main world markets of the corresponding goods'. However, the world market price is a most ephemeral conception. Prices vary from one 'main' world market to another and there is, of course, the problem of comparing commodities; even some raw materials are by no means homogeneous. The difficulty is particularly marked in the case of manufactured goods but, as we have seen, these formed a diminishing proportion of Ghana's imports from the USSR. This change in favour of raw materials and the growing sophistication of Ghanaian importers seems to have kept Soviet prices competitive. This may best be seen by reference to Ghana's imports of cement and crude petroleum. These products are of a fairly consistent quality so that a comparison of the price charged by various suppliers is a reasonably accurate indicator of competitiveness. Petroleum also has the merit that it is currently Ghana's largest import from the USSR. Table 4.7 shows the unit price paid by Ghana for these commodities from the USSR and from all other suppliers. It can be seen that, taking several years together, the Soviet Union is a competitive supplier.

It does not seem, therefore, that the USSR can be held fully responsible for the anomalous excess of Ghanaian exports over imports. This conclusion is reinforced by reference to the experience of the other countries which trade bilaterally with the USSR. The balance of trade between the Soviet Union and its other payments agreement partners for the period 1960–7 reflected $7,790 million (f.o.b.) in exports and $4,046 million (f.o.b.) in imports. With non-payments agreement trade the respective figures were $3,506 million and $4,355 million.[19] Soviet exports to the former group constituted 65.5 per cent of its total trade with payments agreement partners, whereas its exports to the latter group accounted for only 44.5 per cent of total trade. The normal situation, it appears, is for the USSR to have an export surplus with payments agreement partners, possibly because some partners are receiving goods as part of Soviet aid.

TABLE 4.7. UNIT PRICE PAID BY GHANA FOR IMPORT OF
CEMENT AND PETROLEUM OVER A NUMBER OF YEARS

Commodity and year	Imports from USSR	All other imports
Imports of cement (SITC 661 200):	Ghanaian £ per ton	
1960	7·65	8·20
1961	7·40	8·05
1962	5·65	6·60
1963	5·25	5·80
1964	6·05	6·55
1965	5·80	7·00
1966[a]	6·40	6·25
Average	6·31	6·92
Imports of petroleum (SITC 313010):	New pesewas per gallon	
1967	4·1	5·2
1968	7·1	6·1
1969	7·3	8·2
1970	7·0	6·6
Average	6·4	6·5

Sources: *Annual Report on External Trade Statistics of Ghana*, vol. 1 (Accra: Central Bureau of Statistics) for 1959–60, 1961–63, and 1964–65, and *External Trade Statistics of Ghana*, for December 1966–70.
[a] Figure for cement clinker (SITC 661 210).

Other explanations for the shortfall of imports are that Soviet products were unfamiliar to conservative Ghanaian importers and consumers and that import licenses were issued inefficiently. An attempt was made to overcome the former problem when the Ghana National Trading Corporation was established 'in order to make full use of these bilateral agreements . . .'[20] This organisation has been quite successful, although in 1963 it was still reported that unfamiliarity with products was one of the factors exerting a downward pull on imports from the bilateral pact countries.[21] The problem was made worse because the government lacked the necessary statistical information with which to prepare an adequate plan for increasing consumption. The Abraham Commission reported: 'We regret to say that trade statistics and data available for research and planning in the country are either non-existent or unsuitably combined. From the moment when goods enter this country to the time when they are offered to consumers, the government knows very little about what happens' and concluded that, 'policies concerning the flow of goods are therefore exercised somewhat in the dark'.[22]

The lack of an adequate administrative and planning mechanism initially hindered the issuing of import licenses. During 1963–5 a number of measures were introduced to encourage trade with the Soviet bloc by issuing import licenses requiring certain commodities to be purchased from the centrally planned economies. There were numerous administrative problems but, by 1965, trade was in balance.[23]

The failure of Ghana to import sufficient goods to offset her exports was a disadvantage, but the crucial point to consider when evaluating the worth of bilateral trade for Ghana is not whether the agreements were used to extract aid but whether they stimulated the centrally planned economies' demand for cocoa. If they did then Ghana benefited by reducing the amount of cocoa available on the traditional markets and thus increasing the price. There can be no doubt that the Soviet's demand for cocoa has increased, but this might have been an autonomous development quite independent of bilateral trade with Ghana. It is difficult to give a definite answer on this point, but the circumstantial evidence certainly favours the proposition that bilateral trade was a spur.

The government of President Nkrumah certainly believed that there was a link between the two, and similar views were held by policymakers in other African countries.[24] On his return from a tour of Eastern Europe in 1965, a spokesman for a Nigerian produce marketing team explained that

> the reason for the slow rate of development of trade [between Nigeria and the centrally planned economies] despite the existing agreements, is probably that Nigeria has not signed the type of agreement which Ghana and the UAR have signed, that is agreements that stipulate quantity, volume, and value of goods to be exchanged annually.[25]

Such views also find support in Soviet statements.[26] There certainly appears to be a historical relationship between the adoption of bilateral trading and the growth of Soviet demand for cocoa. The 1960 trade agreement listed cocoa as one of the products to be exported by Ghana, but officials of the Cocoa Marketing Board had great difficulty in persuading the Soviet Union to import any, and when they did so there was a strong suspicion that some had been resold on the free market. A protocol to the first bilateral agreement in 1961 specified that the USSR would increase its cocoa imports; indeed, tables 4.2 and 4.3 show that both Soviet and Eastern European imports of cocoa have increased steadily since 1961, the greatest increase in Soviet cocoa imports being in 1963–65. Oleg Hoeffding's work on the Soviet Union's attempts to balance its trade accounts with the non-communist world in this period suggests that imports purchased on a barter basis are less likely to be cut back in a balance of payments crisis than are hard currency imports.[27]

Perhaps the strongest confirmation of the value of bilateralism is to be found in the actions of successive Ghanaian governments. After the 1966 coup, all bilateral trade and payments agreements concluded with the Eastern European socialist countries and the People's Republic of China were suspended with a view to reviewing them all in the light of Ghana's interests.

Concerned to ensure that her supplies of cocoa would continue, the Soviet Union began to investigate the possibility of increased buying from other producers; however, all the agreements other than those with China and Albania were retained by Ghana.[28] In 1969, the payments agreements with Eastern Europe were allowed to lapse, but the agreement with the USSR, which now mainly concerns the bartering of cocoa for petroleum, was renewed. After the 1972 coup, the new government expressed its intention of increasing bilateral trade.[29] Thus, four different governments with widely differing outlooks have all, with greater or lesser enthusiasm, considered some bilateral trade with the socialist world to be in their interests.

III. Aid and Technical Assistance

During the first two to three years of independence, the new Ghana government took little interest in the USSR, largely because there seemed to be no pressing reason for diversifying established international contacts. By 1960, the picture was beginning to alter: Ghana's foreign exchange reserves, which had formerly borne most of the brunt of economic development, were dwindling while development needs were growing; at the same time, development activities began to emphasise industrialisation and an expansion of the State sector of the economy. The first of these changes required more foreign investment and aid, while the second made it unlikely that the UK and USA would be willing to provide all the funds. Consequently, Ghana began to take more interest in the Soviet bloc. In 1960, Kojo Botsio took up a long-standing invitation to visit Moscow, and four months later the two countries signed an agreement on economic and technical cooperation.[30] The following year Nkrumah himself toured the communist bloc with great success in terms of aid offers received; afterwards Krobo Edusei was deputed to follow up the verbal agreements reached by the Ghanaian president and another agreement on economic and technical cooperation resulted.[31]

As with trade, the Nigerian government was more reticent than the Ghanaian. After Ghana began to receive offers of Soviet aid the Nigerian government's reluctance to solicit development assistance from the same source came under attack on the grounds that Nigeria was losing out because of official prejudice.[32] Despite this pressure, the civilian government set its face against aid from the Soviet Union. To mollify its critics it showed some public interest in Soviet aid, but these initiatives were not followed through. In 1961, for example, a joint Regional and Federal Economic Mission to Europe included the Soviet Union and Eastern Europe in its itinerary. While in the USSR they met Khrushchev and, according to some estimates, the Soviet government expressed its willingness to make available development assistance of up to $44·5 million.[33] Nothing more was heard of this offer, however, and domestic critics claimed that the tour was merely an exercise in window-dressing.[34] Despite a statement in 1964 by the Minister of

Finance, Chief Festus Okotie-Eboh that 'during the last three years my
colleagues and I have not spared ourselves in our efforts to make our needs
known to all countries which might be able to offer assistance',[35] the only
tangible example of Soviet aid received under the civilian government was
a gift of 650 books for the National Library. More interest was shown in
Soviet development aid after the military coup of 1966, but the civil war
intervened before anything substantial could materialise. After the end of
the civil war, a fairly modest list of Soviet projects was agreed, and since
1972 the scope of Soviet aid has increased substantially by its involvement
in the iron and steel mill to be built at Ajaokuta.

A. *The Size and Nominal Terms of Soviet Aid*
By the Ghana government's estimate, the Soviet Union provided almost
US$50 million of medium and long-term credits to Ghana between 1960
and 1966.[36] This is substantially less than a Soviet commitment estimate of
Rb76 million.[37] The difference may stem from the mode of administering
loans: the Soviet Union consents initially to a broad skeleton agreement
and commits itself to an upper limit on the amount of aid it will provide.
This agreement is not binding until specific projects for which the credit is to
be used are hammered out. The amount of aid used is thus normally less
than the amount committed because administration takes time and because
there may be failure to agree on projects. In the 1961 aid agreement, for
example, provision was made for the construction of a textile mill, and in
May 1962 specific proposals were adopted for a mill at Tamale. However,
disagreement arose over the size of the enterprise; the Ghanaian Ministry
of Industries sought to expand the capacity from 6 to 20 million square yards
per annum and to have a finer cloth product that the originally agreed-upon
khaki. The mill had been planned to use locally grown fibre, but there were
inadequate quantities to supply an enlarged mill. Consequently, the
Soviet government preferred phased increments in production. No agreement
could be reached and the project was dropped in January 1966.[38]

By the time of the 1966 coup, the Soviet Union was owed 6 per cent of
all medium-term debts (which comprised 60 per cent of Ghana's total debts)
and Eastern Europe as a whole was owed 16 per cent. Most of the Soviet
loans were at low interest rates ($2\frac{1}{2}$ per cent) and, although they were classified as medium term, were repayable over 12 years in Ghanaian goods and/
or convertible currency.[39] A few were on more commercial terms, such as
the finance arranged for Ilyushin aircraft, fishing trawlers, and agricultural
machinery, for which there was a down payment of 10–40 per cent, a
repayment period of 5–8 years, and interest rates of up to 4 per cent.[40]

Soviet project aid normally covers only the cost of equipment and
technical assistance that cannot be provided locally – in general, about one-
third of total project costs.[41] In Ghana's case, however, extra assistance
was forthcoming in the form of a commodity credit made available under a
protocol signed in March 1963 which provided that the Ghana government

would receive Rb 20 million of Russian goods between 1963 and 1966 which were to be sold to raise funds to cover local costs. Like the other Soviet credits, the interest was 2·5 per cent with a provision for repayment in Ghanaian goods or convertible currency. Although the credit was to be used exclusively for Soviet-assisted projects, the Ghanaian Ministry of Finance pooled its receipts so that the loan contributed to the government's overall financial resources rather than to any specific project.[42]

There can be little doubt that the terms under which Soviet aid was made available were generous. The advantages of Soviet aid are particularly marked when compared with Ghana's main alternative source of external finance — Western European suppliers' credits. The terms of these loans by Western companies to facilitate the export of their machinery and equipment were only slightly, if at all, more favourable than commercial credits and were guaranteed by the donor firm's government. In January 1962, the US promised over $40 million for finance towards the Volta Dam. With such a large part of its African aid budget already committed to Ghana, it was improbable that the US government would have been prepared to provide much more even if it had not become concerned at Nkrumah's domestic and foreign policies, and in 1963 Kennedy instructed AID to extend no further long-term credits to Ghana.[43] Similarly, the UK government had neither the funds nor the inclination to undertake a major investment in Ghana. Other Western countries (including the Federal Republic of Germany, Israel, and Italy) provided aid, but by 1963 the only two major sources of foreign capital available to Ghana were Western suppliers' credits and communist aid.

The difference in the nominal terms of these two forms of aid, if suppliers's credits can be so called, is quite striking. Even the Soviet Union's less generous loans for the Ilyushins, trawlers, and so on compare favourably with the credit provided to finance an extension to Tema Harbour the terms of which required a down payment of 60 per cent with the remainder to be paid over $2\frac{1}{2}$ years at 5·5 per cent.[44] While this is an extreme case, the same conclusion is borne out by Table 4.8 which gives a breakdown of all medium-term contractor-financed projects, including official Western government aid. It does not, however, include finance for the Volta Dam which was long-term. The distinction between IMF and non-IMF states is, with the exception of Czechoslovakia and Yugoslavia (members of the IMF), the same as the distinction between Western and communist countries. The Nigerian government also accepted in principle that Soviet aid was in some respects more desirable than suppliers' credits. It noted in particular that suppliers' credits were liable to involve distortions caused by 'side attractions and vested interests'. However, in practice, despite a commitment to make 'strenuous attempts' to attract Eastern bloc aid, nothing materialised.[45]

An important consideration when evaluating the effectiveness of aid is whether the chosen investment will begin to generate an income before the loan which financed it needs to be repaid. The average repayment period

for Western credits was about 5 years, and it can therefore be seen from
Table 4.8 that only 8·6 per cent of the IMF loans could have paid for themselves during the repayment period. In the case of the non-IMF loans, however, over 61 per cent could have paid for themselves. This difference was
due to the cost of IMF member credits and the types of projects financed.
The largest IMF member commitment was to infrastructure; the largest non-
IMF member commitment was to manufacturing and agriculture.

If the terms of the non-IMF countries were more favourable to Ghana
than those of the IMF states, the same is true of rescheduling agreements
since the 1966 coup. After the coup the new regime exhibited clear anti-
communist tendencies, and it was not out of the question for them to
repudiate the non-IMF loans completely. In this situation the communist
countries played a shrewd hand, and their policy toward debt rescheduling
was cautious. They agreed to accept whatever terms Ghana managed to negotiate with her Western creditors, and when these terms left the determination of the rate of moratorium interest to individual creditors, the non-
IMF states were markedly more generous than their IMF counterparts.[46]
The effect of rescheduling by IMF and non-IMF creditors is striking.
Whereas the moratorium interest imposed by the latter was 16 per cent of
the original interest and principal, that of the former was 39·4 per cent
of the original.[47] A report submitted by the Ghana government to the creditor
nations in April 1970 noted wryly that 'it is a sad reflection on the comparative relations between Ghana and the two groups of countries that the IMF
countries imposed the harsher terms even though she has long-standing
economic and other ties with them'.

B. *The Effective Terms of Soviet Aid*
Such considerations indicate only the nominal terms of Soviet aid which take
account of rates of interest, periods of repayment, and similar technical
points. The effective terms, by contrast, include the price and quality of the
equipment and personnel provided under the aid agreement. Unfortunately,
little systematic research was carried out on these aid projects while they
were in operation. Work on them ceased after the 1966 coup and since
then documents have been lost while memories have faded and been
coloured by new prejudices. Any assessment of the effective terms of
Soviet aid must therefore be largely impressionistic.

Save for the state farms which, while unsatisfactory, were subject to
special problems, no Soviet-financed productive enterprise was in operation
by the time of the 1966 coup, although a fish-processing factory, a gold
refinery, and a prefabricated housing plant were nearly completed. Some
projects, such as the textile mill at Tamale, were not built because of differences between Ghanaian and Soviet conceptions of feasibility. Others
were prolonged through the rigidity of Soviet practices. However, the
most important reason for their noncompletion is that it was a long time
before Soviet projects got off the ground. Only two of these projects

TABLE 4.8. ANALYSIS OF CONTRACTOR-FINANCED PROJECTS IN GHANA
(NC: MILLION.)[2]

| Sector | Expected to generate income | | | | | | | | Total | |
| | Less than 6 years | | 6–12 years | | More than 12 years | | Other | | | |
	IMF	non-IMF	IMF	non-IMF	IMF	non-IMF	IMF	non-IMF	IMF	non-IMF
Agriculture & Fisheries	30·1	4·5	32·7	11·2	0·0	0·0	0·0	0·0	62·8	15·7
Mining	0·0	0·0	0·0	0·0	0·0	2·4	0·0	0·0	0·0	2·4
Manufacturing	0·0	0·0	58·4	31·3	0·0	0·0	0·0	0·0	58·4	31·3
Construction	0·5	0·0	0·3	0·2	64·6	2·9	0·0	0·0	65·4	3·1
Transport & Communications	3·1	0·2	40·1	8·0	46·9	4·9	4·7	0·0	94·8	13·1
Electricity, Gas, & Water	0·0	0·0	0·0	0·5	66·2	1·7	0·0	0·0	66·2	2·2
Unallocated[1]	0·0	0·0	0·0	0·0	0·0	0·0	43·0	23·5	43·0	23·5
Total	33·7	4·7	131·5	51·2	177·7	11·9	47·7	23·5	390·6	91·3
As per cent of total	8·6	5·1	33·7	56·1	45·5	13·1	12·2	25·7	100·0	100·0

Source: J. H. Mensah, *The State of the Economy and the External Debts Problem* (Accra, 1970).

Notes: Figures include credits for imports of raw materials and consumer goods as well as projects that do not generate any directly-measurable economic returns.

[1] The following contracts are excluded: (1) purchase of frigate, (2) Drevici Group projects, and (3) atomic reactor, agricultural equipment, pharmaceutical industry, and automobile factory, for which contract prices are not known.

[2] Until July 1965 the Ghanaian Pound was the unit of currency and was valued at par with the Pound Sterling. On 19 July 1965 Ghana changed to a decimal currency, the Cedi based on 100 pennies. This was considered to be impractical for calculation and on 23 February 1967 the New Cedi was introduced, valued at 10 shillings sterling. Since then it has been devalued and revalued several times.

had passed the feasibility stage by 1963. The record does not show the Russians to be particularly fast workers, but neither does it reveal them as sluggards.[48]

Despite the non-completion of the projects there is enough evidence from Russian activities to give rise to concern over the quality of Soviet equipment and technical assistance. Criticisms have been made of the price, quality, and suitability of Soviet machinery. Officials of Ghana's Geological Survey Department, with whom a team of Soviet geologists worked, complained that Russian vehicles consumed too much fuel, while a civil servant sent to Moscow to sign a contract for Soviet machinery for the state farms objected that much of it was unnecessary or unsuitable.[49] It is difficult to evaluate these criticisms, for while there have been problems in adapating Soviet machinery, particularly vehicles, to Ghanaian conditions, similar difficulties have been experienced with some Western suppliers and may owe much to the absence of adequate maintenance facilities. Some complaints have been made that equipment was secondhand, in contravention of specific provisions in most of the agreements, but this is hotly denied by the Soviet government. What may be concluded is that Soviet equipment is generally less sophisticated than equivalent Western products and that these differences may be magnified in a difficult tropical environment. The justified criticisms levelled at Soviet personnel are that they were expensive and sometimes inefficient. It is impossible, however, to say whether these problems render Soviet projects valueless, since the only ones put into operation were the state farms where the difficulties experienced were particularly severe.

Despite these handicaps, a certain amount was achieved by Soviet assistance. Apart from the fish-processing plant, gold refinery, and prefabricated housing factory which were not quite completed by the 1966 coup, the major Soviet activities were a geological survey of northern Ghana, aid for four state farms, and educational aid. During 1962–6 a Soviet geological survey team operated in northern Ghana and represented the largest external contribution to mineral exploration.[50] Work was scheduled to finish in January 1965 but the contract was extended to September 1966 but was, of course, terminated by the coup. The geologists' maps, instruments, and reports (still in Russian) were left behind in disorder, but no effort was made to preserve or use them.

The record of Soviet aid to state farms is fairly dismal, but this was due in part to the general failings of the state farms where expansion was too rapid, lines of authority were confused, and political and economic objectives were often at loggerheads. However, Soviet aid did little to improve the situation. Norman Uphoff writes that 'the Ghanaian agriculturalists who had to deal with the Soviets were uniformly dissatisfied with Soviet aid'.[51] In 1966, new accounting methods were introduced to the State Farms Corporation, making it possible to extract deficits for individual farms. The average losses made by the Soviet farms were over six times as great (or four times if no account is taken of depreciation) as the average for all farms.[52] Only part of the higher than average deficit can be explained by the greater than average size of a Soviet farm.

Educational assistance is possibly the most widespread form of Soviet aid and both Nigeria and Ghana have experience of it. While the Nigerian government was slow to accept Soviet help for development projects inside the country, Nigerian students were quick to take up offers of education in the USSR. The Nigerian government was initially opposed to the idea of accepting Soviet scholarships,[53] but it soon discovered that its hand had been forced. In the early 1960s the USSR was happy to make scholarships available through either governmental or non-governmental channels. The Nigerian authorities found that despite their reticence, young Nigerians were going to the Soviet Union on scholarships administered by individual politicians, trade union leaders and others. In order to exercise some control over the type of people awarded scholarships and over the subjects studied, the Federal government centralised the control of all foreign scholarships in 1962,[54] and the number of young Nigerians leaving annually to study on officially approved Soviet awards rose from 16 in 1962 to 161 in 1970.[55] By 1972 there were some 678 Nigerians studying in USSR about whom the Federal government had details; most were on technical courses with 44 per cent studying medicine, engineering and related subjects.[56]

In Ghana, Soviet aid to education took the form of Russian teachers, Russian-financed educational institutions built in Ghana, and Ghanaian students sent to Russian educational institutions. Soviet teachers began to arrive in Ghanaian secondary schools in 1963 and by the 1964–65 academic year they formed the second largest contingent of foreign teachers provided on an aid basis in these schools. They were fairly evenly distributed among mathematics, physics, and chemistry and none taught social sciences.[57] Many Ghanaian students travelled in the reverse direction to Soviet educational institutions. Although a Scholarships Secretariat was established by the Ghana government, it was bypassed by some students so that the authorities had no clear idea of how many of their young people were studying in Eastern Europe. This situation arose largely because at first the Soviet Union claimed to be able to educate anyone, irrespective of their qualifications. After serious rioting among African students in 1963, the Soviet authorities became more 'elitist' and cooperated with the Scholarships Secretariat in selecting candidates. In 1966 there were 642 Ghanaians on scholarships in the Soviet Union, making her the second largest provider of overseas awards. In 1970, she still maintained this position, although the number of Ghanaians on foreign scholarships had decreased all round.[58]

With respect to the subjects being studied, there is a close similarity between the Nigerian and Ghanaian situations. Of the 289 Ghanaian students known to be in the USSR in 1969, almost half were studying medicine and a further 81 were studying engineering or agriculture and related subjects. There is, of course, the problem of comparing academic standards. Some Soviet-trained medical doctors who returned to Ghana after the fall of

Nkrumah were re-examined by the Ghanaian medical authorities and found
wanting. Some said that their training was inadequate, others that it was
different from that received in the West but of the same standard. The current
military government has now resolved the issue by decreeing that all
Ghanaians qualified as doctors, engineers, and technicians in Eastern Europe
are henceforth to be accorded equal treatment with their Western-trained
counterparts subject to whatever 'orientation' may be considered necessary.[59]
While the flow of students was largely uncontrolled, there were real grounds
for fearing that those who 'qualified' in the USSR might have little aptitude
for their newly acquired discipline. However, now that there is a check on
the academic backgrounds of those awarded Soviet scholarships, there
seems no reason why it should prove any more difficult to assess Russian
educational standards than it is to do the same for American standards. In
1968, the Soviet and Nigerian authorities agreed on the mutual recognition
of academic awards. In addition to teachers and scholarships, the Soviet
Union provided Ghana with aid to equip and staff three technical schools,
of which only one was in operation by the time of the coup. The completed
school was for tractor operators. It was expensive and the Soviet teachers
appeared rather rigid in their approach, although they were energetic and
might have improved had they not been repatriated after the coup.[60]

IV. Lessons from the Experience

The experience of Ghana in its commercial dealings with the Soviet Union
suggests that there is a light at the end of the tunnel, but that the tunnel
itself is by no means straight and narrow. The main lessons would seem to
be that commerce in the USSR is organised in a fashion different from
the West or in many less developed countries, and that there are some
things the Soviet Union can do well and some things that it cannot. The
major issues facing African governments or those in other developing
countries when considering whether to export to the Soviet Union may be
phrased as simple questions, although the answers are more complex. First,
does the USSR offer a stable market; if not, does its instability counter-
balance or exaggerate instability in the market economies? Second, does the
Soviet Union pay better prices than the market economies; if not, are there
any other ways in which export receipts will be increased by diverting some
goods from traditional purchasers into new markets? Third, there is the
problem of bilateralism; what are the advantages and disadvantages of agreeing to trade with the USSR on a barter rather than a cash basis? These questions may be illuminated, if not answered categorically, by studying the
experience of Ghana and cocoa. Cocoa beans are a fairly homogeneous
commodity, but Ghana produces the prime quality. Soviet imports of cocoa
are long standing, and for most of the period under consideration Ghana has
been its major supplier. During the 1960s a determined effort was made by

the Ghana government to increase cocoa sales to the centrally planned economies, and the USSR in particular. The trade between the two countries has been conducted both within and without the framework of a payments agreement. Finally, throughout the period under consideration the world cocoa market has been unstructured with no world commodity agreement to complicate the picture. The tentative conclusion that may be drawn from Ghana's experience is that in a situation where a primary producer is a major exporter of a particular good, where demand on the free market is price inelastic, and where the primary producer can absorb appropriate quantities of relatively homogeneous Soviet commodities, bilateral trade with the USSR may be markedly beneficial. If these assumptions do not hold, the situation is of course more complicated, but trade may still be beneficial. On balance, Ghana's strategy was a success. It should be possible to assess whether this success will be mirrored by other commodities to which different market structures apply.

Ghana's experience with Soviet aid adds further support to the argument that offers of assistance should be treated with caution by developing countries. Soviet aid was superficially very attractive both because its nominal terms were generous and because it was well suited to the projects it financed. Herein lies the root of much criticism of Soviet aid. Investment in directly productive industry was ambitious but also risky. If successful, the factories would be highly beneficial to the recipient, but because of their ambitiousness, Soviet projects were also more liable to failure. Investment in a road or railway or agricultural extension scheme runs little risk of failure. Once a road is built it simply needs to be kept in good repair. It may or may not act as a catalyst for new investment and may or may not transform the economic situation prevailing in the localities through which it passes, but these are not the concern of the aid donor who is unlikely to be criticised if the recipient fails to make full use of the project. A factory is a quite different proposition; not only must the building be erected and the machines set in motion but they must remain in motion, must be supplied with raw materials and their products must be conveyed to an adequate market for sale. If the project fails in any of these respects the donor is blamed, and there is little that it can do to extricate itself. In Ghana it was agreed that the Russians would not be responsible for the management of the state farms established with Soviet equipment, but this was to no avail in saving the USSR's reputation – when the state farms failed, responsibility was laid at the Soviet door.

There is, therefore, something of a threshold with Soviet aid and trade; economic relations with the USSR and other centrally planned economies require a certain commitment before they will mature from sporadic contacts to a fuller relationship. The USSR has constructed effective and valuable projects in various parts of the Third World. The lesson from Ghana would appear to be that for success a recipient should have a clear and realistic set of priorities and should exercise effective control over the project's implementation. Unfortunately, this is tantamount to insisting that a State with an underdeveloped economy should have a fully developed polity.

Notes

[1] See for example, House of Representatives *Debates* cols 279–80, 334, 607, 655, 834, 1022, 1046, 1070, 1245, and 1267 1 April, 2 April, 5 April, 6 April, 8 April, 10 April and 11 April 1963.

[2] UN Statistical Office *Monthly Bulletin of Statistics* Vol XXV: 7 July 1971, Special Table B.

[3] House of Representatives *Debates* cols 2898–9, and 3003, 16 November 1961.

[4]*African Foreign Trade Statistics: Series B. Trade by Commodity* (New York: UN Economic Commission for Africa, 1965), no. 11. The equivalent figures for Nigeria in 1970 are even more extreme — 100% of exports to USSR were in SITC categories 0–2 although only 33% of total exports fell under these 2 headings.

[5]Tony Killick, 'The Economics of Cocoa' in W. Birmingham, I. Neustadt, and E. N. Omaboe *eds. A Study of Contemporary Ghana*, (London, 1966), vol 1.

[6] *West Africa*, 27 February 1965, p. 240.

[7] *West Africa*, 1965, p. 407.

[8] Gill and Duffus Ltd., *Cocoa Market Reports*, no 242 (London, 1971).

[9] *Ibid*, no 191 (1966), p. 8.

[10] Egon Neuberger, 'Is the USSR Superior to the West as a Market for Primary Products?' *Review of Economics and Statistics* 46 (August 1964) pp. 287–93, and S. H. Goodman, 'Eastern and Western Markets for the Primary Products of Ghana', *Economic Bulletin of Ghana* 10 (1966): 23–28.

[11] Philip Hanson, 'Soviet Imports of Primary Products: A Case Study of Cocoa', *Soviet Studies* 23 (July 1971) pp. 59–77.

[12] Ghana, *Parliamentary Debates* (Accra, 1966), vol. 43, cols 6478–88.

[13] Ghana, *Economic Survey 1960* (Accra): Central Bureau of Statistics, par. 315, and *United Nations Treaty Series* (New York, 1960), vol. 421, p. 27.

[14] *Ibid*, Par. 335.

[15] This point is linked with the earlier discussion on prices. To the extent that sales to the centrally planned economies reduced the supply of cocoa to the free market they also increased the value of Ghana's exports to the West and therefore its foreign exchange earnings. The improvement in Ghana's foreign exchange position thus came about by improving its foreign earnings in the West rather than by increasing its foreign exchange savings on imports.

[16] *Ghana Treaty Series* (Accra, 1961), no. 57.

[17] Ghana, *Economic Survey 1964*, par, 108.

[18] *West Africa*, 1 May 1965, p. 493. See also 'Joint Recommendations of the Ghana Government and the USSR Government', art. 5, *Ghana Treaty*

Series (Accra, 1963) p. 12, for evidence of Ghanaian dissatisfaction.

[19] UNCTAD Secretariat, *Approaches to Multilateral Settlements in Trade between the Socialist and Developing Countries* (TD/B/AC 7/3), annex 11, table 1, prepared by the Institute for Economic and Market Research, Budapest.

[20] Ghana, *Economic Survey 1961*, par. 337.

[21] Ibid., *1963*, par. 108.

[22] W. E. Abraham, *Report of the Commission of Enquiry into Trade Malpractices in Ghana* (Accra: 1965), par. 47.

[23] For a fuller discussion of the problems see C. Stevens 'In Search of the Economic Kingdom', *Journal of Developing Areas*, vol. 9: 1 (October 1974) and also C. Stevens, *The Soviet Union and Black Africa* (Macmillan, London 1976). According to Ghanaian statistics, imports from the USSR were slightly less than exports in 1965. According to Soviet statistics, Ghana's imports from the USSR were slightly larger than her exports to the USSR in that year.

[24] K. Amoaka-Atta in *Parliamentary Debates*, vol. 43, cols. 6487–88.

[25] Home Service Broadcast in English, Lagos, 1800 GMT, 6 July 1965, *Summary of World Broadcasts* (London).

[26] See for example, T. S. Khachaturov, *The Development of External Economic Relations of the Soviet Union* (Paper delivered at the Congress of International Economic Association, Montreal, 2–7 September 1968) p. 3.

[27] 'Recent Structural Changes and Balance of Payments Adjustments in Soviet Foreign Trade', in Alan A. Brown and Egon Neuberger *eds. International Trade and Central Planning*, (Berkeley, 1968), pp. 312–37.

[28] Ghana, *Economic Survey 1966*, par. 116.

[29] *N.R.C. Budget Statement for 1972–73* (Accra, Ministry of Finance 1972), par. 65.

[30] *United Nations Treaty Series* (1960), vol. 399, p. 61.

[31] *Ghana Treaty Series* (1961), no. 58.

[32] See House of Representatives *Debates*, cols. 1046 and 1061, 8 April 1961, and cols. 843, 874, 878 and 884–5, 4 April 1962.

[33] Kurt Muller, 'Soviet and Chinese Programmes of Technical Aid to African Countries', in S. Hamrell and C. G. Widstrand *(eds.) The Soviet Bloc, China and Africa*, Uppsala 1964 p. 117.

[34] House of Representatives *Debates* col. 3024, 18 November 1961, and cols. 730–3, 24 March 1964.

[35] *Ibid*, cols. 1846–7, 7 April 1964.

[36] This figure is calculated from an estimate of NC30·99 million in medium-term loans in Mensah, *State of the Economy*, app., and an estimate of NC11·7 million in long-term loans and NC6·9 million suppliers' credits made by the Bank of Ghana for private enterprise.

[37] *The USSR and Developing Countries: Economic Cooperation* (Moscow: 1966), p. 7.

[38] N. Uphoff, *Ghana's Experience in Using External Aid for Development 1957–1966: Implications for Development Theory and Policy* (Berkeley, California, Institute of International Studies, 1970), pp. 559–60.

[39] UN Treaty Series (1960), vol. 399, p. 61, art. 8, and *Ghana Treaty Series* (1961), no. 58, art. 2.

[40] 'Statement of Public Debt: Foreign Credits as at 30 June 1967' in *Report and Financial Statements by the Controller and Accountant-General for the Year Ended 30 June 1967* (Accra).

[41] B. R. Stokke, *Soviet and Eastern European Trade and Aid in Africa* (New York 1967), p. 73.

[42] 'Protocol to the Agreements on Economic and Technical Cooperation of 4 August, 1960 and 4 November 1961', *Ghana Treaty Series* (1963), esp. art. 2; 'Protocol on the Deliveries on Credit from the USSR of Consumer Goods, Construction and Other Materials in 1963–66', *Ghana Treaty Series* (1963); and Uphoff, *Ghana's Experience*, chapter 5, fn. 238.

[43] Arthur M. Schlesinger, Jr., *A Thousand Days* (New York, 1967).

[44] 'Statement of Public Debt: Foreign Credits as at 30 September 1962' *Report and Financial Statements by the Account-General and Report of the Auditor General for the Year Ended 30 September 1962* (Accra).

[45] *National Development Plan: Progress Report 1964* (Lagos), March 1965 p. 34.

[46] The moratorium interest is a rate of interest imposed on that proportion of the contractual principal and interest that is deferred by rescheduling, which extends the period over which the loans are to be repaid by a smaller amount each year. The debtor must thus pay the original rate of interest plus a moratorium rate of interest on the difference between the amount actually repaid each year and the amount due prior to rescheduling. The total burden of debt is thus increased while the repayment period is extended.

[47] IMF member states were owed 212·6 million New Cedis in original principal and interest; their moratorium interest amounted to NC83·7m for a total of NC296·3m. Non-IMF member states were owed NC37·4m originally with NC6·0m in moratorium interest for a total of NC43·4m. Mensah, *State of the Economy*.

[48] For further details of the practicalities of Soviet aid see the author's article 'In Search of the Economic Kingdom', op. cit., and book *The Soviet Union and Black Africa*, op. cit.

[49] Uphoff, *Ghana's Experience*, pp. 347–50 and Chap. 6, N. 90.

[50] *Ibid*, pp. 347–50.

[51] *Ibid*, p. 509.

[52] Calculated from *Balance Sheet and Operating Statement for the Year Ended 31 December 1966* and *Balance Sheet and Operating Statements for the Year Ended 31 December 1967* (Accra: State Farms Corporation).

[53] House of Representatives *Debates* cols. 1684, 14 April 1962, *West Africa* no. 2344, 5 May 1962, p. 494.

[54] House of Representatives *Debates* cols. 2546–52, 21 August 1962.

[55] *West Africa* No. 2369, 27 October 1962, p. 1196 and information from Bureau of External Aid for Education, Lagos.

[56] These were not the only Nigerian students in the USSR. For further details see C. Stevens, *The Soviet Union and Black Africa* op. cit.

[57] Uphoff, *Ghana's Experience*, op. cit. chap. 5, nn. 119, 123.

[58] Figures from the Ghana Scholarships Secretariat, 1971.

[59] *West Africa*, 13 November 1972, p. 1544.

[60] Uphoff, *Ghana's Experience*, op. cit., p. 374.

5 India's Trade with the Socialist Countries

DEEPAK NAYYAR

The last two decades have witnessed a phenomenal growth in trade between the less developed countries of the Third World and the socialist countries. India has been very much a part of this trend. In 1952/53, the value of India's trade with the socialist bloc was a mere $9·2 million. By 1972/73, it had risen to $910·3 million. As a result, the combined share of Bulgaria, Czechoslovakia, East Germany, Hungary, Poland, Romania, the USSR and Yugoslavia in India's total trade increased from less than 0·5 per cent to more than 18 per cent. This remarkable expansion occurred in a framework of bilateral trade agreements,[1] the principal feature of which was that payments for all transactions were made in rupees.

The main object of this paper is to evaluate the benefits derived by India from its trade with the socialist countries of Eastern Europe. In a broader context, such an exercise would also shed some light on the possible contribution of socialist countries to economic development in India. However, given the unusual framework in which the trade was carried out, it is necessary, as a preliminary step, to examine the working of the trade and payments arrangements. After that, we can move on to the crux of the paper.

I. The Mechanism of Trade and Payments Agreements

Bilateral trade is an integral part of the overall system of economic relations between the socialist countries and India. All trade is channelled through agreements which have three distinct features: (a) the mode of payment; (b) a long-term contractual approach coupled with specific annual arrangements; and (c) an automatic conversion of aid, as well as debt repayments, into trade flows. We shall discuss each of these characteristics in turn,[2] and, in the process, highlight the mechanism and the working of the trade and payments arrangements.

Consider first, the mode of payment. To begin with, in the early fifties, all payments were made in convertible currencies. Gradually, the emphasis of trade agreements shifted to bilateralism and, by 1956, the Eastern European countries had adopted the rupee as the unit of account in their trade with India. In practice, however, trade did not balance each year and the surpluses or deficits which arose had to be settled in sterling. In 1959/60, there was a radical change in the payments mechanism. It was decided that payments for *all* transactions were to be made in inconvertible rupees. Balances outstanding each year were to be settled through exports or imports of mutually agreed products. The complete transition to rupee payments brought about a genuine shift to bilateralism in India's trade with the socialist countries. For this reason, our empirical analysis focuses attention on the period after 1960. Throughout the subsequent years, India's exports to, and imports from, these countries were effected through the mechanism of bilateral rupee trade. However, in the agreements, the exchange value of the rupee was pegged to its gold equivalent, so that the Eastern European countries were protected from the devaluation of the rupee in June 1966.[3]

The second distinct feature of the bilateral arrangements is their long-term contractual approach. Generally, the duration of trade and payments agreements was three to five years, although they were sometimes extended for longer periods.[4] Originally, the main purpose of such agreements was to outline the long-term objectives of economic cooperation between the partner countries. But after 1960, more specific clauses were introduced. For example, in some cases, quantitiative targets for the expansion of trade, the value of goods to be exchanged, or the intention of increasing the proportion of manufactures in India's exports,[5] were written into the agreement as special provisions. All the same, even such clauses were quite general and aggregative in their very nature. In actual fact, trade flows were determined by the annual trade plan. At the beginning of each year, the contracting parties decided upon the aggregate total value of trade between them for that year. A list of possible importables and exportables were appended to this plan, but the commodity pattern of trade remained flexible. Therefore, it is clear that although the long-term agreement provides the framework, '. . . the annual trade plan continues to be the specific operational document'.[6]

The *ex-ante* determination of the annual value of trade is most interesting. The trade target is calculated in such a way that after taking the credit inflows from the socialist countries to India and the debt servicing outflows from India to the socialist countries into account, the trade is bilaterally balanced each year. Hence, it is apparent how aid from the socialist countries and debt repayments by India are automatically converted into trade flows through the bilateral agreements.[7] However, this does not preclude the possibility of short-term imbalances that might arise during, and at the end of, each plan. Surpluses and deficits outstanding at the end of a year are usually adjusted for in the next annual trade plan. In the very short run, imbalances are met through an extension of temporary swing credit facilities by the partner in surplus.

So much for the principles underlying rupee trade. It is also quite crucial to understand how the trade transactions actually take place in this frame-work. The procedure is indeed quite complex. Each Eastern European country maintains four accounts with banks in India: (i) a central clearing account with the Reserve Bank of India; (ii) another special account with the Reserve Bank in which it deposits any credits extended to India as aid; (iii) a similar corresponding account, again with the Reserve Bank, in which debt repayments by India are deposited; and finally (iv) a current account with one or more commercial banks. In this system, India pays for its imports from the socialist countries by depositing inconvertible rupees into the first central account or by withdrawals from the second account. On the other hand, socialist countries finance their imports from India by incurring expenditure through their current account with commercial banks. If they want to spend their credit in the third account, it must be transferred to their account with a commercial bank through the central clearing account. Despite the complexity in accounting, the equilibrating mechanism is fairly simple. If a particular socialist country exhausts its rupee balances, India extends temporary swing credit facilities, and the repayment is made as soon as possible. In the opposite situation, when a socialist country accumulates a large rupee surplus, India uses import licensing to restore the balance. Whatever happens, in the long run, the accounts are bilaterally balanced.

The central accounts of the socialist countries are protected against any alterations in the exchange value of the rupee, and these countries are free to transfer the rupee balances from any of their other accounts into it. For this reason, accounts in the commercial banks hold just what is necessary for current transactions.

In this section, we have been concerned with the operational aspects of bilateral trade and payments arrangements. It would now be in order to outline the growth in trade that occurred, and to specify the criteria on which an evaluation of India's economic ties with the socialist countries ought to be based.

II. An Outline of the Approach

Table 5.1 shows that, since the transition to rupee payments in 1960, India's trade with the socialist bloc increased very rapidly indeed. In fact, taken together, the value of exports to, and imports from, the rupee trade countries in 1972/73 was 360 per cent higher than in 1960/61. At the same time, the share of these countries in India's foreign trade more than trebled. While rupee trade increased at an average rate of 15 per cent per annum, it is apparent that the growth was not quite continuous. The particularly rapid expansion in the first half of the sixties was interrupted by a slight drop in the level of trade during 1966/67 and 1967/68. This was followed by another phase of expansion in trade, which was certainly slower than before and was also interrupted by a reduction in the value of trade, for two years,

TABLE 5.1. INDIA'S TRADE WITH SOCIALIST COUNTRIES

Year	Total value of trade: imports and exports (US $million)	Value index 1960/1 = 100	Percentage share in India's total trade
1960/61	197·5	100	5·3
1961/62	319·7	162	8·7
1962/63	426·4	216	11·2
1963/64	500·8	254	11·8
1964/65	607·5	308	13·3
1965/66	658·2	333	14·1
1966/67	604·7	306	14·0
1967/68	597·5	303	14·0
1968/69	768·0	389	17·6
1969/70	788·3	399	19·7
1970/71	785·8	398	18·7
1971/72	727·0	368	15·9
1972/73	910·3	461	18·3

Source: Director General of Commercial Intelligence and Statistics (DGCIS), *Monthly Statistics of the Foreign Trade of India* (Calcutta: Government of India).
Notes: (i) Statistics relate to Indian fiscal years beginning 1 April.

(ii) The value of trade has been converted into US dollars @ $1 = Rs 4·76 for the period up to 1965/66 and $1 = Rs. 7·50 for the period 1966/67–1971/72 which were the official exchange rates. As explained earlier in the text, this has been done in order to facilitate comparison over the entire period under study. Thus, the dollar is used only as a *numeraire*. For the year 1972/73 we have used an exchange rate of $1 = Rs 7·55, which is the conversion factor in the UN *Yearbook of International Trade Statistics, 1972/73*.

(iii) The value index and the percentage share of the socialist countries in India's total trade have been computed.

(iv) The group of socialist countries is constituted by Bulgaria, Czechoslovakia, East Germany, Hungary, Poland, Romania, USSR and Yugoslavia.

at the beginning of the 1970s. There were several factors underlying the somewhat uneven nature of the trend, and we shall go into these a little later.

From India's viewpoint, the benefits of bilateral rupee trade seem fairly obvious. First, trade with the socialist countries could not have grown as rapidly as it did, except through the media of bilateral agreements. Second, in the absence of this trade, economic assistance in the form of development credits may not have been extended by the centrally planned economies of Eastern Europe. Third, given the extreme shortage of foreign exchange in the Indian economy, the introduction of rupee trade added to India's import capacity, at the same time underwriting an expansion in exports. This is particularly significant in view of the stagnation in exports during the fifties. What is more, the existence of the payments arrangement described above reduced the burden of debt servicing, in so far as repayments could be made in exports or domestic currency, instead of scarce convertible foreign currencies.

Although the benefits appear to be quite straightforward, any measurement or quantification poses a problem. It is clear that an expansion of bilateral trade *per se* is no index of the gain to India. After all, it is perfectly possible that a part of the increase in exports to the new bilateral agreement markets is illusory, in as much as it represents a diversion of exportable commodities away from the other traditional markets. Alternatively, the prices received for exports may not be favourable. Even if they are, the real benefit of rupee trade would also depend upon the choice of imports offered by the socialist countries and the import prices charged. In principle, therefore, an analysis of the costs and benefits of the bilateral trade and payments agreements, for India, must be based on some assessment of: (i) the *net* increase in exports, (ii) the composition of imports, and (iii) the terms of trade obtained.

There are two reasons why the net growth in exports may have been less than the apparent increase. In the first place, it is possible that India met a part of its commitments under the bilateral agreements by diverting exports from the convertible currency markets to the new trading partners. Secondly, socialist countries may have re-exported Indian products to the rest of the world. This kind of practice is easily distinguishable if shipments from India are directly reconsigned to other ports without being actually unloaded in any socialist country, or if distinctly Indian products are re-exported after import. However, when we consider commodities which were produced and exported by the socialist countries even before they began trading with India, several complications arise. It is no longer possible to identify the Indian origin of such exports. But to the extent that imports of these commodities from India enhance the exportable surplus in socialist countries, there is an implicit re-export. As far as India is concerned, all such re-exports are the equivalent of exports diverted from her traditional markets to her bilateral trading partners, and do not constitute a net increase in exports. On their part, the socialist countries might re-export Indian goods for the following reason. Many of them suffer from foreign exchange shortages, and the resale of products imported from India (under rupee agreements) might be one way of obtaining convertible currencies. Alternatively, it is possible that under the bilateral arrangement they have to import some Indian products for which there is little demand; these products might then be dumped on the world market, again for the purpose of obtaining foreign exchange. Apart from diversion, such dumping would probably reduce world prices thereby worsening India's terms of trade with the rest of the world.

Given that export earnings from rupee trade could only be used to finance imports of goods and services from the socialist countries, the composition of imports is clearly of considerable importance. The question is whether India's imports under the bilateral agreements were high-priority items necessary for its development programme, or were they low-priority goods which it was forced to buy in order to exhaust available rupee balances? Of course, the price and quality competitiveness of these imports is equally important.

Under bilateral agreements, the terms of trade are directly dependent

on prices received for exports and prices paid for imports. Therefore, in
order to compare the terms of trade obtained from the socialist countries
with those obtained from the rest of the world it is necessary to compare:
(i) prices fetched by exports under rupee trade and in the world market; and
(ii) prices paid for imports under rupee trade and in the world market.

The above discussion makes it clear that if the terms of trade obtained from
the bilateral partner countries are no worse than those obtained from other
countries, and imports are constituted by high priority items, *any* net increase
in exports as a result of rupee trade constitutes a real benefit to India.[8] Having
thus set out a clarification of the theoretical issues involved, it is now possible
to attempt an evaluation of India's trade with the rupee payment countries.

The issues outlined above are discussed as follows: the next section reviews
the pattern and composition of India's exports to, and imports from, the
socialist countries. This is followed, in section IV, by an assessment of the
net increase in exports. Section V is devoted to an analysis of the terms of
trade obtained. The final section of the paper attempts to draw together the
threads of the argument and to provide an overall evaluation of India's
trade with Eastern Europe and the USSR.

III. Pattern of Trade

We have shown that bilateral arrangements led to a rapid growth in the aggregate value of India's trade with the socialist bloc. Clearly, it is necessary to go
beyond such aggregative data and analyse the pattern and composition of
rupee trade in some detail. Three important questions arise in this context.
First, what were the trends in exports, imports and the balance of trade?
Second, how was the total trade distributed as between the different Eastern
European countries? And third, what were the changes, if any, in the commodity composition of exports and imports?

A. *Balance of Trade*
The trends in India's exports to, and imports from, the rupee trade countries,
during the period 1960/61–1972/73, are outlined in Table 5.2. The growth
in exports is indeed striking, and their value in 1972/73 was six times that in
1960/61, rising at a compound rate of 18·7 per cent per annum. In fact,
between 1960/61–1962/63 and 1970/71–1972/73 the average annual share
of the socialist countries in India's export earnings rose from 10·4 per cent
to 23·6 per cent; what is more, over the same period, increased exports to
these countries accounted for 43·2 per cent of the total increment in India's
exports.[9] Except for the slight decline in 1966/67, 1967/68 and 1971/72,
the expansion in exports was continuous. This break in trend can be explained
in terms of the following factors. First, 1965/66 was a very poor agricultural
year which affected exports to *all* markets adversely. Second, the devaluation

of the rupee in June 1966 had a dislocating effect, particularly on trade with the socialist countries, because the agreements had to be adjusted for the exchange rate alteration and this took some time.[10] Presumably the uncertainties surrounding exchange rate policy in late 1971, as well as the subsequent changes in it, were responsible for the lower value of exports in 1971/72.

Imports under the bilateral agreements increased as rapidly as, if not faster than, exports in the first half of the 1960s. There were three factors underlying this trend in imports: (i) the transition to payment in inconvertible rupees;[11] (ii) the increase in exports, to which imports were tied under the new payments arrangement; and (iii) the aid offered by socialist countries in the form of development credits.[12] However, the growth in imports did not continue beyond 1965/66. The figures in Table 5.2 do indicate a higher level of imports in 1968/69 and 1969/70, but this was followed by a decline and imports appear to have stabilized at a lower level, close to that which prevailed in the mid-sixties. To some extent, of course, the trend described here was inevitable, if the import surplus of past years had to be compensated for by an excess of exports over imports. This point becomes very clear if we consider changes in the balance of trade during the period under study.

From our point of view, the balance of trade between India and the socialist countries in the fifties is not so important, because, until 1959/60, the surpluses or deficits which arose had to be settled in convertible currencies, such as sterling. Trade was still largely governed by the usual considerations of international commerce. On the other hand, the period since 1960 has been characterised by a radically different payments mechanism, which gave rise to bilateral rupee trade. We are, in fact, interested in an evaluation of this arrangement.

A glance at the data in Table 5.2 reveals three distinct phases in India's balance of trade with the socialist countries. In the early sixties, India ran a trade deficit which was obviously financed from development loans extended by the partner countries. This was followed by a period of four years, when trade was bilaterally balanced. Finally, starting in 1969/70, India maintained a trade surplus, the magnitude of which increased markedly in the early seventies. Given that loans had to be repaid through exports, the last phase of the trend was unavoidable, and, if India wanted to reduce its dependence on aid, it was also necessary. In other words, debt servicing could only be sustained through a net export surplus. An overall view of these interdependent economic transactions would clearly be useful. Unfortunately the Indian government does not publish any statement of the country's balance of payments with the socialist bloc. This may be so for reasons of security, because imports of military equipment are an important constituent of trade with Eastern Europe. However, it is possible to construct a summary statement of the balance of payments on the basis of indirect evidence available from different sources. Such an exercise has been done elsewhere for the period up to 1965/66.[13] Therefore, in the following analysis, we shall concern our-

TABLE 5.2. INDIA'S BALANCE OF
TRADE WITH SOCIALIST COUNTRIES
(IN $ MILLION)

Year	Exports	Imports	Balance
1960/61	104·4	93·1	+11·3
1961/62	135·6	184·1	−48·5
1962/63	195·1	231·3	−36·2
1963/64	229·2	271·6	−42·4
1964/65	302·9	304·6	−1·7
1965/66	329·0	329·2	−0·2
1966/67	301·0	303·7	−2·7
1967/68	301·2	296·3	+4·9
1968/69	355·2	412·8	−57·6
1969/70	410·1	378·2	+31·9
1970/71	482·3	303·5	+178·8
1971/72	458·0	269·0	+189·0
1972/73	621·8	288·5	+333·3

Source: Statistics published by DGCIS, Calcutta.
Note: Figures relate to Indian fiscal years beginning
1 April, and have been converted into US dollars.

selves with the subsequent years as that was also the period in which the trade
surplus became very significant.

Table 5.3 sets out the broad aggregates of economic transactions between
India and its bilateral trade partners in the seven years from 1966/67 to
1972/73. We find that, taken together, export earnings and gross credits

TABLE 5.3. STATEMENT OF INDIA'S ECONOMIC
TRANSACTIONS WITH THE SOCIALIST COUNTRIES,
1966/67−1972/73
(IN $ MILLION)

Credits		Debits	
Exports, fob	2929·6	Imports, cif	2252·0
Credits utilised	488·3	Debt servicing	578·7

Sources: (i) For exports and imports: Table 2.

(ii) For credits utilised: Government of India, *Economic Survey,
1973−74* (New Delhi) p. 105. The figures have been converted
into US dollars at the official exchange rate.

(iii) For debt servicing: Government of India, Ministry of
Finance, Department of Economic Affairs, *External Assistance,
1971/72 and 1972/73* (New Delhi, 1974). This gives data on
total repayments, including amortisation and interest up to
31 March 1973. From this we have deducted the repayments
made in the Second and Third Plan periods (figures in Dharm
Narain, op. cit., p. 25), in order to obtain the figure for debt
servicing in the period 1966/67−1972/73. Once again, the statistics
have been converted into US dollars.

utilised exceeded the import and debt servicing payments by a sum of $587·2 million. Clearly, this substantial net surplus of credits over debits needs some explanation. Logically speaking, the answer must be found in unrecorded imports, payments for invisibles, errors or an *actual* surplus in India's favour.

In pursuit of an explanation, we compared India's imports from the socialist countries as recorded by trade statistics in India *with* exports to India from the socialist countries as reported in their statistics. During the period 1967 to 1972, the cif value of India's imports from these countries added up to $1891·1 million, whereas the fob value of exports from the socialist countries to India worked out at $2161·2 million.[14] It is obviously not appropriate to compare a cif figure with an fob figure. To make them comparable, the costs of insurance and freight must be added to the latter. Assuming that a margin of 10 per cent is a reasonable approximation, the value of Eastern European exports to India can be estimated at $2377·3 million. Therefore, it would seem that India's imports under bilateral trade, between 1967 and 1972, were recorded as $486·2 million *lower* than exports to it as recorded by its partners. This still leaves a net surplus of $101 million in India's favour which needs to be accounted for. We know that import data in the official trade statistics of India do not include payment for invisible items such as technical assistance, shipping and insurance facilities. It is quite likely that these payments amounted to 15 per cent of the gross development credits utilised,[15] which works out at $73·2 million. The remaining surplus of $27·8 million is probably attributable to errors, omissions and time lags involved in the recording of statistics.[16]

The obvious question that arises is why was the underrecording of imports, on the part of India, so large? In our view, the gap of $486 million can be explained largely in terms of imports of defence and military equipment. For political reasons, the Indian government probably did not want to reveal the magnitude of these imports, which were consequently left out of the trade statistics.[17] Admittedly, this is pure conjecture, but available evidence suggests that our estimate of defence imports is quite plausible. Firstly, the USSR, Czechoslovakia and Yugoslavia, which were the principal suppliers of military equipment, accounted for 75 per cent of the unrecorded imports.[18] Secondly, defence imports in the Third Plan period are estimated in the range $158–210 million,[19] so that a figure of $486 million is not unreasonable for a seven-year period that witnessed two wars.

B. *Market Distribution*

Consider now the distribution of total trade as between the different bilateral arrangement partners. Table 5.4 outlines the market distribution of India's rupee trade and brings out the changes in relative shares of different countries. The main trends emerging from these figures can be summed up as follows.

(i) Among the socialist countries, the USSR was by far the most important market for exports and source of imports. Its share in India's total trade with the Eastern Bloc countries averaged at more than 50 per cent for most of the

TABLE 5.4. MARKET DISTRIBUTION OF INDIA'S TRADE WITH
SOCIALIST COUNTRIES
(AVERAGE ANNUAL RELATIVE SHARES: IN PERCENTAGES)

Country	1960/61– 1962/63	1963/64– 1965/66	1967/68– 1969/70	1970/71– 1972/73
Bulgaria	1·5	2·2	2·4	4·5
Czechoslovakia	15·8	12·6	10·9	8·3
East Germany	7·4	8·2	7·8	6·3
Hungary	5·1	5·0	4·7	4·4
Poland	9·3	8·3	8·5	10·9
Romania	4·3	1·9	2·5	4·6
USSR	47·6	54·0	57·0	55·8
Yugoslavia	9·0	7·8	6·2	5·2
Total	·100·0	*100·0*	*100·0*	*100·0*

Source: Statistics published by DGCIS, Calcutta.
Note: Figures relate to an average of three-fiscal-year periods.

period under study. In absolute terms also its trade with India grew very
rapidly, rising from an annual average of $150 million in the three year period
1960/61–1962/63 to $452 million during 1970/71–1972/73.

(ii) Although trade with Bulgaria, Hungary and Romania increased substantially in the 1960s, they remained relatively unimportant trading partners,
on the average, accounting for less than 11 per cent of India's bilateral rupee
trade.

(iii) Apart from the Soviet Union, India's main trading partners in Eastern
Europe were Czechoslovakia, East Germany, Poland and Yugoslavia. In
general, trade with East Germany and Poland kept pace with the overall
expansion in India's trade with the socialist countries. However, the share of
Czechoslovakia and Yugoslavia in India's bilateral rupee trade declined
steadily over the period 1960/61–1972/73. In this context, it is worth noting
that, with effect from January 1973, India's trade with Yugoslavia ceased to
be on a bilateral basis, and payments for all transactions are now made in
convertible currency.[21]

C. *Trends in Exports*

From market distribution, let us turn to the question of changes in the composition of trade. The trends in India's principal exports to the rupee payment
countries, since 1960, are outlined in Table 5.5. These twenty commodity
groups accounted for most of India's rupee trade exports, which is hardly
surprising, as they also constituted her major exports to the rest of the
world.[22] An examination of the data reveals the following trends.

(i) Exports of some products like cashew kernels, coffee, mica and
leather increased rapidly throughout the period under study, although the
growth tapered off in the late 1960s or early 1970s.

TABLE 5.5. INDIA'S PRINCIPAL EXPORTS TO RUPEE TRADE COUNTRIES
(IN $ MILLION)

	1960/ 61	1961/ 62	1962/ 63	1963/ 64	1964/ 65	1965/ 66	1966/ 67	1967/ 68	1968/ 69	1969/ 70	1970/ 71	1971/ 72	1972/ 73
1. Jute manufactures	9·6	21·7	22·6	32·5	53·2	71·5	66·8	56·1	48·9	41·0	63·2	60·7	89·1
2. Tea	17·0	19·5	24·3	26·6	36·3	36·7	28·4	30·8	30·7	35·7	39·7	53·5	50·4
3. Cashew kernels	5·3	7·5	9·3	10·9	18·1	16·4	22·1	14·9	28·2	36·1	24·5	26·9	36·1
4. Oilcakes	4·9	8·2	25·1	33·3	49·8	41·2	35·9	44·9	46·6	34·0	48·2	35·3	59·9
5. Coffee	4·5	6·1	12·6	8·0	16·1	17·3	11·7	14·0	17·7	19·5	26·4	16·8	18·3
6. Iron ore	13·8	14·6	20·0	18·2	18·3	18·2	14·2	17·0	18·4	18·3	17·8	21·0	22·1
7. Pepper	9·1	5·1	4·5	6·7	7·8	11·6	8·7	12·5	9·3	15·6	10·7	15·4	12·9
8. Engineering goods	—	0·1	0·2	0·5	1·2	3·0	4·0	8·8	12·0	14·2	16·4	17·5	26·3
9. Chemicals and related products	0·3	1·0	2·0	1·2	5·2	7·4	4·5	5·8	7·8	12·9	16·1	11·8	17·9
10. Mica	4·2	4·4	5·4	6·1	5·8	8·6	6·2	8·9	8·8	10·3	11·9	13·4	14·1
11. Tobacco	1·5	3·0	12·6	17·3	21·0	13·9	4·4	7·1	6·3	10·0	8·4	23·3	39·6
12. Hides and skins	12·6	9·5	15·0	12·5	12·5	12·4	16·3	7·4	3·8	7·3	4·4	—	—
13. Footwear	3·4	1·9	2·0	3·6	3·7	5·7	5·6	5·6	4·2	4·1	6·2	4·7	6·5
14. Vegetable oils	3·1	4·9	5·3	7·0	4·9	3·6	—	2·5	8·1	4·4	7·7	8·1	12·3
15. Cotton piecegoods	—	—	0·5	0·3	2·3	8·6	5·1	0·5	7·8	8·7	13·7	12·6	45·8
16. Raw wool	3·4	8·6	6·9	3·6	7·7	8·5	4·1	4·6	3·9	3·2	4·4	2·6	2·0
17. Manganese ore	2·7	2·2	3·2	3·5	3·5	5·3	2·3	1·8	2·6	1·7	1·1	1·2	1·0
18. Lac	1·2	1·4	1·5	2·0	1·4	2·2	1·1	1·0	1·2	1·5	0·9	1·0	1·3
19. Leather	0·3	0·9	3·4	5·1	5·0	3·9	24·1	17·9	28·1	49·6	46·6	41·7	59·0
20. Clothing	0·2	0·1	0·3	0·9	3·3	5·9	6·1	7·8	12·0	12·2	23·2	26·7	28·9
Total including others	*104·4*	*135·6*	*195·1*	*229·2*	*302·9*	*329·0*	*301·0*	*301·2*	*355·2*	*410·1*	*482·3*	*458·0*	*621·8*

Source: Statistics published by DGCIS, Calcutta, except for engineering goods, for which data published by the Engineering Export Promotion Council are used.
Note: (i) All data relate to Indian fiscal years beginning 1 April and have been converted into US dollars.
(ii) Chemicals and related products include manufactures of wood, cork, paper, paperboard, glass and rubber.

(ii) There were other products such as jute manufactures, tea, oilcakes and unmanufactured tobacco, exports of which also registered a substantial increase between 1960/61 and 1972/73, but a significant proportion of the growth occurred before 1965/66. In fact, in the latter half of the sixties, jute and tobacco exports fell markedly, whereas exports of oilcakes and tea were quite stagnant. However, 1972/73 witnessed a recovery in the earnings derived from all these export commodities.

(iii) Exports of hides and skins, vegetable oils, raw wool, manganese ore and lac fluctuated widely, but the general picture is one of decline or stagnation. The value of iron ore, pepper and footwear exports also fluctuated, but on balance showed a slight increase over the entire period.

(iv) In the late sixties, some new products acquired importance in the export basket; these were engineering goods, clothing, cotton piecegoods, and chemicals and related products. Export earnings from these commodity groups increased rapidly but remained only a small proportion of the total.[23]

Although the above trends identify the commodities which were responsible for the rapid export growth, they provide no index of the changes in commodity composition. In order to see if there was any diversification in India's exports to the socialist countries, it is necessary to group products according to the degree of processing involved in the output finally exported. Table 5.6 does just that by classifying India's rupee trade exports into raw materials, food, beverages, tobacco, etc., and manufactured goods. It shows that, between 1960/61 and 1972/73, exports of manufactured goods grew

TABLE 5.6. COMMODITY COMPOSITION OF INDIA'S EXPORTS TO THE SOCIALIST COUNTRIES

	Annual average 1960/61– 1962/63		Annual average 1965/66– 1967/68		Annual average 1970/71– 1972/73	
	$m	%	$m	%	$m	%
1. Raw and crude materials	43·5	30·0	46·7	15·0	40·1	7·7
2. Food, beverages, tobacco, etc.	64·5	44·5	126·2	40·7	187·9	36·1
3. Manufactured goods	21·7	15·0	108·2	34·9	211·5	40·6
Total of above	*129·7*	*89·5*	*281·1*	*90·6*	*439·5*	*84·4*
Total rupee trade exports	*145·0*		*310·4*		*520·7*	

Source: Table 5.
Notes: (i) Group 1 includes iron ore, mica, hides and skins, raw wool, manganese and lac; Group 2 includes tea, cashew kernels, oilcakes, coffee, pepper, tobacco and vegetable oils; Group 3 includes jute manufactures, engineering goods, chemicals and related products, footwear, cotton piecegoods, leather and clothing.

(ii) The three groups together do not add up to the total exports because our data are not exhaustive, i.e. there are items other than the twenty principal exports on which this table is based.

very rapidly; exports of food, beverages, tobacco, etc. (a group constituted mostly by primary and semi-processed agricultural products) also increased substantially, but raw material exports were quite stagnant. However, it is the changes in relative shares that are more important. We find that, in the early sixties, the bulk of India's exports to the socialist countries consisted of primary and semi-processed agricultural products and raw materials. In the period 1960/61—1962/63, unprocessed raw materials, food, beverages and tobacco accounted for nearly three-fourths of the total rupee trade exports. Since then the situation has changed considerably. Manufactured goods, which were only 15 per cent of the total in 1960/61—1962/63, increased their share to 40 per cent during 1970/71—1972/73. At the same time, the share of raw materials fell sharply from 30 per cent to a little less than 8 per cent. This diversification was largely the result of specific clauses about increased exports of manufactures from India in the trade and payments agreements. Despite this change, however, the socialist countries absorbed a relatively lower proportion of manufactures as compared with the rest of the world.

D. *Composition of imports*

To complete the discussion on the pattern of trade between India and the socialist countries of Eastern Europe, it now remains for us to consider the commodity composition of imports and the changes in it. Table 5.7 shows the trends in India's principal imports under the bilateral trade agreements. Over the twelve-year period, these eleven commodity groups accounted for more

TABLE 5.7. INDIA'S PRINCIPAL IMPORTS FROM SOCIALIST COUNTRIES
(ANNUAL AVERAGES: IN $ MILLION)

Commodity group	1960/61– 1962/63	1963/64– 1965/66	1966/67– 1968/69	1969/70– 1971/72
Base metals	36·5	44·1	36·7	38·9
Metal manufactures	6·1	5·4	3·8	1·8
Machinery	75·5	168·6	145·4	146·0
Transport equipment	4·0	7·6	8·5	10·0
Chemicals	7·5	12·1	15·2	23·7
Paper and paper manufactures	4·1	5·0	8·0	8·9
Medicinal and pharmaceutical products	1·5	2·5	4·4	8·4
Fertilizers	5·7	5·7	20·5	21·5
Petroleum products	6·0	18·9	10·3	13·2
Scientific instruments	4·6	6·2	6·1	7·3
Dyeing and Tanning Materials	1·2	1·1	1·1	0·5
Total including others	*169·5*	*301·8*	*337·6*	*316·9*

Source: Statistics published by DGCIS, Calcutta.
Note: All figures relate to Indian fiscal years and have been converted into US dollars. The annual averages have been computed.

than 85 per cent of total imports. A glance at the table also confirms that
rupee trade provided India with high-priority imports. Machinery and transport equipment constituted 50 per cent of the total import bill, while intermediate goods such as base metals, chemicals, fertilisers and petroleum products made up another 28 per cent.[24] There is no doubt that these capital
goods and intermediates were *essential* to India's development programme,
and were by no stretch of the imagination low priority goods which India
was forced to import in order to use up its rupee balances with the Eastern
Bloc countries. Of course, it is possible to argue that such imports could,
alternatively, have been obtained in the world market. Indeed they could,
but not with the same ease, because India suffered from acute shortages of
convertible foreign exchange, which, in turn, made payment in inconvertible
rupees a welcome facility.

It was established earlier that if the imports purchased under rupee trade
were constituted by high-priority items, the benefits derived by India from
its bilateral agreements with the socialist countries would depend on the net
increase in exports and the overall terms of trade obtained. We now turn to
an analysis of these aspects.

IV. Net Export Growth: An Assessment

In section III, we have shown that any attempt at a quantification of net
export growth must determine two things: first, the extent to which India
diverted export supplies from convertible currency areas to the socialist
countries; and second, the proportion of Indian products re-exported by
the latter. Once such diversion has been estimated, it is fairly simple to discern
the net impact of bilateral rupee trade on export growth.

A. *Export Supplies Diverted by India*
As long as there is no constraint on increasing the domestic production of an
exportable product, the question of diversion does not arise. However, supply
conditions might be such that domestic production cannot be stepped up
adequately to meet all increases in demand. If the supply of Indian exportables was less than infinitely elastic during the period under study, it is quite
possible that India diverted export supplies away from her traditional markets
to meet her export commitments under the bilateral agreements. An exact
measure of this diversion would be the difference between the actual exports
to convertible currency areas, and what these exports would have been in
the absence of rupee trade with the socialist countries. Such a hypothetical
question raises immense problems of measurement, and can only be answered
by extrapolating past trends. However, the extrapolation methodology suffers
from the limitation that the factors underlying the trends might well change
over time, and there may be no past trends in the case of non-traditional
exports. In view of this conceptual problem and the consequent statistical

difficulties involved, it would be extremely difficult to estimate what India's exports to the rest of the world would have been in the absence of trade with the Eastern Bloc countries.

A less exact, but more pragmatic, approach would be to measure the visible reduction in India's exports to the rest of the world as a result of increased exports to the socialist countries.[25] For this purpose, it is necessary to distinguish between India's exports to the rupee payment countries from her exports to convertible currency areas, and then compare the trends over the period under study. For each commodity, statistically, there are four possible combinations: an increase in India's exports both to the socialist countries and to the rest of the world; an increase in exports to the rest of the world accompanied by a fall in exports to the socialist countries; an increase in exports to the socialist countries accompanied by a reduction in exports to the rest; and finally, a falling trend in exports to both groups of countries. Let us consider the possibility of diversion in each case.

(i) An increase in exports to both sets of countries means that, as a result of bilateral trade, there is no visible reduction in exports to convertible currency areas, but it does not eliminate the possibility of implicit diversion. It might be argued that were it not for trade with the socialist countries, exports to the rest of the world may have increased even more. However, such a proposition rests on the assumption that there would have been sufficient import demand in the convertible currency areas. This might be difficult to establish one way or another, because one does not know what the world demand would really have been in the absence of socialist countries. All the same, on the basis of evidence available about trends in world demand, we shall try to assess the possibility of implicit diversion. It would be worth remembering that such an exercise may yield somewhat uncertain results.

(ii) If an increase in exports to the convertible currency areas is accompanied by a reduction in exports to the socialist countries, it would be perfectly reasonable to assume that there is no diversion.

(iii) A reduction in exports to the rest of the world accompanied by an increase in exports to the socialist countries suggests a strong possibilty of diversion, but may not always mean that India diverted export supplies from the former to the latter. Firstly, it is possible that there was a falling trend in exports (of a particular commodity) even before the socialist countries emerged as important markets, in which case, the decline may be independent of increased exports to rupee payment areas. Secondly, there may be exogenous changes in factors such as world demand and India's relative competitiveness. These may be quite independent of the expansion in rupee trade and might yet lead to a fall in India's exports to the rest of the world. But if there are no such factors, and the decline in exports to convertible currency areas began only after the socialist countries became important markets, it is most likely that India diverted export supplies.

(iv) By itself, a falling trend in exports to both groups of countries does not establish or refute the possibility of diversion. However, if exports to the socialist countries fall faster, or even at the same rate as exports to the rest of the world it would be reasonable to assume that there is little likelihood of diversion. On the other hand, if exports to convertible currency areas fall relatively more than those to rupee payment countries, it is likely that India diverted export supplies from the former to the latter.

So much for a general methodology. Let us now consider the trends in each of India's principal exports to the Eastern Bloc countries in order to determine the extent to which limited exportable supplies were diverted from convertible currency areas. The method outlined above provides us with a broad framework which is supplemented with other available and relevant evidence for particular exports.

(1) *Jute manufactures.* Table 5.5 shows that India's exports of jute goods to the socialist countries increased most rapidly between 1960/61 and 1965/66; they rose from an average annual value of $18 million during 1960/61–1962/63 to $52·4 million in 1963/64–1965/66. At the same time, exports to the rest of the world increased from $287 million to $303·8 million.[26] This was roughly in the same proportion as the increase in import demand in the two sets of countries.[27] Moreover, throughout the first half of the 1960s India maintained her share of the world market at a little over 70 per cent.[28] Clearly, in this period, increased exports to the socialist countries did not reduce India's exports to the rest of the world.

In the following years, the trend was completely different. After 1965, India rapidly lost her share of the world market to Pakistan and there was a marked decline in her exports of jute manufactures. I have shown elsewhere that this was largely because of the poor competitive position of the Indian jute industry.[29] Exports to convertible currency areas fell sharply from the peak level of $312·6 million in 1965/66 to an average annual value of $247 million during the period 1966/67–1971/72: a decline of 21 per cent. But over the same period of time, exports to the socialist countries fell by 21·5 per cent, declining from a peak level of $71·5 million to $56·1 million. Thus it seems extremely unlikely that India diverted any export supplies even after 1965/66.

It is, however, possible that the year 1972/73 was an exception. In that year exports of jute manufactures to the socialist countries were distinctly higher than the average of previous years, at $89·1 million, whereas those to convertible currency areas were slightly lower at $238·3 million. The demand conditions in the world market were such that extra exports under rupee trade are not likely to have been at the expense of Western markets. This is because the bulk of India's jute exports to the Eastern Bloc countries were constituted by sacking cloth and jute bags,[30] which were increasingly difficult for India to sell in the rest of the world on account of the development of substitute materials and handling techniques in the Western countries.[31] To the extent that this was true, bilateral agreements offered India additional markets for her jute goods, not only in 1972/73, but also in earlier years.

(2) *Tea.* India's exports of tea to the socialist countries grew rapidly in

the early sixties, stagnated thereafter and registered an increase once again in the seventies. The average annual value of tea exports to the rupee payment countries rose from $26·7 million in the period 1960/61—1965/66 to $38·5 million during 1966/67—1972/73, but at the same time exports to the rest of the world fell from $225·6 million to $164·2 million. Given the fact that the increasing pressure of domestic demand reduced the supplies available for export,[32] it is likely that India might have diverted some export supplies from convertible currency areas. However, it is interesting that although exports to the socialist countries increased by only $11·8 million per annum, exports to the rest of the world fell by $61·4 million. Clearly, most of the fall in India's tea exports to convertible currency areas *cannot* be explained in terms of supplies diverted to the rupee payment countries. In fact, it has been shown that the main reasons for India's poor export performance were increased competition from East African teas in the UK market, and the relative attractiveness of the domestic market.[33] Both these developments were quite independent of bilateral rupee trade.

In view of these factors, it is difficult to say how much of the increase in exports of tea under rupee trade was diversionary. To the extent that the traditional markets were saturated and the world demand for tea was quite stagnant, the Eastern European countries did provide a new source of demand for Indian tea. All the same, if India could have surmounted competition from the East African countries, at least a part of the tea sold to the socialist bloc could have been sold for convertible currency.

(3) *Cashew kernels*. Exports of cashew kernels from India increased substantially during the period under study. The annual average value of cashew exports to the socialist countries increased from $11·3 in 1960/61—1965/66 to $27 million during 1966/67—1972/73. At the same time, exports to the rest of the world also increased from $35·8 million to $47·2 million. The expansion in rupee trade did not reduce exports elsewhere. On the other hand, it is very likely that the additional demand created by the socialist countries pushed up the world cashew prices thereby improving India's terms of trade.[34] However, given the rising trend in world demand, it might be argued that a portion of the cashew kernels sold under bilateral agreements could have been sold in the western markets. This sounds plausible, but, given the increasing competition from Brazil, Tanzania and Mozambique, it would have been difficult.

(4) *Unmanufactured tobacco*. India's exports of tobacco to the socialist countries increased at a fast pace in the early sixties, rising from an annual average value of $2·3 million in 1960/61—1961/62 to $17 million during 1962/63—1964/65. Over the same period, exports to the rest of the world were virtually unchanged, falling very slightly from $27·8 million to $27·4 million. However, between 1960/61 and 1964/65, India's total tobacco exports increased faster than world exports,[35] as a result of which her share in the world market also increased. Therefore, it would seem that bilateral trade provided India with additional markets for her tobacco at the cost of

a very minimal diversion of export supplies.

After 1964/65, however, the trends were completely reversed. Exports to the socialist countries dropped sharply, falling from the peak level of $21 million in 1964/65 to an average of $8·3 million during 1965/66–1970/71, whereas exports to the rest of the world increased from $30·2 million to $32·7 million. The contrast in export volume trends is even more pronounced. Exports to the rupee payment countries fell from 42·2 million kgs in 1964/65 to an annual average of 10·4 million kgs during 1965/66–1970/71, while exports to convertible currency areas increased from 35·2 to 38·8 million kgs.[36] It appears that tobacco exports were actually diverted from socialist countries to convertible currency markets.

In recent years tobacco exports under rupee trade have recovered somewhat and, during 1971/72–1972/73, averaged 29·8 million kgs, fetching a sum of $31·5 million. However, this has not been at the cost of diverting supplies from Western markets, exports to which also increased in these two years, attaining a level of 47·2 million kgs, and earning $37·7 million in foreign exchange.

(5) *Iron ore.* Although India's total exports of iron ore grew at a phenomenal pace, her exports to the socialist countries were quite stagnant. The average annual value of iron ore exported to the rupee payment countries hardly changed from $17·2 million during 1960/61–1965/66 to $18·4 million in 1966/67–1972/73, whereas exports to the rest of the world more than doubled rising from $41·5 million to $107·1 million. Thus it seems most unlikely that export supplies were actually diverted from convertible currency areas to meet commitments under bilateral agreements.

(6) *Manganese ore.* There was a distinct falling trend in India's exports of manganese ore during the period under study. Her exports to the convertible currency areas fell from an average annual value of $19·3 million in the period 1960/61–1965/66 to $14·2 million during 1966/67–1972/73: a decline of about 26 per cent. But, at the same time, exports to the rupee payment countries fell by 50 per cent from $3·4 million to $1·7 million. Obviously, there was no diversion of export supplies. In fact, given the deteriorating quality of the ore, and the restricted nature of the world market,[37] India was having problems in selling its manganese. Any sales through bilateral agreements were therefore a welcome addition.

(7) *Mica.* Since 1960, India's total mica exports have been virtually stagnant. However, exports to the socialist countries increased from an annual average of $5·8 million in 1960/61–1965/66 to $10·5 million during 1966/67–1972/73, while exports to the rest of the world fell from $15·4 million to $9·6 million. Thus, *prima facie*, it would appear that exportable supplies were diverted from convertible currency areas in order to meet commitments under bilateral agreements. However, it should be pointed out that, owing to the importance of the US market, the changes in American demand for mica were an extremely important factor underlying these export trends. The following facts provide further confirmation.[38] Between

1960/61 and 1964/65, when American demand for mica registered a slight increase, India's exports to the Eastern Bloc countries were quite stagnant. In the subsequent years, American import demand fell sharply, because of the decision to run down the stockpile and the new technological developments in the electronics industry.[39] Both these factors were completely independent of rupee trade and would have led to a much greater fall in India's mica exports, had it not been for the additional demand created by the socialist countries.

(8) *Oilcakes*. These emerged as an important commodity in India's export basket during the sixties. Between 1960/61 and 1964/65 total oilcake exports nearly trebled, rising from $30 million to $83·5 million. In this period, exports to the socialist countries jumped from $4·9 million to $49·8 million, and exports to the rest of the world increased only moderately. In view of the fact that world import demand for oilcakes, particularly in Western Europe, rose sharply in these years,[40] it is quite likely that a significant proportion of the oilcakes exported by India under bilateral trade agreements could have been sold in convertible currency areas.

However, the growth in exports of oilcakes came to an abrupt end after 1964/65 and there was a marked change in the trends. Exports to the Eastern Bloc countries fell from their peak level of $49·8 million to an average annual value of $40·9 million during the period 1965/66—1971/72, but in proportional terms exports to the rest of the world registered a greater decline from $33·7 million to $23·3 million. The difference is even more pronounced if we compare the trends in export volume. The quantity of oilcakes exported to the convertible currency countries dropped sharply from 609 million kgs in 1964/65 to an annual average of 311 million kgs during 1965/66—1971/72, whereas the quantity exported to the rupee payment countries declined only from 654 million kgs to 482 million kgs.[41] It is worth noting that there was a recovery in the level of exports during 1972/73, when India sold 565 million kgs of oilcakes to the socialist countries for $59·9 million and 436 million kgs to the convertible currency countries for $39·1 million.

What must have happened is quite apparent. In the latter half of the 1960s there was a shortfall in India's production of oilcakes which was met by a cut in exports. Perhaps because of the commitment under bilateral agreements, the reduction in exports to the socialist countries was far less than exports to the rest of the world. Available evidence suggests that, owing to the growth of livestock and dairy farming, the rapid expansion in West European demand for oilcakes continued during this period.[42] Therefore, it is most likely that India implicitly diverted scarce supplies of oilcakes to rupee trade countries, when they could have been sold in convertible currency areas. There were two main reasons for this diversion: (i) some West European countries restricted imports of groundnut oilcakes, which constituted the bulk of Indian oilcake exports;[43] (ii) the landed cif prices of Indian oilcakes in Western Europe were not competitive.[44] In other words, India may not have been able to sell all its oilcakes in Western markets.

(9) *Coffee*. India's exports of coffee to the socialist countries increased substantially over the period under study, rising from an average annual value of $10·8 million in 1960/61—1965/66 to $17·8 million during 1966/67—1972/73. There is little point in comparing the trend in exports to the rest of the world because all of India's coffee trade with the convertible currency areas between 1962 and 1972 was regulated by an International Coffee Agreement. Except for two years, India filled her export quota throughout this period.[45] In 1965/66 and 1969/70 her exports fell short by 6·1 and 8·8 million kgs respectively.[46] Valued at prices prevailing in the world market at that time, these two shortfalls amount to a foreign exchange loss of $11 million. We know that none of the Eastern Bloc countries were signatories to the Agreement.[47] Therefore, it is clear that all of India's coffee exports to the rupee trade countries, except for the diversion worth $11 million in 1965/66 and 1969/70, were a net addition to her exports.

(10) *Pepper*. It is difficult to extract a general trend from statistics on pepper exports owing to sharp fluctuations, which in turn are attributable to erratic supplies and consequent variations in world pepper prices.[48] To some extent, the fluctuations can be eliminated by averaging the data. Table 5.5 shows that the average annual value of pepper exports to the socialist countries increased from $7·5 million in the period 1960/61—1965/66 to $12·2 million during 1966/67—1972/73. However, exports to the rest of the world declined from $8.9 million to $6.5 million. On the surface it appears that $2·4 million worth of pepper exports were diverted from convertible currency areas to bilateral trade markets each year. But, in fact, it is quite possible that India's poor export performance in the convertible currency markets was because of the competitiveness factor. Throughout the sixties, Indian pepper prices were consistently higher than the prices of her main competitors, Indonesia and Malaysia.[49] As such, in years when Indonesia and Malaysia had a normal crop, it would have been difficult for India to sell more of its pepper in convertible currency markets, and it is unlikely that there was any diversion of export supplies by India. On the other hand, in years when exports of the two main competitors dropped sharply, as they did in 1962, 1965 and 1970 because of poor crops,[50] India could have sold more pepper than she did to the convertible currency countries. If we assume that *all* the pepper exported to the socialist bloc during these three years could have been sold in western markets, the diversion amounts to $26·8 million.

(11) *Leather*. India's exports of leather and leather manufactures were virtually stagnant in the early 1960s, but grew rapidly thereafter. A considerable proportion of this growth was attributable to bilateral rupee trade. The average annual value of India's leather exports to the socialist countries rose from $3·1 million in the period 1960/61—1965/66 to $38·1 million during 1966/67—1972/73. At the same time, exports to the convertible currency areas increased from $50·8 million to $77.3 million. To the extent that India's principal market for leather, viz., the UK, was relatively stagnant,

the shift in markets probably helped exports.[51] What is more, increased exports to the Eastern European countries did not reduce exports elsewhere.

In the sixties, however, there was a substantial expansion in the import demand for leather in many of the Western European countries such as Italy, France, Spain and West Germany.[52] Thus, it is quite possible that India could have sold more leather in these convertible currency markets. In fact, Pakistan, which exported roughly the same type of leather, did achieve a remarkable growth in exports, and most of its markets were in the West.[53] Hence, it seems likely that there was some implicit diversion of exportable supplies under the bilateral trade agreements, in the absence of which India's exports of leather to convertible currency areas might have increased faster than they actually did.

(12) *Other exports.* So far we have considered the important traditional exports to the socialist countries. Apart from jute manufactures and leather, these consisted entirely of raw materials and primary or semi-processed agricultural products. However, in the late 1960s, there was a change in the commodity composition of exports and some non-traditional products were also sold to the rupee payment countries. In this category, the most important groups were clothing, engineering goods and chemicals and related products. Between 1965/66 and 1972/73, exports of engineering goods to the Eastern Bloc countries increased from $3 million to $26·3 million, and of chemical and related products from $7·4 million to $17·9 million. Over the same period, exports to the rest of the world increased from $36·7 million to $173 million in the case of engineering goods and from $15·9 million to $35·6 million in the case of chemicals. The story was much the same in clothing, exports of which to the socialist countries increased from $5·9 million to $28·9 million, while exports to the rest of the world rose from $6·1 million to $45·3 million. It is patently clear that the growth of these non-traditional exports under bilateral rupee trade did not displace exports to the convertible currency areas. In fact, the socialist countries provided additional markets for these products without the uncertainty, the sales efforts and the advertising expenses which would have been unavoidable in the convertible currency markets.[54]

The commodities discussed above accounted for the bulk of India's exports to the socialist countries during the period under study. Our analysis has shown that except in the case of oilcakes and to some extent in leather, tea, pepper and coffee, India did not divert scarce export supplies from convertible currency areas in order to meet her bilateral trade commitments. We have made some estimates of diversion in coffee and pepper. If we assume that in addition two-thirds of the oilcakes, half the leather and one-fourth of the tea sold to the socialist bloc could have been sold in Western markets, then 14·1 per cent of India's total exports to the rupee payment countries constituted a diversion on her part.[55] These assumptions are necessarily arbitrary, but have been selected so as to provide some index of the maximum diversion possible. To some extent, they are based on our knowledge

of the world market for Indian exports.[56] While oilcakes could have been
sold most easily, Indian leather had some quality problems, and Indian tea
faced intense competition from East African countries. It should, of course,
be kept in mind that any attempt at a quantification of diversion is bound
to be conjectural and, therefore, the above figure should be treated as a
rough approximation.

B. *Re-exports by the Socialist Countries*

There are two methods by which the Eastern European countries could have
resold the products obtained from India under bilateral agreements in convertible currency markets. In the first place, shipments from India could
have been directly reconsigned to ports in the Western countries without
ever actually arriving in a socialist country. Alternatively, Indian products
could have been re-exported after import. Let us explore each of these
possibilities in turn.

(1) *Reconsignment in transit*. Cargoes loaded in transit may be diverted
from their stated destinations in Eastern Europe, either by reconsignment
at an intermediate port or by unloading in transit at a West European port.
In both cases, such shipments do not constitute a net addition to India's exports and amount to switch trading on the part of her bilateral partners.
Clearly, it is almost impossible to measure the extent of this diversion
separately for every commodity. Even if all the necessary data on shipping
were available, which is inconceivable, it would be a stupendous task to
estimate the extent of switch trading in each of India's exports to the
socialist countries during the period under study.

It would be far more practical to resort to an aggregative test. If there is
switch trading, and some of the purchases made in India do not actually
reach the socialist countries, it is only reasonable to infer that these products
do not enter their import statistics. Therefore, a comparison of: (i) India's
total exports to the socialist countries as reported in Indian trade statistics
with (ii) total imports from India by the socialist countries as reported in
their statistics, should provide us with some idea of the extent of switch
trading. Such comparisons of trade figures, however, are not free from
limitations. Firstly, it is possible that the basis of recording import and
export statistics varies from country to country. As it turns out, this is not
a serious problem because all Indian exports are recorded fob and, fortunately,
most Eastern Bloc countries also record their imports on an fob basis. But
import data in the case of Hungary and Yugoslavia is on a cif basis, for
which some adjustment might be necessary. Secondly, the time lag inevitable
in shipping, i.e., the ocean journey for the cargo, might lead to discrepancies
in annual trade statistics between countries. We have tried to overcome this
problem by aggregating the data for the entire period 1960–1972.

The results of the exercise are outlined in Table 5.8, which shows a very
close correspondence between the statistics of partner countries involved
in bilateral rupee trade. In fact, the percentage difference between the total

TABLE 5.8. A COMPARISON OF INDIAN AND EASTERN EUROPEAN
TRADE STATISTICS, 1960 TO 1972
(IN US $ MILLION)

Country	(1) Imports from India as recorded by the socialist countries	(2) Exports from India as recorded by Indian trade statistics	(3) Percentage difference $\frac{(2)-(1)}{(2)} \times 100$
USSR	2352·9	2399·1	1·93
Bulgaria	112·7	111·4	−1·17
Czechoslovakia	456·7	458·8	0·46
East Germany	314·4	294·0	−6·94
Hungary	270·6	183·5	−47·47
Poland	319·8	328·4	2·62
Romania	120·2	125·5	4·22
Yugoslavia	338·0	323·5	−4·48
Total	*4285·3*	*4224·2*	*−1·45*

Source: For Column (1): United Nations, *Yearbooks of International Trade Statistics, 1964, 1969, 1972–73* (New York). For Column (2): Statistics published by DGCIS, Calcutta.

Note: From 1960 to 1969, all figures have been converted into US dollars at the official rates of exchange. The exact conversion factors used for *one* US dollar are: 1·17 Bulgarian leva, 7·2 Czech korunas, 4·2 East German marks, 11·737 Hungarian forints, 4 Polish zlotys, 6 Romanian lei, 0·90 USSR roubles and 12·50 Yugoslav dinars. However, for the period 1960/64, the exchange rate in Yugoslavia was $1 = 300 dinars, and this has been used for those years. For the years 1970–1972, the UN data are published in terms of US dollars.

value of Indian exports to the rupee payment countries as reported in India's trade statistics and as recorded by the socialist countries works out at less than 5 per cent for each Eastern European country,[57] with the exception of Hungary and East Germany. There seems to be no feasible explanation for the 47 per cent difference between the Hungarian and Indian trade figures.[58] The fact that Hungary records its imports on a cif basis can account only for a part of this gap, but certainly not all of it. However, it is sufficient to know that the Hungarian figure substantially exceeds the Indian one and that eliminates the possibility of Indian shipments being diverted from their original destination. Similarly, the East German figure exceeds the Indian one by about 7 per cent, and it can be inferred that the German Democratic Republic did not re-export Indian goods.

Thus, inasmuch as any sanctity can be attached to trade statistics, it seems that there was no significant or apparent switch trading of Indian products by the socialist countries.

(2) *Re-export after import.* Consider now, the possibility of actual re-exports of Indian products by the socialist countries of Eastern Europe. It is most unlikely that they could have resold any of India's non-traditional ex-

ports like clothing, engineering goods, footwear, chemicals and other related products in convertible currency areas, for the simple reason that, in such goods, product differentiation and brand names are rather important and exporting involves marketing expenses like advertising, etc.

Among the traditional exports of manufactures, exports of cotton textiles to the bilateral trade markets were quite insignificant throughout the period under study.[59] On the other hand, exports of jute manufactures under the bilateral agreements were indeed substantial. The bulk of these exports comprised jute bags and sacking. As such, it is quite unlikely that these could have been re-exported to the convertible currency areas because competition from substitutes had reduced the demand for jute bags and sacks in the Western countries to a minimum level.[60] Although there was a substantial import demand for leather in Western Europe, it is highly unlikely that Indian manufactured leather was re-exported because exports of leather from the socialist countries of Eastern Europe were negligible throughout the period under study.[61]

We are now left only with raw materials and primary or semi-processed agricultural products that could have been re-exported by India's bilateral rupee trade partners. These commodities can be classified into two groups: those which were *not* produced domestically in the socialist countries, and those which were produced domestically.

In the first group, the three main Indian exports were pepper, coffee and cashew kernels. In the absence of domestic production, any exports of these products by the socialist countries would certainly suggest re-export. An examination of official international trade statistics shows that none of the Eastern Bloc countries exported black pepper throughout the period 1960 to 1973.[62] Exactly the same is true for coffee.[63] In fact, with the inception of the International Coffee Agreement in 1962, the socialist countries, which were non-quota countries, could not have legally exported coffee to convertible currency areas which were quota countries under the Agreement.[64] Cashew kernels are generally included in the broader category of 'edible nuts' in most trade statistics, so that it is virtually impossible to identify the extent of cashew exports, if any, from the socialist countries. However, there have been reports of Indian cashew nuts being resold by the socialist countries; in fact, some are reported to have been sold at a price discount in New York.[65] But, owing to the lack of necessary data, it is not possible to quantify the extent of re-export.

An analysis of re-exports in the second group of commodities is far more difficult, because most of these products were produced and exported by the socialist countries even before they began trading with India. We shall restrict our analysis to three commodities, viz., tea, tobacco and oilcakes, the choice of which was determined entirely by the statistical information available.

(a) *Tea*. The bulk of India's tea exports under bilateral rupee trade was absorbed by the USSR, which was also the only socialist country that exported tea in the period 1960–72.[66] During this period, however, there was a marked increase in its exports which rose from an annual average of 8·7 million kgs in the period 1961–66 to 11·6 million kgs during 1967–72.[67] At the same time, the annual average imports of tea from India increased from 17·5 million kgs to 29·7 million kgs.[68] On the surface, this seems to suggest that Indian tea must have been re-exported, but we find that the annual average domestic production of tea in the USSR also increased from 47·6 million kgs to 62·4 million kgs.[69] Therefore, it is extremely difficult to say what proportion of the growth in the Soviet Union's tea exports in the sixties was due to re-exports of Indian tea, although some element of re-export is implicit. But this may not have been any loss to India in the convertible currency markets, because available evidence suggests that almost all Soviet tea exports went to other Eastern Bloc countries and Mongolia.[70]

(b) *Tobacco*. After a careful and detailed examination of statistics relating to exports of unmanufactured tobacco by the Eastern Bloc countries and their imports from India, Dharm Narain has shown that in the period 1961/62–1965/66 there were no significant re-exports of Indian tobacco by the socialist countries.[71] The possibility of such re-exports after 1965/66 is even more remote because of the very rapid decline in exports of tobacco from India under bilateral rupee trade.

(c) *Oilcakes*. Among the socialist countries, Poland was by far the most important buyer of oilcakes from India,[72] and official international trade statistics show that Poland did not export any oilcakes in the period 1960 to 1973.[73] Except for very small quantities in the early sixties, there were no exports of oilcakes from Bulgaria, East Germany, Hungary and Romania.[74] The Soviet Union was always a large exporter of oilcakes and exported substantial quantities of oilcakes even before it started importing them from India.[75] Therefore, it is impossible to say how much of its imports from India were re-exported. In the case of Czechoslovakia and Yugoslavia, the evidence is more definite in as much as exports of oilcakes from these countries showed a marked increase after 1960.[76] This suggests that Indian oilcakes were probably re-exported, but once again it is extremely difficult to quantify the extent of it, owing to the lack of data on domestic production and consumption of oilcakes in these countries.

The above discussion on the re-export of Indian goods by the socialist countries is certainly not exhaustive, but it does cover most of India's exports to these countries under bilateral agreements.[77] On the basis of limited statistical evidence, our analysis has shown that: (i) there was no switch trading on a significant scale; (ii) it seems extremely unlikely that manufactured goods imported from India could have been re-exported by the socialist countries; and (iii) as for primary or semi-processed agricultural products, some of them were definitely not re-exported (at least legally), whereas others were, but it is not possible to estimate the extent of such re-exports. However, these findings should not be taken to mean that the socialist countries did not indulge in any switch trade or re-export of Indian

products. In fact, during the sixties, there were several instances of such
practices, and a parliamentary committee specifically pointed to the resale
of Indian cashew nuts, oilcakes, hides and skins, coffee, tea and spices, by
the socialist countries in convertible currency markets.[78] The Indian government was quite aware of some of these instances,[79] but in the absence of
definite proof, it was unable to do anything about it.[80]

All the same, in so far as any reliance can be placed on available statistical
evidence, it seems that only a very small proportion of Indian exports under
bilateral rupee trade were resold by the socialist countries through reconsignment or re-export. Given the limitations of the data examined, any
attempt at a quantification of such resale must necessarily be based on
guesswork. Dharm Narain estimated it at 3·5 per cent of India's total
exports to the socialist countries,[81] and 'official circles' evidently put it at
around five to ten per cent.[82]

V. The Terms of Trade

Thus far, we have been concerned with an analysis of the extent to which
bilateral rupee trade led to a net increase in India's exports. However, in
order to evaluate the benefits of this export growth, in particular, and of
trade with the socialist countries, in general, it is necessary to examine the
terms of trade obtained from the socialist countries under bilateral agreements.

We have shown that the terms of trade are directly dependent on the
prices paid for imports and the prices received for exports. A detailed investigation of the prices paid by India for the commodities imported from the
Eastern Bloc countries would be quite complex, and is beyond the scope of
the present essay. Hence, we shall rely on available evidence on this point.
Information on import prices is scarce, but all the studies so far have shown
that the prices of goods imported from the socialist countries have generally
been lower and very rarely higher than the prices of similar goods imported
from the rest of the world.[83] According to Dave, '. . . a study of about 100
unit values of imports of chemicals, fertilisers, newsprint and iron and steel
products from these countries for three years 1957—59 suggests that no higher
prices were charged . . . [and] . . . the findings indicate that except for some
dyes, chemicals and high grade steel, prices charged by these countries were
less than the multilateral prices.'[84] For the period 1961/62—1965/66,
Dharm Narain also computed average unit values of selected imports namely,
base metals, paper, petroleum and petroleum products, organic and inorganic
chemicals and iron and steel products, and found that, except in one year,
the prices charged by the socialist countries were significantly lower than
the prices India paid to convertible currency countries.[85] However, these
selected imports constituted only 35 per cent of India's total imports from
the East European countries in the first half of the sixties.

In a more recent study, relating to the period 1958/59—1969/70, Sebastian compared the average unit value of twenty-four items, which accounted for 60 per cent of India's imports from the USSR, with the unit value of the same imports from Western countries.[86] He concludes that, except in a few cases, the prices charged by the Soviet Union were definitely lower than those charged by other countries.[87] Nevertheless, a sizeable proportion of total imports is constituted by machinery and transport equipment, for which it is quite impossible to obtain comprehensive price data, and unit value comparisons are meaningless because of the wide quality variations.[88] Asha Datar suggests that '. . . a significant proportion of the imports of machinery and equipment from the East European countries has been financed by tied credits.'[89] Therefore, even if price comparisons were possible, it would not be appropriate to compare these prices with the prices from the cheapest source.[90]

There is a widely held view that the machinery and capital equipment imported from the socialist countries was of relatively inferior quality, and, what is more, India may have paid excessively high prices for it. Evidence in support of such a view is extremely hard to find, and wherever statements of this kind are made, they are rarely documented. As we have stressed before, price and quality comparisons for machinery, over a large range, are well-nigh impossible. However, it is worth pointing out that in any market for manufactured goods, low prices are often a substitute for adequate quality. Thus it is unlikely that bilateral agreements lumbe'red India with poor quality imports that were also overpriced. Clearly, importers in the private sector would not have entered into such transactions. Available evidence suggests that the government, too, was careful on this account.[91] And if capital goods bought from the socialist countries did not have the same quality as the equivalent from Western countries, it may well have been the result of a conscious decision to buy lower-price equipment. Of course, the decision not to purchase the latest, most sophisticated, equipment from the West may also have been a wise one, and the machinery supplied by the socialist bloc may have been more 'appropriate' for India's needs.[92]

Although the evidence adduced above is not exhaustive, and it is not possible to say anything definite about the prices or quality of machinery imports, to a limited extent it does indicate that imports under bilateral agreements were sometimes cheaper and usually not any dearer than in the world market. As such, it would be reasonable to assume that the purchasing power of Indian exports under rupee trade varied directly with the prices received for them.

Data on export prices are extremely hard to come by. Thus we have to resort to a comparison of the average unit value of exports to the socialist countries and the average unit value of the same exports to the rest of the world. The major drawback of this method is that it does not take any account of quality differences. However, it is only way by which one can get some idea of the terms of trade.

For a comparison of unit values we have selected ten commodity groups which constituted about two-thirds of India's exports to the Eastern Bloc countries during the period under study. These are: jute manufactures, tea, cashew kernels, oilcakes, iron ore, coffee, pepper, manganese ore, lac and unmanufactured tobacco. Admittedly, there are quality differences within each of our selected commodity groups, but they are much less than would be in the case of non-traditional manufactured exports.

Table 5.9 outlines the trend in the average unit value of the selected exports and brings out the differences between the prices received from the socialist countries and the prices received from the rest of the world. It shows that except for jute manufactures, cashew kernels and tobacco, the Eastern Bloc countries paid consistently higher prices than the convertible currency countries. In the case of tobacco and jute manufactures the price difference is almost certainly attributable to the quality composition. It is generally accepted that as compared to the rest of the world, the Eastern Bloc countries bought relatively low quality virginia tobacco from India;[93] this fact was bound to be reflected in the average unit value. As for jute manufactures, the bulk of the socialist countries' imports consisted of jute bags and sacking, whereas a large proportion of India's exports to the Western countries consisted of carpet backing. We know that gunny bags fetch a much lower price per unit of weight as compared to carpet backing.[94] Thus it is not surprising that the average unit value works out slightly lower for the socialist countries, even though they paid higher prices than the rest of the world for jute bags.[95] In the case of cashew kernels, however, the rupee payment countries did pay lower prices than the convertible currency countries.

In view of the fact that differences in the quality composition of exports can significantly affect the average unit values, it might be useful to compare the unit prices of more specifically defined qualities in some of these products. Table 5.10 does just that, and also compares the unit values obtained in selected exports of chemicals during the years 1970/71 and 1971/72. In all the selected qualities and products, the socialist countries were important buyers. Although these figures relate to only a few products in two particular years, they do suggest that the socialist countries paid better prices than the rest of the world even in some comparable-quality products.

One might ask if it is at all possible to make an overall comparison of export prices obtained in the world market. A weighted average of the price differentials provides one obvious solution. Starting from the data on the quantity and value of exports, from which Table 5.9 is derived, we computed an index of the unit value obtained from socialist countries expressed as a percentage of the unit value obtained from the rest of the world, for each commodity in each year. These indices were then weighted by the corresponding share of each commodity in the total exports to socialist countries in that particular year, and finally averaged for each year. This weighting method eliminates the importance of large price differentials in individual

TABLE 5.9. A COMPARISON OF AVERAGE UNIT VALUES FOR SELECTED INDIAN EXPORTS TO SOCIALIST COUNTRIES AND THE REST OF THE WORLD
(ANNUAL AVERAGES)

Export commodity group	In Rs per:	1960/61–1962/63		1963/64–1965/66		1967/68–1969/70		1970/71–1972/73	
		Socialist countries	Others	Socialist countries	Others	Socialist countries	Others	Socialist countries	Others
Jute manufactures	kg	1·89	1·71	1·79	1·83	2·88	3·47	3·77	3·95
Tea	kg	6·76	6·06	6·49	5·78	9·06	7·76	8·07	7·39
Cashew kernels	kg	4·52	3·86	4·81	4·97	8·80	9·50	9·73	10·64
Oilcakes	kg	0·36	0·35	0·39	0·34	0·64	0·56	0·67	0·59
Iron ore	ton	55·00	28·57	43·28	32·79	61·43	55·01	63·05	52·47
Coffee	kg	3·88	3·19	4·43	4·00	6·41	4·91	6·69	6·57
Pepper	kg	4·06	3·66	3·81	3·68	5·98	5·89	7·84	7·03
Manganese ore	ton	133·43	108·86	119·62	78·66	163·91	95·89	155·11	94·08
Lac	kg	2·49	2·27	2·68	2·54	3·11	1·98	5·79	5·59
Tobacco	kg	1·67	3·40	2·48	4·12	5·67	6·30	7·73	6·31

Source: Statistics published by DGCIS, Calcutta.
Notes: (i) The figures have been computed from statistics on the quantity and value of exports, and averaged for the three-year periods.
(ii) All figures are in rupees and no adjustment has been made for the devaluation in June 1966, because it affects the unit value to both groups of countries equally.
(iii) The year 1966/67 has been left out of account, data for which are difficult to aggregate owing to the devaluation part of the way through.

TABLE 5.10. A COMPARISON OF UNIT VALUES IN SOME SPECIFIC
EXPORT ITEMS
(IN RUPEES PER KG)

	1970/71		1971/72	
Product	*Socialist countries*	*Rest of the world*	*Socialist countries*	*Rest of the world*
1. Black leaf tea	8·22	7·37	8·06	7·37
2. Coffee: Arabica planta- tion 'A'	8·28	7·84	6·66	6·35
3. Jute hessian bags	3·55	3·39	4·12	4·04
4. Jute sacking bags	2·72	2·51	2·98	2·80
5. Varnishes	6·45	2·66	6·19	3·69
6. Synthetic enamels	5·72	3·52	5·76	3·15
7. Potassium permanganate	4·65	4·03	4·80	4·17

Source: Statistics published by DGCIS, Calcutta.
Note: Calculated from data on the quantity and value of exports.

commodities which might have constituted only a small proportion of total
rupee trade exports. It also provides us with one overall relative price index
for each year. The results of the statistical exercise are outlined in Table 5.11,
which reveals that except for 1968/69, when the prices received from
socialist countries were marginally lower than those obtained from other
countries, India obtained higher prices for her exports under bilateral rupee

TABLE 5.11. AN AGGREGATE INDEX OF PRICES PAID
BY SOCIALIST COUNTRIES EXPRESSED AS A PER-
CENTAGE OF PRICES PAID BY OTHER COUNTRIES
FOR SELECTED INDIAN EXPORTS

Year	*Relative price index*	*Selected exports as a percentage of total Indian exports to the socialist bloc*
1960/61	118·5	67
1961/62	136·6	66
1962/63	123·0	70
1963/64	101·9	69
1964/65	108·4	74
1965/66	108·3	71
1967/68	103·2	66
1968/69	99·3	59
1969/70	114·6	52
1970/71	105·3	50
1971/72	109·1	56
1972/73	108·0	53

Source: Statistics published by DGCIS, Calcutta. The method of
computation is explained in the text.

trade than she did in the world market, throughout the period under study. It must be noted that the rupee payment countries offered much higher prices in the early sixties, but once trade flows through the bilateral agreements became regular, the price differential registered a marked decline.

Although price data are not available for about one-third of India's exports to the East European countries, the evidence that we have examined does show that, in general, they paid higher prices than the rest of the world.[96] A comparison of import prices is even more difficult, because machinery and equipment accounted for more than half of India's imports under rupee trade. However, available evidence does suggest that the prices paid for imports to the socialist countries were no higher than those paid to the rest of the world. Hence, it is quite reasonable to infer that India obtained somewhat better, and at any rate no worse, terms of trade from the socialist countries.

VI. An Overall Evaluation

The main conclusions emerging from the above analysis can be summed up as follows: India's trade with the socialist countries increased most rapidly after 1960. This rapid growth occurred in a framework of bilateral trade agreements, the distinct feature of which was that payments for all transactions were made in rupees. The USSR was by far the largest market for Indian goods, as well as the principal source of imports, although Czechoslovakia, East Germany, Poland and Yugoslavia were also important trading partners.

The growth in exports was quite remarkable, and continued throughout the period under study. To begin with, the bulk of India's exports to the Eastern Bloc countries consisted of raw materials and primary or semi-processed agricultural products. Gradually, however, the commodity composition shifted towards manufactured goods. Imports under the bilateral agreements increased a little faster than exports until the mid-sixties. Among other things, this was attributable to the development credits extended by the socialist countries. The expansion of imports did not continue at the same pace thereafter. To some extent, of course, official statistics understate the value of imports because they exclude defence imports, which were indeed significant in the period 1965/66–1972/73. Besides, it was inevitable that India should generate an export surplus to compensate for the balance of trade deficits in past years. In this context, it should be stressed that imports from the socialist countries were predominantly constituted by capital goods and intermediate products that were essential to India's development programme.

An analysis of bilateralism showed that if the imports purchased under rupee trade were high priority items, the benefits derived by India from its trade relations with the socialist countries would depend upon the net increase in exports and the terms of trade obtained.

The estimation of net export growth raised several conceptual and statistical difficulties. However, a detailed examination of available evidence showed that, except in the case of oilcakes and to some extent leather, tea, coffee and pepper, India did not divert any scarce exportable supplies from convertible currency areas in order to meet her export commitments under the bilateral agreements. In fact, in the case of traditional exports like manganese ore and mica and non-traditional exports such as clothing, engineering goods and chemicals, the socialist countries provided welcome new markets. As for the resale of Indian products by the Eastern Bloc countries in convertible currency markets, the problems of measurement were even more acute. Although there were some instances of switch-trading and re-exports by the socialist countries, it was not on any significant scale. A comparison of Indian and Eastern European trade statistics revealed almost no evidence of switch trading. We also found that there was little possibility of the socialist countries having re-exported Indian manufactured goods. The lack of necessary data prevented a complete commodity-wise analysis of the remaining primary product and raw material exports. However, we did examine some commodities on the basis of available statistical information and found that the Eastern Bloc countries did not re-export any pepper, coffee, tobacco or tea to the convertible currency markets. On the other hand, it is quite possible that they re-exported some of the cashew nuts and oilcakes imported from India to the Western countries, but no quantification was possible.

On the whole it is clear that the diversion of export supplies by India and the re-export of Indian products by the socialist countries constituted a relatively small proportion of India's exports under bilateral rupee trade. It is evident that precise estimates of net export growth are extremely difficult, and putting a figure on it would be conjectural. Nevertheless, on the basis of evidence examined, it appears that about 80 per cent of the increase in India's exports to the socialist countries was a real one.

The terms of trade under bilateral agreements were, on balance, probably favourable to India and, at any rate, no worse than those obtained from other countries. Existing work on the subject suggests that the prices of a significant proportion of goods imported from the socialist countries were not higher than prices of similar goods imported from the rest of the world. On the other hand, the evidence we examined clearly showed that socialist countries paid higher prices for Indian exports compared with the rest of the world.

Bilateral rupee trade provided India with imports which were essential for its development programme and was also responsible for a little more than 40 per cent of the growth in India's total exports over the period under study. In view of the fact that a large proportion of it constituted a net increase in exports and was probably at better terms of trade, the benefit derived by India so far is unquestionable. In the coming years, gains from this trade would, of course, still depend upon the pattern, the composition and the terms of trade. However, it is difficult to predict the future of India's economic relations with the socialist countries as it is likely to be influenced by a variety of economic and political factors.

Notes

[1] Trade agreements were not unique to the socialist countries. In the 1960s, India negotiated trade agreements with several other countries. However, most of them, such as those with France, Greece, Indonesia, Iran and Iraq, were no more than a gesture of political good-will and economic co-operation between the signatories. Although a list of tradable commodities was generally incorporated in the agreements, nothing was specified, and the pattern as well as volume of trade were determined by the usual considerations of international commerce. As we shall show later, bilateral trade agreements with the socialist countries of Eastern Europe, including the USSR, were substantially different.

[2] This discussion is based on three main sources: (i) A study by the Indian Institute of Foreign Trade, *India's Trade with Eastern Europe* (New Delhi, 1966) pp. 46–8; (ii) Dharm Narain, *Aid through Trade*, UNCTAD document TD/B/C.3/57 (Geneva, December 1968) pp. 20–4; (iii) Asha Datar, *India's Economic Relations with the USSR and Eastern Europe* (Cambridge, 1972) pp. 87–90. It should be noted that none of these studies goes beyond 1965/66, and, since then, there have been significant developments in India's trade with the socialist countries.

[3] India had to fulful the unimplemented portions of its long-term export contracts in terms of the earlier value of the rupee. It follows that the sudden increase in the rupee value of India's exports to the socialist countries after June 1966 does not reflect a genuine increase in trade. Therefore, in order to make post-devaluation trade figures comparable with the earlier ones, it is necessary to deflate them. We have tried to solve the problem by converting all statistics into US dollars at the official exchange rate. This might appear paradoxical as all trade was actually transacted in rupees, but the dollar should be looked upon only as a *numeraire*, which has been used for no reason other than its convenience. Its parity remained unchanged throughout most of the period under study. The US dollar was devalued by 8·5 per cent in December 1971, and once again by 10 per cent in February 1973. However, the rupee too was devalued marginally in December 1971, and six months later it was pegged to the pound and floated. As such, even for the year 1972/3, the dollar is the most suitable approximation as a *numeraire*.

[4] For a detailed description of India's trade and payments agreements with the socialist countries, see a case study prepared by the UNCTAD Secretariat, *Trade and Economic Relations between India and the Socialist Countries of Eastern Europe*, TD/B/129 (Geneva, July 1967) pp. 20–30.

[5] To take an illustration, the 1966 agreement with the USSR stipulated that the proportion of manufactures in India's exports to the Soviet Union would increase from less than one-third in 1964 to 40 per cent in 1970; cf. ibid., p. 24.

[6] Dharm Narain, op. cit., p. 21.

[7] In other words, aid and trade cannot be treated as separate issues. Thus the value of development credits extended by the socialist countries would depend on the terms of trade obtained under the bilateral payments agreements, and not on the prices of aid-financed imports alone.

[8] Diverted exports are obviously not a gain, but they do not necessarily constitute a loss. That would happen only if the terms of trade actually worsen on account of bilateral trade. However, some economists argue that a premium attaches to convertible foreign exchange earned, so that even at equivalent terms of trade any diversion of exports constitutes a 'cost' imposed by rupee trade. On the other hand, it might be said that the uncertainty and risk of convertible currency markets are largely eliminated in bilateral trade markets owing to the contractual nature of long-term agreements, thereby yielding a 'benefit'. Although these types of arguments have some element of truth, such costs and benefits are extremely difficult to quantify.

[9] The average annual value of India's total exports increased from $1392 million in 1960/61−1962/63 to $2262 million in 1970/71−1972/73, an increase of $870 million. (Calculated from statistics published by DGCIS, Calcutta.)

[10] For an enumeration of the short-run administrative problems encountered in rupee trade following the devaluation, see *Economic and Political Weekly* (22 October 1966) pp. 396−7.

[11] In the period 1956/67−1959/60, before this transition, India's imports from Eastern Europe were stagnant around a level of $70 million.

[12] During the Third Five-year Plan, i.e. 1961/62−1965/66, aid financed 38·3 per cent of imports from the socialist countries. Over the entire period, 1952/53−1972/73, aid financed only 29·2 per cent of total imports from this group of countries. (Calculated from statistics published by (a) DGCIS on trade, and (b) Ministry of Finance on external assistance.)

[13] See Dharm Narain, op. cit., p. 23 and Asha Datar, op. cit., p. 97.

[14] Calculated from the UN, *Yearbooks of International Trade Statistics, 1970−1971* and *1972−1973* (New York), including both 1967 and 1972.

[15] Evidence available from the early sixties confirms this assumption; cf. Asha Datar, op. cit., appendix 3.

[16] Our estimate of unrecorded imports is based on calendar year figures, and as such does not include the last nine months of 1966 or the first three months of 1973 both of which are included in the financial year figures.

[17] Under the *note pass* system, government departments can clear import shipments without going through Customs.

[18] Calculated from the UN, *Yearbooks of International Trade Statistics*, op. cit.

[19] See Asha Datar, op. cit., p. 95.

[20] Calculated from DGCIS statistics.

[21] Cf. Reserve Bank of India, *Report on Currency and Finance, 1972−73* (Bombay) p. 232.

[22] They constituted 89·5 per cent of India's total exports to the socialist countries in 1960/61−1962/63 and 84·4 per cent in 1970/71−1972/73; see Table 5.6.

[23] For example, during the three-year period 1970/71−1972/73, they constituted only 16·4 per cent of the exports to rupee payment countries.

[24] In this context, it is worth noting that although the Eastern European countries provided a relatively small proportion of India's total imports, they were important suppliers in these commodity groups. For instance, in the period 1969/70–1971/72, the socialist countries accounted for only 14 per cent of India's total import bill, but supplied 34 per cent of the machinery and transport equipment, and 18 per cent of the said intermediate goods, bought by India. (Calculated from statistics published by DGCIS, Calcutta.)

[25] A similar approach is adopted by Dharm Narain, op. cit., p.6.

[26] Exports to the rest of the world have been calculated as the difference between India's total exports and the exports to socialist countries. The figures for the former have been taken from statistics published by DGCIS, and for the latter, from Table 5.5. Unless specified otherwise, the same sources have been used to calculate exports to convertible currency areas in the following analysis.

[27] Between 1961–63 and 1964–66, imports of jute goods by the centrally planned economies increased from 56 thousand tons to 162 thousand tons, whereas imports by the rest of the world increased from 1170 thousand tons to 1291 thousand tons; cf. FAO, *Monthly Bulletin of Agricultural Economics and Statistics* (Rome, February 1971).

[28] See Deepak Nayyar, *India's Exports and Export Policies in the 1960s* (Cambridge University Press, 1976), Chapter 3.

[29] ibid.

[30] In the period 1968/69–1972/73 jute bags alone accounted for 56 per cent of the value of the jute manufactures exported by India to the rupee payment countries. A large proportion of the remainder was constituted by sacking and hessian cloth. (Calculated from statistics published by DGCIS, Calcutta.) For evidence on the overwhelming importance of sacking in the early sixties, see Datar, op. cit., p. 146.

[31] For a detailed discussion, see Deepak Nayyar, op. cit., chapter 3.

[32] ibid., chapter 5.

[33] ibid.

[34] For evidence, and a more detailed discussion of this point, see ibid., chapter 6.

[35] Cf. FAO, *Trade Yearbook 1966* (Rome) p. 247.

[36] Calculated from statistics published by DGCIS, Calcutta.

[37] For details, see Deepak Nayyar, op. cit., chapter 7; the section on manganese ore.

[38] ibid.

[39] The replacement of electronic tubes and valves, which used mica, by transistors, reduced the demand for it.

[40] See FAO, *Trade Yearbook, 1965*, p. 212.

[41] Calculated from statistics published by DGCIS, Calcutta.

[42] For an analysis of the growth in demand, see a study by the UNCTAD–GATT International Trade Centre, *The Major Import Markets for Oilcake* (Geneva, 1972).

[43] ibid., pp. 10–11.

[44] Cf. Asha Datar, op. cit., p. 153.

[45] See documents EB/1189/72 and EB/1296/74 of the International Coffee Organization, London.

[46] ibid.

[47] Cf. *International Coffee Agreement, 1962*, p. 230, and *1968*, p. 39, published by HMSO, London.

[48] Pepper crops in the main producing countries, India, Indonesia and Malaysia, are constantly vulnerable to diseases that can destroy the entire crop. Therefore a good crop gluts the market and a poor crop sends prices shooting up. For a detailed discussion, see *Factors Affecting the World Pepper Economy*, FAO document CCP 71/9/1 (Rome, July 1971).

[49] ibid., p. 14.

[50] ibid., and FAO *Commodity Review, 1973–74* (Rome, 1974) p. 137.

[51] For a detailed discussion, see Deepak Nayyar, op. cit., chapter 8.

[52] See *The World Hides, Skins, Leather and Footwear Economy*, FAO Commodity Bulletin Series No. 48 (Rome, 1970) and *Hides, Skins & Leather*, UNCTAD–GATT International Trade Centre (Geneva, 1968).

[53] In the period 1967/68–1969/70, only 14 per cent of Pakistan's leather exports went to the Eastern Bloc countries, and the rest were sold in convertible currency markets; cf. M. Kidron, *Pakistan's Trade with Eastern Bloc Countries* (New York, 1972) p. 78.

[54] Bilateral trade agreements do away with the risk and uncertainty of convertible currency Western markets. This indirect benefit is particularly crucial in the case of non-traditional exports wherein product differentiation, brand names and selling costs are an all-important part of any successful export effort.

[55] Calculated from Table 5.5 for the period 1960/61–1972/73.

[56] Cf. the study on Indian exports by the present author, op. cit.

[57] Even these small differences can be explained in terms of the time lag for exports effected at the end of the period; particularly as Indian data relate to fiscal years so that exports during January–March 1973 are also included in the 1972 figure, whereas statistics from the Eastern European countries relate to calendar years. In any case, the Bulgarian and Yugoslav figures are higher than the Indian ones, thereby ruling out a direct reconsignment of shipments from India.

[58] It is possible that the Hungarian trade statistics are based on an exchange rate different from the official one; alternatively the discrepancy may be the result of price reforms carried out in the Hungarian economy.

[59] It should be pointed out that cotton textile exports to the socialist countries were rather high in 1972/73 but this was part of a special deal with the USSR which supplied India with raw cotton to process and re-export. At the same time, exports to the rest of the world were more than maintained.

[60] Cf. Deepak Nayyar, op. cit., chapter 3. Of course, re-exports in small quantities were always possible but these could not have been significant. For the period 1961–65, Dharm Narain has shown that even if all the jute goods exported by the socialist countries were Indian in origin (and if this figure was larger than actual Indian exports, he took the latter as the maximum possible re-export, such re-exports could not have been more than 8·6 per cent of India's exports of jute goods to the East European countries (op. cit., appendix B, pp. 18–19).

[61] Cf. *The World Hides, Skins, Leather and Footwear Economy*, op. cit., pp. 76–7.

[62] See FAO, *Trade Yearbooks, 1965*, p. 201, *1971*, p. 262 and *1973* p. 313, except for Romania, which exported 0·03 million kgs in 1966.

[63] ibid., *1965*, pp. 185–6, *1971*, pp. 243–4, and *1973*, pp. 289–90, except for the USSR which exported small amounts of coffee in 1960 and 1961.

[64] There were, however, some illicit inflows of 'tourist' coffee from the non-quota countries into Western Europe; see Paul Streeten and Diane Elson, *Diversification and Development: The Case of Coffee* (New York, 1971) p. 20. But no quantitative estimates are available, and it is extremely difficult to pinpoint how much of this coffee was Indian.

[65] See M. Goldman, *Soviet Foreign Aid* (New York, 1967) pp. 110–11.

[66] None of the other East European countries exported any tea except for minute quantities in one or two stray years; cf. FAO, *Trade Yearbooks, 1965*, pp. 192–3, *1971*, pp. 252–3, and *1973*, p. 306.

[67] Calculated from FAO, *Trade Yearbooks*, ibid.

[68] International Tea Committee, *Annual Bulletin of Statistics* (London, 1973).

[69] See FAO, *Production Yearbook, 1971*, p. 270, and *1972*, p. 169.

[70] Dharm Narain, op. cit., Table A-7.

[71] ibid., appendix B, pp. 20–21.

[72] In terms of volume, exports to Poland accounted for 25 per cent of India's oilcakes exports to the socialist countries during the period 1960/61– 1965/66. (Calculated from ibid., Table A-10.) This proportion was 29 per cent in 1970/71–1972/73. (Calculated from statistics published by DGCIS.)

[73] Cf. FAO, *Trade Yearbooks, 1965*, pp. 210–11, *1971*, pp. 274–5, and *1973*, p. 327.

[74] ibid.

[75] ibid. For example, in 1960, the USSR exported 496·4 million kgs of oilcakes.

[76] ibid. It is worth noting that, in the 1970s, exports of oilcakes from Yugoslavia, Czechoslovakia and USSR fell sharply to very low levels; cf. FAO, *Trade Yearbook, 1973*, p. 327. Thus, in these years, the possibility of re-export was very little.

[77] It is not possible to comment on the remaining exports owing to the lack of necessary data.

[78] Eleventh Report of the Fourth Lok Sabha's Estimates Committee, *Utilisation of External Assistance* (New Delhi, Lok Sabha Secretariat, August 1967) pp. 228–9.

[79] Personal discussions with the people concerned at UNCTAD in Geneva, and with the officers of the Foreign Trade and Shipping Ministries in New Delhi, confirmed this awareness. It was felt that there were very few complaints about reconsignment and re-export against the USSR, but evidently all the other Eastern European countries had indulged in these practices. In his study on *Pakistan's Trade with Eastern Bloc Countries*, op. cit., Michael Kidron also found (p. 26) that the USSR absorbed all its imports, whereas the others indulged in switch trade.

[80] This was the testimony of the Ministry of Foreign Trade Representative to the Lok Sabha Committee, op. cit.

[81] op. cit., p. 13.

[82] Reported in Asha Datar, op. cit., p. 161.

[83] See Dharm Narain, op. cit., pp. 16–19; Asha Datar, op. cit., pp. 175–6; and *India's Trade with Eastern Europe*, op. cit., pp. 26–8 and 69–76.

[84] S. Dave, 'India's trade with East European countries—rejoinder', *Indian Economic Journal* (April 1962) p. 482.

[85] The unit value comparisons were made for narrowly defined 'homogeneous' products within each of the broad commodity groups. A weighted average of the unit import prices yielded the following interesting result:

Ratios of unit values of imports of selected industrial materials and intermediate products from socialist countries and rest of the world: 1961/62 92·4; 1962/63 92·1; 1963/64 88·7; 1964/65 93·2; 1965/66 101·1. (Source: Dharm Narain, op. cit., p. 18. The prices paid to socialist countries are expressed as a percentage of those paid to the rest of the world.)

[86] See M. Sebastian, 'Does India buy dear from and sell cheap to the Soviet Union?', *Economic and Political Weekly* (1 December 1973) pp. 2141–50. Some of the selected imports were: fertilisers, newsprint, iron and steel, copper alloys, refractory bricks, tractor ploughs, drilling machines, bulldozers, etc.

[87] ibid., p. 2146.

[88] Dharm Narain compared the unit values of ten specific items of machinery (ibid., Table A-28) and found that import prices under bilateral trade were lower than world prices for seven of these items. In the remaining three items the prices charged by the socialist countries were slightly higher. However, this sample is much too small for any general conclusions to be drawn from it.

[89] op. cit., p. 176.

[90] There have been reports that credit-financed imports from Eastern Europe were priced higher than world prices. But, in this, the socialist countries were not unique. It has been shown that aid-tied imports from the Western countries were also overpriced significantly: cf. Michael Kidron, *Foreign Investments in India* (London, 1965) pp. 122–3 and Jagdish Bhagwati, 'The tying of aid', in J. Bhagwati and R. Eckaus (ed.), *Foreign Aid* (Penguin, 1970) pp. 267–8. According to Asha Datar (op. cit., p. 257), '. . . there is no evidence that the prices charged by East European credits are higher than in the case of tied credits from other sources.'

[91] Estimates Committee Report, *Utilisation of External Assistance*, op. cit., pp. 229–30.

[92] For a detailed discussion on the question of 'appropriate' technology in less developed countries, see Frances Stewart, 'Trade and Technology', in Paul Streeten (ed.), *Trade Strategies for Development* (London, 1974).

[93] National Council of Applied Economic Research, *Export Prospects of Tobacco* (New Delhi, 1966) pp. 111 and 116.

[94] Carpet backing fetched more than Rs 4 per kg in 1970/71, whereas jute hessian bags and jute sacking bags fetched only Rs 3·39 and 2·51, respectively.

[95] See Table 5.10.

[96] A recent World Bank report also found that India's exports to the socialist countries fetched prices that compared favourably with world prices; quoted in *The Financial Times*, London (5 April 1974).

6 East European Aid to India

PRAMIT CHAUDHURI

I. Introduction

This essay attempts to outline the basic features of the aid-relationship between India and the East European countries from the early 1950s to the early 1970s. For reasons that will emerge shortly, it is in these years that the flow of foreign credit designated specifically as aid began to flow from the latter. Aid from the East European countries has played a significant part in the development of the Indian economy. From time to time I shall illustrate the relative orders of magnitude involved, by comparing the volumes and terms of aid from these countries, with those received from other donors. To avoid misinterpretation, I should state that it is not my purpose to derive normative conclusions from such comparisons. Although aid administrators might argue endlessly about relative shares, there are no unambiguous criteria on the basis of which an economist can lay down how much aid country X, as opposed to Y, should give to country Z. Moreover, the formal and nominal terms of aid received from alternative sources are not always a reliable index of the benefits which accrue to the recipient country from such aid. There are certain distinctive characteristics of the mechanism of aid-transfer between East Europe and India, that make such comparisons even more difficult to draw.

In what follows, I shall begin by describing briefly the sources of aid statistics and point out some of the limitations of such statistics. Given that aid is seen by both India and the East European countries as part of a wider framework of economic cooperation between them, I shall then discuss some of the explicit policy-decisions that define and circumscribe the aid-relationship. In the rest of the paper, I shall present the basic statistical features of that relationship, ending with some discussion of problems that have arisen at the project level with the utilisation of economic aid from the East European countries.

Broadly speaking, there are three major sources of statistics relating to aid. The Indian Ministry of Finance publishes aid statistics in the *Economic Survey* and *External Assistance*, and the Reserve Bank of India in the *Report on Currency and Finance*. Although the data are superficially plentiful, there

* The empirical material used in this chapter was partly collected under a research project financed by the Social Science Research Council.

are some major discrepancies in the three sources. Without going into much detail we can note that the most reliable figures for total aid authorised and utilised are given in the *Economic Survey*. The publication *External Assistance* gives a very detailed breakdown of particular loans and of the terms of such loans. However, it almost certainly overstates the total volume of aid received and utilised. The figures for total aid from this source are also non-comparable, to some extent, between the period before and after devaluation.[1] For these reasons, we have used the former source for data on total value of aid, while using the latter for information relating to terms of aid, as well as the sectoral composition of such aid.[2]

The attractions to India of economic cooperation with the East European countries are many. They are a significant source of foreign aid, albeit not the largest source. This is true, especially of the USSR, which holds the dominating position within this group, even more ostentatiously than the USA's similar primacy amongst the capitalist countries. During the period 1951/52–1969/70, the USSR ranked fifth amongst the major aid donors and supplied 78.2 per cent of total aid utilised from the East European countries. Quantities apart, the special significance of aid from the socialist countries lies in the fact that they are willing to give aid for projects which have not always been favoured by some of the other donors. I refer, of course, to the capital goods industries in the public sector and the unwillingness of the USA, as the major donor, to finance such projects in the past. Not the least important, it is widely felt that the East European countries are more sympathetic to India's effort to develop within the context of a development strategy that assigns a dominant role to the development of a public sector.[3] Finally, the presence of this group of countries considerably strengthens India's bargaining position *vis-à-vis* the capitalist countries.

The fact that India looks to the East European countries both as a source of supply of capital goods, as well as capital imports, together with the fact that the latter are centrally planned economies, has led to the development of a particularly close relationship between the aid and trade aspects of economic cooperation. Although we are not concerned here with the details of these arrangements, the important point to bear in mind is that the aid-relationship is seen rather consciously as part of a total relationship that embraces the movement of both goods and funds between India and the donor countries. It is important to bear this in mind in interpreting some features of the aid-relationship.[4]

There are two other points that we must also bear in mind. One is that, whether one thinks it sensible or not, both sides have as a matter of policy ruled out the provision of large-scale grants as a means of providing assistance. The other is that, since 1960, the East European countries have accepted payment of loans in non-convertible rupees. For a country like India which suffers from acute scarcity of foreign exchange, this reduces the burden of servicing foreign loans, compared with those that are repayable in hard currencies. Insofar as accumulated rupee balances have to be liquidated by the movement of goods, there is obviously a real resource cost of repaying these loans.[5]

II. Aid Flows: Volume and Composition

We can turn now to a study of the quantitative aspects of aid flows. Before doing this, we have to bear in mind that the figures are given in rupees and not in foreign currencies. This means that the same amount of foreign resources gives a higher figure for aid, after the 1966 devaluation (that is, from the fiscal year 1966–67, the devaluation falling in the second quarter of 1966). Table 6.1 gives the total values of non-food aid in the form of loans and grants authorised by the major donors. As the East European countries give no food aid, this method of comparison understates the relative magnitudes of aid given by countries such as the USA, which have given substantial parts of aid in the form of food aid. Moreover, the USSR and others also do not offer grants, as a matter of mutually agreed policy and the figures, therefore, stand for loans authorised for this group of countries.[6] It will be seen that offers of economic assistance from the USSR came early on in the life of planned development in India. This was during the period of the First Five Year Plan, when the only other donors were the USA and the IBRD. The USSR's commitments came to a head during the Second Plan period, when aid was committed for such projects as the steel plant at Bhilai and the Heavy Engineering Corporation at Ranchi. Thereafter, the emphasis fell increasingly on bilateral trade agreements as a channel for

TABLE 6.1. TOTAL NON-FOOD AID (LOANS PLUS GRANTS)
AUTHORISED
(RS MILLION)

Source	*1951/52 to 1955/56*	*1956/57 to 1960/61*	*1961/62 to 1965/66*	*1966/67 to 1970/71*
Total non-food aid of which:	*3,649*	*14,063*	*24,868*	*32,095*
Total loans of which:	*2,314*	*12,808*	*23,490*	*29,954*
US	1,095	3,386	8,380	10,802
USSR	647	3,191	1,005	2,500
IBRD/IDA	572	2,608	4,222	6,628
UK	–	1,227	2,420	3,830
West Germany	–	1,341	3,081	2,410
Japan	–	268	1,381	1,642

Source: Government of India, Ministry of Finance, *Economic Survey*.
Note: Rates of Conversion: $1 = Rs 4·76 up to 1965/6; $1 = Rs 7·50 since 1966/67.

economic cooperation between the two countries. Roughly speaking, the
time-pattern of aid from other East European countries is the same.[7]

One aspect of Soviet aid to India which needs to be emphasised is that
it was the first country to commit aid for a duration of a whole Plan, rather
than on a year-to-year basis. The advantages of such assistance for planned
development have been stressed by economists like Patel and Reddaway in
the Indian context.[8] Needless to say, this was made possible by the different
political systems under which government policy is formulated in the USSR.
On the other hand, it has been argued by some authors that this procedure
imparts a certain rigidity to Soviet assistance, although it must be added
that such rigidities are not entirely absent from the aid policy of other
donors.

From the point of view of development efforts, a relevant magnitude is
the volume of aid that is actually utilised by the recipient during any period
of time. These figures are given in Table 6.2, which gives the amounts by
donor groups. Of the East European countries, India did not have any aid
transactions with the DDR, while the contributions of Bulgaria and
Romania are negligible and can be ignored for all practical purposes. For aid
utilised, as for aid that is authorised, the USSR is by far the most dominant
partner of the group. It is followed by Czechoslovakia, Poland and Hungary,
roughly in that order. As for the time-pattern of aid utilised, it is different
from that of aid committed. It was only during the period of the Second

TABLE 6.2. TOTAL LOANS (NON-FOOD) UTILISED BY MAJOR DONORS (RS MILLION)

	1951/52 to 1955/56	*1956/57 to 1960/61*	*1961/62 to 1965/66*	*1966/67 to 1970/71*
East European Countries of which:	–	*749*	*2,539*	*3,281*
Czechoslovakia	–	–	126	461
Poland	–	–	113	112
USSR	–	749	2,072	2,253
Yugoslavia	–	–	97	443
Other Countries of which:	*1,264*	*7,248*	*19,208*	*27,944*
UK	–	1,219	1,705	3,824
USA	926	1,537	7,952	11,275
West Germany	–	1,199	2,197	3,037
IBRD/IDA	338	2,228	3,239	6,470
Japan	–	160	882	2,267
Others	–	157	693	1,071

Source: Government of India, Ministry of Finance, *Economic Survey.*
Note: Rates of conversion; as in Table 1.

Plan that India began to draw on Soviet assistance, as the investments in steel and heavy machinery plants actually came to be undertaken. Utilisation of aid from the other East European countries began from the Third Plan period. The peak in Soviet assistance came during the Second Plan also. At the time of writing, a substantial part of Soviet aid remains in the pipeline, mainly to finance the completion of Bokaro, the outstanding amount at the beginning of 1973/74 being Rs. 3289·9 million.

It will be seen from Table 6.2 that, quantitatively, the USSR and other East European countries made a significant contribution to aid flows, although they provided only a small part of the total foreign aid received by India. As we have indicated earlier, this point has to be qualified by the existence of the bilateral trade agreements between the two sides.[9]

Limiting ourselves to the aid side of the picture, we can go on to attempt partial answers to some of the relevant questions that have been raised. Is it true, for example, that the sectoral composition of Soviet aid makes it particularly beneficial to India, given her commitment to a particular development strategy that emphasises the role of heavy industries? Or is it that Soviet assistance is available on more favourable terms of repayment? Or does the relative insulation of the East European economies from international trade and their régime of administrative prices lead India to pay relatively higher prices for aid-tied imports? Although I cannot attempt a complete answer to any of these questions in the light of existing information, it is possible to indicate the directions in which answers are likely to lie.

III. Uses and Terms of Aid

It is, perhaps, worthwhile to dispose of a certain distortion that has crept into the assessment of the contribution of East European aid. There is a lively debate in the literature on foreign aid about the pros and cons of project-tied aid. The question whether project-tying helps or does not help recipient countries is not a question that is capable of an unequivocal answer. Much depends on the particular circumstances of the case. Most people would agree, however, that from the Indian point of view, there are substantial benefits to be achieved from the availability of non-project-tied aid.[10] Now, it is a fact that all aid received from these countries is 100 per cent tied to specific projects. It has been argued, therefore, that project-tying reduces the benefit of such aid to India.[11] This is, of course, true and follows directly from the premises of the argument. It does, however, overlook the fact that between India and the East European countries an elaborate mechanism of commodity trade has been set up that is supposed to take into account the requirements of the Indian economy for maintenance imports, insofar as they can be met from the latter economies.

Table 6.3 gives the sectoral composition of Soviet loans and roughly

TABLE 6.3. SECTORAL COMPOSITION
OF PROJECT AID UTILISED, 1956—70
(PERCENTAGES)

Sector	USSR	All donors
Steel	49·8	27·7
Heavy Machinery	9·0	11·5
Mining	5·0	—
Power	15·5	21·4*
Oil	17·8	—
Transport	—	23·5
Others	3·1	15·9
Total	*100·0*	*100·0*

Source: Government of India, Ministry of
Finance, *External Assistance.*
Note: Figures may not add up to the total
due to rounding.
*Includes investment in mining and irrigation.

compares it to the sectoral composition of *project* loans received from the
capitalist countries. The comparison is a rough one because the sectoral
distribution for all donors includes the East European countries. However,
as the percentage of loans from the latter is on average not higher than 10
per cent of the total, it is unlikely to alter our conclusions substantially if
they were left out. We have to bear in mind that while for the USSR project aid is equivalent to total aid, for the capitalist countries project aid is
only a proportion of total loans. For the major donors in this group, for
example, project aid was roughly 60 per cent of the total in 1963—65. By
the end of the sixties, the ratio had fallen to somewhere between 10 to 30
per cent of loans from the USA, the UK and West Germany, Japan and the
IDA, while remaining at the same level for France and the IBRD. It will
be seen that while it is true to say that the sectoral composition of Soviet
aid was different from that of aid received from the capitalist donor countries, the differences do not conform easily to the pattern that is intuitively
imagined. It is not the case that the aid given by the Soviet Union has been
heavily concentrated on creating capital-goods capacity, while capitalist aid
has gone into creating capacity for consumer goods industries. As far as
the heavy machinery sector itself is concerned, there is not a great deal of
difference between the two, especially if we classified investment in mining
financed by Soviet aid with heavy machinery. For the capitalist countries,
mining has been classified as part of the investment in power, which again
will explain part of the discrepancy we can see between the two groups. The
significant differences lie mainly in the fact that the proportion of aid given
to the steel industry is very much higher for the Soviet Union, while the
capitalist countries, including the IBRD, have given over more than a fifth
of total loans to finance the building up of an infrastructure in transport.

The other interesting point is the significant share of Soviet aid devoted to the production and exploration of oil in India.[12]

As far as the other donors in this group are concerned, out of a total of Rs. 574·1 million of Czechoslovak aid utilised until 1969/70, 79·3 per cent went to the heavy machinery sector, the rest going to the setting up of thermal power stations. The bulk of the total of Rs. 197·4 million of Polish aid utilised up to 1969/70 went to power generation, a small amount going into machine tools production. Therefore, of the major aid donors from East Europe, aid from Czechoslovakia alone conforms closely to the generally implied pattern that most of the socialist credit has gone into machines for producing machines.

It is commonly said that the rate of utilisation of aid has been lower for the East European countries. Table 6.4 illustrates this point with reference to the Soviet Union. It will be seen that the statement is correct for the two periods 1956–61 and 1966–70 but not for the intervening period. It is not clear how much of the problems of utilisation of Soviet aid is due to the alleged rigidities of the system. It is likely that the lower rate of utilisation of Soviet aid can be explained by two factors. One is that all Soviet aid is project-tied, and project aid, from whatever source, has a slower rate of utilisation. The second is that half of Soviet aid has been concentrated on two projects – the steel plants at Bokaro and Bhilai – and the rate of aid utilisation has been dependent on the progress made on these two projects. There does not seem to be any evidence that the delays in implementing Soviet projects have been higher than that in projects built with aid from other donors.

So far we have been talking about the gross flow of aid. Given that fresh aid commitments from the East European countries ceased after 1968/69, and that aid has to be repaid, the question might be asked, how much net aid has been received by India from this group of countries in recent years.

TABLE 6.4. RATE OF UTILISATION OF NON-FOOD LOANS,
BY MAJOR DONORS

	Percentage of authorised aid utilised during		
	1956/57–1960/61	*1961/62–1965/66*	*1966/67–1969/70*
USA	45·3	94·7	116·3
UK	99·3	70·4	104·6
USSR	23·5	207·2	73·0
West Germany	89·8	71·3	134·8
IBRD	85·3	85·3	144·2
IDA	–	72·0	124·4
Japan	59·7	63·9	107·0
Canada	100·0	37·3	58·3

Source: Calculated from Government of India, Ministry of Finance, *Economic Survey.*

Some figures are given in Table 6.5, which shows the proportion of debt servicing to total aid utilised in particular years. Although there are wide fluctuations in the ratio from year to year, it is clear that India has been receiving progressively less net aid from the group, as past loan repayments continue in the face of no fresh commitments.[13] In this context, the USSR and other socialist countries compare very unfavourably with the USA, the UK and the IDA, but not all that unfavourably with donors such as West Germany, France, Japan or the IBRD.

TABLE 6.5. DEBT SERVICE AS A PERCENTAGE OF
TOTAL AID UTILISED

	1966/67	*1967/68*	*1968/69*	*1969/70*
Czechoslovakia	4·0	38·4	56·7	82·8
Poland	76·9	137·5	255·6	77·0
USSR	98·7	135·5	76·3	121·9
Yugolsavia	9·4	100·2	114·6	27·6
UK	47·6	46·4	72·5	49·4
USA*	18·3	21·8	32·8	38·3
IBRD	247·7	188·6	200·1	195·0
IDA	1·9	2·3	8·1	6·4
West Germany	57·6	57·5	84·1	99·7
France	84·1	15·7	86·3	84·8
Japan	65·3	59·0	69·7	112·5

Source: Calculated from *Economic Survey* and *External Assistance*.
*Figures for USA exclude rupee payments.

The question can now be asked whether the East European countries have given aid to India on particularly favourable terms. One might expect this to have happened, given the widely-held belief that they are sympathetic to the 'socialist' policies followed by the Indian government. The actual terms of aid offered by the East European countries, and by some of the Western countries, are given in Table 6.6. The point has first to be made that there was relatively little aid from these countries for 1971; the figures simply refer to the terms of outstanding loans rather than to fresh commitments. Whereas, for the other donors, the comparison between columns 1 and 2 of Table 6.6 brings out the significant softening of the terms of new loans, it will be seen that the East European countries have given loans at very low rates of interest, the rate being typically $2\frac{1}{2}$ per cent. However, loans have also been given for much shorter periods than those offered by some, though not all, of the other donors and there have not been any significant grace periods for repayments. To a large extent, the short duration of the loans offsets the advantages of lower rates of interest and overall the terms do not come out very favourably. For example, if we use the concept of 'grant element' as a ranking device, the USSR terms will come out more unfavourably than

TABLE 6.6. TERMS OF AID FROM SELECTED DONORS

	Interest rates (per cent)		Maturity (years)		Grace period (years)	
	(1)	(2)	(1)	(2)	(1)	(2)
Czechoslovakia	2·5	2·5	4 to 6	8 to 12	1	nil
Hungary	2·5 to 4·5	2·5	10	10	1	nil
Poland	2·5	2·5	10	8 to 12	3	nil
USSR	2·5	2·5	12	12	1	nil
Yugoslavia	3	3	6 to 8	11	nil	nil
France	5 to 6	3·5 to 8·0	10	10 to 25	nil	nil
West Germany	3 to 5·5	2·5	15 to 25	30	4 to 7	8
Japan	5·8	5·25	15	18	5	5
IBRD	5·5 to 6·0	7·0	10 to 20	30	nil	10
IDA	0·75	0·75	50	50	10	10
UK	3·5	nil	25	25	7	7
USA (1)	0·75	2 to 3	5 to 6	40	2	10
(2)	5·75	6	40	10 to 20	10	3

Source: As for Table 3.
Notes: Col. (1) Up to 1966/67. Col. (2) 1971.
For USA, row (1) refers to DLF/AID loans; row (2) to Eximbank loans.

those of West Germany, the IDA, the UK and the AID/DLF loans from the USA, but more favourably than those for Eximbank loans or IBRD loans. The ranking will remain unaltered both before and after 1966/67.[14] It has to be borne in mind, however, that the burden of debt-servicing imposes quite different forms of sacrifice on India for East European compared with Western loans. The latter have to be repaid in convertible hard currencies, while the former are repaid essentially in terms of domestic resources, where the shadow price of foreign exchange is higher than the official rate of exchange. The real burden of servicing the East European debt depends on the prices secured by India for her exports at the margin, as opposed to the free market price for these goods.[15]

There does not seem to be any reason for holding the view that the East European countries have overall offered particularly favourable terms to India. However, we have to bear in mind that the existence of this group as an alternative source of aid has probably helped India to get both more aid and more favourable terms from other donors. At least as far as the USA is concerned, the growing volume of US aid to India and the considerable softening of the terms of aid during the time of the Second Five Year Plan are not coincidental.

We can now turn to the question of the cost of aid-tying to India. There are clear indications that the practice of aid-tying by major donors has considerably reduced the foreign purchasing power that is nominally transferred to India through aid.[16] Elsewhere, I have tried to show that the overall incremental cost to India of aid-tying is in the region of some 30 per cent, on the basis of a fairly conservative estimate. We are here concerned with

the cost of tied aid from east European countries. Unfortunately, we do not
have at the moment a countrywise breakdown of the cost of aid-tying for
different donors. There is a fairly widespread belief in India, both in the
government and in the private sector, that the East European countries drive
a hard bargain. However, there are no firm data available to establish the
point and such folklore is not always a reliable index of the true state of
affairs. Casual empiricism indicates that, given the fact that the overall
cost of tied aid to India is in the region of 30 per cent, there is no *a priori*
reason for thinking that the degree of overvaluation is higher for East
European sources than for aid donors generally. On the basis of a comparison
of unit import values for 39 commodity groups in 1963/64 and 48 commodity
groups in 1968/69 we find the following: for 1963/64 in 44 cases the unit
value of commodity imports from the East European countries was *higher*
than the weighted average for the particular commodity group; in 53 cases
it was *lower* than the weighted average. For 1968/69, the figures are 43
and 88, respectively. While this is a casual exercise and says nothing about
the degree of over- or undervaluation in particular, it does not suggest that
the cost of aid-tying is relatively greater for East European aid.[17]

The question arises whether one can be firmer about the degree of over-
or underpricing of imports from the East European countries, compared
with prices charged by other suppliers. For example, Dharm Narain has
calculated some figures for the period 1961/62 to 1965/66 which gives a
mean index of 93·5.[18] This can be interpreted as saying that, on average
the East European countries prices are 6·5 per cent lower than prices
charged by other suppliers. It is difficult to see what emphasis should be
attributed to such an average value. Firstly, even over the limited period,
the Dharm Narain index shows no clear trend. Secondly, the standard
deviation related to the mean difference is rather high, being 4·12, and
almost all the negative deviations fall within this range. Most important, perhaps, is the fact that there are very substantial differences in unit values
for different suppliers within particular commodity groups. Moreover,
across commodity groups there is no clear ranking pattern between suppliers,
either within the group as a whole or within the sub-group of East European
countries. A system of value weighting, which is a practical method and
which in fairness to Dharm Narain we too have fallen back upon, is not
a very satisfactory one, because it slips in an implicit assumption about
the possibilities of substitution. In the face of these difficulties, it seems
better to rest on the weaker hypothesis, that there is no obvious reason
for supposing that the East European countries have charged prices that
are typically higher than those charged by other countries.

IV. A Micro-view of Aid

So far we have confined ourselves to the aggregate quantitative data, to outline the basic aid-relationship between India and the East European countries. As has been said earlier, aid from these sources has been tied to specific projects. A study of the experience of these projects, at stages of formulation, construction and operation, throws interesting light on the aid-relationship. What follows is highly selective and tentative, indicating problems and questions which will merit further detailed study rather than a firm and exhaustive analysis.[19]

Much that is highly critical has been written about the performance of public-sector plants in India. There have been major delays and problems in the formulation of such projects. During construction, they have far exceeded their expected costs and taken much longer to bring to completion than was originally planned. After completion, their operational performance has been poor. Frequent breakdowns and stoppages, failure to reach targets of output, and low rates of utilisation of capacity are fairly common; at best, low profitability and at worst, cumulative losses, have also marred their performance. We have argued elsewhere that the picture, at least until the end of the sixties, is not as uniformly black as is sometimes painted by critics of the public sector.[20] However, it is undeniable that there is much truth in these criticisms and the development of public sector industries in India, to put it mildly, has not been an unqualified success.

Our concern here is with a somewhat narrower issue. Given the overall picture relating to the development of the public sector, what has been the relative performance of those enterprises which have been financed out of East European aid and equipped with East European technology and equipment? Have they suffered from the various shortcomings of public-sector industries to a greater or a lesser degree? To what extent can such shortcomings be attributed to certain aspects of the aid relationship? A detailed study of the issues is not possible within the present context. In what follows, we do no more than sketch out the bare outlines, illustrating our points with reference to some specific cases.

For convenience, the main conclusions of this section may be briefly summarised here. A number of problems which have been faced by East European aid projects turn out to be common to a number of public sector projects, irrespective of the source of aid for such projects. In turn, such problems are fairly closely related to the general economic strategies and policies followed by the Indian Government. Some, indeed, are related to the stage of industrial development reached by the Indian economy. It is difficult, and quite often impossible, to separate questions of aid, let alone East European aid, from the larger and more general questions of development policy.

As pointed out in Section III, the bulk of the East European aid has come from the USSR and about half of Russian aid has gone into the steel industry. In addition, there has been investment in the capital goods sectors, including engineering goods, electrical equipment and mining machinery, precision instruments and the pharmaceutical industries. Of the other East European countries' aid the most notable are Czechoslovak projects in foundry forge plants and machine tools. The largest, and the most talked about of the Russian aid projects have been the two steel plants, at Bhilai and Bokaro. In addition, there is the Heavy Engineering Corporation at Ranchi, the Hardwar plant of Bharat Heavy Electricals Ltd., Indian Drugs and Pharmaceuticals Ltd. and many others, including oil refineries.[21]

It is important to note that the development of public-sector industries in India was initially conceived as a key element in a particular development strategy, the so-called Soviet type of industrialisation policy. We need to stress here two characteristics of such a strategy that are important in the present context. The first is that the Government tried, quite consciously, to set up a number of industrial plants producing intermediate and capital goods, which involved large-scale investment and relatively advanced technology; such industries had hardly existed before in underdeveloped economies. Secondly, it was logically implicit in the strategy, although neither sufficiently nor explicitly recognised by policy makers, that the public sector be able to generate and maintain a high rate of development expenditure and an increasing rate of real investment in the economy. The significance of these two factors for the problem at hand will become clear in our discussion.

Broadly speaking, the problems faced by public-sector industries, including the East European aid projects, can be classified into those relating to faulty planning at the stages of project preparation and construction and those relating to the operation of the completed projects. Here it must be admitted that some of the sweeping criticisms of public-sector projects, such as those contained in the otherwise very valuable reports of the Committee on Public Undertakings of the Lok Sabha, do not give sufficient attention to the difficulties of pioneering a capital goods sector in a poor, semi-industrialised country and of establishing norms of performance which are initially derived from the rich, industrialised economies of the West. Nonetheless, it is undeniable that many avoidable and highly costly mistakes were made in carrying out the investment programme for the capital goods and intermediate goods industries in India. The major problems that arose were of three different kinds.

(1) The completion of the projects took very much longer than expected. Delays of up to eighteen months or more for parts of a project were by no means untypical. Indeed, it is known that some priority projects of the Second Plan were not even complete by the end of the Third Plan. Part of the explanation for these delays, as Datar very rightly pointed out, lay in bad project preparation.[22] In some cases, radical changes in the design of projects were required by the Government to fit in with actual or perceived changes in need. Russian as well as German project estimates turned out not to have provided for essential facilities, which had later to be incorporated into the project.

In other cases, delays were occasioned by the failure of Indian suppliers to provide various parts and components on time or to complete parts of the site construction works. Equally, delays were caused by failure to keep to the schedule of deliveries for plans, designs and equipment, as well as the supply of faulty equipment, blame for which has to be attached to foreign suppliers of equipment. The point is that such experiences were in no way unique to projects financed by East European aid donors. They arose as much in the case of the Bhilai steel plant and the Heavy Engineering Corporation at Ranchi, which were Russian projects, as in the case of the German steel plant at Rourkela or the British heavy electrical plant at Bhopal.

An extreme and somewhat ludicrous example is that of the steel plant at Bokaro, which was initially conceived to go into production in 1965–66 and which was barely complete in 1974.[23] The case underlines the difficulty of drawing simple morals from such cautionary tales. A substantial part of the delay arose initially from the insistence of US contractors on re-preparation of project reports and the subsequent breakdown of negotiations between the US and the Indian authorities, when the whole project had to be started afresh. However, much delay was also caused during the process of construction under Soviet aid. Just as the Soviet willingness to build Bokaro was a political act, so was the US unwillingness to help build a steel plant in the public sector.[24]

(2) The equipment chosen initially, turned out to be either unsuitable for Indian conditions or inferior in relation to comparable equipment available.[25] An example of the latter is the failure of the Soviet project plan for Bokaro to provide for large-capacity LD-converters which, according to the original Indian consultants Dasturco, would have significantly reduced the cost of production of steel. Similar problems have arisen in the case of the Russian built plant for the Indian Drugs and Pharmaceuticals plant.[26] The Fertilizer Corporation of India also encountered such problems in the construction of their newer plants. In this respect, the problems related to the supply of unsuitable equipment or feedstock for projects aided by different Western donors. Equally, it is very widely held in India that even for private-sector technical collaboration agreements, plants embodying the latest and the most efficient technologies are not generally made available to the Indian counterparts.

The evaluation of the suitability of a particular technology for a poor country which has a very different industrial infra-structure is made difficult by the fact that appropriateness of a particular technology is not simply a question of the degree of scientific sophistication of the technology under consideration. Its appropriateness has to be evaluated in terms of the environment in which it is to operate, and in terms of availability of types of skilled labour, complementary resources and services.[27] Moreover, owing to differences in specifications, performance and prices, it is extremely difficult to make cost comparisons between different projects for producing capital goods and intermediate goods. For what it is worth, it is true that the average cost per unit of output is expected to be much higher for the Russian-financed Bokaro, say, than was estimated for its US counterpart or that was regarded as a feasible target by Dasturco. There is no guarantee, however, that either of the latter two would have been the actual cost. Indeed, cost escalation has been the common fate of public-sector projects. On the other hand, Bhilai, which has been set up with Russian aid and uses simpler and cruder equipment is said to succeed in producing cheaper steel. By and large, it is true to say the East European countries tend to favour projects which involve heavier initial investment, larger scales and longer gestation period, as a trade-off against lower long-run average costs for reasonable levels of capacity use. This can be illustrated, for example, with reference to the experience of both Bokaro and the Heavy Engineering Corporation.[28] In Indian experience, for which aid donors do not and should not bear the larger share of the blame, such a strategy has turned out rather badly. The expected cost savings have not materialised and the economy has been saddled with heavy investment costs and a large measure of excess capacity. This is a factor of the utmost significance in relation to the role of public-sector industries as a potential mobiliser of funds. It stands out as an example of the serious consequences of the failure of the Indian Government to devise policies that are necessary for the implementation of a Soviet-type industrialisation strategy, rather than an example of inefficiency of the aid-relationship.

An underlying feature of the Indian economic strategy has been to encourage the use of foreign exchange-saving, indigenous resources. How does the experience with East European aid compare with that of projects aided by other donors, in this particular respect? Have the East European countries encouraged the use of Indian know-how and materials to a greater extent? Have they at least acquiesced to such a policy with greater willingness? As with so many things, we must give a somewhat equivocal answer to this question. For a number of comparable projects, the foreign exchange component does appear to have been significantly lower for Russian aid projects. The data in Table 6.7 support such a conclusion but only to a limited extent. The data at the macro-level, therefore, suggest that the import content of Russian aid projects has tended to be lower. While there has been a greater willingness on the part of the Russian donors to use a larger proportion of domestic resources in the construction of investment projects, the same cannot be said about their attitude to the use of Indian technology. They have shown no greater willingness to allow for a higher degree of Indian participation in design and construction of investment projects or in the sharing of industrial know-how, then other donors.

(3) The combined effect of these two factors has been to produce very high cost escalations in the public-sector capital goods industries. Substantial discrepancies between the planned and the actual investment costs of projects have been a very common experience in India. Datar gives an

TABLE 6.7. FOREIGN EXCHANGE COST AS A PERCENTAGE
OF TOTAL COST OF COMPLETED PROJECTS

Project		Donor	Cost per cent
Steel:	Bhilai	USSR	48·3
	Bokaro	USSR	30·4
	Durgapur	UK	56·6
	Rourkela	West Germany	60·5
Bharat Heavy Electricals:			
	Hardwar	USSR	33·6
	Bhopal	UK	32·7
Heavy Engineering Corporation		USSR	43·6

Source: Government of India, Bureau of Public Enterprises, *Annual Report of the Working of Industrial & Commercial Undertakings of the Central Government,* various issues.

average figure of 63 per cent as a measure of cost escalation for projects financed out of East European aid. According to her, this is a high figure relative to the costs of other projects.[29] However, it is also clear from her figures that the degree of cost escalation has been much lower for some East European projects. The three steel plants of the Hindustan Steel Ltd., Bhilai, Durgapur and Rourkela, financed respectively out of Russian, British and German aid, yield roughly the same measure of cost escalation of around 80 per cent.[30] As Datar concluded: All the public sector plants seem to have had similar troubles — delays and cost escalation![31] There is no simple correlation between long gestation, wrong technology and higher costs. Part of the increase in costs no doubt reflects the normal process of inflation in the international economy, part genuine improvements in plant design and capacity and part simply the result of avoidable and unavoidable wastes of a bureaucratic system pioneering the development of a capital goods industry in an underdeveloped country.

On the operational side, the record of public sector enterprises has been somewhat depressing on the average. Three shortcomings stand out the most strongly: failure to reach output targets, low levels of capacity utilisation over extended periods of time and low profitability. With very few exceptions, public sector enterprises have failed to show reasonable levels of profits and most have accumulated substantial losses over their period of operation. Needless to say, the low profitability is, at least in part, the consequence of the first two factors mentioned above. For highly capital-intensive industries, the rate of profit is extremely sensitive to the rate of capacity utilisation. In addition, there have been complaints about the quality of the output of public sector industries. However, such complaints have also been frequently made against the private sector.

Table 6.8 gives some figures for the profits and losses of some of the major

TABLE 6.8. PROFITS (+) AND LOSSES (−) OF SELECTED PUBLIC SECTOR ENTERPRISES

Project	Donor	Cumulative profits (+) or losses (−) 1959/60–1968/69 Rs. million	Average annual profit (+) or loss (−)	
			1968–1970 Rs. million	1973–1974
Hindustan Steel Ltd.	UK, USSR W. Germany	−1,449	−252	−116
Heavy Electricals Ltd.	UK, USSR	−224	−6,837	+209
Hindustan Machine Tools Ltd	Various	+53	+817	+7
Heavy Engineering Corpn.	USSR	−333	+15,675	−119
Fertilizers & Chemicals (Travancore)	UK	+4	−919	−22
Fertilizer Corporation of India	Various	+75	+32	+6
Indian Drugs & Pharmaceuticals	USSR	−120	−9,134	−28
Hindustan Antibiotics	USSR	+56	+5	+5

Source: Government of India, Bureau of Public Enterprises, *Annual Report of the Working of Industrial & Commercial Undertakings of the Central Government*, various issues.

public sector enterprises during the period 1959–60 to 1973–74. It is true that not all public sector industries have made losses and that a few appear to have turned the corner into profit-making enterprises. However, in terms of capital invested, the record of public sector industries has been somewhat appalling. As far as the plants set up under East European aid are concerned, their experience would seem to be somewhat mixed. They figure prominantly amongst the loss makers, partly because they figure prominently in the public sector but they do not figure exclusively. They are often, so to speak, in good company.

A very brief consideration of the performance of three of the public sector steel plants, Bhilae, Durgapur and Rourkela, throws some interesting light on the problem. Of the three, the Russian financed Bhilai has so far had the best record of performance. It was the first to be commissioned and since then, its production record has been the best, both in terms of levels and of continuity. Thus, the average rate of capacity usage in the three plants during 1972–1974 was as follows: Bhilai – 80 per cent, Durgapur – 47 per cent and Rourkela – 62·5 per cent. During the period 1968–1970, both Bhilai and Durgapur made substantial losses (Bhilai – Rs. 77·0 million; Durgapur – Rs. 328·7 million), Rourkela making a small profit of Rs. 38·6 million. Over the period 1972–1974, both Bhilai and Rourkela made a profit (Bhilai Rs. 237·8 and Rourkela Rs. 109·3 million), while Durgapur made a substantial loss of Rs. 441·6 million.

It is commonly agreed that Durgapur has for a long time been dogged with serious labour unrest and its performance is affected by factors that are not purely economic. Of the two other plants, the Russian Bhilai and the German Rourkela, the commonly held view is that the former is the better and the cheaper of the two. However, the actual situation is a little more complicated. Both plants from time to time, have developed major production difficulties. More importantly, the product composition of the two plants is quite different. Bhilai produces basically structurals, while Rourkela specialises to a much greater extent in flat products, although both plants, in common with all Indian steel plants, are required to produce too many types of products over too short production runs to be efficient. By and large, demand for structurals has been more buoyant in the economy than that for flat products, while the Government's price policy has also had an unequal incidence on the two. Because of Indian conditions it would be a little unfair to lay the poor performance of various public sector plants on one or more of the aid donors. Indeed, frequently the main cause of poor performance can be seen to have been purely domestic in origin. Nor are such causes always to be found in some traditional inefficiency of Indian industry, that is so beloved of some economic commentators. Quite often the problem lies in the ability and the willingness of the Indian Government to pursue particular investment policies, maintain particular patterns of expenditure within the economy and use or abuse particular instruments of control to regulate the economy. The inability of the Government to maintain a high rate of investment in the economy has had very serious repercussions on capacity utilisation and rates of profit – especially in the capital goods industries.

To return to the more general experience of public sector industries, there have been five major causes of poor performance: problems arising in the supply and quality of raw materials; breakdowns in plant and of major equipment; a product mix unsuited to the pattern of demand in the market; poor financial and production management; and labour unrest. Aid donors and suppliers of equipment can sometimes be held responsible, as far as the imposition of a particular product mix or equipment failure is concerned. For example, the Soviet financed pharmaceuticals factory at Pimpri produces a particular combination of drugs, for many of which there is no demand in India. As far as equipment is concerned, this has often been due to faulty maintenance and is therefore attributable to poor management at the plant level, witness the collapse of part of the factory roof at Rourkela. For the other reasons of poor performance, that is quality and supply of raw materials and for labour unrest, aid donors – East European or others – can hardly be said to have been responsible.

In conclusion, the aid-relationship is part of a wider economic relationship between India and the East European countries, in a far more integrated sense than is true of India's relationship with her other donors. The group has been a significant though not a dominant supplier of aid to India, the USSR being the most important member of the group. While there is no reason to believe that they charge higher prices for their aid-financed exports than the other donors, they do give aid on relatively hard terms. The kind of projects which their aid has financed have made a mixed showing, sharing many of the problems that have arisen within the public sector inustrial plants, irrespective of the source of the aid. This is, indeed, not surprising, because these problems reflect mainly some deeper structural malaise within the Indian economy, raising in their turn some very basic issues relating to the overall strategy of development. However, their main usefulness to India has lain in their willingness to give aid for particular projects that are regarded as high-priority investment and to give such aid for public sector development, at times when other major donors, such as the US, have shown an extreme reluctance to do so. Last, but not least, their existence as an alternative source of imports and aid has considerably strengthened India's hand in her aid-negotiations with the capitalist group of donors.

Notes

[1] A large number of methodological and practical problems arise in the course of using the published data for purposes of analysis. These are discussed at some length in Pramit Chaudhuri, 'The impact of aid on the Indian economy, 1950–70', 1974 (mimeo).

[2] The sectoral composition of aid among donors and projects, or the terms of aid received from different donors, are not affected by the overvaluation of the foreign exchange value of aid received.

[3] Here, we evade the question of the extent to which Indian development strategy can be labelled 'socialist' or likened to the Soviet strategy.

[4] On bilateral trade, see Deepak Nayyar, Chapter 5.

[5] A precise theoretical formulation of this point will be somewhat complicated. Broadly speaking, loans repayable in hard currencies impose the heaviest burden, whereas loans repayable in domestic currency, e.g., PL480 food aid from the USA, impose the least burden. Loans repayable in domestically produced goods fall in between, depending on the terms of trade obtaining between the donor and the recipient.

[6] The figure for loans *authorised* excluded the East European countries other than the USSR. As explained in the text, the bulk of the aid from this group came from the USSR.

[7] For a discussion of East European countries' aid to India, see Asha Datar, *India's Economic Relations with the USSR and Eastern Europe, 1953–1969* (London: Cambridge University Press, 1972) and Marshall I. Goldman. *Soviet Foreign Aid* (New York: Praegar, 1967). Also P. J. Eldridge, *Politics of Foreign Aid in India* (London: Weidenfeld & Nicolson, 1969); M. Sebastian, *Soviet Economic Aid to India* (New Delhi: NV Publications, 1975) also contains some useful information on aid.

[8] I. G. Patel, 'Foreign capital and domestic planning', in J. H. Adler (ed.), *Capital Movements and Economic Development* (London: Macmillan, 1970) and W. B. Reddaway, *The Development of the Indian Economy* (London: Allen & Unwin, 1962).

[9] See Datar, op. cit., and Nayyar, op. cit.

[10] Such aid enables India to finance imports necessary for utilisation of existing capacity – the so-called 'maintenance imports'.

[11] Datar, op. cit.

[12] For a detailed discussion, see B. Dasgupta, Chapter 7.

[13] After 1968/69, the bilateral trade agreements were meant to incorporate both the trade and aid aspect of economic cooperation, with the exception of the financing of the Bokaro steel project.

[14] On 'grant element' see for example Göran Ohlin, *Foreign Aid Policies Reconsidered* (Paris: O.E.C.D., 1966). Our conclusions also show that the view held by some economists that the interest terms are the major determinants of the 'grant element' is somewhat too simple.

[15] For such a price comparison, see Deepak Nayyar, op. cit.

[16] On the cost of aid-tying in general, and to India in particular, see Jagdish Bhagwati, 'The tying of aid' in Jagdish Bhagwati and Richard Eckaus (eds.), *Foreign Aid* (London: Penguin, 1970); I. G. Patel, 'Foreign aid: retrospect and prospect', *Commerce* Bombay (30 March 1968); Chaudhuri, op. cit.

[17] Chaudhuri, op. cit. The range of commodities covered excludes equipment, due to problems of comparing heterogeneous equipments in terms of price and efficiency. They cover the same range of goods as the study by Dharm Narain referred to in footnote 18, e.g., chemicals, non-ferrous metals, basic iron and steel products, etc.

18 Dharm Narain, 'Aid through trade: case study of India', in Pramit Chaudhuri (ed.), *Aspects of Indian Economic Development* (London: Allen & Unwin, 1971).

19 This section if based on the following sources: Datar, op. cit.; Goldman, op. cit.; Padma Desai, *The Bokaro Steel Plant: A Study of Soviet Economic Assistance* (Rotterdam: North Holland, 1972); Government of India, Lok Sabha, Committee on Public Undertakings: (1) 3rd Lok Sabha, (a) 11th Report — *Rourkela Steel Plant*; (b) 22nd Report — *Indian Drugs and Pharmaceuticals Ltd*; (c) 29th Report — *Durgapur Steel Plant*; (d) 30th Report — *Bhilai Steel Plant*; (2) 4th Lok Sabha, (a) 12th Report — *Heavy Electricals (India) Ltd*; (b) 14th Report — *Heavy Engineering Corporation Ltd*; (c) 67th Report — *Production Management in Public Undertakings*; (d) 68th Report — *Bokaro Steel Plant*; (3) 5th Lok Sabha, (a) 38th Report — *Hindustan Machine Tools Ltd*; (b) 40th Report — *Role and Achievements of Public Undertakings*; (c) 56th Report — *Indian Drugs and Pharmaceuticals Ltd*; 77th Report — *Steel Authority of India Ltd.*

20 See Pramit Chaudhuri, 'India: objectives, achievements and constraints', in Chaudhuri, op. cit., p. 77f, cited in footnote 18.

21 The experience of the oil industry is not covered in this paper.

22 Datar, op. cit.

23 Desai, op. cit.

24 A. Kapoor — *International Business Negotiations: A Study in India*, (New York: New York Unviersity, 1970).

25 See, for example, Jack Baranson, *Manufacturing Problems of India: The Cummins Diesel Experience* (Syracuse: Syracuse University, 1967).

26 Desai, op. cit., and CPU, 5th Lok Sabha, 56th Report, cited in footnote 19.

27 Baranson, op. cit.

28 Desai, op. cit., and CPU, 4th Lok Sabha, 14th Report, cited in footnote 19.

29 Datar, op. cit.

30 CPU, 3rd Lok Sabha, 11th, 29th and 30th Reports, cited in footnote 19.

31 Datar, op. cit., p. 243.

7 Pakistan and the Socialist Countries: Politics, Trade and Aid

AKBAR NOMAN*

Economic relations are frequently also political relations, especially between countries. Trade and flag are not entirely unlike chicken and egg in that their mutual causality is often inextricable. Hence, in examining the economic relations between Pakistan[1] and the socialist countries,[2] this paper begins by outlining the political relations which constituted the framework for the former. Section II examines the development and nature of trade between Pakistan and the socialist countries. Section III focuses on aid.

I. Politics

The first of the four phases in Pakistan's political relations with the socialist countries distinguished here (1947–50) was characterised by a measure of cordiality in marked contrast to that which followed. The first state in modern times to be created on the basis of religion lost little time in establishing diplomatic and trading relations with the USSR and the then infant socialist regimes of Eastern Europe. The first trade agreement with a socialist country was signed with Czechoslovakia in October 1948, followed by the signing of similar agreements with Yugoslavia in April 1949,[3] Poland in July 1949, and Hungary in November 1950.

By the time that the last of these agreements was signed, Pakistan's political relations with the socialist countries had begun to deteriorate sharply with her involvement in the cold war. This came in Prime Minister Liaquat's visit to the USA in May 1950, as a result of an invitation received in December 1949 which was given precedence over an invitation, extended six months earlier, to visit the USSR. During his visit to the USA, Liaquat expressed strong support for the US stance in the cold war in general, and on Korea in particular. The Soviet invitation to the Pakistani Prime Minister was, it seems, discreetly and unofficially withdrawn.[4]

*The views expressed in this paper are entirely personal and should not be taken to reflect, in any way, those of any institution or organisation with which the author may be associated.

163

In January 1950, Pakistan recognised the newly founded People's Republic of China and, on his US visit, Liaquat explained that Pakistan had done so because the People's Republic was an 'established fact and in order to ease the flow of trade'.[5] The context in which this decision was made is most relevant. Pakistan's flow of trade had been drastically disrupted (at exactly the same time as the People's Republic of China was established) by the dispute with India, over the exchange rate, which was, in effect, a dispute over the possible worsening of India's terms of trade with Pakistan, entailed by Pakistan's decision not to devalue along with sterling and the Indian rupee in September 1949.[6] This had brought trade between the two countries to a virtual standstill. In China, Pakistan found an alternative supplier of coal, which had been a vital import from India. Since India has been by far the largest single market for exports of raw jute and raw cotton, accounting for about 85 per cent of the value of Pakistan's exports, Pakistan was also anxiously in search of alternative markets for these raw materials. This anxiety was, however, soon to disappear with the raw materials boom and the sellers' market for cotton and jute engendered by the Korean war; but it reappeared with the collapse of that boom. The then Prime Minister Nazimuddin said in 1953 that the contemplated US blockade of China 'would affect many friends of the US who want to trade with China. In our case we want to sell our cotton.'[7]

Pakistan had been selling significant quantities of her raw cotton and some raw jute to the USSR, Czechoslovakia and China during 1947/48–1949/50 when exports to these countries, consisting almost entirely of these two items, accounted for something of the order of 7–8 per cent of the value of total exports.[8]

The signing of a number of trade agreements with the Eastern European countries during 1948–50 was probably partly motivated by the political desire to reduce economic dependence on India. As noted above, the incentive to search for specific markets for raw jute and cotton in socialist countries was much reduced by the Korean boom. By the time the boom petered out, the direction of Pakistan's trade had changed drastically away from India and towards Western Europe, Japan and the US. At the same time, Pakistan had become involved in the cold war on the side of the Western countries.

The ensuing political hostility between Pakistan and the countries of the socialist bloc, in the context of the highly charged international politics of that period, was not particularly conducive to the development of trade and other economic relations with these countries, especially after 1954, when Pakistan became a formal ally of the USA by signing a mutual defence pact and joining the US-sponsored system of military alliances. This coincided with a sharp rise in US military and economic assistance to Pakistan.[9] It also led to a sharp decline in the value of Pakistan's trade with the socialist countries (see Table 7.1) so that their share in the somewhat stagnant value of Pakistan's total trade fell from nearly 7·5 per cent in the early 1950s to less than 4 per cent during the mid-1950s, rising only marginally to 4·5 per cent by the end of the decade. Not surprisingly, Pakistan did not receive any economic or military aid from the socialist countries in the 1950s.

Relations with the communist world in general remained strained through-out the 1950s, though this is perhaps less true of Sino-Pakistan relations than of relations with the other socialist countries. There were, however, occasional attempts at conciliation and temporary, limited thaws which included tenta-tive, informal offers of aid from the Soviet Union. In 1956, a Soviet delega-tion of forty headed by First Deputy Premier Mikoyan was sent to Pakistan to participate in the ceremonies inaugurating Pakistan as a republic. On this occasion, Mikoyan publicly declared Soviet willingness to provide economic aid to Pakistan. He invited a parliamentary delegation to visit the USSR and stated that a visit from Bulganin and Khruschev (who had toured India and Afghanistan a few months earlier) only awaited Pakistan's invitation. At the same time, Foreign Minister Molotov is reported to have informally indicated, at a diplomatic reception, Soviet interest in assisting Pakistan to build a steel mill similar to that which the USSR was constructing in Bhilai, India.[10] The temporary improvement in Pakistan–Soviet relations in 1956 included the visit of a Pakistani parliamentary delegation to the USSR and the signing of the first barter trade agreement between the two countries. However, it was not for another eight years that barter became a regular feature of Pakistan–Soviet trade.

It was probably not entirely coincidental that the next major occasion for an improvement in Soviet–Pakistan relations coincided with some disquiet in Pakistan at the large increase in US aid to India and the related formation of the Aid-to-India Consortium in 1958, following a food and foreign exchange crisis in India. In the same year, a Soviet parliamentary delegation visited Pakistan. In 1959, negotiations between the governments of Pakistan and the USSR about Soviet assistance for oil and gas exploration were initiated. These negotiations were on the point of completion when the U-2 incident soured relations between the two countries and led to a suspension of the talks.[11] An agreement providing for Soviet technical assistance and equipment for oil and gas exploration, to be financed by a loan of $30 million, was finally signed in March 1961.

This improvement in relations with the USSR occurred at around the same time that Pakistan's relations with China worsened to what was perhaps their lowest point. Possibly this was a sign of the Sino-Soviet split, which had not quite become public at that time. Until 1958, the year of General Ayub Khan's *coup d'état*, relations with China had remained on considerably better terms than those with the USSR, partly because China had been fairly successful in balancing relations with India and Pakistan. In 1956 Chou En-Lai had made equally cordial visits to both countries; and, earlier that year, the Pakistani Prime Minister had visited China. The statement in Washington by Ayub's foreign minister in 1959 that 'expansionist tendencies were more noticeable in China than in Russia,[12] seemed to represent a reversal of a major presump-tion of Pakistani foreign policy. In 1959, when the Sino-Indian border dispute, after simmering for a long time, was showing signs of coming to the boil, and again in 1960, after the Chinese ousted the Dalai Lama from Tibet, Ayub offered India a joint defence pact, an offer which India did not accept. There was, hence, an element of irony in the effect of the Sino-Indian border clash of 1962 on the system of inter-relations which represented the international politics of the Indian subcontinent. For Ayub's government the most important outcome of the Sino-Indian conflict was probably the speed and scale of US arms deliveries to India. Consequently, Pakistan's relations with the US deteriorated markedly. As a corollary, relations with China in particular, and with the other socialist countries in general, improved dramatically. The period 1963—65 witnessed a flurry of exchange visits by official delegations and heads of governments between Pakistan and China. During this period Ayub visited both China and the USSR.

Increased trade and aid quickly followed the improvement in Pakistan's relations with the socialist countries. In January 1963 Pakistan and China signed their first trade agreement. Later in the year, an air transport agreement was signed providing for Pakistan International Airlines to operate in China, thereby giving PIA a lucrative virtual monopoly on China's air link with the world for the next decade or so. This was followed by the first barter trade agreement between China and Pakistan which was signed in September 1963.[13]

During 1963 and 1964 Pakistan also signed a number of trade agreements with the USSR and Eastern European countries. In August 1963, the USSR committed a loan of $30 million, and in early 1964 China pledged a loan of $60 million to Pakistan. The latter was subsequently converted into a grant. Other socialist aid commitments followed. As we shall see in the next section, the flurry of trade and aid agreements with socialist countries resulted in a phenomenal spurt in Pakistan's trade with these countries. Trade turnover increased fivefold during the 1960s.

President Ayub's visit to the USSR in April 1965 consolidated the new stage in Pakistan—Soviet relations in this third phase in Pakistan's relations with what was by now a divided Socialist bloc. Ayub spoke with frankness of the poor relations that had existed between the USSR and Pakistan 'only a few years ago' and gave his 'sincere assurance' that nonetheless 'the people of Pakistan have always entertained the most friendly feelings towards the people of the Soviet Union'.[14] Mikoyan, in turn, praised him for 'displaying the boldness and vision of a great statesman'.[15] A trade agreement, aimed at doubling Soviet—Pakistani trade by 1967, was signed during this visit.

At around the same time (1965—66) China became a significant source of arms supplies, bringing to an end the US role of the virtual sole supplier of arms to Pakistan. In 1968 the governments of Pakistan and the USSR signed an agreement for the sale of Soviet arms to Pakistan.[16]

The essentially neutral posture of the USSR in the disputes between Pakistan and India, including the 1965 war, came to an end in 1971, with strong Soviet support for India and Bangladesh, particularly during the fully-fledged outbreak of hostilities in December 1971 which resulted in the establishment of the state of Bangladesh. The much impaired relations between the USSR and the reduced Pakistan staged a considerable recovery in 1973 following Prime Minister Bhutto's visit to the USSR, with the signing of a debt relief accord and a new trade agreement, fresh commitments of aid and the inauguration of the Soviet-assisted steel mill project. Under the debt relief accord, Pakistan was no longer held liable for the repayment of Soviet loans, amounting to Rs 260 million, utilised in the former East Pakistan.[17]

Political relations between China and Pakistan remain cordial, though they have lost much of their speciality and vitality, but this has far more to do with the change in China's international position than with the division of Pakistan. The events of 1971 afflicted relations with the USSR, the future course of which remains somewhat uncertain, especially in view of the heightened tensions between Pakistan and Afghanistan, a country whose friendly relations with the USSR have a long history.

The changes in the political relations with the socialist countries since the break-up of Pakistan do not appear to have had a significant impact on its economic relations with those countries, unlike the changes in the early 1950s and early 1960s. None of these alternations, of course, has had much to do with changes in the nature of the political regime or internal political developments in Pakistan. As we have seen, most of the political alignments and re-alignments referred to above were the product of international political developments.

II. Trade

Each of the two widely separated regions of the Indian Customs Union which became Pakistan in 1947 had a similarly elemental trading pattern, which consisted essentially of exporting an agricultural raw material and importing all manner of manufactured consumer goods. Raw jute and raw cotton accounted for about 85 per cent of Pakistan's export earnings in the late 1940s. Until the devaluation disagreement with India in September 1949, and the consequent virtual standstill in trade between the two countries, India was by far the most important trading partner, accounting for 40–50 per cent of Pakistan's trade.[18] The UK followed with a share of around 20 per cent.

The only significant socialist trade partners in the late 1940s were the USSR and Czechoslovakia. Pakistan's exports to the USSR during 1947–50 steadily averaged about Rs 45 million a year, which was nearly three times the average annual value of exports to Czechoslovakia.[19] Exports to these two countries accounted for 4–5 per cent of Pakistan's total exports, consisted almost entirely of raw cotton, and exceeded the value of imports from them by about five times.

By the early 1950s Pakistan had signed trade agreements and established substantial trading links with a number of Eastern European countries, the USSR and the People's Republic of China. There were large year-to-year fluctuations in trade with the socialist countries, both individually and collectively, throughout the 1950s. In an attempt to overcome this problem, the data in Table 7.1 are presented as three-year averages centred on the year indicated. As can be seen from that table, the share of the socialist countries in the value of Pakistan's foreign trade had risen to 7·5 per cent in the early 1950s from about 2—3 per cent in the late 1940s. This increase was accounted for by the addition of China to the socialist camp and the expansion of trade with Eastern European countries. However, the value of Pakistan's trade turn-over with the USSR actually declined to an average of Rs 33 million per annum during 1951/2—1953/4 compared with an annual average of Rs 55 million in the late 1940s. The deterioration in Pakistan's political relations with the countries of the socialist bloc led to a sharp contraction in trade with *all* these countries. Their share in the somewhat stagnant rupee value of Pakistan's total trade had halved by the mid-1950s. Some recovery in the late 1950s raised their share to 4·5 per cent by the end of the decade, but the trade turnover with the socialist countries was still 21 per cent lower in current rupee terms, as compared to the annual average over the period 1951/2—1953/4.[20]

The structure of Pakistan's trade with the different socialist countries in the 1950s was similar to her overall trade structure, inasmuch as exports of jute and cotton accounted for 80—90 per cent of total export earnings and imports were largely constituted by assorted manufactured goods. But where-as at the beginning of the decade almost all of Pakistan's jute and cotton was exported in raw form, by the end of the 1950s the share of these raw materials in total exports had fallen to about 60 per cent. Basically, this was due to the increasing exports of jute manufactures and cotton textiles. However, it is worth noting that the proportion of manufactured exports in Pakistan's trade with the socialist countries did not increase significantly, and, by the end of the 1950s, jute and cotton in their raw form still accounted for about three-quarters of Pakistan's exports to Eastern Europe, USSR and China. There was some change in the structure of Pakistan's imports from these countries and textile imports were virtually eliminated by the late 1950s. In fact the structure of imports from the socialist countries was highly diversified, and Pakistan imported an assortment of manufactured intermediate and capital goods.

The striking feature of this trade was that exports to the socialist countries far exceeded imports from them, and Pakistan had an almost continuous and substantial trade surplus with Eastern Europe, USSR and China, both as a group and individually. Table 7.2 shows the cumulative trade surplus with these countries in absolute and in relative terms. The former is measured in current rupee values and the latter is expressed as the ratio of imports to exports.

What the table reveals is rather startling. In the period 1951/2—1955/6, Pakistan's trade with the socialist countries was almost a one-way flow with the resulting Pakistani trade surplus exceeding Pakistan's total cumulative trade surplus during these five years. In other words, Pakistan's trade with the rest of the world was in deficit over this period, but the moderate deficit of Rs 163 million was considerably more than offset by the Rs 808 million cumulative surplus with the socialist countries.

TABLE 7.1 PAKISTAN'S TRADE WITH SOCIALIST COUNTRIES: TURNOVER IN THE 1950s
(THREE-YEAR AVERAGES CENTRED ON THE YEAR INDICATED*)

A. Value and Share

Value and Share	1952/3		1956/7		1959/60	
	Value (Rs million)	Share (Per cent)	Value (Rs million)	Share (Per cent)	Value (Rs million)	Share (Per cent)
1. Total foreign trade of which trade with:	3181·3	100·0	3508·0	100·0	4064·7	100·0
2. Eastern Europe†	50·1	1·6	31·9	0·9	66·4	1·6
3. USSR	32·7	1·0	15·7	0·4	37·4	0·9
4. China	153·7	4·8	83·8	2·4	82·5	2·0
Sub-total (2 + 3 + 4)	236·5	7·4	131·4	3·7	186·3	4·5

B. Annual growth rates (%)

	1952/3–1956/7	1956/7–1959/60	1952/3–1959/60
World	2·5	5·0	3·6
Eastern Europe†	−10·7	27·7	4·1
USSR	−16·8	33·5	1·9
China	−14·1	− 0·5	−8·5
Socialist countries	−13·7	12·4	−3·4

Source: Central Statistical Office (CSO), Government of Pakistan, *25 Years of Pakistan in Statistics: 1947–72* (Karachi, 1972) pp. 383–400.

Note: The Pakistani rupee was devalued in 1955 from Rs 3·31 = $1 to Rs 4·76 = $1, so that in dollar terms the value of Pakistan's total trade actually declined during the 1950s.

* A year is the Pakistani fiscal year i.e., July to June.

† Bulgaria, Czechoslovakia, East Germany, Hungary, Poland and Romania. The bulk of Pakistan's trade with these countries in the 1950s was accounted for by Poland and Czechoslovakia.

TABLE 7.2 THE BALANCE OF PAKISTAN'S TRADE WITH THE SOCIALIST COUNTRIES IN THE 1950s
(CUMULATIVE FIGURES)

| | 1951/2–1955/6 | | | | 1955/6–1959/60 | | | |
	(1) Merchandise exports (Rs million)	(2) Merchandise imports (Rs million)	(3) (1)–(2)	(4) (2)/(1) (%)	(5) Merchandise exports (Rs million)	(6) Merchandise imports (Rs million)	(7) (5)–(6)	(8) (6)/(5) (%)
1. World	7812	7167	645	91·7	7982	9749	–1767	122·1
of which:								
2. Eastern Europe	152·3	37·5	114·8	24·6	160·0	58·6	101·4	36·7
3. USSR	96·1	3·8	92·3	4·0	87·7	32·4	55·3	36·9
4. China	623·0	21·7	601·3	3·5	286·3	122·0	164·3	42·6
Sub-total (2 + 3 + 4)	871·4	63·0	808·4	7·2	534·0	213·0	321·0	39·9

Source: CSO, 25 Years of Pakistan in Statistics, op. cit., pp. 383–98.
Note: Eastern Europe includes Bulgaria, Czechoslovakia, East Germany, Hungary, Poland and Romania.

Beginning in 1955/6, Pakistan's overall trade balance went into a large and growing deficit, financed by sharply rising inflows of foreign aid. However, Pakistan continued to export substantially more to the socialist countries than she imported from them. It should be noted in passing that all of Pakistan's foreign trade deficit, and considerably more, was accounted for by West Pakistan, the former East Pakistan being in continuous and substantial surplus throughout the 1950s.[21]

The whole of Pakistan's trade surplus with the socialist countries during the 1950s accrued in convertible foreign exchange. The trade agreements that Pakistan had signed with these countries did not feature barter deals or bilateral payments arrangements, but were confined to granting Most-Favoured-Nation treatment and indicating items of possible trading interest.

As we have seen, barter trade came in the mid-1960s, following closely in the footsteps of the political rapprochement between Pakistan and USSR/ Eastern Europe on the one hand, and China on the other. In the 1960s trade between Pakistan and the socialist countries grew extremely rapidly, largely under the aegis of the flurry of barter or 'commodity exchange' agreements concluded during 1963–66.

Over the decade as a whole, trade with the socialist bloc increased five-fold in terms of current rupee values, and about three times as rapidly as Pakistan's total foreign trade. The year-to-year fluctuations, however, remained large. The three-year average annual value of trade with socialist countries grew at the rate of 20 per cent per annum during 1959/60–1969/70. Table 7.3 shows that the share of such trade in Pakistan's total foreign trade rose from 4·5 per cent at the turn of the decade to nearly 14 per cent at the end of it.

The published data underestimate the expansion of Pakistan's socialist trade in the 1960s, for, as Kidron points out, they exclude Pakistan's imports of military equipment which 'appear to have switched from wholly Western to predominantly EBC (East Europe, USSR, China) suppliers over the decade' and which 'might have accounted for as much as $100 million a year'.[22]

The spurt in trade with the socialist countries was concentrated in the years 1963/4–1966/7, during which period the systematic and substantial Pakistan trade surplus with these countries disappeared[23] and the structure of trade altered considerably. This structure differed greatly between the former East and West Pakistans, as did the relative importance of the growth in trade with different socialist countries. Over the decade, the rise in trade with the USSR was evenly distributed between the two former wings of Pakistan, while East Pakistan's trade with China and West Pakistan's trade with Eastern Europe increased at rates more than twice that of the other wing. Table 7.4 outlines the difference in the experiences of West Pakistan and East Pakistan/ Bangladesh.

The data in the table suggest that the differences between East and West Pakistan were not very significant. There were, of course, other respects in which the experience of the two wings of the former Pakistan differed greatly. Much of the dissimilarity in the economic experience of East and West Pakistan

TABLE 7.3 PAKISTAN'S TRADE WITH THE SOCIALIST COUNTRIES: TURNOVER IN THE 1960s
(THREE-YEAR AVERAGES CENTRED ON THE YEARS INDICATED)

| | 1959/60 | | 1969/70 | | 1959/60–1969/70 |
	Value (Rs million)	Share (Per cent)	Value (Rs million)	Share (Per cent)	Annual growth rate (Per cent)
1. Eastern Europe	66·4	1·6	651·3	7·8	25·5
2. USSR	37·4	0·9	249·7	3·0	21·0
3. China	82·5	2·0	250·0	3·0	11·7
4. Sub-total (1 + 2 + 3)	186·3	4·5	1151·0	13·8	20·0
5. World	4064·7	100·0	8302·3	100·0	7·5

Sources: 1958/59, 1959/60 and 1970/71 data from CSO, 25 Years of Pakistan in Statistics, op. cit.; 1960/61, 1968/9 and 1969/70 data obtained from Michael Kidron, Pakistan's Trade with Eastern Bloc Countries (New York, 1972) Table II–1, pp. 72–5.
Note: The official exchange rate throughout the 1960s was Rs 4·76 = $1.

TABLE 7.4 TRADE WITH SOCIALIST COUNTRIES IN SELECTED YEARS: BY REGIONS OF THE FORMER PAKISTAN

	1960/1		1964/5		1969/70	
	E. Pak.	*W. Pak.*	*E. Pak.*	*W. Pak.*	*E. Pak.*	*W. Pak.*
A. Value of trade (Rs million)						
1. Eastern Europe	71·2	28·3	93·8	113·3	229·7	298·9
2. USSR	14·1	21·0	10·4	58·7	81·4	113·6
3. China	35·8	54·5	148·9	130·3	145·8	103·1
4. Sub-total (1 + 2 + 3)	121·1	103·8	253·2	302·3	456·9	515·5
5. *World*	*2273·5*	*2713·3*	*2970·0*	*4812·0*	*3475·9*	*4893·6*
B. Share in trade with socialist countries (per cent)						
6. Eastern Europe	58·8	27·3	37·1	37·5	50·3	58·0
7. USSR	11·7	20·2	4·1	19·4	17·8	22·0
8. China	29·5	52·5	58·8	43·1	31·9	20·0
C. Share in total foreign trade (per cent)						
9. Socialist countries (1 + 2 + 3)	5·3	3·8	8·5	6·3	13·2	10·5

Source: Michael Kidron, op. cit., pp. 72–6.

during the days of the Union is reflected in the dissimilarity in their trade structures by the end of the 1960s. Broadly speaking, West Pakistan started off as an exporter of raw cotton and ended the 1960s as an exporter of cotton textiles and a variety of manufactured goods, in addition to raw cotton. East Pakistan began as an exporter of raw jute and ended as an exporter of raw and processed jute. Tables 7.5 and 7.6 show the structure of exports of the former Pakistan and of its two regions to the world as a whole and to the socialist countries.

As measured by the two criteria of Table 7.5, Pakistan's exports to the socialist countries, which were heavily concentrated in 1960, had diversified considerably by the end of the decade but remained less diverse than her exports to the rest of the world. Further evidence of the diversification is provided by the sharp decline in the share of raw cotton and raw jute from about 90 per cent of the value of Pakistan's exports to socialist countries before the surge in trade beginning in 1963/4, to about 50 per cent during 1967/8–1969/70.[24] Almost all of the diversification in Pakistan's exports as measured in Table 5 was attributable to West Pakistan, which is somewhat misleading, as there was a significant relative shift from raw jute to jute textiles in East Pakistan's total exports during the 1960s. There was, however, no such shift in East Pakistan's exports to the socialist countries and, on the eve of that region's transformation into Bangladesh, the structure of its exports to the socialist countries was much the same as the structure of its total exports at the time that it was transformed from East Bengal to East Pakistan. In other words, during 1967/8–1969/70 raw jute accounted for about 86 per cent of East Pakistan's exports to the socialist countries, whereas its share in the total merchandise export earnings of that region was somewhat less than 50 per cent. This is confirmed by the data in Table 7.6, which outlines the share of major exports in the value of exports to the socialist countries and to the world as a whole during 1967/8–1969/70 for each of the two regions of former Pakistan. The thirteen such West Pakistani exports accounted for about 93 per cent and 70 per cent respectively of West Pakistan's total exports to the socialist countries and to the world as a whole; that is, West Pakistan's exports to the socialist countries differed significantly from its exports to the rest of the world by the virtual absence of minor exports which consisted largely of 'miscellaneous manufactures' – a wide variety of manufactured goods that Pakistan began to export in the 1960s, exports of which to the world grew at annual rates of 20–25 per cent throughout the decade, accounting for a large part of West Pakistan's very respectable export performance during the 1960s.

In the first few years following the independence of Bangladesh, the value of Pakistan's exports increased quite sharply. Over the period 1969/70–1973/4 the dollar value of exports, in current prices, rose at an annual rate of 32 per cent. A large part of that growth in export earnings was attributable to rising unit prices of exports, which accounted for about 77 per cent of the increase in the value of exports during 1971/2 and 1972/3. While export value

TABLE 7.5 STRUCTURE OF PAKISTAN'S EXPORTS TO THE WORLD AS A WHOLE AND TO THE SOCIALIST COUNTRIES, 1960/61, 1964/65 AND 1969/70

	1960/61			1964/65			1969/70		
	Pak.	E. Pak.	W. Pak.	Pak.	E. Pak.	W. Pak.	Pak.	E. Pak.	W. Pak.
A. Number of commodities* providing 1 per cent or more of total exports to:									
World	8	4	8	13	2	11	12	4	18
Socialist countries	4	3	1	6	3	6	14	5	13
USSR	3	2	1	2	1	3	10	2	10
East Europe	1	4	1	6	2	10	12	5	12
China	3	3	1	5	2	3	4	2	3
B. Proportion of total exports accounted for by top three commodities* exported to:				(Percentages)					
World	66	92	53	54	89	42	47	91	27
Socialist countries	97	98	100	91	98	92	60	92	55
USSR	98	99	99	100	100	100	67	100	61
East Europe	99	95	99	68	100	85	50	89	51
China	98	99	100	95	100	99	97	100	99

Source: M. Kidron, op. cit., 94—95.
* Distinguished at the four-digit level of the Pakistan standard trade classification.

TABLE 7.6 EAST AND WEST PAKISTAN'S MAJOR EXPORTS:* SHARE IN TOTAL EXPORTS TO THE WORLD AND TO THE SOCIALIST COUNTRIES, 1967/68–1969/70

	Percentage of total exports to the world	Percentage of total exports to the socialist countries	Exports to socialist countries as percentage of exports to the world
A. East Pakistan			
Raw Jute	48.1	85.8	20.8
Jute fabrics	25.5	2.6	1.2
Bags & sacks of textile	16.9	5.0	3.4
Leather skins	2.3	3.0	15.2
Leather	1.5	0.8	6.6
Total	*94.3*	*97.2*	*12.0*
B. West Pakistan			
Raw cotton (except linters)	20.1	37.1	30.4
Cotton yarn, unbleached	9.4	3.8	6.7
Rice	8.0	9.0	18.4
Cotton cloth, unbleached	7.8	12.2	25.6
Cotton cloth, bleached	4.7	12.0	41.8
Cotton yarn, bleached	4.2	6.6	26.0
Leather, skins	4.0	3.2	13.3
Knotted carpets, rugs	2.5	0.8	5.1
Molluscs, crustacea	2.4		0.4
Raw wool	2.1	1.7	13.6
Calf leather	1.6	2.3	2.9
Footwear	1.6	3.9	39.5
Sporting goods	1.6	–	0.9
Total	*70.2*	*92.6*	*21.6*

Source: M. Kidron, op. cit., pp. 84, 89.

increased by about 40 per cent in each of these two years, the growth in export volume, at about 8 per cent per annum, was not inconsiderable, representing in part the fair amount of success that Pakistan had in diverting to the world market goods previously exported to the former East Pakistan. The export boom came to an abrupt end in 1974/75.

Exports to the socialist countries did not share in the export boom after 1970/71, in which year their dollar value increased by about 25 per cent, while their share in Pakistan's total exports reached a peak of 20·2 per cent. As Table 7.7 shows, after increasing by about 11 per cent in 1971/2, exports to the socialist countries declined sharply in 1972/3 and 1973/4. In the latter year, their value at $68 million was down to the level of 1969/70 and their share in total exports had fallen to 6·6 per cent. This was reversed in 1974/5 when, with total exports stagnating, the share of socialist countries rose to nearly 9 per cent.

The sharp decline in exports to the socialist countries in 1972/3 and 1973/4 was a result of deliberate policy to reduce barter exports, as Pakistan had accumulated a surplus of $63 million on barter trade by the end of 1971/2. These bilateral balances had been virtually eliminated by the end of 1973/4 and consequently the restraint on barter exports was eased at the beginning of 1974/5.

The share of bilateral or barter trade in trade with socialist countries rose from nothing in the early 1960s to 66 per cent in 1969/70 and to about 70 per cent in 1972/3, but declined to 51 per cent in 1974/5. The shift away from bilateralism in trade with socialist countries is likely to continue with the termination of bilateral payments arrangements with Hungary, Romania and Yugoslavia in 1975.[25] Throughout the era of barter trade, Pakistan had been unwilling to sell as much of its traditional foreign exchange earning raw materials as the socialist countries had been wanting to buy under barter agreements. This was particularly true for raw cotton and raw jute before December 1971, and raw cotton since. Another difficulty in matching supply and demand in barter exchanges has been the Eastern European desire to sell complete manufacturing plants under barter and Pakistan's preference to purchase them piecemeal, and under medium- or long-term credits.

Apart from the usual gains from trade, Pakistan has experienced an unusual gain in trading with socialist countries insofar as she has obtained higher prices on average for her exports to these countries compared with the rest of the world, while the prices of imports from the socialist countries were, on average, comparable with rest-of-the-world prices. Thus Kidron found that over the period 1960/61—1969/70 the weighted average of export prices obtained from socialist countries exceeded those obtained from other countries by 10·6 per cent.[26] Kidron did not find that the advantage of higher export prices was cancelled out by higher import prices, so that the terms of Pakistan's trade with the socialist bloc were substantially better than Pakistan's global terms of trade.[27]

On the other hand, there was possibly some loss to Pakistan on account of

TABLE 7.7 PAKISTAN'S TRADE WITH THE SOCIALIST COUNTRIES, 1969/70–1974/75* (US$ MILLIONS AND PERCENTAGES)

	1969/70 Value	1969/70 Share	1970/71 Value	1970/71 Share	1971/72 Value	1971/72 Share	1972/73 Value	1972/73 Share	1973/74 Value	1973/74 Share	1974/75 Value	1974/75 Share
A. Exports												
1. World	337.9	100.0	419.8	100.0	589.1	100.0	826.3	100.0	1026.4	100.0	1039.0	100.0
of which:												
2. Socialist countries (3 + 4 + 5)	67.4	20.0	84.9	20.2	94.7	16.0	78.2	9.5	67.9	6.6	91.9	8.8
of which:												
3. Eastern Europe	43.2	12.8	46.2	11.0	45.5	7.7	39.2	4.7	38.0	3.7	44.7	4.3
4. USSR	16.8	5.0	34.0	8.1	23.7	4.0	21.1	2.6	25.9	2.5	32.0	3.1
5. China	7.4	2.2	4.7	1.1	25.5	4.3	17.9	2.2	4.0	0.4	15.2	1.5
B. Imports												
1. World	690.1	100.0	756.8	100.0	611.1	100.0	811.4	100.0	1370.7	100.0	2113.6	100.0
of which:												
2. Socialist countries (3 + 4 + 5)	69.6	10.1	77.6	10.2	80.4	13.1	88.4	10.9	137.7	10.0	165.4	7.8
of which:												
3. Eastern Europe	43.0	6.3	45.6	6.0	48.4	7.9	37.6	4.7	61.7	4.5	70.0	3.3
4. USSR	16.0	2.3	20.4	2.7	14.7	2.4	15.8	1.9	18.3	1.3	41.4	2.0
5. China	10.6	1.5	11.6	1.5	17.3	2.8	35.0	4.3	57.7	4.2	54.0	2.6
C. Trade turnover												
1. World	1028.0	100.0	1176.6	100.0	1200.2	100.0	1637.7	100.0	2397.1	100.0	3152.6	100.0
2. Socialist countries	137.0	13.4	162.5	13.8	175.1	14.6	165.9	10.1	205.5	8.6	257.3	8.2

Source: Government of Pakistan, Finance Ministry, *Pakistan Economic Survey, 1973/74* and *1975/76* and CSO, *Foreign Trade Statistics* (June, 1974).

Note: Until 12 May 1972, the official exchange rate was Rs 4·76 = US$1. From 12 May 1972 to 15 February 1973, it was Rs 11·00 = US$1. Since 15 February 1973, the exchange rate has been Rs 9·9 = US$1. Rupee values were converted into dollar values at Rs 5·72 = $1 for 1971/72, Rs 10·35 = $1 for 1972/73 and Rs 9·9 = $1 for 1973/74 and 1974/75, which are the implicit exchange rates used in the *Pakistan Economic Survey.*

* Refers to the former West Pakistan till December 1971, and to the reduced Pakistan thereafter.

her exports to the socialist bloc being resold in third countries. Such reswitching does not appear to have occurred on a large scale, but was not insignificant in the 1960s and is accounted for entirely by Eastern European countries other than the USSR and Yugoslavia.[28] On barter exports, some loss from reswitching might arise because more widely usable convertible foreign currency is foregone in favour of narrowly usable bilateral claims on the trade partner in question. This loss may be compounded or offset by losses or gains in terms of trade. To assess whether Pakistan gained or lost on reswitched exports on this count, and if so, to what extent it is necessary to compare the terms of trade she obtained on those particular reswitched exports with those she could have obtained in the world market. Unavailability of data precludes such an assessment, though it can be assumed that such losses could not have been significant since Pakistan's overall terms of trade *vis-à-vis* the socialist countries as a group compare favourably with those *vis-à-vis* the rest of the world.

The impact of Pakistan's trade relations with the socialist countries on her structure or pattern of production does not appear to have been particularly noteworthy. In fact, the composition of Pakistan's exports to the socialist bloc indicates that trade with these countries did not particularly assist her in diversifying her production structure by finding markets for new and manufactured exports. Indeed, as noted above, the composition of Pakistan's exports to the socialist countries as compared with those to other countries was noticeably more biased towards traditional and primary exports.

Since the separation of Bangladesh, the relative importance of socialist countries in Pakistan's trade has diminished, particularly in the case of exports, with the socialist bloc taking about 9 per cent of Pakistan's exports in 1974/5, compared with about 20 per cent of West Pakistan's exports at the turn of the decade.[29] Further, an increasing proportion of Pakistan's trade with these countries has been taking place on a convertible currency basis and it appears that the decline in the relative importance of barter trade is likely to continue.

III. Aid

Socialist aid to Pakistan began in March 1961 with a $30 million loan from the USSR for oil and gas exploration. As with politics and trade, however, the turning point came in 1963–64, which marked the beginning of a systematic and significant aid relationship between Pakistan and the socialist countries. Apart from the above mentioned Soviet loan of $30 million, the whole of the $126 million of aid commitments by the socialist countries during the Second Plan period (1960–65) were made from 1963 onwards. As Table 7.8 shows, socialist aid increased quite dramatically during the Third Five-Year Plan, when loans and grants from five socialist countries amounted to $444 million, or nearly 15 per cent of all foreign loans and grants received by Pakistan. The two Chinese grants of $60 million and $47·5 million were originally loans which were transformed into grants in early 1972.

Table 7.8 reveals the USSR and China have been the principle socialist aid donors, together accounting for about 85 per cent of all socialist aid. The USSR, with $381 million worth of aid commitments till the end of 1973/4, has been the largest socialist donor. About $300 million of Soviet aid is accounted for by two major projects. The Oil and Gas Development Corporation has received more than $50 million worth of Soviet equipment and technical assistance for oil and gas exploration. The Corporation was established in 1961 with Soviet assistance and the total expenditure that it had incurred till June 1974 amounted to Rs 606 million, of which the USSR contributed Rs 271 million.[30]

The biggest Soviet commitment was made in 1973 and as yet remains largely undisbursed. This is a loan of approximately $250 million for a steel mill to be located near Karachi. Construction of the mill commenced recently and it is expected to go into production by 1978/9, reaching its full capacity of 2 million tons by 1980/1. The total cost of the project was originally estimated at Rs 9360 million ($945 million), but this has since been revised upwards quite substantially, and Pakistan is seeking additional Soviet finance for the project.

Until mid-1974, four Eastern European countries — Yugoslavia, Czechoslovakia, Poland and Romania — had together committed $128·8 million or about 15 per cent of total socialist aid commitments. Somewhat more than half of that amount was accounted for by Yugoslavia. All Czech and Polish aid came during the Third Plan quinquennium (1965—70). Romanian aid consists of a $13·1 million export credit, committed in 1973/4. Indeed, export credits have been almost the exclusive form of Eastern European lending to Pakistan. Moreover, the terms of Eastern European and Soviet loans and credits have been much the same, with interest rates ranging from 2·5 to 3 per cent, and amortisation periods varying from 10 to 12 years.

Chinese aid, however, has been provided on much softer and uniform terms. Loans are interest-free and repayable over forty years. The $60 million and $47·5 million Chinese contributions to Pakistan's Second and Third Plans, respectively, were converted into grants in early 1972 when Pakistan was facing considerable debt-servicing difficulties and was about to embark on debt-relief negotiations with members of the Aid-to-Pakistan Consortium. In early 1970 the Chinese committed $220 million within the framework of the Fourth Pakistan Plan.[31] Chinese economic aid is intended largely to finance machinery imports from China.

The USSR and Eastern European countries also provided substantial debt relief in 1972. All the relevant agreements with these countries relieve Pakistan of the debt liability in respect of credits obtained from these countries and utilised in the former East Pakistan. Debt worth $49 million was written off.

The USSR and Eastern European countries have shown a marked preference for medium-term project aid to industry. The latter, particularly Yugoslavia, have not been entirely averse to providing assistance for private sector projects.

TABLE 7.8 SOCIALIST AID TO PAKISTAN* (COMMITMENTS IN US$ MILLIONS)

	Pre-2nd Plan 1947–60	2nd Plan 1960–65	3rd Plan 1965–70	Post-3rd Plan 1970–74	Total 1960–74
A. Loans and credits					
1. China	—	—	220·0	—	220·0
2. Czechoslovakia	—	—	40·1	—	40·1
3. Poland	—	—	9·8	—	9·8
4. Romania	—	—	—	13·1	13·1
5. USSR	—	36·9	93·0	251·2	381·1
6. Yugoslavia	—	29·1	33·7	3·1	65·8
7. Sub-total (1 to 6)	—	66·0	396·6	267·4	729·9
8. Total loans and credits from all sources	640·7	2042·8	2677·7	2409·9	7771·1
9. Socialist countries as percentage of total	—	3·2	14·8	11·1	9·4
B. Grants					
10. China	—	60·0	47·5	2·9†	110·4‡
11. Total grants from all sources	741·1	1572·1	355·7	97·3†	2766·2‡
12. Socialist countries as percentage of total	—	3·8	13·4	3·0†	4·0‡

Source: Government of Pakistan, Finance Ministry, *Pakistan Economic Survey, 1973/4*, Statistical Appendix.
Notes: Years refer to fiscal years.
*Refers to East and West Pakistan until December 1971; and to former West Pakistan only thereafter.
†1970–73.
‡1960–73.

Chinese assistance has been about equally divided between commodity and project aid and, like Soviet aid, has been directed exclusively at the public sector.[32]

The expansion of socialist aid and trade links with Pakistan from 1963 onwards was, of course, interrelated; export credits financed about two-fifths of Pakistan's imports from the socialist countries at the end of the 1960s. The root of these trade and aid relationships was, as it always is, political; in Pakistan's case, perhaps, more visibly so than it usually is. And notwithstanding the analogy drawn in the opening paragraph of this essay between flag and trade on the one hand, and chicken and egg on the other, there can be little doubt that for the case at hand, the political flag came first and the economic links, through trade and aid, later.

Notes

[1] Pakistan includes Bangladesh before 1971 and excludes it after that. Suitable qualifications are made to the term as and when necessary.

[2] The term 'socialist country' refers to a country which claims to be either socialist, or in the process of becoming socialist, in the strict Marxist sense. Apart from that claim, such countries are distinguished by much greater state ownership of the means of production. Since the predominance of state ownership is not a sufficient condition for socialism, the extent to which some of these countries are, in fact, socialist is a disputed question, which the author wishes to ignore for the purposes of this essay.

[3] This agreement, however, was not ratified.

[4] Cf. S. M. Burke, *Pakistan's Foreign Policy: An Historical Analysis* (London: Oxford University Press, 1973) pp. 100–1.

[5] Speech made at a luncheon meeting of the National Press Club in Washington. Quoted, in ibid., p. 102.

[6] Pakistan was the only member of the sterling area which did not devalue along with the pound sterling in September 1949.

[7] Quoted in Mushtaq Ahmed, *The United Nations and Pakistan* (Pakistan Institute of International Affairs, 1955) p. 85.

[8] See Section II. Foreign trade statistics of the period are not easy to handle. There are no data on trade with India until April 1948. From April 1948 to July 1949 foreign trade statistics include seaborne but not landborne trade with India, which is a significant limitation. Pakistan's exports to the USSR, Czechoslovakia and China accounted for 14·6 per cent in 1947/48 (August to March), 10·9 per cent in 1948/49 and 9·0 per cent in 1949/50 of Pakistan's recorded seaborne exports. The data refer to the former Pakistani fiscal year which ran from 1 April to 31 March.

[9] Commitments of US non-military grants and loans during 1955–60 (the first plan period) totalled $792 million, the cumulative total up to 1955 was $169 million. (See Government of Pakistan, *Pakistan Economic Survey 1973/74*, Statistical Appendix, pp. 89–90.)

[10] Cf. Burke, op. cit., pp. 211–212. According to Burke these Soviet aid offers were not taken up by Pakistan.

[11] Gary Powers had taken off in his ill-fated U-2 from the American Communications base near Peshawar in May 1960.

[12] The then foreign minister, Manzur Qadir, is quoted in ibid., p. 216.

[13] The day after the signing of the air agreement, the US State Department announced the suspension of a $4·3 million loan to Pakistan for the improvement of Dacca airport. A few weeks earlier the meeting of the Aid-to-Pakistan Consortium had been postponed. Pakistan–US relations probably reached their nadir.

[14] Quoted in R. A. Yellon, 'Shifts in Soviet policy towards developing areas 1964–1968', in W. R. Duncan (ed.), *Soviet Policy in Developing Countries* (Waltham, Mass., 1970) p. 266.

[15] Quoted in ibid., p. 266.

[16] In April 1968 Pakistan informed the US that the lease on the American Communications base near Peshawar would not be renewed upon its expiry in July 1968. Later in April, Kosygin visited Pakistan. In July 1968 a Pakistan military delegation visited the USSR and obtained Soviet agreement to supply arms to Pakistan. See S. M. Burke, op. cit., pp. 364–5.

[17] See section III below and Khalida Qureshi, 'Pakistan and the USSR', *Pakistan Horizon,* Vol. XXVII, No. 1 (First Quarter, 1974). Qureshi argues that this Soviet gesture strengthened Pakistan's hand in the debt relief negotiations with other creditors.

[18] This is a rough estimate. As noted earlier, foreign trade statistics for the late 1940s are incomplete and of poor quality. There are no data on trade with India for the period 15 August 1947 to 31 March 1948. From April 1948 to July 1949 trade statistics include seaborne but not the substantial landborne trade with India. During 1948/9 (March–April) India's share in Pakistan's seaborne trade was 25 per cent for exports and 41 per cent for imports. It should be noted that almost all raw jute exports to India were landborne. See Walter Godfrey, *Pakistan,* Board of Trade, Overseas Economic Surveys (London: HMSO, 1951).

[19] In the period 15 August 1947 to 31 March 1948 exports to the USSR amounted to Rs 40 million, and to Czechoslovakia Rs 3 million. During April–March of 1948/9 and 1949/50 Pakistan's exports to the USSR amounted to Rs 44 million and Rs 45 million, or 5·2 per cent and 5·8 per cent respectively, of Pakistan's total *seaborne* exports. Exports to Czechoslovakia represented 1·9 per cent of total *seaborne* exports in 1948/9 and 1·7 per cent in 1949/50. See Walter Godfrey, op. cit., pp. 7–11.

[20] 1951/2 and 1953/4 are Pakistani fiscal years which run from July to June. Unless otherwise indicated, all such references are to the Pakistani fiscal year.

[21] For details of the trade triangle, East Pakistan–West Pakistan–World, see Government of Pakistan, Planning Commission, *Report of The Panel of Economists on the Fourth Five Year Plan* (Islamabad, May 1970).

[22] Michael Kidron, op. cit., p. 25.

[23] And was replaced by a small deficit. The cumulative Pakistani trade deficit with the socialist countries (including Yugoslavia) over 1964/65–1969/70 amounted to Rs 237·9 million. The ratio of imports to exports rose from 0·92 in 1964/5–1966/7 (this over-all trade surplus with socialist countries was largely attributable to China) to 1·22 in 1968/69–1969/70.

[24] Calculated from CSO, *25 Years of Pakistan Statistics,* op. cit.

[25] Pakistan continues to maintain bilateral payments arrangements with Bulgaria, China, Czechoslovakia, Poland and the USSR.

[26] M. Kidron, op. cit., ch. 4.

[27] 'All in all and despite much evidence to the contrary, the [socialist countries'] machinery prices do seem cheaper than world prices for comparable items, cheaper than might be justified by differences in quality or in servicing . . . The same does not seem to be true of imported raw materials.' (ibid., p. 53.)

[28] Kidron, *op. cit.,* pp. 25–7.

[29] The principal change in the direction of Pakistan's exports during the 1970s has been towards the Middle East and the Far East (particularly Hong Kong).

[30] The Corporation has so far succeeded in finding three natural gas fields with estimated reserves of 0·131 million mill. cubic feet and an oil field (Tut) with estimated reserves of 30·8 million barrels.

[31] The civil war of 1971 and its aftermath led to the abandonment of the Fourth Five-year Plan.

[32] Cf. I. Brecher and S. A. Abbas, *Foreign Aid and Industrial Development in Pakistan* (Cambridge University Press: 1972) pp. 80–1.

8 Soviet Oil and the Third World

BIPLAB DASGUPTA

I. Introduction

Whenever we talk about oil we usually think of the Middle East. This is only natural; the Middle East accounts for a third of the world's crude oil production, and for three-fifths of world oil exports, in addition to owning more than half of the world's proved oil resources.[1] But the Middle East is not a country, it is a region containing a group of countries. If we take individual countries into account, the United States and the Soviet Union emerge as the two largest oil-producing nations of the world.[2] Ever since the birth of the modern petroleum industry in the 1850s these two countries have almost always been at the top of the league of the oil-producing countries.[3] What differentiates them is their high rate of self-consumption (unlike the Middle East which despite its enormous oil wealth consumes only 3 per cent of world oil production), which leaves no exportable surplus – in fact, a growing deficit in the case of the United States, and a comparatively small surplus in the case of the USSR. Hence, their impact on *trade* in oil is much less than proportionate to their production.

Similarities between these two economies do not end here. Both countries make significant gains in foreign exchange by selling oil. In the case of the USSR, oil exports are the most important source of its hard currency earnings; while the USA, although a net importer of oil as a country, earns enough through profit-remittances of US-based multinational companies, arising from their foreign operations, to more than compensate for the oil import bill.[4] Because of the importance of oil, both as a source of energy and as a strategic material for military purposes, both of these countries have assigned a high priority to this commodity in their respective foreign policies, particularly in relation to the Middle East. As the history of the oil industry shows, their decisions with respect to oil have always been motivated by a mixture of political and economic factors.[5]

Differences in the foreign oil policies of the USA and USSR arise from differences in the structure of their oil economies. The US government is closely identified with the US-based multinational oil companies, particularly the five top ones – Standard Oil of New Jersey (Exxon), Gulf Oil, Texas Oil,

185

TABLE 8.1. WORLD ESTIMATED CRUDE OIL PRODUCTION
(IN THOUSAND TONNES)

	1972	1973	1974
USA	528,454	514,297	494,850
Canada	86,485	100,117	97,000
North America	*614,939*	*614,414*	*591,850*
Venezuela	168,232	175,388	156,000
Caribbean Area	*185,612*	*193,466*	*173,700*
Latin America	*63,846*	*70,705*	*73,550*
Saudi Arabia	285,583	364,685	412,000
Iran	252,339	293,908	301,000
Kuwait	151,097	138,255	112,000
Iraq	72,350	99,371	95,000
Abu Dhabi	50,424	62,525	68,000
Neutral Zone	30,497	27,415	28,000
Qatar	23,262	27,495	24,700
Middle East	*915,941*	*1,065,396*	*1,094,240*
Nigeria	89,784	101,306	112,000
Libya	105,751	104,586	77,000
Algeria	50,085	51,154	49,000
Africa	*263,290*	*278,687*	*263,500*
Western Europe	*15,743*	*15,507*	*16,010*
Indonesia	53,730	66,407	71,500
Far East	*92,272*	*109,852*	*112,300*
USSR	400,440	427,250	457,000
Rumania	14,128	14,200	14,200
China	30,000	50,000	65,000
Communist bloc	*452,631*	*499,822*	*545,110*
World	*2,604,274*	*2,847,849*	*2,870,260*

Source: *Petroleum Economist* (January 1975).

Socony Mobil Oil, Standard Oil of California — which, together with British
Petroleum (British-owned) and Royal Dutch Shell (British-Dutch in registra-
tion, but with a high percentage of its equity now in the hands of US companies), are collectively known as the 'seven sisters' or 'majors' in the oil
industry[6] and which, even in 1973, accounted for half of the world's crude
production.[7] These five mammoth organisations, which vertically integrate
all types of activities in the oil sector, from oil exploration through refining
and transport to marketing, within one corporate framework, operate
through literally hundreds of affiliates and subsidiaries all over the world.
They maintain close relationships with one another in matters of pricing
or production, ranking among the largest ten corporate entities in the United
States. Moreover, their activities are not confined to the oil sector alone: these

majors account for 30 per cent of coal resources and 50 per cent of uranium reserves in the United States; in addition they promote ventures for producing oil from non-conventional sources such as shale rocks or tar sands. Given their importance in the US economy and their 'multinational' character, conflicts between them and the governments of foreign countries almost always involve the foreign office of the US government — for example, the negotiations for the participation of US companies in the Middle Eastern operations during the twenties,[8] or the decision to suspend US aid to Ceylon following nationalisation of US world oil marketing companies in that country in 1963.[9] On their part, the major US companies have always been vocal in their support for US foreign policy.[10]

In contrast, the oil industry in the USSR is owned by the government. Its public enterprises do not operate through subsidiaries and affiliates in the foreign countries. Although at one time the Western governments feared that the USSR would attempt to set up marketing networks in the oil-consuming countries in order to compete with the 'majors',[11] such fear has been proved to be without foundation. The Soviet Union prefers either to trade directly with other governments, or it relies on the already existing marketing organisations for distributing oil. In exchange for its participation in the

TABLE 8.2. CRUDE OIL PRODUCTION IN
THE USA, THE USSR AND THE WORLD,
1861—1950
(IN MILLION TONNES)

Year	World	USA	USSR
1861	0·3	0·3	negligible
1884	5·0	3·3	1·5
1890	10·5	6·2	3·9
1897	16·8	8·2	7·5
1898	17·2	7·5	8·5
1899	18·0	7·7	9·1
1900	20·5	8·6	10·4
1901	23·0	9·4	11·7
1902	25·0	12·0	11·1
1903	26·8	13·6	10·4
1904	30·0	15·8	10·8
1905	29·6	18·2	7·6
1914	56·1	35·9	9·2
1920	94·8	59·8	3·5
1926	151·0	104·2	8·9
1930	194·1	121·3	17·5
1940	295·2	182·8	30·7
1950	522·8	270·0	37·6

Source: Henrich Hassman, *Oil in the Soviet Union* (Princeton, 1953).

oil industry, the Soviet Union does not ask for equity ownership, nor even part ownership; whereas the 'majors', until very recently, demanded a share in the equity ownership as a precondition for their participation. For this reason, many of the oil-consuming countries, particularly the poor ones, whatever their political or ideological affiliations, are eager to establish relations with the USSR for buying oil, for establishing refineries, or for prospecting. They are not afraid of Soviet involvement in their economy, since such involvement is specific to a particular project or agreement, and is not of a continuing nature. The Soviet agreements with Turkey, Pakistan, Ceylon or Ethiopia are obvious examples.

The emergence of the Soviet Union as an important source of oil has provided the oil-consuming countries with the option of bypassing the multinationals. While, as a percentage of total Soviet oil exports, the amount going to less developed countries is small (see Table 7.3), its impact on their economy and trade relations has been no less significant.

The primary aim of this essay is to examine the impact of Soviet oil on the economies of the Third World countries. But some of the important oil-consuming developed countries of the world, such as Japan and Italy, which played an important role in promoting Soviet exports, will also be considered in our analysis.

II. The Soviet Oil Industry

Oil was discovered in the present-day Soviet Union in 1860, but it was not until the 1880s, when the Baku oil fields were developed, that production became significant.[12] Towards the end of the nineteenth century the Soviet Union became the leading producer, accounting for half the total world supply of crude oil (Table 8.2); but its supremacy was short-lived. In 1904 production in the Baku oil fields was hampered by a prolonged strike, followed by riots and revolutionary activities; and by 1906 production from this oil field had virtually stopped. Recovery began in 1909, and the production figures reached the 1899 level of 9 million tonnes in 1914, but the conflicts following the Communist revolution of 1917 again hampered production for several years, bringing it down to 3–4 million tonnes during 1918–21. From the late twenties until the beginning of the Second World War production grew rapidly; but again, between 1943 and 1947, production declined. Over the forties, production grew from 30·7 million tonnes to 37·6 million tonnes, less than 7 million tonnes in ten years.

This brief history of the Soviet oil industry shows that it was plagued by frequent interruptions in production until the end of the Second World War. But these were due to causes which originated outside the oil industry. Soviet oil reserves were always known to be large, larger than the reserves in the United States. The most recent estimates of world proved reserves show the Soviet Union ahead of any region outside the Middle East and

TABLE 8.3. USSR OIL IMPORTS AND EXPORTS, 1971–73
(IN THOUSAND TONNES)

Exports to:	1971	1972	1973
Finland	8,567	8,627	10,028
Italy	9,002	8,430	8,652
West Germany	6,092	6,195	5,849
France	4,539	3,078	5,348
Netherlands	1,631	2,433	3,220
Sweden	4,569	4,363	3,215
Japan	3,284	1,011	2,022
Belgium	2,038	2,516	1,673
Austria	1,128	967	1,250
Morocco	868	934	943
UK	–	267	834
Greece	1,011	909	797
Switzerland	805	822	658
Denmark	861	772	633
Ghana	598	625	614
Norway	628	447	603
Spain	214	784	509
India	473	378	477
Iceland	379	439	468
Egypt	1,604	1,442	352
Others	1,392	1,361	2,414
Non-communist countries	49,683	46,800	50,559
Communist countries	55,417	60,200	67,741
Total	*105,100*	*107,000*	*118,300*
of which:			
Total crude	74,800	76,200	85,300
Total products	30,300	30,800	33,000
Imports			
Total	*6,600*	*9,100*	*14,700*
of which:			
Total crude	5,100	7,800	13,200
Total products	1,500	1,300	1,500
Net exports	*98,500*	*97,900*	*103,600*

Source: *Petroleum Economist* (August 1974).

North Africa, containing about double the proved reserves in the United States.[13] The current production figure is 457 million tonnes (Table 8.1), the expected production figure in 1980 being 800 million tonnes.[14]

The main obstacle to the oil production in the Soviet Union is the vast size of the country and the geographical spread of its oil fields. Many of its oil fields, particularly the new discoveries, are located in less accessible regions of Western Siberia where production is costly and time-consuming, and the cost of transport is a major component in the ultimate consumers' price in the developed western part of the country. The influence of the economies of transport on Soviet production is best seen from figures of imports of both oil (from Iraq and other countries in the Middle East)[15] and gas (from Afghanistan and Iran)[16] in order to correct regional imbalances and to avoid heavy costs of transporting Soviet oil and gas to the relevant consuming areas.[17] Recent talks about borrowing technology from Japan and USA to develop Siberian oil and gas fields at lower cost is another indication of the problems facing the USSR oil industry.[18]

III. Ownership and Trading Patterns until the Mid-fifties

In the early part of the history of the Russian oil industry, the leaders were Rothschild, famous Paris bankers, and the Nobel group from Sweden. A group of English firms, owned by W. N. Gladstone (son of a former British Prime Minister) and Alfred Stuart also came to own a large part of the Russian crude during the last part of the nineteenth century. Besides these three groups there were a larger number of Russian entrepreneurs, such as Mentascheff and Lianosov, who together in 1912 formed the Russian General Oil Corporation (RGOC). Before the revolution of 1917, the Nobel group came to hold the majority of shares in the RGOC, and Rothschilds sold their share to Royal Dutch Shell.[19]

After the revolution, the new government nationalised the oil industry by a decree in June 1918, but by September of that year the Baku oil fields were taken over, first by the Turks and then by the British, and the latter handed them back to the oil companies again. Both Standard Oil of New Jersey and Royal Dutch Shell at that time purchased shares in the Nobel group and TGOC, respectively, in the expectation that the Soviet regime would soon collapse. However, the Baku oil field was run over by Soviet forces again in May 1920, and the companies were nationalised for the second time.[20]

Soon afterwards, in 1922, the foreign oil companies formed a united front for pressurising the USSR for the return of oil properties, and, as an alternative, for compensation. But the unity was short-lived: while negotiations were going on, many international oil companies, including both Shell and Standard Oil of New Jersey, were trading in oil with the Soviet Union. But, by 1926, it had become clear that the negotiation for compensation was not going to succeed. Royal Dutch immediately stopped purchasing Soviet oil, but Standard Oil of New Jersey concluded a three-year agreement with the Soviet Union for selling Soviet oil. Royal Dutch Shell considered the agreement to be 'immoral' and the oil to be sold by the former as 'stolen oil', and began a price war when the first consignment of Soviet oil landed in Bombay in 1927.[21] The global price war that followed continued for about nine months, involving almost all the major companies and markets and jeopardised the interests of all the oil companies. This was the background against which the first steps towards cartel control of the world markets were taken in 1928 by the oil companies.[22] The 1928 agreement, popularly known as the 'as is' agreement, was followed by a number of others during the 1930s for establishing a common policy of pricing, market-sharing and calculating shipping costs by oil monopolies. Any company violating the agreements was liable to pay fines.[23]

However, not all the oil producers of the world were under the control or ownership of the majors. Romanian production, though small, was difficult to control because the producing companies numbered more than thirty and had diverse, often conflicting, interests; and Soviet oil was mainly under government ownership. One of the objectives of the various agreements among the companies was to bring the distribution of Soviet oil under their control; and, in fact, during that period, most of it was channelled through the major oil companies.[24] But a part of it was sold to smaller companies ('independents') outside the international cartel, who would sell it in consumption centres at prices lower than those charged by international majors. To the extent that they undercut the majors, they posed a serious threat to the 'world-parity' price structure, and the majors reacted against this competition by selling oil almost at 'give away' prices in the centres where the Soviet imports arrived. The independents had no marketing network to compare with that of the established companies; the supply of Soviet oil was irregular; and their financial resources were not big enough to stand up to a price war with the majors. Most of the independents were eventually swallowed up by the majors.[25]

Soviet exports increased from a meagre 0·1 million tonnes in 1921/22 to 1·3 million tonnes in 1924/25, 2·8 million tonnes in 1927/28 and 6 million tonnes in 1932. Oil exports reached Italy, France, Germany, England, Belgium, Spain, Sweden, and Denmark. It earned more foreign currency than any other item, except timber, and enabled the USSR to buy machinery from the West.[26] The Soviet Union accounted for 14 per cent of the oil imported by European countries. But, with the increase in domestic Soviet consumption, the pace of exports slackened. These declined to less than 5 million tonnes in 1933 and to less than 1 million tonnes in 1938. Rapid industrialisation of the economy and the growth of motor transport were important factors behind this decline, as also was the need for military preparations with the rise of fascism in Germany. By the end of the thirties Soviet oil had disappeared from the world market. During the war years the Soviet Union became a net importer of oil, and it was not until 1955 that it emerged again as a net exporter of oil.[27]

IV. The Soviet Oil Export Offensive

The period after 1955 witnessed a rapid increase in Soviet crude oil production and was accompanied by an even more rapid increase in exports. Whereas, in 1950, the USSR exported only 3 per cent of its production, in 1955 the figure was 11·3 per cent, and by 1959, had reached 19·6 per cent.[28] Most of the exports in this period were concentrated in Eastern Europe, but also included some other countries (for example, Israel, until the 1956 Middle East war). But net exports amounted to only 3·6 million tonnes in 1955, and 4·8 million tonnes in 1956. Within three years, however, gross exports had jumped to 25·4 million tonnes (21 million tonnes net of imports), and in 1960 the figure had risen to 30 million tonnes.[29] Japan was one of the earliest buyers. In 1959, the Soviet Union entered into an agreement with Japan to supply 7·5 million barrels a year during 1960—2; and Idemitsu Kosan, an independent refiner which bought about 30,000 tonnes in 1955, decided to buy 6 million tonnes in 1961.[30]

There were several explanations for the rapid growth in Soviet exports during 1959 and 1960. The main explanation was that Soviet oil was cheaper, the price being between 10 and 25 per cent less than the Persian Gulf oil prices, while ocean freight was calculated from either the Black Sea or the Persian Gulf, according to which was nearer the consumption centre.[31] Moreover, payment could be made in local currency or with non-oil commodities. Egypt paid for oil with cotton, Cuba with sugar, Greece with tobacco, Israel with citrus fruit and Italy with steel pipes.[32] Soviet oil trade usually formed a part of a big package deal involving other non-oil commodities as well as both crude oil and oil products; and the prices of the individual components of the packages were not specified.

This sudden growth in Soviet exports immediately brought the USSR into open conflict with the established major international oil companies. The latter were worried on many counts. The low Soviet prices disrupted the standardised world-parity pricing system they had maintained for so long. Soviet supplies made serious inroads into markets which were traditionally supplied by the majors, and the presence of Soviet oil tempted even many anti-communist governments to buy oil from this new source in order to reduce their dependence on the major oil companies. Moreover, unlike the latter, the Soviet Union was prepared to help in the construction of oil refineries, or in prospecting for oil, without asking for equity ownership. The Soviet Union also encouraged the setting up of public sector marketing companies in various oil consuming countries which displaced the marketing affiliates of majors.

One major cause of conflict was the attempt by governments of various countries — particularly India and Cuba — to induce the oil refineries owned by major oil companies to process cheaper Soviet crude in place of crude supplied by their own parent companies. In early 1960 the Indian government concluded an agreement to buy 3·5 million tonnes of crude oil from the USSR at a reported discount of 20—25 per cent on the price of Gulf crude oil of the same quality. Since the government had no refinery of its own, it asked the three refineries owned by the major international companies to process it. The latter at first undertook to examine the crude, but then refused to refine it on the ground that they had had longstanding agreements with their suppliers of crude, which could not be easily set aside. This, however, was not a true position, since the suppliers of crude were no different from the majors themselves. Their opposition to Soviet crude was based on commercial grounds: their reluctance to sacrifice an outlet for their Middle East crude in India, and their long-standing fear of Soviet competition in the world market.[33]

These companies took a similar stand against Soviet crude also in Cuba and Finland, in order to retain their grip on world oil supply. The politics of the cold war also played its role, as could be seen from various statements made by business or political interests on this issue. However, different governments responded differently to the situation. The government of Finland managed to persuade the companies to refine Soviet oil, the Cuban government nationalised the oil refineries, while the Indian government capitulated and broke off the agreement with the USSR. But even in the last case the major oil companies were quick to realise the need for making some adjustments in view of Soviet competition and allowed a discount of 15 US cents per barrel.[34]

Another major area of conflict was the marketing of oil products. In 1960, the Ceylon government concluded a deal with the USSR for buying 1·25 million tonnes of oil products at a price 25 per cent below the world parity level, and asked the major oil companies which owned the oil distributing organisations to sell it. When they refused, in 1962, the government of Ceylon responded by taking over 175 oil distribution pumps, and putting them under a newly created state-owned company, the Ceylon Petroleum Corporation.[35] This prompted the US government to take the side of the oil companies and suspend economic aid until suitable compensation was offered to the latter.[36] In India also the Soviet Union and Romania became the chief suppliers of imported kerosene and diesel, which were sold through the state-owned Indian oil company formed in 1959.[37] In 1965 import trade in oil products was declared to be the monopoly of the Indian Oil Corporation (IOC), the state-owned company, which became the largest distributing company in the country towards the end of the sixties. Here again, the major companies did not give up without a fight. As soon as the first consignment of Soviet diesel oil reached Bombay in 1961, the major oil companies offered diesel at prices even lower than those quoted by IOC for its Soviet products. As a consequence, a large part of IOC's supply remained unsold for a period of time, which also created storage problems, and forced IOC to sell its products at an even lower price. However, the objectives of this price war were limited to pressuring the government and it did not last long.[38] The availability of Soviet oil products also encouraged the government to prescribe ceilings on oil product prices at levels below those given by the world-parity pricing formula.[39] Among others, Soviet oil products were sold to Algeria, Morocco, Ghana, Guinea and Turkey.

Soviet oil was also sold to independent refining companies. In Italy, ENI, the state-owned oil company, reached an agreement with the USSR in 1960 to import 30 million barrels of oil a year for five years,[40] which it used effectively in its campaign against the major international companies for reduced oil product prices and a greater share of the oil market.

In Japan, independent refining firms like Idemitsu Kosan or Daikyo used Soviet oil in the same way; to reduce costs and prices of oil products in competition with the majors. Many of the Japanese refineries were jointly owned by the majors with the independent national companies; the latter now put pressure on the majors (with the support of the government) to reduce the price of crude oil imported from the Middle East.[41]

In some of the Latin American countries — notably Brazil, Mexico, Argentine, and Uruguay — the practice has been for the state-owned oil refineries to invite tenders for supplying crude. Now the Soviet Union had also become a big competitor in supplying crude, although (except for two state-owned companies, Petrobras of Brazil and YPF of Argentina in 1958–9)[42] the Latin American governments were usually reluctant to buy from the Soviet Union.

As an official report by the US Senate stated, 'US political influence has been a restraining factor in a number of countries in Latin America.'[43] But the inevitable result of Soviet competition was a reduction in the price quoted by the major international firms to those markets; sometimes they quoted prices which were lower than the offer from the USSR.[44]

The Soviet Union was also prepared to build refineries in poor oil-consuming countries. From the point of view of the oil-importing countries, the establishment of a domestic refining industry ensures regularity of oil supplies, makes them less dependent on the powerful international oil companies, makes a significant contribution to the industrial development of the country, and also saves a substantial amount of foreign exchange. The saving on foreign exchange is equivalent to the difference in the import prices of oil products and crude oil (*net* of the foreign exchange costs specific to the operation of the refinery). The major international companies are not usually interested in building refineries of less than a certain size; they are interested in fewer and larger refineries, subject to the relative costs of transportation of crude oil and products. Moreover, they have little to gain from building refineries which would be owned by the government and which would replace oil products supplied from their own refineries. In contrast, the Soviet Union, which did not possess any marketing or refining establishments in those countries, had no difficulty in agreeing to the construction of oil refineries in oil-consuming countries. These refineries were operating outside the control of the large international firms, they were not tied to particular sources of crude oil, and hence were able to buy crude from non-major sources including the Soviet Union. Refineries were built and offered by the Soviet Union in countries as diverse as India,[45] Turkey[46] and Ethiopia.[47]

Finally, the Soviet Union also emerged as an alternative source of supply of technology for oil exploration. In 1961, it entered into an agreement with Pakistan to conduct a detailed survey of oil prospects and to cover the costs with a credit of $35 million payable over 17 years. Unlike the major oil companies, it did not ask for any share in the oil or gas to be found as a result of its activities. This agreement came about at a time when the Western oil companies were closing down their exploratory work in that country.[48] In India a body of Soviet experts visited the country in 1965, prepared a six-year plan for oil development, recommended the formation of a state-owned Oil and Natural Gas Commission (ONGC), and helped the latter after its formation to find some of the richest oil deposits in the country (in Gujarat in the early sixties).[49] This success in Gujarat followed the withdrawal of Standard-Vacuum (jointly owned by two US majors) from oil exploration in India in 1960. The major oil companies, who already owned vast oil refineries in the Middle East, were not keen to explore for oil in areas where the probability of finding oil was not high, and where new discoveries would only have the effect of replacing crude oil supplies from the Middle East.[50]

The Soviet Union was not alone in challenging the hegemony of the major international oil companies over the oil market during the late fifties and early sixties. Their activities coincided with the discovery of a number of new oil fields by several smaller companies ('minors') which were not organisationally linked with the majors. Notable among these were ENI, the state-owned company of Italy; Philips, Continental, Standard Oil of Indiana and Occidental, US independents and Arabian Oil, a Japanese company. These companies discovered oil in various parts of the Middle East, particular in the neutral zone (between Saudi Arabia and Kuwait) and Libya. Since these companies did not possess elaborate marketing facilities they were willing to sell crude oil and products at lower than world-parity prices. Like the Soviet Union they were willing to build refineries in various countries if that assured them an outlet for crude oil for a long period. The discovery of big oil deposits in Algeria, Nigeria, Libya and Abu Dhabi in the late fifties also raised the expectation that prices would fall. These factors, the Soviet intervention, and the entry of several newcomers at a time when the supply of oil to the world market was plentiful, helped to transform conditions in the oil market from being under the virtually exclusive control of a small group of large oligopolistic firms towards more openness and competition.

V. The Impact of the Soviet Oil 'Offensive'

We are now in a position to summarise the major consequences of the Soviet oil 'offensive'.

First of all, it undermined the world-parity pricing system. The latter was a 'basing point' system with the Persian Gulf or the Gulf of Mexico as the base. Under this system, the price at a given consumption point

equalled the fob price at base ('posted price') *plus* the transport cost
from the base to the consumption point, no matter where the oil actually
came from.[51] But now this price structure crumbled. Discounts of up to
25 per cent off parity prices were available from the Soviet Union or the
independents, and even the major oil conpanies were forced to reduce prices.
'Only fools and affiliates pay posted prices' became the joke in the oil industry;
but soon it became difficult even for the affiliates to stick to posted prices.

Secondly, it made the oil consumers more knowledgeable about the intri-
cacies of the oil industry. Before the Soviet intervention, knowledge about
the affairs of the oil industry was highly imperfect. The major oil companies
knew everything, but were unwilling to part with their knowledge. Although
it would seem improbable today, even the basic information about the way
the world-parity pricing formula worked or about the vertically integrated
nature of the major oil firms was not known or understood by the majority
of oil-consuming countries. For example, in India, for a long time the oil
refineries owned by the major companies concealed the fact that they received
their crude supplies from their own affiliates in the Middle East, and preten-
ded the existence of a long-term contract with crude suppliers at the 'posted'
price which could not be rescinded.[52] The major oil companies were either
unwilling to prospect for oil, or to provide data on such work to governments;
and even when such data were provided their authenticity was often subject
to doubt. They were not interested in training local personnel, or to put them
in responsible positions (except for some symbolic appointments); and the
knowledge gap which existed between them and the local government could
not be bridged as long as the former retained their dominant position in the
world market. If any oil-consuming country wanted to examine the technical
and economic consequences of building a refinery or of undertaking oil
exploration, they were forced to be guided by the advice of the major oil
companies; and there was no way of verifying whether the advice they
offered was not prejudiced by their own marketing considerations. The entry
of the Soviet Union and the other newcomers now provided the oil-
consuming countries with another source of technology and knowledge.

Thirdly, it improved the bargaining position of the oil-consuming companies *vis-à-vis* the major oil companies. Earlier, they were vulnerable to
threats or blackmail from oil companies if they refused to accept the latters'
demands. There were few alternative sources they could turn to if the oil
companies decided to turn off the oil tap. In the past various governments
of poor countries were subject to such threats, for example, India, Ceylon or
Cuba. But the position changed after 1959–60. In the case of Cuba, the conflict with the oil companies resulted in their expulsion and the running of oil
refineries with Soviet help. In Ceylon a public sector oil-marketing company
based on oil products from the USSR and Egypt replaced the major oil companies. In India the growth of the public sector in exploration, production,
refining, and distribution, could not have been possible without Soviet and
Romanian help.[53]

Fourthly, paradoxically enough, it even improved the bargaining position of the governments of oil-producing countries with which Soviet oil was in direct competition for the supply of oil. In order to meet the intense competition of Soviet oil in the world market, the majors reduced 'posted' prices; but this led to serious conflicts with oil-producing countries who had been eligible since the early 1950s to a half share in the profits from oil; and the decline in oil prices meant for them a lower oil revenue per barrel of oil sold. The Organization of Petroleum Exporting Countries (OPEC) was formed in 1960 with the primary objective of halting this decline in prices, and it succeeded in its aim of stabilising profits.[54] Previously, oil-producing countries were dependent on the major oil companies for markets, technology and managerial expertise. To the extent that Soviet intervention weakened the control of the majors on the markets of oil-consuming countries and made the latter more knowledgeable about the affairs of the oil industry, the problems of finding buyers of oil, from the point of view of producing countries, was no longer that acute. Whereas, during 1951–54, the nationalised Iranian oil industry could not find buyers of oil because of a boycott by the major oil companies, such a situation could not arise after 1960. Moreover, while technologically the oil-producing countries continued to be dependent on foreign sources, they could now acquire personnel or technology from concerns not connected with the majors. For example, when the French-owned CFP withdrew personnel from the Algerian refinery they could be replaced by East Europeans; and the development of North Rumailla oil field in Iraq could be undertaken with Soviet help.[55]

In short, the Soviet entry into the oil market radically transformed the international oil scene, and made it more competitive. Although its immediate impact was to reduce oil prices, in the long run it was a contributory factor in the price increases which took place in the 1970s.

VI. Political Factors in Soviet Exports

Many observers attribute political motives to the Soviet offensive in the field of oil trade. Even as early as in the early fifties one author, Henrich Hassman, commented: '. . . at present Russian oil is no threat to other oil producing countries. However, it could become a danger again if the Soviet government should shatter the international price structure with a deliberate dumping of even small quantities.'[56] A study sponsored by the Rand Corporation in 1961 commented: 'Growing reliance on the Soviet bloc for such a strategic commodity as oil exposes non-Soviet consumers to the danger that the incoming flow of oil can be cut off at the whim of the Soviets.'[57] In the foreword to a report of a committee of the US Senate in 1962, on 'Problems raised by the Soviet oil offensive', Senator Kenneth B. Keating stated:

Sold at prices determined by political rather than economic considerations, accompanied by propaganda, technicians, and all the prerequisites

of a communist marketing system, and designed to undermine the commercial activities of the free enterprise system, Soviet oil has already begun
to injure the West. Unless steps are taken now, the onrush of Soviet oil
over the next 5 or 10 years may seriously undermine the economic independence of Western Europe and the future of private enterprise in
the underdeveloped countries.[58]

The report itself explained the significance of the 'Soviet oil offensive'
in terms of the following four factors: (a) it was communist oil, (b) it displaced
oil from other sources, (c) it tended to disrupt a well-established oil-pricing
system, and (d) it showed a phenomenal rate of increase in Soviet production.
It quoted the Managing Director of Caltex as saying, 'This is really an economic
war between East and West; and it's gone far beyond the point of private companies being able to fight it on its own.' The report also mentioned attempts
by Standard Oil of New Jersey to force a boycott of Soviet oil-carrying vessels,
and a suggestion from a joint congressional sub-committee on foreign economic policy to develop an effective multilateral control on export credits and
strategic shipments that help support the Soviet military and industrial base.
It also mentioned the US decision to scrap the agreement with the Japanese
firm Idemitsu Kosan for supplying fuel to US forces in Japan, when the
latter decided to buy a large amount of oil from the Soviet Union; and that
the government of Japan was induced to take legislative measures against
heavy Soviet oil imports.

Another report by a team which visited the Soviet oil-fields in 1961
commented:

> Once the USSR has established itself in the European markets as the
> flow of Soviet oil increases but the demand for Western equipment
> declines, the motivation in this area may shift to political rather than
> economic gains.[59]

The anxiety of Western interests over the rapid increase in Soviet oil
exports was reflected in the large number of reports, documents and books
written on this subject during this period. Fears were expressed about the
Soviet policy of dumping cheap oil on the free market with the objective
of driving out the established oil companies and thereby establishing control
over the supply of this strategic material. The proof of dumping was their
charging 10—20 per cent less than the world-parity price for the East
European communist countries. The danger of relying on Soviet oil supplies
was evidenced by their decision to cut off supplies to Israel after the 1956
Middle East war.[60] But if one takes the argument about lower prices of Soviet
oil, these were certainly not give-away prices, but were well above production costs and kept a good profit margin for the Soviet Union. In fact these
'low' prices became the normal prices during the sixties. A comparison with
prices charged for East European consumers is also of doubtful validity unless

one takes into account the full set of trade relationships among the COMECON countries.[61] While the point about the stoppage of Soviet supplies to Israel is valid, such political use of economic power is not a new phenomenon in the oil industry. The Western oil interests have been no less guilty of such practices in the past.[62]

There is no doubt that political factors do play a certain role in Soviet trade decisions, as also in the trade activities of the USA and other Western countries. But it is possible to explain Soviet oil export policy independently of political motives. The price policy they followed might have been followed by almost any private company entering a new market in order to win away customers from existing suppliers; and, as we have already noted, the prices they offered still left them with a good profit margin. Even if they discriminated between communist and non-communist buyers of oil in favour of the latter, such a policy could again be explained in terms of differences in price elasticities in the two markets. The majors also charge higher crude prices to their own refinery affiliates (whose demand is price-inelastic), compared with the prices they charge to independent refineries, such as Petrobras of Brazil. Even the amount involved was not very large; during the period 1955–65 Soviet oil accounted for six per cent of West European imports compared with a figure of 14 per cent during the 1930s.[63] One observer – Lawrence R. Marks, who compiled a report for investors in international oil – even went to the extent of saying: '. . . its influence may not even be greater than the future combined effect of oil being produced and marketed by several newcomers to the international oil scene.'[64] A report prepared by Petroleum Economics Limited, a consultant firm, commented that Soviet traders 'are hard bargaining businessmen who will not enter into business deals which are not commercially advantageous to them', but that the prospects for Soviet oil exports were not large as a percentage of world consumption, which 'does not suggest the existence of a master plan for Soviet domination of world markets'.[65] A more recent study by Walter Laquer in 1969 stated: '. . . while political motives did play a certain part in the Soviet oil offensives, the exports were profitable business from Moscow's point of view, even at the low price level. The Russians did not want simply to disrupt the old price schemes but to become charter members of a new club of oil producers, based on a more stable commodity agreement.'[66]

The experience of the past sixteen years has vindicated that statement. Soviet oil exports have remained more or less steady as a percentage of world oil exports, at about $4\frac{1}{2}$ per cent. Their prices had been only marginally less than the prices charged by Western concerns during most of the sixties, and occasionally they were outbid by the latter.[67] They have not gone out of their way to push the Western oil companies out of the world market, or to set up their own distribution network. However, their very presence, and the ability to offer crude, oil products and technology, and even military support if necessary, made all the difference between conditions existing in the oil industry before 1959–60 and after.

VII. Soviet Oil and Opec

The relationship between the Soviet Union and OPEC contains elements of
both conflict and complementarity of interests.

Economically, the conflict arises from the role of Soviet oil as an alternative to oil from the Middle East. Gains made by Soviet oil during the sixties
had almost always been at the cost of Middle East oil deliveries. Soviet competition brought down oil prices during the sixties, which also affected the
revenues of OPEC. Competition was so keen during the period that OPEC
never considered asking the USSR to become one of its members, although
non-Middle Eastern exporters like Venezuela, Indonesia and Nigeria were
invited to join.

The economic interests of OPEC's members and the Soviet Union converge
in their policies towards the major international oil companies. As we have
already noted, Soviet competition weakened the marketing position of the
majors and thereby strengthened OPEC's bargaining position. The formation
of OPEC was the direct consequence of the trend of falling crude prices due
to Soviet competition, and its success was largely due to the failure of the
majors to undertake punitive action against its members under changed
conditions in the world market. On the other hand, over time, the intensity
of Soviet competition is declining. After having established a certain share
in the world oil market, the Soviet Union has now developed a vested interest
in stable and high oil prices.[68] The demand—supply conditions in the seventies
are so much in favour of oil suppliers that there is hardly any serious need
for price competition for capturing new markets. And as we shall see, the
quantum of Soviet exports is not going to rise as fast in future as was once
predicted, for a variety of reasons. Whether the USSR joins OPEC or not, the
threat of Soviet competition is not an important policy parameter from the
viewpoint of OPEC today.

Politically, the members of OPEC are basically anti-communist and therefore anti-Soviet. Only Algeria and Iraq among them are close to the Soviet
Union, and could be considered left wing. Most oil-producing countries in
the Middle East — Abu Dhabi, Kuwait, Qatar, Bahrain, Saudi Arabia or Iran —
are feudal autocracies, and Libya has a theocratic anti-communist nationalist
régime. The major oil-exporting countries outside the Middle East — Indonesia, Nigeria and Venezuela — are also likewise under strong US influence.
Some of these countries do not have diplomatic relations with the Soviet
Union.

But again, their political interests converge on one or two issues. On Israel,
the Soviet Union is strongly on their side; and while the NATO countries
have attempted to form a political pressure group against OPEC, the Soviet
Union has been consistent in its support for Arab policies on oil and in general
for Arab nationalism against Western imperialism.

Militarily most of the oil-producing countries are dependent on the West.
The small sheikhdoms of the Persian Gulf are afraid of their bigger neighbours

who are looking for excuses to swallow them; Iran, Iraq and Saudi Arabia would be only too pleased to take over Bahrain, Kuwait and Abu Dhabi, respectively. The huge economic disparities between the oil-rich enclaves and their poorer Arab neighbours in the Middle East and North Africa are attracting migrants to the former to such an extent that the original inhabitants are already a minority (although politically in power) in Kuwait, Bahrain and Abu Dhabi; and it is only a matter of time before the underprivileged majority demand equal political rights. A 'Sikkim-type' situation can only be averted with the backing of a big military power. Furthermore, the OPEC régimes — feudal and autocratic as they are — are under the constant fear of mass uprisings. Both for fighting the revolutionaries and for securing refuge if the revolution succeeds, they are virtually dependent on Western support. Despite their occasional anti-US rhetoric and differences with the USA on the Israel issue the military dependence of these régimes on the United States is an overwhelming factor in their economic and political decisions. This is true not only in the case of the small sheikhdoms, but also of Iran, Saudi Arabia, and Indonesia outside the Middle East.

On the other hand, Soviet military support to Arab countries such as Egypt, Iraq and Syria is an important factor in their collective operations against Israel. Moreover, these feudal regimes also fear military intervention from the US (which would require no more than a minor paratroop operation for transferring power to a more obliging prince in a sheikhdom) on the excuse of 'strangulation' of the US economy; their best bet against such a threat is the restraining influence of the Soviet union because of the strategic importance of the Middle East.

In brief, the political, economic and military aspects of the Middle East situation in relation to the Soviet Union are neither clear-cut nor easy to follow in ideological terms. Despite their political antagonism towards the USSR and their military dependence on the USA, on issues connected with oil and Israel these countries benefit from Soviet support.

VIII. The Future of Soviet Oil Exports

As seen from Table 8.4, the quantum of Soviet oil exports to the non-communist countries has remained virtually stable ever since 1967 at around 50 million tonnes a year, or 1 million barrels a day; while imports have increased from a meagre 17,000 barrels a day in 1967 to 358,000 barrels a day in 1973. As a consequence, net exports are declining — by about a third between 1967 and 1973. Reports from various countries indicate that the Soviet Union is not very keen to enlarge its export commitments in coming years.[69]

Table 8.3 shows that during 1971–73 Soviet oil exports to less developed countries have been confined mainly to India, Egypt and Ghana; but these three together account for less than ten per cent of total Soviet oil exports

TABLE 8.4 ESTIMATED COMMUNIST
BLOC OIL TRADE, 1967–73
(IN THOUSAND BARRELS PER DAY)

Year	Exports	Imports	Net exports
1967	984	17	967
1968	981	16	965
1969	961	66	895
1970	1008	131	877
1971	995	150	845
1972	1036	243	793
1973	999	358	641

Source: *Petroleum Economist* (June 1974).

to countries outside the Communist bloc. The great bulk of Soviet oil exports goes to Western Europe, from where the Soviet Union buys industrial goods in exchange for the hard currency earned. About half of the total Soviet oil exports go to the communist countries.

Table 8.3, however, underestimates the qualitative significance of Soviet oil to countries of the Third World. Soviet oil has been instrumental in the growth of public sectors in oil distribution and refining in many countries, including India, Egypt, Cuba, Ceylon, Turkey and Ghana. Even when not much oil was imported from the USSR, the possibility of their securing supplies from that source induced the major international companies to reduce prices or offer good terms.

Secondly, much of the help came in the form of expert advice on exploration and technical assistance for building refineries, factors — important though these are — not represented by Table 8.3.

Thirdly, in the past, on many occasions the poor oil-consuming countries themselves have been reluctant to rely heavily on Soviet crude oil for political reasons. They have used Soviet oil for extracting better terms from the major or minor Western oil firms, for building public sector refining and marketing enterprises, and for achieving self-sufficiency in refining and crude oil production; but at the same time they have tried to keep their dependence on the USSR at the lowest possible level. India, for example, while making the most of Soviet help to curb the influence of the foreign oil monopolies and to achieve its goals of self-sufficiency in refined products and part-self-sufficiency in crude oil production, has refrained from using Soviet crude in the refineries partly or fully owned by the government.

In future, Soviet oil exports to less developed countries will depend upon the following four factors:

(i) Soviet crude oil production: as we have already indicated, production is expected to achieve a level of 800 million tonnes in 1980; but much of the increase will come from the distant West Siberian oil reserves, which will add to costs of production and transport.

(ii) The pace of industrialisation in the Soviet Union, and the corresponding needs of domestic consumption: not surprisingly, the Soviet Union gives a high priority to the needs of domestic industry and, given a rate of growth in oil demand of seven per cent a year, by 1980, very little of the expected production by then will be available for exports.[70] The demand for oil is also growing in other COMECON countries, so much so that in 1973 they imported 18 million tonnes of oil from the Middle East.[71] According to one estimate, East European consumption will grow from 40 million tonnes in 1968 to 119 million tonnes in 1980, only 30 million tonnes of which will come from local sources, mainly Romania.[72] If there is a serious shortage of oil in East Europe, it is likely that the latter will receive a high priority in the allocation of Soviet exports.

(iii) The development of alternative energy sources in the Soviet Union: the latter is rich in coal and gas reserves. In fact, until very recently, coal was the main source of energy in the Soviet Union.[73] In 1972, coal and oil each accounted for one-third of energy consumption, while gas accounted for a quarter.[74] Recent increases in oil prices might induce more intensive production of other energy sources and the transfer of as large an amount of oil as possible for exports.

(iv) The three factors mentioned above will determine the amount of oil available for export; but the distribution of such exports between the less and the more developed countries will largely depend on the relative needs for Western technology and equipment and for building economic and political relationships with less developed countries in competition with the West. If the much-discussed and debated trade relationship with the USA materialises, the former might get precedence over the latter. If, on the other hand, the Soviet Union decided to forego such technical help, it will be more willing to enlarge its trade activities with the less developed countries.

Three other points need to be noted. First, as indicated before, in the future more than in the past, Soviet technological help (as also its presence in the oil market) will play a much bigger role than the actual supply of oil to the less developed countries. Secondly, under the changed political condition in the oil industry since October 1973 – with the OPEC governments emerging as the decision-makers with regard to the price and allocation of oil and as owners of crude oil, in place of the major oil companies – Soviet oil cannot play the role it did in the late fifties and the early sixties as an alternative source of crude, oil products and technology to the major oil companies. As a consequence, its role as supplier of oil is bound to be peripheral in the coming years, unless of course OPEC tries to use its monopoly power against individual less developed countries under Soviet patronage.

A third point is about the likely emergence of China as an important factor in world export trade in the future. An oil-importing nation until recently, China's crude oil production jumped from 10 million tonnes in 1968 to 50 million tonnes in 1973 and 65 million tonnes in 1974; and by the end of the seventies it is expected to reach a high figure of 400 million tonnes.[75] Given its present low level of industrialisation, and the need for foreign currency for rapid industrialisation, a great part of this production is likely to be exported. Already China is exporting to a number of countries, mainly Japan and the Philippines; over time, more and more countries will come within its supply orbit. The nature of the relationship between the USSR and China and the Middle East will be an important determinant of the pattern of the oil trade in the coming years.

Notes

[1] *International Petroleum Encyclopaedia* (1973).

[2] See Table 7.1.

[3] See Table 7.2.

[4] For a detailed account of the advantages accruing to the US by way of foreign-exchange earnings and access to an important raw material, see Michael Tanzer, *The Political Economy of International Oil and the Underdeveloped Countries* (London, 1969).

[5] Walter Laquer, *The Struggle for the Middle East* (Pelican, 1969); George Lenezowski, *Oil and State in the Middle East* (1960).

[6] See Biplab Dasgupta, 'Large international firms in the oil industry', Institute of Development Studies *Bulletin*, Special issue on Oil and Development, Vol. 6, No. 2; Edith Penrose, *The Large International Firm in Developing Countries: The International Petroleum Industry* (London, 1967).

[7] *Petroleum Times* (26 July 1974). Esso, Gulf, Mobil, Standard Oil California, and Texas, accounted for 10·15 per cent, 5·06 per cent, 2·96 per cent, 5·75 per cent and 7·07 per cent respectively.

[8] Lenezowski, op. cit.

[9] *Petroleum Times* (8 March 1963).

[10] Zuhayer Mikdashi, *The Community of Oil Exporting Countries: A Study of Governmental Cooperation* (London, 1972).

[11] Harold Lubell, *The Soviet Oil Offensive and Inter-Bloc Economic Competition* (Rand Corporation, 1961).

[12] Henrich Hassman, *Oil in the Soviet Union* (Princeton, 1953). F. C. Gerretson, *History of the Royal Dutch*, 4 volumes (1953–7), also contains a great deal of information on the early days of the Russian oil industry.

[13] *International Petroleum Encyclopaedia* (1973); British Petroleum, 'Statistical review of the world oil industry, 1972'.

[14] In 1973 about a quarter of crude oil production came from West Siberia, and by 1980 about half its expected production is likely to come from this source. See *Petroleum Economist* (May 1974).

[15] *Petroleum Economist* (June 1974). About 18 million metric tons were supplied by Iraq, Libya, Iran and two other countries in 1973.

[16] *Petroleum International* (August 1974).

[17] Until 1956, the USSR's imports from Romania exceeded its exports to Eastern Europe. The southwest part of the USSR is distant from oil fields but is nearer Romania, and a product pipeline runs from Romania to Odessa. See Petroleum Economics Limited, 'The oil and natural gas industries of the USSR', 1959 (mimeo).

[18] Several agreements were reached during 1974 between Japanese and US firms on the one hand and the USSR on the other; but in early 1975, these were rescinded because of restrictions imposed on trade with the USSR by the US Senate. See *Petroleum Economist* (January 1974, May 1974, June 1974, February, 1975).

[19] Hessman, op. cit., Gerretson, op. cit.

[20] ibid.

[21] For details, see Biplab Dasgupta, *The Oil Industry in India: Some Economic Aspects* (London, 1971) chapter 2.

[22] United States, Federal Commission, *International Petroleum Cartel* (1952).

[23] ibid.

[24] ibid.

[25] See Biplab Dasgupta, *the Oil Industry in India: Some Economic Aspects* (London, 1971) pp. 58–60.

[26] Hessman, op. cit.

[27] In that year, imports and exports were 4·39 and 7·99 million tonnes respectively; see Petroleum Economics Limited, op. cit.

[28] Robert E. Ebel, *The Petroleum Industry of the Soviet Union* (American Petroleum Institute, 1961). (Report of a team of US oil experts who visited the USSR oil fields in 1961).

[29] Ebel, op. cit.

[30] US Senate, Committee on the Judiciary, *Problems Raised by the Soviet Oil Offensive* (Washington, 1962).

[31] Lubell, op. cit.; *Platts Oilgram Press Service*, of 1959 and 1960.

[32] See *Platts Oilgram Press Service* (24 January 1961); US Senate, op. cit.; Lubell, op. cit.; Ebel, op. cit.

[33] *Capital* (2 July 1960); Government of India, *Report of the Oil Price Enquiry Committee* (Delhi, 1961).

[34] *Platts Oilgram Press Service* (29 July 1960).

[35] *Petroleum Times* (3 March 1962; 23 August 1962; 8 March 1963).

[36] Agreement on compensation was not reached until late 1965. See *Petroleum Intelligence Weekly* (17 May 1965).

[37] Although both the USSR and Romania were offering oil products since early 1959, it was not until mid-1960 that an agreement with the USSR was signed for deliveries of 1·5 million tonnes of diesel oil, jet fuel and paraffin. See Y. Yershov, *India: Independence and Oil* (Moscow, 1965).

[38] See Government of India, 28th Report of the Estimates Committee of the Third Lok Sabha on *The Indian Oil Corporation* (1962–3). See also *Capital* (16 November 1961; 23 November 1961).

[39] Government of India, *Report of the Oil Price Enquiry Committee* (Delhi, 1961).

[40] US Senate, op. cit.

[41] In the late sixties with the reduction in Middle East prices, Japan's imports of Soviet crude oil declined. But even in 1965 the USSR accounted for 3·6 per cent of imports to Japan. See *Petroleum Intelligence Weekly* (1 November 1965).

[42] Petroleum Economics Limited, op. cit.

[43] US Senate, op. cit.

[44] *Petroleum Intelligence Weekly* (28 January 1968).

[45] So far the Soviet Union has built two refineries in India — at Koyali and Barauni — both under public ownership; and Romania has built the public sector refinery of Nunmati. Both countries have given long-term easy credits for refinery construction at a $2\frac{1}{2}$ per cent interest rate. See Dasgupta, op. cit., and Yershov, op. cit.

[46] *Petroleum Intelligence Weekly* (1965).

[47] US Senate, op. cit.

[48] US Senate, op. cit.

[49] About a quarter of Soviet aid to India up to mid-sixties, amounting to Rs 85 million, was spent on oil. The credits were repayable over 12 years (which began one year after completion of deliveries) and carried $2\frac{1}{2}$ per cent interest. In comparison, loans from the US Export–Import Bank and the World Bank carried $5\frac{3}{4}$ per cent interest, and most other sources charged about $5\frac{1}{2}$ to $6\frac{1}{2}$ per cent during that period. Of the total foreign exchange requirements of ONGC in 1963, 60 per cent came from the USSR, Romania and Yugoslavia, 20 per cent from Italy and France and the rest from other foreign sources. Moreover, about 5000 Indians were trained up to mid-sixties as geologists, geophysicists, drillers, mechanics, welders and electricians in the oil centres of the USSR and Romania, and soviet experts also organised crash courses at Bombay. See Yershov, op. cit., for details.

[50] Dasgupta, op. cit., chapter 9.

[51] Dasgupta, op. cit., chapter 6. See also, H. J. Prank, *Crude Oil Prices in the Middle East: A Study in Oligopolistic Price Behaviour* (1966). Until 1945, the Gulf of Mexico was the only 'base'. This formula was followed even when no oil was imported from the USA by a given consumption centre, in order to minimize disputes about prices between oligopolists and the consequent risks of a price war. One consequence of this price policy, from the point of view of many oil-consuming countries, was that they did not benefit from their possible proximity to oil producing areas, since for the purpose of price fixing it was only their distance from the Gulf of Mexico which mattered. For example, the price of oil produced in Burma was cheaper in London than in Calcutta (which was 7,000 miles nearer to Burma) because London was closer to the Gulf of Mexico.

[52] Government of India, *Report of Oil Price Enquiry Committee* (Delhi, 1961).

[53] Yershov, op. cit.

[54] Mikdashi, op. cit.

[55] *Petroleum International* (December 1974).

[56] Hassman, op. cit.

[57] Lubell, op. cit.

[58] US Senate, op. cit.

[59] Ebel, op. cit.

[60] Lubell, op. cit.

[61] Laquer, op. cit.; Robert W. Campbell, *The Economics of Soviet Oil and Gas* (Johns Hopkins, 1967).

[62] The embargo on trade in Iranian oil imposed by the USA and the UK after the nationalisation of the Anglo-Iranian oil company in 1951 is one such example.

[63] Laquer, op. cit.

[64] Lawrence R. Marks, *Communist Bloc Oil: A Report fo Investors in International Oil* (1959).

[65] Petroleum Economics Limited, op. cit.

[66] Laquer, op. cit.

[67] *Platts Oilgram Press Service,* various numbers during 1960—65, in particular 28 February 1963. In recent years, following the October 1973 escalation of prices, the Soviet Union is charging very high prices. For example, it recently asked for $18 a barrel from West Germany. See *Petroleum Economist* (April 1974).

[68] See *Petroleum Economist* (April 1974).

[69] For example, although India asked for 1.5 million tonnes of kerosene, 0·5 million tonnes of diesel, and 2 million tonnes of fuel oil during 1975 from the Soviet Union, it is not expected to get more than 1 million tonnes of kerosene, 0·1 million tonnes of diesel and 1 million tonnes of fuel oil. See *Petroleum International* (January 1975).

[70] Laquer, op. cit.

[71] *Petroleum Economist* (June 1974).

[72] Laquer, op. cit.

[73] Coal accounted for 64·6 per cent of total energy consumption in 1950, but its share fell to 52.2 per cent in 1960 when oil's share rose from 17·6 per cent to 28·7 per cent and the share of natural gas trebled from 2·3 per cent to 7·4 per cent. See Ebel, op. cit.

[74] In 1973, 668 million tonnes of coal were produced and the target is to increase the figure to 1000 million tonnes by the turn of the century. Gas deposits are also large, so large that some economists believe priority should be given to gas production over oil. Nuclear power generation is also another alternative which is being extensively researched. See *Petroleum Economist* (March 1974).

[75] See *Petroleum International* (November 1974); *Petroleum Economist* (September 1974, January 1975).

9 China's Economic Relations with Less Developed Countries: 1950–1976

SUZANNE PAINE*

I. Introduction

On 14 July 1976 the 1162 mile-long Tanzam railway was officially handed over to the Tanzanian and Zambian governments after nine months of successful trial operation. During this time it had already carried 159,000 tons of copper and zinc from Zambia, 130,000 tons of grain, chemical fertiliser, steel products and machinery to Zambia, 100,000 tons of railway building material and 250,000 passengers. The foreign costs of the project were financed by an interest-free loan of $401 million in addition to which the Chinese gave the Tanzanians a grant of 106 million yuan in July 1976.[1] The local costs were financed by proceeds from sales of Chinese commodities by local state-owned corporations, mainly consumer goods, thus avoiding the need for any local budgetary allocation.[2] The labour-intensive construction methods used generated employment for as many as 40,000 Tanzanians alone, while after its completion, 10,000 Tanzanians and Zambians were occupied in running it.[3]

Clearly this is a model instance of successful foreign economic aid to an LDC — and a case of a project rejected by Western aid sources.[4] As the Tanzanian Ambassador to the USA put it, China's assistance

> was the sole offer we had. We had no other alternative. Ironically it turned out to be the softest we had ever hoped to get. And it wasn't from a Super-Power. It successfully challenged the invincibility of western technological superiority and dominance. It was a demonstration of our potential and capabilities — if only the Third World [had] stopped to exploit it.[5]

The Chinese, of course, were not oblivious of the latter point:

> It [the railway] is also a triumph for the third world countries and people who rely on their own efforts and support each other in developing their

*I should like to thank Deepak Nayyar, the editor, for extremely helpful and constructive suggestions, as a result of which the content of this paper has been substantially improved.

national economies. It is of far-reaching political and economic significance. It helps Tanzania to exploit the coal and iron deposits in its souther region and Zambia to break the Rhodesian and South African racists' blockade. It helps consolidate the independence of Tanzania and Zambia and develop their national economies and strengthen relations between both countries and between the east and central southern African countries.

The successful completion of the railway is a telling blow to imperialism and a great encouragement to the people of the Third World. The two super-powers, the United States and the Soviet Union, and other imperialist countries had all refused to help build the railway.[6]

This paper has begun with a sketch of the Tanzam railway project because, in a nutshell, it embodies many of the most fundamental aspects of the theory and practice of Chinese economic relations with Third World countries.[7] These are examined in greater detail in subsequent sections. More specifically, the principles according to which the Chinese claim to manage their Third World policies are outlined in Section II. Section III reviews the data available up to 1976 on the magnitude, direction, commodity pattern and terms of Chinese trade, and Section IV surveys the corresponding evidence on aid. However, given the recent availability of data on Chinese trade and aid,[8] the major aim of this essay, apart from providing an integrated and updated survey, is to consider certain basic issues concerning China's economic relationships with LDCs. As a result, Section V identifies a methodological approach to the evaluation question, which is applied in Section VI in order to shed as much light as possible on the former. Questions are raised mainly about the nature of Chinese trade and aid relations with LDCs, including the extent to which the record matches up to Chinese claims, marks a new departure from the records of western and other socialist countries, and could have been improved. Some brief comments are also made about the political economy of its effects. Section VII summarises the main conclusions. It should be noted that military transactions are not discussed.

II. The Principles Underlying China's Economic Relations with LDCs

A. *Background: Foreign Relations*
China's economic relations with LDCs — just like those of the USA and USSR — have been as much an extension of foreign as of economic policy. Indeed, China's analysis of the position of poorer African, Asian and Latin American countries and her overall relations with the less developed countries has been influenced substantially by her political relationship with the Soviet Union. While the USSR was still regarded by the Chinese as being in the 'socialist camp', the major world contradictions were defined as those

(a) between the socialist and the imperialist camp,
(b) between the proletariat and bourgeoisie in capitalist countries,

(c) between the oppressed and imperialist countries, and

(d) among imperialist countries and among monopoly capitalist groups.[9]

In Lin Piao's speech of the mid-1960s 'Long live the victory of the People's War', the contradiction between the revolutionary peoples of Asia, Africa, and Latin America and the imperialists headed by the United States had been elevated to the status of being the principal contradiction in the contemporary world. And when, after Czechoslovakia, the Chinese characterisation of the Soviet Union progressed from being 'revisionist' to 'social imperialist' (a term to be discussed further below), the characterisation and ranking of contradictions was modified accordingly: the major contradictions were listed as those

(a) between the oppressed nations and both 'imperalism' and 'social imperialism',

(b) between the proletariat and bourgeoisie in the capitalist and 'revisionist' countries,

(c) between imperialist and 'social imperialist' countries and among 'social imperialist' countries, and

(d) between socialist countries and both imperialism and 'social imperialism'.[10]

At this point, a few comments on the Chinese concept of 'social imperialism' seem apposite – not least because the rousing polemic which so frequently accompanies their use of it can make it seem like a catch-all term of abuse to cover any and every criticism levelled against the USSR. The basis of the Chinese analysis is that:

The economic base of the Soviet Union today is state monopoly capitalism which came into being after the all round restoration of capitalism by the Soviet revisionist renegade clique. There the ownership of the means of production and the relationships between man and man and distribution are all dominated by the bureaucrat monopoly capitalist class. The characteristics inherent in this economic structure make Soviet social imperialism even more brutal in its aggression and expansion abroad and in its struggle for world hegemony ... To grab maximum profits, it redoubles its efforts to ... annex new territories, plunder cheap overseas raw materials, sell goods overseas in quantity, export capital and shift the burden of crises on to others. Incomplete statistics show that the total amount of Soviet capital exported to the third world between 1952 and 1972 was more than 13,000 million dollars. This opened the way for the expanded exports of commodities by flooding a number of third world countries with large quantities of unmarketable goods. Between 1955 and 1973, high priced Soviet manufactured goods were sold to these countries for more than 16,000 million dollars, from which huge profits amounting to several thousand million dollars were taken away.[11]

Numerous other charges are made concerning, for instance, the living standards of the Soviet people, the allegedly excessive militarisation of the Soviet economy, etc., but these are not of direct relevance here. Nor will any critical appraisal of the concept of social imperialism itself be attempted. Two points, however, should be made. Firstly, the concept *can* be understood to have a clear meaning in terms of the policies listed above to which it is supposed to lead, irrespective of whether these have actually taken place. Secondly, there is the question of whether the term 'social imperialism' is appropriate to describe such a package of characteristics and policies, or whether this is an unjustifiably forced usage given the conventional Leninist use of the word. We do not, however, venture into such controversial territory here. Instead, we follow the Chinese use of the term *without implying anything whatsoever* about the justification of applying it to the Soviet case.

That the 'imperialist' and 'social imperialist' superpowers (i.e. the USA and USSR) are the main enemies of both socialist and Third World countries is still the position held by the Chinese today, at least at the time of writing. This explains the strong support by the Chinese for the 'Group of 77' (which in fact includes 110 states) in their demands for a new international economic order (NIEO), even though if the proposed policies were actually implemented in anything more than a superficial way, it appears likely that they would effect little more − at least in the short term − than a redistribution of income between capitalists in advanced countries and in certain better-off capitalist LDCs.[12] To understand this, given the emphasis which the Chinese place on the need for socialist revolutions in the third world, it is necessary to recapitulate briefly some of the analysis underlying Chinese foreign policy − expressed in typical Chinese fashion:

1. The USA and USSR are the two 'superpowers', 'the biggest international exploiters and oppressors of today', whose 'ferocious contest for world hegemony' makes war increasingly likely.[13] The USA 'desperately clings to the old order, opposes the establishment of a new international order, in order to preserve its vested interests. It painstakingly preaches about "interdependence" as "the core of maintaining international order" alleging that "global prosperity" rests on its leadership.' The other superpower (the USSR) 'is even more greedy and more cruel than the old-line imperialism in its plunder and exploitation of the people of the Third World. Following the footprint of transnational corporations of the West, it sets up joint ventures abroad for capital export, seizure of markets and grabbing natural resources ... It extorts fabulous profit by practising trade exchange of unequal values and reselling at high prices. It uses "aid" as a means controlling other countries and practising usury ... It ferociously presses recipient countries for repayment of debts and servicing of interests.'[14] China is not a superpower and never will be; it is a socialist country.
2. The world is divided into the First World (the two superpowers), the Second World (the remaining industrialised countries) and the Third World (all LDCs, including China).[15]
3. Both the Second and Third World countries have been struggling 'to rid

themselves of the control, intervention, subversion and bullying of the super-powers', and this struggle has intensified during recent years, with 'the basic contradictions in the world . . . sharpening'.[16] In the celebrated words of Mao Tse-tung, the outcome has been that 'the current international situation is characterised by great disorder under heaven, and it is excellent.'[17]

4. Although 'countries want independence, nations want liberation and the people want revolution',[18] 'revolutionary movements can be neither exported nor imported'; rather they have to be effected by the efforts of the masses, especially workers and peasants, in the countries concerned.

5. Such self-reliance has to be the basis of economic as well as political progress. In the case of China itself this has meant that even during the most 'open' foreign trade phases, the share of trade in the national product has still remained low, and its purpose — apart from certain political and foreign aid components — has been confined to acquiring such inputs essential for the current development plan as could not be obtained or produced domesti-cally (see Section III below). The recommended counterpart to this for small LDCs, firmly trapped by participation in international markets, is through the mass efforts of their own peoples, to grasp internal sovereignty and control of their own resources, and to combine with other LDCs to smash the old international economic order so as eventually to make possible much more self-reliant development strategies and to enable international economic and trade affairs to 'be handled jointly by all countries of the world, instead of being controlled and monopolised by either of the superpowers or both';[19] in other words, 'to safeguard national independence and develop the national economy' and 'to strengthen economic co-operation and mutual support among developing countries'.[20] In international economic policy terms this implies, for instance, an integrated programme for commodities and price indexing; expanding opportunities for LDC exports (particularly manufactur-ing) to provide foreign exchange for key imports; interest-free or low interest foreign aid with the possibility of deferred repayment; practical, effective and cheap transfer of technology; revision of the international patent system and reform of international monetary institutions — i.e. support for the Third World's NIEO proposals.[21]

To sum up, the Chinese 'line' of recent years has been that the 'masses' in non-socialist LDCs must make their own revolutions and that, in the mean-time, China would support the combined efforts of the governments of these countries in their attempt to establish a NIEO. However, except for a brief comment on the need for special assistance to the poorest LDCs,[22] there appears to be no analysis of the distributional changes such a NIEO might make, not just between members of the 'Group of 77' but, more funda-mentally, between classes within individual LDCs: central issues, such as capitalist growth in richer LDCs at the expense of poorer ones and the inter-relationship between trade and class, are eschewed completely.

B. *Trade*

Nonetheless, the Chinese have stated certain clear principles which they believe should govern all their trade, with whomsoever it is conducted. Firstly, self-reliance − *not* to be confused with self-sufficiency − and secondly, equality and mutual benefit. 'Self-reliance' is essentially about gaining control of, as well as mobilising and using, all available own resources to accelerate own development before bringing in other resources from outside, and is the main theoretical rationale for treating foreign trade as a residual in national economic planning: in Mao's words, 'rely mainly on our own efforts while making external assistance subsidiary' and 'make foreign things serve China'. On the other hand, at times, these dicta are almost conveniently imprecise, being consistent with statements as polarised as the following:

To develop industry by depending on importation of foreign techniques and equipment not only is not a shortcut, but is a tortuous, evil path[23]

The Chinese people wish to have friendly co-operation with the people of all countries and to resume and expand international trade in order to develop production and promote economic prosperity[24]

Self-reliance in no way implies 'self-seclusion' or rejection of external assistance, but means relying mainly on one's own efforts while making external assistance subsidiary . . . making up for each other's deficiencies and learning from each other.[25]

Such substantial differences in interpretation have frequently arisen since liberation, as can be seen from the fact that fluctuations in the constant price data on the magnitude of trade presented in Table 9.1 coincide in part with political events such as the Cultural Revolution and Sino-US détente. However, these interpretative differences become easier to explain if the various motives for Chinese trade are analysed. The first of these has been to obtain commodities and inputs, particularly machinery and new technologies, deemed essential for maintaining and accelerating growth performance or, very occasionally, to make up at short notice key shortfalls in planned production. In other words it 'is putting into practice the principle of making foreign things serve China . . . '[26] Such trade has quantitatively dominated Chinese trade; it was largely carried out during the 1950s with the Soviet Union, but since the Sino-Soviet split, it has taken place instead mainly with advanced capitalist economies, except when important raw materials have been purchased from Third World suppliers. It has also been the main source of the often-heated controversy within China over the extent to which trade is desirable, a typical recent example of which were the criticisms by the Chiang Ching group of 'servility to things foreign'.[27]

Of the other important factors which have determined the growth and magnitude of Chinese trade, possibly the most striking has been political −

the export or re-export of key supplies to the People's Revolutionary Movements in Vietnam and other Indo-Chinese countries, and to other countries, such as Albania, with whom China has had special political ties. A third factor has been China's foreign aid programme, which has naturally generated commodity trade flows. Finally, China has normally sought to export sufficient in value terms both to ensure a balanced trade account on multilateral transactions and to meet bilateral commitments (see below).

Thus in principle one can separate Chinese non-military imports and exports as follows:

$$I = I_G + I_P + I_A + I_B$$

$$E = E_P + E_A + E_B$$

where G indicates predominantly arising from own growth considerations, P indicates predominantly arising from political considerations, A indicates predominantly arising from aid policies, B indicates predominantly arising from trade balancing/financing considerations, and where normally

$$I_G + I_P + I_A + I_B = E_P + E_A + E_B$$

For instance, G would mainly apply to advanced technology and essential raw material imports, P to exports of key consumer and capital goods to newly socialist countries and revolutionary movements in Indo-China, to occasional trade deals designed to help out non-socialist governments deemed to be sympathetic, and to commodities imported by China for re-export for these purposes, etc. Note however that it is not always easy to identify which factor is in fact dominant in any real transaction. For example, bilateral imports from an Asian socialist country could simultaneously fall under P and B and bilateral exports to the same under both P and A; imports from a non-socialist LDC could simultaneously be G and B (balancing consumer exports to that country), or, having been acquired as part of a bilateral deal, could be re-exported to earn foreign exchange or to provide aid, etc. Indeed the formula could in principle be disaggregated still further to incorporate the bilateral-multilateral distinction. Thus letting b represent bilateral and m multilateral transactions,

$$I_{bG} + I_{mG} + I_{bP} + I_{mP} + I_{bA} + I_{mA} + I_{bB} + I_{mP}$$
$$= E_{bP} + E_{mP} + E_{bA} + E_{mA} + E_{bB} + E_{mB}$$

C. *Aid*

In many respects, it is easier to identify clearly the principles according to which the Chinese claim to run their aid programme, since these were enunciated by Chou En-lai during his African visit of 1974. Briefly, the eight principles are (1) equality and mutual benefit (as with trade); (2) recognition of the recipients' sovereignty without any privileges for China (excluding some aid tying); (3) low interest or interest-free loans with long repayment periods; (4) emphasis on recipient self-reliance; (5) labour-intensive projects which yield quick returns and hence surpluses for reinvestment more rapidly; (6) 'best quality' equipment at 'international market prices'; (7) training recipient country personnel; (8) local living standards for Chinese aid personnel.[28] At the time these principles were seen by many to be as much a political statement (in the form of a poorly disguised attack on the Soviet Union) as an agenda for the promotion of international economic development: they almost appeared to have been phrased to cover the most common criticisms voiced against Soviet aid. Although their precise interpretation in the positive sense is not always clear, what they certainly do *not* involve is apparent. Chinese aid would not mean the overpriced supply, financed by 'hard' loans, of quasi-obsolete technology for highly capital-intensive projects with long gestation periods and requiring the presence of an élite of foreign technicians, such as Soviet aid was alleged to involve. Leaving aside for the moment the controversial question of the veracity of these implicit criticisms of the USSR, most of the above would be regarded by all commentators as very desirable, with the possible exception of the emphasis on labour-intensive projects, since in practice this meant intrastructural projects and light industry rather than the capital goods and heavy industry essential for the ultimate creation of an indigenous industrial base. Futhermore, since the Chinese *had already* been carrying out these principles during the years before Chou's speech was made,[29] they cannot be dismissed as a cheap attempt to make political capital out of the problems into which certain Soviet aid programmes had run.

III. China's Trade with LDCs: The Statistical Evidence

A. *Seven General Features of China's Foreign Trade*
It may be useful to begin by recapitulating certain familiar features of China's trade as a whole. Firstly, all trade is managed through eight state-owned foreign trade corporations which act as agents, carrying out a trade plan under the guidance of the Ministry of Foreign Trade, with some aid from the China Council for the promotion of International Trade (CCPIT).[30]

Secondly, as mentioned above, the Chinese have given great weight to balanced trade — if not always in the short term, at least in the medium term. The two occasions on which China has made use of substantial trade credits were during the 1950s from the USSR, a debt repaid by the mid-1960s, and in the early/mid-1970s from the advanced capitalist countries. This balanced trade policy of keeping China free from foreign debts has been pursued partly for its own sake, but was further reinforced by Chinese fears, based on other LDCs' experience with Western economies and the World Bank, and on their own with the USSR, about the adverse effect on national policies which international creditors can have once a country falls substantially into debt.

TABLE 9.1 CHINA'S EXPORTS, IMPORTS AND TRADE BALANCE, CURRENT
AND CONSTANT (1963) PRICES, 1950–75

	Current prices: $USm			Constant (1963) prices: $USm			Current prices index of	
	E	I	E–I	E	I	E–I	Total trade	Trade with all LDCs
							1962 = 100	
1950	620	590	30					
1951	780	1120	–340					
1952	875	1015	–140	795	1005	–210		
1953	1040	1255	–215	995	1295	–300		
1954	1060	1290	–230	930	1345	–415		
1955	1375	1660	–285	1295	1715	–420		
1956	1635	1485	150	1560	1555	5		
1957	1615	1440	175	1530	1380	150		
1958	1940	1825	115	1940	1825	115		
1959	2230	2060	170	2315	2085	230		
1960	1960	2030	–70	1920	2070	–150		
1961	1525	1490	35	1540	1520	20	113	91
1962	1525	1150	375	1585	1180	405	100	100
1963	1570	1200	370	1570	1200	370	104	107
1964	1750	1470	280	1685	1435	250	120	140
1965	2035	1845	190	2005	1785	220	145	165
1966	2210	2035	175	2155	1915	240	159	168
1967	1945	1950	–5	1930	1840	90	146	146
1968	1945	1820	125	1920	1735	185	141	143
1969	2030	1830	200	1920	1690	230	144	151
1970	2050	2240	–190	1865	1890	–25	160	152
1971	2415	2305	110	2180	1880	300	176	176
1972	3085	2835	250	2570	2115	455	221	231
1973	4960	5130	–170	3040	2850	190	369	349
1974	6515	7490	–975	2980	3200	–220	313	
1975	6800	7200	–400				523	

Sources: 1950–72 Chen in USCJEC 1975, *op. cit.*
1973–5 US CIA

Table 9.1 shows China's trade balance both in current prices and in constant
1963 prices over the period 1950–75, and Figure 9.1 (p. 254) depicts the constant
price data: deficits during the 1950s, mainly on the account with the Soviet
Union, were followed by the requisite surpluses during the early 1960s, even
though this was a period when the Chinese were in the process of rebuilding
their economy after the three bad years 1959–61. No further substantial
deficits were accumulated until the Chinese bought so heavily in the West and
Japan during recent years, and these were to some extent financed at the time
by remittances from the overseas Chinese and profits from Chinese-owned
enterprises in Hong Kong.

Thirdly, implementation of the 'self-reliance' approach, together with the
fact that China is a large economy, has meant that throughout the whole post-

liberation period trade has constituted a fairly low proportion of national product, imports having remained below 4 per cent and reaching only about $3\frac{1}{2}$ per cent in the 'high trade' years of the mid-1950s and mid-1970s.

Fourthly, Chinese trade has been characterised by the comparatively high degree of fluctuation in its total,[31] which is attributable not just to variations in Chinese and/or world economic conditions, but also to the differences, referred to above, in the interpretation of the extent to which trade is consistent with self-reliance.

A fifth, and particularly well-known, point about Chinese trade is the major shift which has taken place in its direction, away from the Soviet Union and Eastern Europe and towards advanced capitalist countries. Goods from USSR and Eastern Europe accounted for 77·8 per cent of imports ($US2135 million at current prices) in 1955, only 8·8 per cent ($US45 million) in 1970 and 6·1 per cent ($US940 million) in 1974, rising somewhat to 17 per cent ($US2333 million) in 1975 — see Table 9.2 — whilst those from advanced capitalist countries, particularly Japan, accounted for almost two-thirds of Chinese imports and about one-third of exports during the 1970s. Indeed, by 1976 Chinese exports exceeded Soviet exports to the USA.

A sixth — and less well known — feature of Chinese trade which is of considerable direct concern here is the multilateral character of a large proportion of it. Based on an analysis of Chinese trade with 44 countries, each of which traded a minimum of $5 million with China between 1969 and 1973, Denny finds that it is much more multilateral than that of other centrally planned economies even when the Hong Kong trade is excluded.[33] This is primarily the result of two factors: firstly, the high proportion of trade which has taken place with non-socialist countries, particularly with advanced non-socialist countries, since the 1960 Sino-Soviet split: and secondly, the key role of exports to Hong Kong and Macao, and re-exports thence to Chinese communities in South East Asia, which greatly exceed imports from these locations. For instance, in 1971, Chinese exports to Hong Kong amounted to $US 424 million, while imports from there were only $US 3 million;[34] in 1975, the corresponding figures were $US 1050 million and $US 5 million.[35] This has been very important in providing the convertible currency with which to finance transactions with the advanced capitalist countries. For instance, in 1975 China's surplus on the Hong Kong account *alone* covered 37 per cent of the deficit on the advanced capitalist country account.

The seventh, and final, characteristic of China's trade to be mentioned at this stage concerns its overall commodity composition. Not surprisingly, as can be seen from Table 9.3, China's exports have consisted primarily of natural or processed primary commodities, and imports primarily of producer goods and certain essential raw material and primary commodities. Until comparatively recently, the former largely meant agricultural produce and textiles; these are however to some extent being superseded by crude oil, which in 1975 amounted to about 15 per cent of total export earnings.[36]

TABLE 9.2 DIRECTION OF CHINESE TRADE, 1950–74(%)

	IMPORTS							EXPORTS						
	Total Socialist	Total Non-Socialist	Total USSR & E. Europe	Total Advanced Capitalist	Total Non-Socialist LDC	Total Socialist LDC	Total LDC	Total Socialist	Total Non-Socialist	Total USSR & E. Europe	Total Advanced Capitalist	Total Non-Socialist LDC	Total Socialist LDC	Total LDC
1950	23·7	76·3	23·7			—		33·8	66·2	33·0			0·8	
1951	46·0	54·0	45·5			0·5		59·6	40·4	57·0			2·6	
1952	67·0	33·0	69·5			0·5		69·1	30·9	66·2			2·9	
1953	70·5	29·5	70·1			0·4		64·4	35·6	60·1			4·3	
1954	75·2	24·8	74·2			0·8		72·1	27·9	64·1			8·0	
1955	78·3	21·7	77·8			0·6		69·1	30·9	61·5			7·6	
1956	68·0	32·0	65·9			2·0		63·9	36·1	57·5			6·4	
1957	61·1	28·9	57·6			3·4		67·2	32·8	61·3			5·9	
1958	60·3	29·7	57·3			2·9		65·9	34·1	60·2			5·7	
1959	66·3	33·7	62·2			4·1		72·4	27·6	65·0			7·4	
1960	63·3	36·7	56·6			6·6		68·1	31·9	59·1			9·0	
1961	48·0	52·0	35·2	40·4	11·6	12·8	24·4	63·3	36·7	45·6	14·7	22·0	17·7	39·7
1962	42·6	57·4	26·1	41·1	16·3	16·5	32·8	60·0	40·0	40·6	14·0	26·0	19·4	45·4
1963	35·8	64·2	19·6	48·3	15·9	16·2	32·1	52·2	47·8	33·7	17·8	30·0	18·5	48·5
1964	26·3	73·5	13·3	47·5	26·0	13·2	39·2	40·6	59·4	23·8	23·7	35·7	16·8	52·5
1965	27·9	72·1	16·3	49·9	22·2	11·7	33·9	31·9	68·1	15·6	28·2	39·9	16·3	56·2
1966	24·8	75·2	15·4	55·9	19·3	9·3	28·6	26·5	73·5	12·5	32·4	41·1	14·0	55·1
1967	17·7	82·3	9·5	69·0	13·3	8·1	21·4	24·9	75·1	8·4	32·8	42·3	16·5	58·8
1968	18·7	81·3	10·6	68·7	12·6	7·9	20·5	25·7	74·3	8·9	32·1	42·2	16·8	59·0
1969	16·1	83·9	8·0	68·1	15·8	8·2	24·0	24·1	75·9	8·6	33·8	42·1	15·5	57·6
1970	17·0	83·0	8·8	71·0	12·0	7·4	19·4	23·3	76·7	8·8	33·1	43·6	14·4	58·0
1971	21·6	78·4	14·2	62·2	16·2	7·4	23·6	24·2	75·8	11·2	33·7	42·1	13·0	55·1
1972	18·9	81·1	13·5	58·8	22·3	5·2	27·5	24·0	76·0	11·9	34·8	41·2	12·1	53·3
1973	14·2	85·8	8·7	69·5	16·3	5·4	21·7	20·3	79·7	8·9	36·9	42·8	11·4	54·2
1974	12·6	87·4	6·1	n.a.	n.a.	6·4	n.a.	21·7	78·3	7·7	n.a.	n.a.	14·0	n.a.

Source: Chen, in USCJEC 1975, op. cit.

TABLE 9.3 COMMODITY COMPOSITION OF CHINESE TRADE, SELECTED YEARS 1969–74; AND BY COUNTRY GROUPS, 1974

		1959	1966	1970	1974 Total	Advanced Capitalist	Non-socialist LDC	Hong Kong & Macao	Socialist
IMPORTS ($US m) TOTAL			2035	2240	7490	5290	1225	20	955
Foodstuffs	%		25	16	21	21	25	0	16
incl. Grains	%		20	13	18	20	8	0	0
Crude materials, fuels	%		17	17	20	12	54	75	16
incl. Oilseeds	%	Not	n.a.	n.a.	2	3	0	0	0
Rubber	%	available	4	4	2	0	12	0	0
Textile fibres	%	in	7	5	8	7	20	0	
Chemicals	%	comparable	12	15	8	10	2	0	6
incl. Fertilizers	%	form	8	10	3	3	2		6
Manufactures	%		45	52	51	57	18	25	60
incl. Textile yarn, fabrics	%		2	2	2	3	0	25	0
Iron and steel	%		11	18	16	21	1	0	5
Non-ferrous metals	%		3	9	6	4	14	0	5
Machinery & equipment	%		22	18	22	23	0	0	39
Other	%		1	0	1	1			2
EXPORTS ($US m) TOTAL		1793	2210	2050	6515	2400	1860	910	1345
Foodstuffs	%	30	28	31	32	17	35	63	35
incl. Animal products	%	9	10	10	8	7	1	35	2
Grains	%	10	7	5	9	2	18	10	11
Fruits and vegetables	%	5	5	8	4	5	4	7	2
Guide materials, fuels, oils	%	9	22	21	21	39	6	8	18
incl. Oilseeds	%	9	4	3	3	4	1	1	1
Textile fibres	%	7	5	5	2	6	0	0	1
Guide animals materials	%	n.a.	4	6	3	5	1	1	2
Petroleum	%	n.a.	n.a.	n.a.	8	17	1	3	6
Chemicals	%	2	4	5	6	8	6	4	4
Manufactures	%	15	42	42	40	36	53	25	40
incl. Textile yarn, fabrics	%	14	14	17	12	15	14	3	9
Clothing	%	⎫ 9	8	8	5	8	3	3	5
Iron and steel	%	⎬	4	2	3	0	6	3	2
Non ferrous metals	%	⎭	n.a.	1	1	2	0	1	1
Machinery & equipment	%	1		n.a.	4	0	6	3	8
Other	%		5	1	1	0	0	0	8

Sources: Usack and Batsavage, *op. cit.*, Chen *op. cit.*, USCIA data.

B. *Trade with LDCs*

1. *Magnitude:*

China's trade with LDCs was quite low during the 1950s, reaching 32 per cent
of the total in 1961 and rising somewhat since then (for instance, 37 per cent
in 1973).[37] In absolute terms this has meant a substantial increase: the
available data show that total trade (exports plus imports) with Asian and
'other' less developed socialist countries increased from $US 5 million in 1950
to $US 460 million in 1961, $US 825 million in 1973 and $US 1360 million in
1974, while that with non-socialist LDCs increased nearly sixfold from
$US 512 million in 1961 to $US 2910 million in 1973. (The group of 'other'
socialist LDCs includes Albania, Cuba and Yugoslavia.) Taking 1962 as 100,
the index for total trade with LDCs had reached 349 by 1973 as compared
with 369 for total trade with all countries. Except for a more rapid rise
during the period 1962–66, fluctuations in the two series have moved very
closely together (see Table 9.1).

LDCs were, however, much more important as export markets than as
sources of import supply: every year since 1964 they have accounted for over
a half of Chinese exports, while non-socialist LDCs alone have absorbed
around 42 per cent. The total LDC share in exports rose rapidly after the
Sino-Soviet split, jumping from 39·7 per cent in 1961 to 56·2 per cent in
1965 and remaining roughly constant since then. In contrast, while the total
LDC share in imports also rose substantially during the early 1960s, reaching
a peak of 39·2 per cent in 1964 (26 per cent if socialist LDCs are excluded),
it has subsequently tended to decline (with certain fluctuations), reaching
21·7 per cent in 1973. Altogether, therefore, China's exports to LDCs have
not only normally exceeded her imports from them, but the former have
grown much more rapidly than the latter; by 492 per cent as compared with
350 per cent between 1961 and 1973 – 620 per cent and 468 per cent respectively, if the Asian socialist countries are excluded. However, such an
export surplus has not been realised on trade with all regional LDC groupings
if taken separately, as we shall see later.

2. *Direction:*

Table 9.4 shows the breakdown of China's LDC trade between regional
groupings. Exports to Hong Kong exceeded those to any other regional LDC
group from 1964 onwards, and went on almost to double their share in total
exports to all LDCs from 18·9 per cent in 1961 to 34·3 per cent in 1973,
though their share in exports to non-socialist LDCs only remained roughly
constant at 43 per cent in both years on account of the declining share of
exports to socialist LDCs. As a proportion of exports to all LDCs, the share
of South Asian, South East Asian and Near Eastern countries combined also
remained roughly constant, averaging a little over 20 per cent. That of African
countries rose by over threefold during the same post-1964 period, while in
the 1970s Latin America, and even certain non-communist southern European

TABLE 9.4 TRADE WITH LDCs: EXPORTS AND IMPORTS TO COUNTRY GROUPS AS PERCENTAGE OF THOSE TO ALL LDCs, AND TRADE BALANCE

| | ABSOLUTE TOTAL FOR ALL LDCs ($US m, Current Prices) | | | Hong Kong & Macao | | | | Malaysia & Singapore | | | NON SOCIALIST COUNTRIES | | | | | | | | | | | | | SOCIALIST COUNTRIES | | | | | |
| | | | | | | | | | | | S.E. Asia, S. Asia & Near East | | | Latin America | | | Africa | | | S. Europe | | | Asian | | | Other | | |
	E	I	B	E	I	B $US m	B as % Total Imports from all Sources	E	I	B $US m	E	I	B $US m	E	I	B $US m	E	I	B $US m	E	I	B $US m	E	I	B $US m	E	I	B $US m
1961	608	364	244	18·9	0·3	114	7·7	8·9	2·5	45	22·7	34·9	11	0·3	2·5	−7	4·8	7·7	1				26·3	26·1	65	18·1	26·1	15
1962	692	378	314	19·9	0·5	136	11·8	9·2	0·1	~64	23·4	34·4	32	0·3	9·0	−32	4·5	5·8	9				24·6	23·8	80	18·1	26·5	25
1963	763	386	377	22·3	0·5	168	14·0	11·8	1·6	84	23·3	31·6	56	0·1	1·8	−6	4·5	14·0	−20				21·6	25·9	65	16·4	24·6	30
1964	919	579	340	27·5	0·3	251	17·1	10·3	0·2	94	23·9	29·7	48	0·2	26·8	−153	5·9	9·3	0				14·7	15·5	45	17·4	18·1	55
1965	1140	625	515	31·1	0·8	350	19·0	10·1	1·6	105	21·9	34·4	35	0·4	16·8	−100	7·5	12·0	10				11·4	14·4	40	17·5	20·0	75
1966	1220	580	640	32·8	0·9	395	19·4	8·2	7·8	55	25·4	31·9	125	0·4	18·1	−100	7·8	8·6	45				12·3	13·8	70	13·1	19·0	50
1967	1145	421	724	27·1	0·2	309	15·9	11·8	11·3	85	23·6	34·4	125	0·4	2·4	−5	9·2	13·1	50				15·7	14·3	120	12·2	23·8	40
1968	1150	376	774	28·3	0·3	324	18·5	14·3	14·6	110	20·4	30·6	120	0·9	0·0	10	7·8	16·0	30				15·7	16·0	120	12·6	22·6	60
1969	1170	441	729	29·1	0·2	339	16·3	13·2	23·8	50	21·8	26·1	140	0·9	0·1	≈10	8·1	20·6	25				12·4	12·5	90	14·5	21·5	75
1970	1190	435	755	31·1	1·1	365	19·1	11·8	11·5	90	21·0	32·2	110	0·8	1·1	5	10·5	16·1	55	0·0	0·1	≈0	10·5	14·9	60	14·3	23·0	70
1971	1335	545	790	33·3	0·9	440	19·1	12·7	6·4	135	15·7	22·9	85	0·7	10·1	−45	13·9	28·4	80	0·0	0·1	≈0	11·2	13·8	75	12·4	17·4	70
1972	1650	820	830	32·4	0·6	530	18·7	10·3	5·5	145	19·4	26·2	105	1·2	25·6	−190	17·3	18·9	40	0·9	0·1	≈15	10·9	9·8	100	11·8	8·5	125
1973	2650	1085	1565	34·3	0·9	815	15·9	12·3	12·4	190	22·5	20·3	375	1·7	23·5	−210	15·8	17·1	100	0·8	0·1	10	13·4	11·5	230	7·5	13·4	55

Source: Calculated from Chen (1975) op. cit.

countries, began to rise over previously almost negligible levels.

Rather a different picture emerges from examination of the import data. Firstly, in contrast to its dominant role in export markets, Hong Kong's share in Chinese imports has been virtually negligible, normally remaining below 1 per cent. The first main group of regions for imports has been South Asia, South East Asia and the Near East, which together accounted for over one-third of all imports in 1961, declining to one-fifth in 1973; the second includes the Asian socialist and 'other' socialist country groups, each of which accounted for over a quarter in 1961 but which have since fallen – the latter less rapidly and sharply. From having comparatively low initial shares, Africa, Malaysia and Singapore, and Latin America have grown in importance. But whereas the share of imports from Africa has grown fairly steadily from about one-fifteenth to almost one-fifth, that for each of the other groups has fluctuated considerably, particularly in the case of Latin America, where it increased from a few percentage points above zero to over a quarter, down to zero and back to a quarter in the space of twelve years.

Correspondingly, the degree of overall trade balance with each of these regional subgroups has varied very substantially: the substantial surplus on total LDC account trade has not been so for all regional LDC groupings taken separately. As would be expected in the political circumstances, there has always been a surplus on trade with the Asian socialist countries and almost always with the 'other' socialist countries, except in 1958, when the total value of trade with them only amounted to $US 5 million in any case. However, by far the most important surplus has been that with Hong Kong and Macao *which in most years since 1962 has financed between 15 per cent and 20 per cent of imports from all sources* (Table 9.4). Furthermore, as can be seen particularly clearly from Figure 9.2 (p. 255), the Hong Kong surplus has consti-tuted the lion's share of the *total* surplus on the *non-socialist* LDC account.[38] Of the other non-socialist country groupings, Malaysia and Singapore made the second largest contribution to this surplus in the early 1960s, but by 1973 had been overtaken by both the Near East, South and South East Asia and African regional group. On the other hand, trade with Latin America has shown a substantially fluctuating deficit during this period (Table 9.4). In other words, there has been considerable heterogeneity in the impact of trade with non-socialist LDCs on the creation of trade surpluses and so on the generation of potential import finance.

Heterogeneity to some extent reappears if trade with individual countries *within* regional LDC groups is examined, since China's trade has by no means been spread evenly. For instance, trade with Argentina, primarily in the form of grain purchases, has dominated the Latin American account. In Africa, the main partners have been Tanzania, Zambia, Nigeria, Egypt, Sudan, Morocco and Uganda; in Asia, Hong Kong, Pakistan, Malaysia, Singapore and Sri Lanka.

3. *Commodity composition:*

As Eckstein remarked over ten years ago, 'it is much more difficult to reconstruct the commodity composition than the direction of Chinese trade.'[39] Data on the overall commodity composition of Chinese trade were reviewed briefly above. However, there are substantial differences between the commodity structure of trade with the various separate country groupings, as can be seen very clearly from the right-hand side of Table 9.3. (It should be noted here that the less developed socialist countries are aggregated with the advanced socialist ones.) For instance, non-socialist LDCs have played virtually no part in supplying any of China's dominant import categories, such as machinery and equipment, iron and steel, or foodgrains; instead, the main category has been 'crude materials, fuels and edible oils', especially rubber, cotton and, until recently, petroleum. In 1974 these imports exceeded half the total from all non-socialist countries excluding Hong Kong, followed by 25 per cent foodstuffs, especially sugar, and 14 per cent non-ferrous metals. The structure of China's exports to these LDCs also differs from her overall export pattern. Again using 1974 data, the most striking feature is that over half were manufactures — mainly of consumer goods — as compared with 40 per cent for all countries, with grains also taking a high share (18 per cent); however textiles and clothing alone had about the same share in Chinese exports to non-socialist LDCs as in total Chinese exports. Exports to Hong Kong, however, deviated somewhat from this, with foodstuffs — most notably animal products — accounting for 63 per cent and 35 per cent respectively in 1974.

The overall picture then for trade with non-socialist LDCs is one of exchange of manufactured consumer goods and some foodstuffs for various mineral and agricultural primary commodities. This compares with the Soviet pattern of exchange of capital goods, plus some consumer goods, for raw materials and some speciality foodstuffs: one which, it can be argued, may be less prone to general developmental problems for less developed partners. At the level of individual countries the Chinese pattern of imports has, for instance, involved purchases of rubber from Indonesia, Malaysia and Sri Lanka, cotton from Sudan, Egypt, Tanzania, Kenya and Uganda, petroleum from Iraq, grain from Argentina, etc. Rubber purchases from Sri Lanka began in 1952 with a five year rubber/rice exchange pact which was effected at prices very favourable to Sri Lanka.[40] This was modified in the second and third five-year pacts with (i) the increasing sale of other Chinese goods, (ii) the introduction of Chinese aid initially for rehabilitation of plantations to compensate for withdrawal of the price premium, but later for a variety of economic goals, and (iii) the subsequent reintroduction of a five cent (later seven cent) price premium. Further, this trade was still sustained when the Chinese harvest was bad by Chinese purchases of rice from Burma for direct shipment to Ceylon. The Indonesian rubber trade was also bilateral, being based on exports of textiles from China instead of rice, and was also backed up with aid, but it was terminated abruptly after Sukarno's fall. On the other hand, the Malaysian trade was until recently based largely on free market purchases, and to some extent tended to fluctuate as a residual to Sri Lankan and Indonesian purchases.[41] From the standpoint of these countries' rubber producers also the Chinese market was of differing significance, never exceeding 17 per cent of the total market in case of Indonesia and 11 per cent in that of Malaya, yet never falling below 21 per cent in that of Sri Lanka and reaching as much as 63 per cent in 1956.[42]

Although the exchange of agricultural or, most commonly, manufactured consumer goods for primary commodities has been the dominant pattern of trade with non-socialist LDCs, there have been other forms of exchanges. For instance, where an aid contract has existed, the pattern of trade has tended to be more diversified, *even if* a good part of that aid is used to support the sort of trade described above; in addition, part is commonly used to import Chinese exports, or on occasion re-exports, of capital goods and intermediates.

Lack of data precludes any detailed analysis of the commodity composition of China's trade with socialist LDCs, to some extent qualitatively different from that with non-socialist LDCs, but a number of patterns appear to have emerged. Firstly, China has exported considerable quantities of commodities which could be regarded as having very high opportunity cost from her own developmental point of view. For instance, during the 1950s Chinese exports of capital goods to North Korea, including complete plants and raw materials, increased her share in Korea's total trade from 9 per cent in 1955 to about 27 per cent in 1957, as compared with a decline in the Soviet share from 80 per cent to 57 per cent over these years.[43] In the mid 1950s Chinese trade with North Vietnam very greatly exceeded Soviet levels,[44] and involved the aid or grant supported export of complete 'turnkey projects'; equipment for the rehabilitation of transport, industry and irrigation works; raw materials for consumer goods industries; and various miscellaneous goods.[45] This pattern changed during the 1960s as the Soviet Union largely took over the role of capital goods supplier while the Chinese exported grain and basic cotton textiles (both on ration in China) to feed and clothe the North Vietnamese. After the Sino-Soviet split, China exported considerable quantities of capital goods, agricultural machinery and grain[46] to Albania. The pattern of trade with Cuba has varied, involving sugar rice exchange plus capital goods exports under aid programmes during the early 1960s,[47] but subsequently settling more into the primary commodity (sugar) for consumer goods category.

4. *Terms:*
At least four factors should be taken into consideration when attempting to evaluate the terms of trade interpreted in a broad sense: (i) its bilateral/ multilateral character; (ii) the prices (actual or nominal) of the commodities exchanged; (iii) the planned regularity or temporary character of the transactions, and (iv) any credit, aid or grant terms contributing to its finance.
(i) *Bilateralism/multilateralism:* China's trade with socialist LDCs has been effected on either a balanced or planned imbalanced bilateral basis — planned imbalance involving Chinese export surpluses, for instance, being built into

much of the trade with the East Asian socialist countries. China's trade with non-socialist LDCs has tended to take place on either the fixed term bilateral or discretionary free market purchase basis (both of these occurred in the case of the rubber trade, as described above). A typical example of the former kind is the five-year Sino-Tanzanian trade agreement signed in 1965, which detailed the annual volume of and growth in exports for both partners, and listed the categories of goods to be exchanged: Tanzanian cotton, sisal, tobacco, copra and other raw materials for Chinese textiles, building materials and stationery supplies.[48] An example of this kind of discretionary purchase is the Chinese grain imports from Argentina which resulted in substantial Chinese deficits on this account, although this should not arise in future years if the trade agreement of February 1977 is implemented. Most Chinese trade with South East Asia falls into this category, with the Chinese running an essentially discretionary export surplus.

(ii) *Prices:* There are no comprehensive price data on Chinese trade in general, let alone on that with LDCs. There is rather a collection of information about individual trading agreements and transactions.[49] This shows plenty of instances in which China has imported a commodity at a price higher than that which probably would have applied had the transaction been effected with the most likely alternative supplier (e.g. the Sri Lankan rubber price described above, the premium for Sudanese cotton, and that for Egyptian cotton in 1955).[50] This is *not* to suggest that China normally pays above the practical equivalent of some world price, but rather that the available evidence does not support the view that China buys its primary commodities from LDCs on the cheap.

Similarly there does not seem to be any consistent evidence to support the hypothesis that China overprices its exports: indeed, if the Soviet literature is to be believed, the complaint would be one of dumping prices.[51] Exports to the Asian socialist LDCs have normally been on highly concessionary terms (see below) although their normal prices are not known. Of exports to non-socialist LDCs, which rose from just over half to just over three quarters of all exports to LDCs between 1961 and 1974, most of those to South East Asia have been on a multilateral 'commercial' basis, i.e. at prices approximating to world levels. Indeed the proportion of exports to non-socialist LDCs accounted for by Hong Kong and Macao *alone* rose from 34 per cent in 1961 to 44 per cent in 1974 in a market where sales depended almost exclusively on commercial competitiveness. In addition, however, there are instances of deliberately concessionary deliveries for political/aid motives to non-socialist LDCs; for instance, in 1964 China sold Sudan $\frac{1}{2}$ million tons of sugar at £51 per ton as compared with an average c.i.f. value of £80 per ton declared by traditional exporters.[52]

(iii) *Discretionary purchases and short and medium term trade agreements:* Not just the bilateral but also part of the multilateral component of Chinese trade has taken place according to planned short/medium term agreements. The Chinese have tended to prefer such contracts, given the importance of fairly accurate projections about trade for domestic planning purposes. The key South East Asian trade is, of course, essentially unplanned, but stability of demand factors particularly in the Hong Kong market, renders it reasonably immune from serious downward fluctuations. However, of the non-bilateral discretionary transactions, some have originated primarily as a means of assistance to the LDC concerned – for instance, the cotton purchases and sugar sales described under (ii), and the purchase of surplus tobacco supplies from Tanzania in 1965.[53]

(iv) *Credits, aid and grants:* The incidence of these has varied very much by region. To preempt the fuller discussion of the ensuing section: (a) most trade with socialist LDCs has been backed by concessionary financial arrangements throughout; (b) a high proportion of trade with African and certain Asian LDCs has been similarly backed: indeed whereas Chinese exports to Africa from 1961–73 amounted to $US 1404 million, total committed aid was $US 1429 million;[54] (c) most of the remaining Asian trade (e.g. to Hong Kong, Malaysia and Singapore) has not been accompanied by aid or concessionary credits; (d) the magnitude of grants/aid under (a) and (b) make it essential to take these into account when calculating the real prices of imports from China.

IV. China's Foreign Aid

Four aspects of China's foreign economic aid concern us at this stage: its magnitude, its country-wise distribution, its terms, and its nature (i.e. the purpose for which it was offered).

1. *Magnitude:*
Just as with trade flows, financial aid commitments and disbursements have fluctuated substantially during the last two decades. Excluding economic aid to the Asian and 'other' socialist countries and revolutionary movements, aid commitments fell to a virtually negligible amount in 1959 and to further, albeit higher, troughs in 1962, 1966 and 1969, with rising peaks in 1961, 1965 and 1970 (see Table 9.5). A rough periodisation helps to outline the trends. In the mid-1950s China followed up her aid to Korea during the early 1950s by starting a modest aid programme to non-socialist LDCs. This was interrupted by the Great Leap Forward, but was started up again at more ambitious levels after the Sino-Soviet split; it was in turn interrupted by the Cultural Revolution, and, despite some small improvement during 1967/8, remained at low levels until a very substantially more ambitious programme was introduced in 1970; the latter has, however, tended to fall off in recent years. Actual disbursements to non-socialist countries have been, on average over the period, about 50 per cent of commitments (as compared with about 55 per cent for the Soviet Union) and have tended to fluctuate in the same way.

Some idea of the comparative international magnitude of Chinese aid to non-socialist LDCs is given in Table 9.6. Taking the years 1974/5, if the lower

TABLE 9.5 CHINA'S ECONOMIC AID TO NON-COMMUNIST COUNTRIES BY REGION 1956–74 (IN PERCENTAGES)

A	Total ($US m)	% Africa	% S. Asia[1]	% E. Asia[2]	% Middle East	% Latin America	% S. Europe	(Total according to Horvath ($US m) 1957–77)
1956	39.1	—	32.5	57.3	10.2	—	—	n.a.
1957	25.6	—	78.1	21.9	—	—	—	38
1958	56.4	8.7	62.9	—	28.3	—	—	51
1959	0.1	—	—	—	100.0	—	—	0
1960	57.6	43.4	36.8	19.8	—	—	—	57
1961	167.2	23.4	76.6	—	—	—	—	125
1962	25.3	—	41.5	39.5	19.0	—	—	10
1963	90.4	81.8	—	—	18.2	—	—	89
1964	231.6	51.5	1.8	—	46.7	—	—	263
1965	308.6	6.8	84.2	—	8.9	—	—	193
1966	35.0	42.9	57.1	—	—	—	—	33
1967	79.8	37.3	50.1	—	12.5	—	—	64
1968	57.6	10.4	72.9	—	16.7	—	—	65
1969	45.0	100.0	—	—	—	—	—	52
1970	722.5	63.6	30.4	—	6.0	—	—	750
1971	565.7	57.2	22.7	—	12.7	7.4	—	505
1972	647.9	43.5	10.5	—	21.3	18.0	6.6	541
1973	428.0	78.3	15.0	—	6.8	—	—	440
1974	197.0*	87.3	—	12.7	—	—	—	197
TOTAL	3780.4							3473

Sources: 1956–72 W. Bartke, *China's Economic aid*, 1975
1973–74 C. H. Fogarty, in USCJEC 1975 (from CIA data)

Notes: * Estimate based on incomplete coverage
1 Pakistan, Sri Lanka, Nepal, Burma, Indonesia
2 Laos and Cambodia

N.B. A. Coverage of Chinese economic aid to socialist E. Asian economics and Albania is excluded, as is economic aid to revolutionary movements.
   B. Technical cooperation agreements are omitted.

TABLE 9.6 CHINESE AID TO NON-SOCIALIST LDCs IN INTERNATIONAL PERSPECTIVE, 1971–3 AVERAGE

	Magnitude ($ mn)	% GDP
China (Economist Estimate)	447	0·24
China (Bartke)	547	0·29
17 Developed Countries	8430	0·32
Including		
France	1278	0·62
Netherlands	277	0·58
Belgium	190	0·52
Sweden	210	0·49
UK	571	0·37
USA	3141	0·27
Japan	703	0·22
Italy	135	0·11
7 Socialist Countries	1547	0·24
Bulgaria	46	0·37
Czechoslovakia	139	0·36
E. Germany	24	0·05
Hungary	78	0·46
Poland	136	0·22
Romania	187	0·80
USSR	945	0·21

Sources: Economist, *Key World Indicators*, London 1976.
Line 2: Bartke (*op. cit.*)

(and sourceless) estimates in total Chinese economic aid given in the table is used, then average Chinese aid as a percentage of GDP was as high as that for the East European socialist countries combined; if instead one of the recognised estimates of the Chinese aid total is used, then the average as a percentage of GDP exceeds the East European. As compared with the share of gross aid in the GDPs of seventeen advanced capitalist countries, China almost reaches their mean of 0·32 per cent and exceeds the values for the USA, Switzerland and Japan. It should of course be noted that 1971–3 were, for China, comparatively 'high aid' years as compared with the 1950s and 1960s, with the implication that her record would compare less favourably if a much longer time period were used. In any case, according to Bartke, total gross Soviet aid to non-socialist LDCs between 1954 and 1972 was 2·6 times that of the Chinese.[55]

China has also channelled substantial economic aid and grant flows to less developed socialist countries. Excluding military aid, Tansky[56] estimated a figure of $US 1·8 billion prior to 1972, which is almost as much as her aid to non-socialist LDCs during the same period. Taking this into account, the

Chinese aid commitment record obviously stands up well as compared with that of the advanced capitalist countries, while its relative position *vis-à-vis* the Soviet Union remains similar to that described above. Note however that, because of its softer financial terms, the comparative Chinese aid record appears better if the evaluation is made in terms of *net* flows.

It is, however, important when examining figures such as these to note that coverage of Chinese economic aid statistics compiled outside China is less than comprehensive. Two main compilations of aid to non-socialist LDCs exist: that by Bartke for 1956–73, which lists aid agreements by country, and details of aid projects both by country and by branch of economic activity,[57] and that by Horvath for 1957–74, which is based on US CIA reports and which lists all the agreements covered.[58] A third, by Fogarty, presents some of the unadjusted CIA data in summary form.[59] Since, overall, Bartke's series yields the higher total *and* since the details of all the projects included are provided,[60] these are normally used here, updated to 1974 by the US CIA data. Both studies are concerned with financial flows, thus excluding those technical assistance programmes unaccompanied by loans, where the Chinese paid the salaries of their aid personnel while the recipient government provided accommodation and certain supplies.[61]

2. *Distribution:*

The pattern of distribution of Chinese aid to *non-socialist* LDCs has changed considerably over a period of time.[62] The earliest non-socialist recipients were from Asia and the Middle East (e.g. Burma, Cambodia, Nepal, Sri Lanka, Indonesia, Egypt, Algeria, Yemen). Aid to Africa started in 1960 with Guinea and continued in 1961 with Ghana and Mali, in 1963 with Somalia, and in 1964–5 with five other countries (including Tanzania). Other important new recipients during these years were Pakistan and Afghanistan in 1965. There were very few new recipients in the low aid interlude during and after the Cultural Revolution, but a large number during the aid revival from 1970 onwards. Some old customers, particularly in Asia and the Middle East, survived throughout the period, but others fell by the wayside – such as Indonesia after the fall of Sukarno and Burma after 1961. Of all regions, Africa got the largest share (virtually half), followed by Asia (one-third), Middle East (about one-eighth), Latin America (one-twentieth), and Southern Europe (just over one-hundredth). (Note that these figures tend to favour recent recipients insofar as the average level of aid commitments increased over that time because of world inflation.) Of single countries, Pakistan alone got one-eighth of total aid commitments to non-socialist LDCs, eight countries out of a total of 47 recipients accounted for one-half and the botton eight recipients got less than 3 per cent.[63] Such a concentration of aid commitments towards selected less developed recipients is also observed in the Soviet case, where the nominal cumulative totals between 1956 and 1973 for the most favoured are also very much higher: for instance, $US 1593 million to India, $US 1198 million to Egypt, $US 826 million to Afghanistan, $US 562 million to Iran,

$US 549 million to Iraq, $US 534 million to Turkey, and $US 474 million to the most favoured Chinese beneficiary, Pakistan, which obtained $US 445 million from China between the same dates.[64] However, whereas the ten major Chinese beneficiaries have been spread widely throughout Africa and Asia, the major Soviet (non-communist) ones have been in very close proximity to its own borders. Indeed, of the cumulative total of $US 11 billion of economic assistance to the non-socialist Third World pledged by the Soviet Union since 1954, *80 per cent* has gone to 'a narrow band of nations, extending from the Mediterranean to China's south-western borders',[65] irrespective of their income levels. Sub-Saharan Africa obtained only 8 per cent, Latin America just over 5 per cent, and East Asia about 1·5 per cent (see Table 9.8).[66] Furthermore, whereas seven out of the top ten non-socialist Chinese beneficiaries up to 1974 had a per capita income below $US 150 in 1973, only three (India, Afghanistan and Pakistan) did in the Soviet case.

Data on Chinese economic aid to socialist LDCs are very fragmentary. According to Tansky's figures,[67] which cover the period prior to 1972, North Vietnam was the main beneficiary, being given a total of $US 962 million, followed by Albania with $US 359 million, North Korea with $US 330 million, Mongolia with $US 115 million and Cuba with $US 100 million.[68]

3. *Terms:*

By far the most important characteristic of Chinese aid is what is widely acknowledged to be the almost unsurpassed generosity of its terms. The typical Chinese aid contract of the 1970s provides an interest-free loan with a twenty year repayment period *and* a ten year moratorium before repayments commence. This differs strikingly from the financial terms of aid from most other sources.[69] The terms of World Bank ordinary loans are related to international interest rates and overall international financial conditions, so that a 1976 contract required repayment over twenty years of almost 9 per cent interest.[70] IDA credits require repayment over thirty to fifty years with about a $\frac{1}{2}$ per cent 'service' charge and ten to twenty years grace.[71] Soviet loans have usually been at fairly soft interest rates (often about 2·5 per cent), but normally with short repayment periods (twelve years) and little, if any, grace period, so that the overall terms do not come out very favourably when the net aid inflow is examined, as happened in the Indian case.[72] Since 1964, a small part of Soviet aid has been on even harder terms – at higher interest rates with a 10–15 per cent downpayment and five to ten year repayment period.[73] Of course, not all Chinese aid has been given on quite such favourable terms: in the early years of the aid programme, interest rates of 2·5 per cent and shorter repayment periods were by no means uncommon – for instance, certain loans were made at this rate in the late 1950s and early 1960s but with ten year repayment and one year grace periods. On the other hand, outright grants have been over four times more common than the 'harder' aid contracts; according to Bartke, such grants constituted 9·1 per

TABLE 9.7 DISTRIBUTION OF CHINESE ECONOMIC AND COMMITMENTS TO TOP TEN NON-SOCIALIST BENEFICIARY COUNTRIES

| | Bartke & CIA 1956–74 | | Horvath 1957–74 | | % GNP (1973) ($US) | Grant ratio (G/L) | | | Adjusted grant ratio (G/L') | | |
	Total (1)	% (2)	Total (3)	% (4)	(5)	→1962 (6)	1963–69 (7)	1970 (8)	→1962 (9)	1963–69 (10)	1970 (11)
Pakistan	495·7	13·1	391	11·3	120	–	·7675	·7822	–	·7024	·7149
Tanzania	402·5	10·7	331	9·5	130	–	·7933	·8410	–	·7262	·7649
Indonesia	255·0	6·8	105	3·0	130	·3327	·4280	–	·3327	·4138	–
Zambia	219·8	5·8	279	8·0	430	–	·7675	·8410	–	·7024	·7649
Somalia	134·0	3·5	133	3·8	80	–	·7886	·8424	–	·7203	·7661
Sri Lanka	132·0	3·5	155	4·5	120	·9309	·5317	·6765	·8412	·5019	·6478
Zaire	130·0	3·4	100	2·9	140	–	–	·8410	–	–	·7649
Egypt	122·0	3·2	134	3·9	250	–	·7675	1·0000	–	·7024	·9000
Algeria 50%	99·9	2·6	100	2·9	570	1·0000	·7844	·8410	·9000	·7204	·7649
Nepal	98·7	2·6	99	2·9	90	1·0000	·5922	·7801	·9000	·5534	·7131

Sources: Cols 1 and 2: as Table 9.6
Cols 3–4, 6–11: Horvath 1976 op. cit.
Col 5: World Bank Economic Atlas

Note: Cols 6–11 calculated from estimates of G/L and G/L' for individual aid commitments by using the nominal magnitude of commitments as weights. G/L and G/L' are defined and discussed on p. 234 and in Appendix 3.

cent of committed aid to non-socialist countries between 1956 and 1973, while zero interest loans with modest grace and long repayment periods have been by far the most important form of aid contract. Indeed, *all* aid contracts with African countries for which interest rate terms have been reported have been at a zero rate.[74] In contrast, only 5 per cent of Soviet aid to non-socialist countries has consisted of outright grants.

Furthermore, the financial advantages of Chinese aid have been enhanced by certain additional factors. The first of these has been the availability of Chinese technical assistance as described above, combined with the assumption of considerate direct responsibility for ensuring that projects get underway successfully. The second factor has been the way in which Chinese aid personnel normally live no more, and often less, luxuriously, than those among whom they are working.[75] This increases the real value of Chinese aid by an estimated 25 per cent compared with that from Western sources, when, as often happens, technical personnel and skill workers are paid out of aid funds.[76] The third factor has been the extent to which the Chinese, and indeed the Soviets, have permitted repayments to be made in soft currency, normally involving the supply of recipient country products to China. This increases the real value of aid to the recipient relative to repayment in hard currency, whereby the donor would have been able to purchase a greater value of recipient country products. However the potential gains from this provision depend crucially on the terms of trade which are set.

Fourthly, the Chinese have adopted a very flexible approach towards

TABLE 9.8 MAGNITUDE AND TERMS OF CHINESE ECONOMIC AID TO NON-COMMUNIST LDCs, 1956–73, AS COMPARED WITH MAGNITUDE OF SOVIET AID 1954–72

(*$US m*)	*Grant*	*Interest Free*	*2·5% Interest*	*Total*	*Soviet Total 1954–72 (Excl. Communist Countries)*
Asia	257·6[1]	711·9	69·7[2]	1089·2	2353·0
Africa	30·6[3]	1612·6	0·5[4]	1643·7	1252·0
Middle East	21·0[5]	428·9	–	449·9	4092·0
Latin America	–	159·0	–	159·0	448·0
Europe	–	42·6	–	42·6	84·0
Total	309·2	2993·4	70·2	3384·4	8229·0

Source: Bartke, *op. cit.* 1975
Notes:
1. Burma 4·2, Cambodia 69·4, Laos 4·0, Nepal 43·7, Pakistan 110·0, Sri Lanka 26·3.
2. Burma 4·2, Indonesia 55·0, Sri Lanka 10·5
3. Algeria 6·9, Kenya 3·0, Mali 8·1, Somalia 3·0, Tanzania 6·6, Uganda 3·0
4. Tanzania 0·5
5. Afghanistan 7·0, Egypt 14·0

assisting beneficiaries with the local costs of aid projects. A typical method is to supply commodities to a state trading corporation in the beneficiary country, and use the proceeds from their sale to the local population to finance local project costs. However, the Chinese have also given direct cash budgetary aid (e.g. to Guinea in 1970). On the other hand, in possible contrast to these 'aid enhancing' factors, the real value of Chinese aid *may* have been reduced to the extent that it was tied to the purchase of products from China which could have been acquired more cheaply elsewhere in the world market. However, even if the effect of tying were to turn out to have been 'aid detracting', this in turn could have been offset by Chinese purchases of commodities supplied as part of repayment terms at above world market prices.

The orthodox literature on foreign aid has attempted to incorporate many of the above mentioned factors in a summary measurement of the real

TABLE 9.9 DISTRIBUTION OF
CHINESE ECONOMIC AID BY
TYPE OF PROJECT

	Number of Projects	
	Completed by 1973	*Total*
Agriculture	16	36
Mining	2	3
Light Industry		
Textile Mills	13	27
Other Plants	63	100
Pharmaceutical Plants	3	3
Heavy Industry	1	1
Oil Industry	1	2
Power Stations	9	16
Electrification	3	7
Transport		
Roads	12	24
Rail	1	4
Bridges	11	15
Misc.	2	4
Communications		
(Broadcasting)	9	9
Irrigation & Water	10	20
Construction		
Buildings	31	41
Hospitals	7	10
Medical Aid	4	14
Other	6	17

Source: Bartke 1975

transfer of resources involved, through the development of the concept of the grant equivalent of a loan, and of the associated concept of the grant ratio. Essentially the grant equivalent (G) of a loan equals the difference between the face value of the loan commitment (L) and the present value of repayments to be made, while the grant ratio is equal to G/L, though both indicators can be broadened to take account of such factors as commodity overpricing, aid-tying, and soft currency repayments.[77] Horvath has made a complete set of computations of the part ratio and grant equivalents of all Chinese aid contracts for each country in an attempt to represent their financial characteristics by readily analysable indicators.[78] However, serious differences are encountered in the interpretation of his work. Briefly, since these issues are discussed in full in Appendix 3, this is partly because of the limited utility of these concepts under any circumstances: their values are extremely sensitive to the precise discount rate chosen, and they in any case only give the grant element from the donor's standpoint. But it is also partly because of the particular assumptions Horvath makes — notably a uniform discount rate of 10 per cent and a uniform 10 per cent adjustment factor for tying. Consequently, (see Appendix 3), (i) the grant element in the early years aid transactions is understated relative to that in later years; (ii) the grant element in Chinese aid commitments in general, relative to those of other countries, is probably understated, given that China is a fast growing planned economy in which the opportunity cost of investible resources used for aid purposes is consequently very high; (iii) inter-country variations in the impact of tying are ignored along with possible changes over a period of time and these have been significant and by no means always negative (see further below). This means that in virtually all cases, his figures can only be used with very careful qualifications. In Table 9.7, weighted averages for the top ten aid receivers for three separate sub-periods have been calculated from Horvath's estimates for individual aid commitments, where the magnitude of such aid commitments were used as weights.[79] Clearly aid was given on very favourable terms during the 1970s, and also in most instances during the 1950s and 1960s; the few relatively low observations for the grant ratio arise because of the short repayment and grace periods (e.g. before 1963, Indonesia received two Chinese aid commitments at between 2 and 2·5 per cent interest, but with eleven-year repayment and one-year grace periods). There are, however, underestimates of the grant ratio for the reasons explained in full in Appendix 3. For these same reasons, the adjusted grant ratio estimates should perhaps be regarded more as an exercise in the calculation of the impact on the ratio of certain additional assumptions, rather than as a more accurate description of the real world situation. Altogether, therefore, these ratios add little, if anything, to the information which can be obtained by direct examination of the terms of the financial contract.

4. *Contracted uses:*
The distribution of Chinese aid to non-socialist LDCs by type of project is

given in Table 9.9. This brings out clearly the predominance of infrastructural and light industrial projects. In value terms, about 35 per cent was committed for transportation projects alone, 23 per cent for light industrial plants, 15 per cent for agricultural and related multipurpose projects, and only 5 per cent for heavy industrial projects — with a wide variety of uses for the residual, including food aid, construction, cash budgetary aid, balance of payments loans, etc.[80] Indeed, aid for heavy industry has been confined to one heavy machine complex in Pakistan. This concentration on relatively labour intensive projects seems to have been an important factor underlying the success of Chinese aid. Such projects tend to be more in tune with the local skills available or easily acquirable, to be implementable with substantial components of Chinese labour if necessary, and to use locally available raw materials. This, as Fogarty points out, has helped China to cope successfully with some of the local shortages which have often created serious problems for aid projects from other donors.[81] Furthermore, the Chinese not only frequently help recipients raise the requisite local funds (as described above), but also provide the administrative and skilled labour immediately required to be paid at local wage rates, simultaneously training local labour to replace them.

Detailed data on the distribution of Chinese air projects to socialist countries are not available, but it has been considerably more orientated to heavy industry or the infrastructure for heavy industry, including 'large' projects such as the 1000 million Kwh Mao Tse-tung hydro-electric installation at Vau i Dejes in Albania. This suggests that Chinese aid to socialist LDCs may have been superior to that given to non-socialist LDCs, insofar as building a heavy industrial base may contribute more to the attainment of national self-reliance and to the development of the productive forces.

The Chinese distribution of projects, particularly to non-socialist LDCs, contrasts sharply with that of Soviet aid, of which as much as three quarters has been committed for heavy industry (including 33 per cent for steel mills), and a further 10 per cent for dams, irrigation and hydroelectric projects.[82] Projects have included steel mills in Iran, Pakistan and India, and the Aswan and Euphrates Dams. As with China, the USSR has backed up its projects with substantial technical assistance, but has on the whole run into more local shortages and difficulties than the Chinese. Furthermore, in certain branches of economic activity (fishing, shipping, herding, irrigation and hydro-electric power) the USSR has ventured into joint ownership with LDCs.

V. Evaluating China's Economic Relations with LDCs: Methodology

Among other things, Section III and IV have demonstrated the following: firstly, that exports to LDCs have not only been a very important component of total exports, but that they have also enabled China to run a substantial surplus on her LDC account; secondly, that a good deal of Chinese trade with

LDCs has been on what may be deemed the 'colonial' pattern of primary commodity imports and manufactured consumer goods exports; thirdly, that aid has been an important background factor to certain parts of China's trade with LDCs, particularly in the case of African and certain South Asian countries, as well as in the case of socialist LDCs; and fourthly, that aid projects have rarely been designed to create the heavy industrial base essential for independent self-reliant (Chinese-style) development.

Evidence such as this has naturally led commentators to ask whether China's trade really differs in practice from that of the West or the USSR, whom she has criticised so fiercely, and whether, despite its comparatively favourable financial terms, her aid to non-socialist LDCs is essentially little more than an instrument for Chinese trade promotion — and one which results more in LDC trade dependency on China than in the stimulation of self-reliant development?

The charges implicit in questions such as these are commonly advanced, and not just in the Soviet literature. For instance:

... outside China, Peking assumes the posture and reality of a hard-boiled and seasoned capitalist. It has learnt all the capitalist gimmicks in sales promotion and advertising, hire purchase, exhibitions and so on. It has mastered the art of watching market trends and adjusting prices on the basis of supply and demand[83]

The main current criticism of Chinese goods in Africa is not of their quality, but the fact that their ready availability inhibits the importing country from setting up light industries to manufacture comparable goods; a more sinister interpretation would be that China is neutralising potential competition[84]

China's aid programme is limited: in most countries it consists of a new factory, a road, an experimental farm, and medical aid teams, but usually not in sufficient depth in a single country nor sufficiently widespread to create a meaningful pattern[85]

Yes despite critical comments such as these in the literature, as well as favourable ones, to date there appears to have been no attempt to construct anything even approximating to a clear set of evaluation criteria, possibly because the exercise is a somewhat difficult one.

The first distinction to be made is that between the *nature* and the *effects* of the trade and/or aid relationship. Three sorts of question may then be raised about the former. The first concerns the extent to which the Chinese record matches up to Chinese claims about their trade and aid policies. The second concerns the extent to which it marks a new departure in international economic relations: is it nonetheless subject to the familiar criticisms levelled against advanced capitalist countries and, by some authors, against the Soviet Union and other centrally planned East European economies? In other words, to what extent does it display the features of 'capitalist' or 'social' imperialism? This in turn involves issues such as excess profitability and penetration, where the former is defined as buying 'cheap' and selling 'dear', and the latter as obtaining control over markets, productive assets, or natural resources. The third issue concerns the hypothetical conditional of the extent to which China could have been expected to 'do better' (in senses to be defined below).

Similarly, questions may be raised about the *effects* of their trade/aid relationships with China on particular LDCs — for instance, what the actual impact has been on variables such as growth, industrialisation, balance of payments, or employment, and what it has been on less straightforward matters such as class differentiation, and the advance of socialism or of capitalism. Conceptually, these questions are quite distinct from those about the nature of the aid/trade relationship since their outcome is determined essentially by the governments of the relevant LDCs and not by the Chinese. However, the two sets of questions cannot be entirely separated in practice since the Chinese can hardly be treated as not knowing that if they give aid to country A, the effects will be very different from those which would obtain in country B owing to, say, the very different political complexion of the government. Thus, although our evaluation will focus on issues connected with the nature of Chinese trade and aid, we shall also discuss briefly certain aspects of its effects.

VI. Evaluating China's Economic Relations with LDCs: The Evidence

A. *The Nature of the Trade and Aid Policies*

1. *Chinese claims vindicated?:*
As mentioned earlier, few would dispute the view that by and large, China has lived up to most of its aid-giving principles. Except in the early years of the aid programme, before China had learned for herself the costs of credits on Soviet terms, aid has been interest-free with long repayment and grace periods. The requisite technical assistance has always been available, and the personnel concerned have not only lived comparatively frugally in the recipient country, but also trained their replacements and left promptly thereafter. Plant and equipment supplied have not usually been the most modern by international standards but *have* tended to operate successfully. As Fogarty puts it,

> Compared with other foreign aid programmes during the past five years, the Chinese have had a good performance record. Earlier frictions . . . have practically disappeared and the LDCs appear satisfied with the operation of the programme. The Chinese have avoided some of the bottlenecks and delays that impede most aid programmes by assuming a larger share of responsibility for implementation. China's success as an aid donor

is also attributable to its understanding of the needs of developing
nations . . .[86]

Even if certain commodities supplied by China under aid programmes could
have been obtained more cheaply from some other source, the rather generous
terms of Chinese loans have normally more than offset such a price advantage
when compared with cheaper initial outlays but more expensive finance. And
although light industrial projects with short gestation periods have probably
accounted for quite a low share of aid commitments (20—25 per cent in non-
socialist LDCs), the remainder have, especially in socialist LDCs, included
important infrastructural and a few heavy industrial projects.

The two main caveats about Chinese fulfilment of her aid principles are
firstly, the impact on the attainment of self-reliance in the recipient country
of the trade flows normally accompanying aid, and secondly, the large gap
between commitments and disbursements. To put the first question another
way; has progress towards national self-reliance made by some Chinese aid
project been more than offset by the opening up of the domestic market to
Chinese goods? Whether for director or indirect reasons, no statistical
formulas are needed to conclude that China has enhanced trade relations with
her aid recipient countries'.[88] The data in Table 9.10 which present the
percentage changes in China's share in the imports and exports of selected
countries between the early 1960s and 1970s show a modest positive net
increase overall for the main aid recipients listed, which would naturally
appear more striking in absolute terms.

Such trade expansion is unlikely to have retarded self-reliance in the
socialist LDCs, where China has supplied capital goods, intermediates
and essential primaries, with manufactured consumer goods being exported
only as specifically required by the recipient. However, in the non-socialist
LDCs, a high proportion of the trade which has accompanied aid has involved
Chinese goods? Whether for direct or indirect reasons, no statistical
formulae are needed to conclude that China has enhanced trade relations with
balances in China's favour. Of the seven countries in Table 9.10 which were
listed among China's top ten non-socialist aid receivers in Table 9.7, only
Pakistan and Tanzania had balances in China's favour for both of the years
covered (1971 and 1973), with Egypt joining them for the year 1973 only.
These surpluses were largely explained by the timing of large aid disbursements
in these particular years: Pakistan had surpluses with China at the end of the
1960s, while Tanzanian total surpluses with China during the 1960s were
almost five times the total of her deficits (i.e. before the exceptionally high
imports related to construction of the Tanzam railway).[89] Altogether, Africa's
total deficit on China trade during the 1960s was roughly equal to the total
value of China's actual aid disbursements. This suggests that special aid-
related deliveries had been responsible for most of the trade deficits of aid
recipients, and that other components of trade have tended to be reasonably
balanced, presumably as a consequence of the bilateral agreements which

AND 1973, AND ITS CHANGE DURING THE 1960s

	Year	Total Trade ($US m)	Trade with China ($US m)	Trade Balance with China ($US m)	Share of China in Total Trade	Share of USSR in Total Trade	Share of No 1 Trade Partner	China's Rank	USSR's Rank	Country with Top Rank	Change in Chinese Share of Imports 1961/6–1967/72 (Selected countries only)	Change in Chinese Share of Exports 1961/6–1967/72 (Selected countries only)
Hong Kong	1971	6,258	567	−547	9.1	0.2	22.9	3	39	USA		
	1973	10,682	1147	−1041	9.8	0.2	20.0					
Malaysia	1971	3,081	84	−48	2.7	1.7	18.8	7	12	Japan		
	1973	5,839	231	−69	4.0	1.9	18.7					
Singapore	1971	4,582	148	−118	3.2	1.1	19.1	9	17	Malaysia		
	*1973	8,680	284	−180	3.3	0.9	17.1					
Sri Lanka	1971	652	61	≃0	9.3	3.3	14.9	2	10	UK	+2.3[a]	+2.9[a]
	*1973	823	70	4	8.5	2.1	8.9					
Pakistan	1971	1,592	65	−5	4.1	3.7	18.7	7	8	USA	+1.5	−0.7
	1973	1,921	62	−34	3.2	1.4	15.0					
Syria	1971	633	17	−4	2.7	8.9	(USSR)	6	2	USSR	+1.6[b]	−2.0[b]
	1973	934	51	4	5.5	10.1						
Iraq	1971	2,224	21	−17	0.9	3.8	16.5	16	4	Italy		
	1973	1,008	42	−30	4.2	8.5	3.4					
Egypt	1971	1,709	44	9	2.5	25.6	(USSR)	14	1	USSR	−0.2[b]	−2.5[b]
	1973	2,031	45	−7	2.2	21.1						
Sudan	1971	687	55	9	8.0	11.2	14.1	3	7	India	+2.1[c]	+3.7[c]
	*1973	893	93	8	10.4	2.9	6.5					
Tanzania	1971	581	96	−72	16.5	0.2	21.9	2	28	UK	+11.4	+0.9
	*1973	766	114	−86	14.9	0.5	17.0					
Zambia	1971	1,231	51	39	4.1	≃0	19.9	9	40	UK		
	1973	1,668	35	6	2.1	≃0	20.3					
Nigeria	1971	3,304	29	−28	0.8	1.9	26.3	14	11	UK		
	1973	5,310	44	−29	0.8	0.8	21.6					
Morocco	1971	1,196	34	3	2.8	3.8	33.1	12	8	France		
	1973	1,975	40	11	2.0	3.5	32.6					
Uganda	1971	425	5	1	1.1	0.6	27.7	19	17	UK	−0.6	−3.9
	*1973	397	7	4	1.7	1.3	23.2					
Somalia	1971	n.a.	1	≃0	n.a.	6.5	25.5	10	3	Italy	+0.9[c]	+0.6[c]
	*1973	98	n.a.	n.a.	1.0	n.a.	n.a.	n.a.	n.a.	n.a.		
Algeria	1971	2,073	21	5	1.0	5.1	31.9	14	5	France		
	1973	n.a.	n.a.	n.a.	n.a.	n.a.	n.a.	n.a.	n.a.	n.a.		

Sources: U.N. Yearbooks of International Trade Statistics; last two

Notes: * Among top ten aid recipients   [a] 1962/6–1967/71   [b] 1960/6–1967/73   [c] 1963/7–1968/72.

regulate many of them. Furthermore, as in Tanzania, part of such deficits may be accounted for by the planned supply of goods for sale to defray the domestic costs of aid projects.

On the other hand, even given the fact that the commodity exchange part of China's trade with this aid-recipient sub-group of LDCs has been reasonably balanced, the stimulus to its growth given by the aid relationship together with its overall character of raw-materials-for-consumer-manufactures, has essentially reinforced the importance of a 'colonial' pattern of trade. And as is well known from the literature on colonialism, this may both destroy existing artisan industry and retard modern industrialisation possibilities, particularly if the exporting partner is not at all that much higher a level of development and is selling labour intensive consumer manufactures.

Four further points have, however, to be taken into account here. Firstly, China largely *replaced* older markets and sources of supply (see for instance Horvath's calculations on the decline in the US share). Secondly, trade-with-aid normally took place in a regular planned fashion in accordance with some negotiated agreement, thus exerting a stabilising influence on the foreign sector. Thirdly, as Table 9.10 brings out extremely clearly, the share in total trade achieved by the Chinese has been comparatively low in most countries. Only in Tanzania in 1971 and 1973 was the share greater than 10 per cent, with Sudan exceeding this in 1973 — and in none of these countries was China the leading trade partner. These figures provide no evidence whatsoever for the general existence of dangerous economic 'dependence' on China by these major aid-recipient non-socialist LDCs: rather Chinese trade often grew at the expense of some leading partner, normally ex-colonial, on which 'dependence' *had* been excessive. In virtually all the black African countries listed in Table 9.10, the share of the number one trading partner *even in the early 1970s* exceeded 20 per cent, and in many exceeded 25 per cent. Much of the 'colonial' pattern of trade was retained, to be sure, but it was at least diversified — and diversified in a way which gave the home country access to almost unprecedentedly 'cheap' loans and technical assistance, which together offered very real opportunities for promoting more self-reliant development. The fourth point arises from the negotiated bilateral character of much of the trade with aid recipients, which means that the precise commodity composition of Chinese exports is arranged with the government of the recipient country. For instance, when the agreement was made to finance the local costs of the Tanzam railway by the sale of Chinese goods, it was also agreed that as far as possible such goods should not include those which were manufactured locally, and a Zambian Industrial and Commercial Association mission visited the twenty-sixth trade fair in Canton to select appropriate goods which were of the best value.[90] Although cutting out all competition with local production was impossible, the consequent planned approach to trade prevented the emergence of any very serious problems on this score. Indeed, Chinese aid projects themselves often play a major role in making Chinese exports re-dundant (e.g. the construction of textile mills in many countries, the establishment of a green tea industry in Morocco, etc).[91] Altogether, therefore, although competition from Chinese imports must have generated some problems in aid recipient countries, its potential impact has been mitigated and controlled as a result of the factors enumerated above.

What then of the second caveat about China's fulfilment of her aid principles, namely the gap between commitments and disbursements? Firstly, the situation has been improving substantially during the 1970s; partly because of the sheer passage of time, with recipients steadily using up aid extensions too large to have been all utilized at one go; partly because of the growing Chinese expertise in implementing aid projects; and possibly partly because of the introduction of ways to help defray the domestic resource costs which were frequently constraining take-up of commitments — a problem to which the Chinese have devoted considerable attention. Secondly, the data are very much affected by political changes, which explain the non-disbursement of substantial quantities of committed aid to, for instance, Indonesia, Burma and Egypt during the 1960s. If the disbursement-commitment ratio after the revival of a high aid strategy in 1970 is examined (using Horvath's data), this rises from 14 per cent in 1970 (when total commitments peaked at $US 750 million) to 65 per cent in 1972, 83 per cent in 1973 and 200 per cent in 1974.[92] This level and pattern of delivery-commitment is respectable by international standards: note that although the whole post-1956 period ratio is roughly equal to that for the USSR, unlike the latter, the Chinese ratio has recorded a very significant improvement — and, of course, the net aid disbursed is higher because of the softer financial terms. Finally, the delivery-commitment ratio for that part of Chinese aid (almost half) which has been extended to socialist countries has naturally been higher, as a result of the much greater possibilities for planned coordination.

Thus to sum up the argument so far, the Chinese aid record appears to have matched up well to most of its aid principles. The associated trade flows may have been 'colonial' in their pattern, but (i) unless it is assumed that primary production could have been cut and resources transferred elsewhere, this normally meant diversification by country on a more stable basis, often away from what previously had been excessive and volatile 'dependence' on one partner, (ii) for most non-socialist LDCs, the relative importance of trade with China still remained comparatively low as compared with that with leading partners, (iii) the potentially adverse impact of imports from China on domestic import substitution has been recognised by both partners and attempts made to control it, and (iv) China has constructed aid projects in production lines which make her own exports redundant.

So far only the trade-aid package component of China's international economic relations has been discussed. But what of China's trade record when it is not accompanied by aid? It is impossible to distinguish precisely between aid related and non-aid related trade flows, but if all trade to Hong Kong, Malaysia and Singapore plus half that to 'other' South East Asian, South Asian, the Near East and Latin American countries is taken as a crude proxy, such non-aid related trade constituted 39 per cent of exports and 20 per cent of imports in 1961, 54 per cent and 29 per cent respectively in 1970, and 59 per cent and 35 per cent respectively in 1973. Here the countries concerned are all non-socialist, the form of the trade is much more likely to be discretionary and multilateral, and those features of the Chinese aid programme which have tended to offset any adverse consequences of the trade relationship are by definition absent. The characteristics of this trade have been large surpluses mainly in hard currency (except in Latin America), and either a 'colonial' or almost one-way pattern (very low imports from Hong Kong; very low exports to Latin America) — hardly what one might expect to be the empirical correlation of the principle of 'equality and mutual benefit'. This is of course not surprising given the trade's overall discretionary and multilateral character, which precludes the sort of bilateral planning essential if inequalities endemic in international economic relations are to be avoided, even if, as may quite possibly have been the case, Chinese goods were not overpriced by international standards. This is not to say that there have been no gains to nationals in these LDCs from trade with China, but simply that such trade has really been no more than capitalist-style participation in the international division of labour.[93]

2. *A new departure?*

Since numerous comparisons with Western and Soviet practice have been made *en passant* in the text, a brief summary only is appropriate here. With respect to the quantity of aid extended relative to GDP, its financial terms, its associated technical assistance, and its successful implementation on a project basis, it compares favourably with both Western and Soviet aid in general. The criticisms of Western aid and trade are very familiar and need no repetition here.[94] Proper appraisal of the typical Soviet aid-trade package is a much more controversial matter, and is obviously beyond the scope of this paper. On the one hand, Soviet aid has played a *decisive* role in the construction of heavy industrial bases in India and Egypt, in the survival and development of Cuba, and most importantly of all, in the industrialisation and development of China herself. On the other hand, it has often been alleged that Soviet aid has involved expensive credits to finance over-priced goods of inferior quality, underpayment to LDCs for exports which may even be reexported subsequently with substantial profits, and growing penetration of and control over recipient partner countries. Evidence from other chapters of this book shows that many of these charges are unsubstantiated or overstated. Indeed, the only ones which seem to merit further scrutiny are the charges of (i) the relative expense of Soviet tied aid;[95] (ii) overpricing of certain machinery exports to LDCs,[96] (iii) engaging in profitable triangular trade by importing a commodity from the Third World and selling exports from the same commodity group to other markets,[97] and (iv) creation of a high degree of economic dependence in one or two LDCs like Egypt and Cuba. Of these, (iii) and (iv) are still probably overstated — (iv) because the situation arose as a result of very special *political* circumstances, and (iii) because firstly, the trade may *still* have been very beneficial to the LDC concerned, and secondly, because the Soviet Union has, like China, often paid premium prices for primary commodities (for instance, the Egyptian cotton example quoted earlier). (ii) has not been conclusively proven either way, though Chandra's evidence on the very substantially higher unit prices of Soviet exports of light vehicles and trucks to the Third World as compared with the West cannot be dismissed lightly.[98] Only (i) seems to stand relatively unscathed.

In the light of all this, how does the Chinese trade-cum-aid package to non-socialist LDCs compare? Its superior financial terms have been reiterated often enough by now, as has the fact that the much greater Soviet extension of heavy industrial projects *may* to some extent offset this on the overall balance sheet. The evidence on Chinese pricing is not sufficiently comprehensive to reach any firm conclusions, but it should be noted that China exports to non-socialist LDCs relatively little of the one commodity group, machinery and equipment, over which the real controversy over Soviet pricing exists. Similarly, no evidence exists on the question of any triangular trade. As concerns pene-tration of aid recipients' economies, China has nowhere approached anything like the peak for the Soviet Union in Egypt, though evidence from socialist recipients, for instance Albania as compared with Cuba, suggests that in special political circumstances this could change.

When compared with the Western record on trade unlinked with aid, China also comes out quite well, as does the Soviet Union, primarily because the socialist principles according to which it attempts to run its internal economy have prevented the emergence of institutions such as multinationals, the instrument through which the vast majority of international 'capitalist' trading and associated investment transactions are carried out. Chinese export compe-titiveness has meant reasonable pricing in line with international levels (if not below), and Chinese shares in non-aid-recipient partners' trade have in general remained low. Indeed, in the early-mid seventies, her share in the trade of her leading LDC trading partner, Hong Kong, was 10 per cent, though this meant a share of 20 per cent in Hong Kong's imports. Here, however, it should be recalled that *nearly two-thirds* of Chinese exports to Hong Kong were food-stuffs (Table 9.3): to put it another way, Hong Kong's import dependency on China has arisen primarily from the peculiar historical circumstances which turned a Chinese city into a foreign-administered enclave located on the Chinese mainland.[99] Hong Kong too exhibits the one instance of Chinese foreign investment, the profits from which constitute an extremely important supplement to Chinese foreign exchange earnings.[100] Again, however, for the historical and geographical reasons indicated above, this cannot be appraised in the same way as would 'normal' instances of foreign investment (e.g. the US in Latin America) or some purely hypothetical case such as, say, Chinese ventures in Sri Lanka.

As compared with the USSR, Chinese 'trade only' differs mainly according to the prevalence of multilateralism: Soviet bilateralism naturally means greater balance and regularity in transactions. A second difference is that, given the USSR's much higher level of development, its exports tend to be much more based on capital goods than do the Chinese, which in principle means that they give a less developed recipient the chance to use them to set up import substitute consumer goods plants. These two factors *may* partially be offset by the alleged problems with Soviet pricing described above, but they are unlikely to be eliminated. On the other hand, it would be unfair to use the greater possibilities for capital goods' export which the USSR's higher level of development permits as a criticism against the Chinese.

Any balance sheet comparing Soviet and Chinese aid-cum-trade packages with socialist LDCs is even more unclear. In both cases, planned cooperation possibilities have materialized successfully, and recipients seem to have been able to obtain and use the aid in a complementary way.

To sum up, therefore, Chinese claims to a new departure in economic relations with LDCs must rest mainly on the qualities of her aid-cum-trade packages with non-socialist LDCs. The quantitative importance of this part of her total trade has increased over the time that her aid programme to these countries has expanded: data do not permit precise identification of its relative magnitude, but it has probably not exceeded one third and on average has been nearer one-quarter since 1961. Non-aid-linked trade with non-socialist countries has also increased in importance from being second to trade with socialist LDCs in 1961 to being the dominant category from the late 1960s onwards; although it has to some extent differed in kind from the corresponding Western record, it has differed in degree only with that of the Soviet Union, with which comparison is extremely complex. It could be argued that access to Soviet capital goods gave Soviet trade an edge over Chinese from an LDC's standpoint: this, however, would have to be weighed up with more conclusive evidence about some of the controversial characteristics of Soviet trade mentioned above. Apropos the Soviet and Chinese aid-cum-trade packages with socialist LDCs, there is no obvious superiority attributable to either side: the fact that all partners had planned economies seems to have enabled all resource transfers to have been used in a complementary and successful fashion.

3. *Better alternatives?*

To what extent could China have improved her international economic relationships with LDCs? The three most serious criticisms emerging from our previous analysis are (i) the extent to which Chinese exports of manufactured consumer goods made successful development of import substitute consumer goods industries more difficult and/or deindustrialised the handicraft sector, (ii) the low proportion of heavy industrial projects offered to non-socialist LDCs under aid agreements, and (iii) the unevenness in her discretionary multilateral trade relationships, particularly with South East Asia.

No rigorous answer can be provided to hypothetical questions of this kind, but certain considerations can be advanced in defence of China's record *vis-a-vis* the first two problems. The third has very much been a product of historical circumstances. Elimination of consumer goods exports would have immediately created substantial problems for China's international payments and so in her subsequent technology export capability. It would also have militated against the balanced trade approach to which she was so firmly wedded as a principle of political economy, and dulled the lessons which she had learned at such cost from participation in international trading relations. In other words, consumer goods exports were in her own interests, and exchange earnings from them substituted for incurring import debts, so helping in an important way to create China as an independent power in the world economy. In fact, most of the surpluses were earned from purchases by overseas Chinese in South East Asian countries, and a good deal from the very special case of Hong Kong; in Africa and South Asia, consumer goods exports were but one piece of the whole trade-cum-aid picture. Furthermore, since trade with non-socialist countries automatically precludes the sort of beneficial outcomes which are in principle possible with socialist countries, there is no point in conducting it as if it did not, given the dominance of the market mechanism in such LDCs' economies. It could be argued that more import substitution with appropriate tariffs would have been a real possibility in the absence of Chinese imports. This however overlooks the differing situations facing China's less developed trade partners. Chinese exports can hardly be claimed to have had a seriously adverse effect on growth in the rapidly expanding countries of South East Asia, while in Africa and South Asia, they came as part of aid agreements actually involving import substitute projects. Furthermore, it is just as likely that the main consequence of any substantial reduction in imports of such goods from China would, in the short term at least, have been a shift in sources of supply.

Increasing the share of capital goods' aid projects would have transferred capital and skilled manpower resources away from heavy industry in China and so again, in this indirect way, have affected the aid programme, given her overall level of development. It would also have undoubtedly affected the success in implementing of Chinese aid which has depended in an important way on the ability to use local materials and manpower. Furthermore, it would have been somewhat inappropriate given the low level of structural development and the very limited planning motivation and expertise in many of the non-socialist LDCs concerned, especially in Africa.

On the other hand, the sheer magnitude of Chinese discretionary multi-lateral transactions with LDCs suggests that there must have been scope for an increase in the negotiated bilateral component. Certainly China would wish to retain some discretionary flexibility to meet unforeseen circumstances, but even this could have been achieved in a more 'planned' way. The quantitative importance of this criticism should not, however, be overstated, since the dependence with China of most of the countries involved in transactions of this kind was fairly low; its qualitative import still persists.

B. *The Effects of China's Trade and Aid Policies*

Not surprisingly, the available evidence suggests that Chinese aid-cum-trade packages have had a positive effect on the promotion of growth and development in the less developed recipients.[101] This, however, poses a fundamental dilemma — has this process in non-socialist LDCs strengthened anti-socialist forces? The answer is obviously unclear and varies from case to case: certainly economic growth plus the creation of new employment opportunities enhances the position of the ruling elite; on the other hand, contact with Chinese aid personnel, and increased knowledge of alternative forms of political economic organisation, may well stimulate the growth of an organised opposition based on the peasantry, industrial proletariat or lumpenproletariat, despite the fact that the Chinese themselves always stay directly out of internal politics.

Detailed examination of the economic effects *per se* is eschewed here for two reasons. Firstly, despite the greater role that the Chinese have normally attempted to play in project implementation (compared with other donors), the actual success of aid projects has been very much the responsibility of the recipient governments. Secondly, the practical evaluation problems are immense — not just involving data problems, but also the question of how to identify the particular contribution of a change in Chinese trade or aid on particular variables in the partner country's economy. Discussion of economic effects in the 'trade only' LDCs is also omitted, since the dominant role of the governments concerned in determining the ultimate effects of trading transactions becomes paramount.

However, a final word on the political implications seems apposite, particularly in view of the criticisms of those such as André Gunder Frank, who writes:

> Nonetheless, when Chinese trade and aid relations with the underdeveloped capitalist countries are examined in the broader international and national political context of which they are an integral part, they appear no better — and often markedly worse — than those of many other countries. It is enough to examine the list of some of the countries or regimes to which — especially since the fall of Lin Piao — Chinese aid has been extended and the particular times at which it has occurred: Yahya Khan's Pakistan at the time of its genocide in East Pakistan/Bangladesh; the Numeiri regime in the Sudan, after it brutally repressed the bid for power by progressive officers and the Moscow allied Communists in 1971; the same year, the Bandaranaike regime in Sri Lanka at the time of the brutal repression of the JVP uprising (in which, notably, the Sri Lanka Government had the support not only of China but also of the Soviet Union, . . .

and continues at considerable length in the same vein.[102] Frank himself does not accept the de facto Chinese view that the dangers from Soviet expansionism are so great that opposition to the Soviet Union must dominate the rights and wrongs of particular political situations from a socialist standpoint, which is why his criticisms are so particularly sharp. However, although we do not agree with such a dismissive attitude (for reasons completely outside the scope of this paper), it seems only correct in a survey and appraisal of Chinese aid and trade to voice the main controversy to which it has led in international political economy.

VII. Summary

It is rather difficult to summarise the preceding discussion of China's economic relations with LDCs; only a few highly selective points will be mentioned here. Firstly, the data situation has precluded any comprehensive survey, the lacunae being particularly severe in the case of economic relations with the less developed socialist countries, but in general owing to the absence of the requisite data from Chinese sources. Secondly, no homogeneous picture emerges. Disaggregation by whether or not a country is socialist and, if not, whether or not it is an aid recipient, is essential, since economic relations with these various subgroups have followed different patterns. For analysing trade relations, further disaggregation according to the bilateral or multilateral character of the trade would also be desirable (see the formulae on p. 214 above), though it was not possible to do this in a systematic way in this paper. Thirdly, to summarise general trends, China's trade with LDCs has, on the whole, grown in line with its total trade, though there have been significant changes in its distribution, with the share of non-socialist countries in total LDC trade rising from around one-half in 1961 to three-quarters in 1973, that of Hong Kong alone from approximately one-tenth to almost one-fifth, and that of Africa from roughly one-twentieth to about one-sixth; trade with non-socialist countries who have not been aid recipients rose from just under one-third in 1961 to two-fifths in 1970 and almost one half in 1973, while trade with non-socialist aid recipients rose from around one-fifth to well over one-quarter. Aid commitments fluctuated substantially, as did trade, with a rising trend. Almost one-half went to socialist LDCs, but of the remainder there was a major shift in its distribution away from the non-socialist economies of Asia and the Middle East towards those located in Africa. Fourthly, the main observable patterns of economic relationships could be divided into three groups: (a) trade-cum-aid packages with socialist countries, (b) trade-cum-aid packages with non-socialist countries, and (c) trade relations with non-socialist countries (these categories are not, of course, exhaustive). The first has involved bilateral exchanges, grants, concessionary loans, and aid in the form of primary commodities, consumer and capital goods projects. The second has also mainly involved bilateral exchanges and occasional grants, but mainly concessionary (interest free) loans with 10 year grace and 20 year repayment periods, and light industrial or infrastructural aid projects; the pattern of trade has been mainly of the primary commodity for consumer goods variety;

surpluses have been in China's favour but have arisen mainly on account of aid deliveries. The third pattern has been rather different, essentially, though not exclusively, involving discretionary free market purchases of primary commodities on a multilateral basis in exchange for manufactured and certain agricultural consumer goods; it is from this pattern that the lion's share of China's overall export surplus on LDC account trade has arisen. Fifth, Chinese aid has by and large lived up well to its avowed principles, and is particularly noteworthy for the comparative generosity of its terms. On the other hand, the low proportion of heavy industrial projects in her aid programme may have reduced the potential benefits from the standpoint of aid recipients, though this was in conformity both with her recommended policy of balanced development and with what could reasonably have been expected given her level of development. Relative to per capita GDP, Chinese aid expenditures stand out well when compared both with advanced capitalist countries and with the East European centrally planned economies. Sixth, Chinese economic relations with non-socialist LDCs have been very much on the basis of conventional participation rather than of socialist participation in the international economy. From the ideological standpoint, her claim to a new departure in her aid-cum-trade packages with non-socialist LDCs must be weighed against her somewhat unquestioning participation in the capitalist international division of labour, even if in practice she has had little alternative. And finally, although any comparative evaluation with the trade and aid policies of the Soviet Union is extremely complicated, it can plausibly be argued that the similarities between them are much greater than the differences.

Notes

[1] This grant was made at the time of handing over the railway so as to cover the increased cost incurred by the Tanzanians because of inflation (C. Mau Fong, *China Now*, 69, February 1977). (Roughly 3·1 yuan = £1 sterling).

[2] Indeed, it seems that where such local proceeds proved insufficient, the Chinese even provided hard currency to cover local costs (see C. H. Fogarty, 'China's economic relations with the Third World', in US Congress, Joint Economic Committee, *China: a reassessment of the economy* (Washington D.C: 1975) (subsequently referred to as USCJEC 1975).

[3] His Excellency Paul Bomani, Tanzanian Ambassador to the US, *Receiving aid from China*, Paper presented to the 30th International Congress of the Human Sciences in Asia and N. Africa, Mexico City, mimeo, August 1976. On a lighter note, as the correspondent of *The Times* pointed out – it runs not just on time but at bargain prices – £5.50 (around ½p a mile) for the cheapest passenger ticket for the complete journey. (See the report by Nicholas Ashford, *The Times*, (Monday 26 July, 1976), who also notes that three categories of passenger fare are offered.

[4] As is well known, two World Bank appraisals and a UN/ECA/FAO all recommended against the viability of the project – see Appendix I for a brief history of the project.

[5] Bomani (1976), *op. cit.*, p. 41.

[6] *Peking Review*, 30, (23 July 1976).

[7] Further unsolicited testimony for both the favourable terms and the success of Chinese aid from the recipient's viewpoint was provided by the Director of the Maltese Department of Information in his letter to *The Times* (16 February 1977).

[8] See for instance Nai-Ruenn Chen, China's foreign trade 1950−74, USCJEC (1975); A. H. Usack and R. E. Batsavage, 'The international trade of the People's Republic of China', in USCJEC *People's Republic of China: an economic assessment* (Washington: 1972); W. Bartke, *China's economic aid* (Hamburg: 1975); J. Horvath, *Chinese technology transfer to the Third World: a grants economy analysis* (New York: 1976); and Fogarty (1975), *op. cit.* Other basic references on Chinese trade and/or aid include F. C. Hung, 'Foreign economic relations', in Yuan-li Wu, ed., *China − a handbook* (1973); A. Eckstein, *Communist China's economic growth and foreign trade: implications for US policy* (New York: 1966); Feng-hwa Mah, *The foreign trade of Mainland China* (Chicago: 1970); R. L. Price, 'International trade of Communist China 1950−65', and CIA, 'Communist China's balance of payments, 1950−65', both in USCJEC, *An economic profile of Mainland China* (New York: 1968); K. C. Chen, 'Relations with third world and "intermediate zone" countries', in Wu (1973) *op. cit.;* P. Timberlake, 'China as a trading nation' in *World Development,* special issue on China, 3, 7−8 (July 1975); L. Tansky, 'Chinese foreign aid' in USCJEC (1972); A. Donnithorne 'Foreign trade as a factor in the foreign policy of the People's Republic of China: in B. Staiger, ed. *China in the Seventies,* German Association for East Asian Studies, (Hamburg: 1975).

[9] Most of these contradictions were regarded as being particularly keenly concentrated 'in the vast areas of Asia, Africa, and Latin America'.

[10] For a useful (though not entirely uncontroversial) survey of all this see P. van Ness, *The third world in Maoist political theory,* paper presented to the 30th International Congress of the Human Sciences in Asia and N. Africa, Mexico City, mimeo, August 1976. See also D. M. Ray 'Chinese perceptions of social imperialism and economic dependency: the impact of Soviet aid', in B. G. Garth, ed. *China's changing role in the world economy.* (New York: 1975) and M. B. Yahuda, 'Chinese conceptions of their role in the world'; *The Political Quarterly,* 45, 1. (Jan−March 1974).

[11] Liang Hsiao, 'Economic cause of Soviet revisionism's world hegemony bid', *Peking Review* 45, 7 November 1975, pp. 18−21 (abridged from *Hongqi,* 10, 1975).

[12] Space precludes proper discussion here of the NIEO. For a somewhat different critical analysis, see Commentary: NIEO, *Cambridge Journal of Economics*, (1, 2, 1977).

[13] 'The continued fierce rivalry between the two superpowers is bound to lead to war some day ... As Chairman Mao Tse-tung pointed out, in an era when classes exist, war is a phenomenon between two periods of peace'. (Speech by Chiao Kuan-hua to UN General Assembly, *Peking Review* 42, (15 October 1976), p. 14.)

[14] Speech by Chou Hua-min, Head of the Chinese Delegation at the 4th UNCTAD Session, Nairobi, 5 May 1976, *Peking Review* 21, (21 May 1976), p. 18.

[15] *Peking Review* 21, (21 May 1976), p. 17.

[16] Thus at the plenary meeting of the UN General Assembly on 5 October, 1976, Chiao Kuan-hua stated that 'Chairman Mao's concept of the three worlds provides orientation for the workers and oppressed nations and oppressed peoples of the world in their fight in the realm of international class struggle', *Peking Review* 42 (15 October 1976), p. 13.

[17] Reiterated by Chiao Kuan-hua, *Peking Review* 42, (*op. cit.*) p. 12. This disorder is 'a good thing' because 'it throws the enemies into disarray . . . while awakening . . . the people, thus pushing the international situation to develop further in a direction favourable to the people and unfavourable to imperialism and social imperialism' (*ibid*).

[18] This position is frequently reiterated by the Chinese, see *ibid*.

[19] Chou Hua-min, *op. cit.* p. 19.

[20] *Ibid* p. 19.

[21] See Appendix 2 for a complete statement of China's position.

[22] Chou Hua-min, *op. cit.*

[23] Quoted by W. Clarke and M. Avery, 'The Sino-American commercial relationship' in USCJEC (1975), *op. cit.* pp. 510–11.

[24] Quotation from Mao Tse-tung, reported in NHNA report of the opening of the 40th China Trade Fair of Canton (1976).

[25] Li Chiang, Speech to UN General Assembly (2 September 1975).

[26] Li Chiang, quoted in Clarke and Avery, USCJEC (1975), *op. cit.* p. 510.

[27] See for instance Kuo Chi, 'Foreign trade: why the "Gang of Four created confusion" ', *Peking Review* (25 February 1977).

[28] Listed in full in *Peking Review*, 34 (21 August 1964). See further F. H. H. King, 'China's foreign aid: theory and practice', in B. Staiger, ed. *China in the seventies*, German Association for E. Asian Studies, (Hamburg: 1975).

[29] For instance in 1961 Mali had been offered a $22 million grant to finance sugar, tea and rice plantations and a $20 million interest free loan with a 10 year repayment and 20 year grace period to finance textile, cigarette and match factories.

[30] On the financing arrangements for Chinese trade, see D. L. Denny, 'International finance in the People's Republic of China', in USCJEC (1975), *op. cit.* (1975a), and D. L. Denny, 'Recent developments in the international financial policies of the People's Republic of China', in B. G. Garth, ed. (1975), *op. cit.* (1975b). Since 1968, the renminbi has been used for denominating and settling contracts with non-socialist countries.

[31] This can be seen from the constant price data in Table 9.1 and Chart 9.1.

[32] The increase represented by the 17 per cent figure is partly accounted for by the fact that in 1975, the Chinese asked that prices should be calculated at international market levels, which means that world inflation affects the figures. See C. MacDougall, 'Useful barter with the Soviet bloc', in *Financial Times* supplement on *Trade with China*, (3 December 1976).

[33] Denny (1975a), *op. cit.* pp. 656–7.

[34] *Current Scene*, X 10 (October 1972).

[35] *Current Scene*, XIV 10 (October 1976). The corresponding figures for 1974 were $US 910 million (exports) and $US 20 million (imports).

[36] *Ibid.*

[37] These figures are calculated from Chen (*op. cit.*) and do not take into account the problem of noncomprehensive coverage of trade with the less developed Asian socialist countries.

[38] Surplus on non-socialist LDC account only is discussed here because of the special factors which have dominated the surplus on socialist LDC account.

[39] Eckstein (1966) *op. cit.*

[40] See J. Wong, 'Chinese demand for South East Asian rubber, 1949–72, *China Quarterly*, 63 (September 1975). In 1953, China bought about three-fifths of Ceylon's rubber exports at a price of 32 pence per pound compared with the average Singapore price of 19 pence per pound, while the corresponding prices in 1956 were 27 and 22 pence per pound.

[41] Thus Malaysia's share in China's natural rubber imports fell from 55 per cent in 1950 to zero in 1952 when the Sri Lankan deal was made, then began again in 1956, rose to 38·3 per cent in 1958, declined to 0·1 per cent in 1964 with the growth of Indonesian purchases, and finally rose to more than half of the total during the years after Sukarno's fall (*ibid, pp.* 492–4).

[42] *Ibid, p.* 513.

[43] Eckstein (1966) *op. cit., p.* 164.

[44] It was 31 times higher in 1955 and seven times higher in 1956. *Ibid.*

[45] *Ibid.*

[46] Including 2·2 million bushels purchased in Canada.

[47] D. Seers, ed., *Cuba: the economic and social revolution.*

[48] G. T. Wu, *China's African policy: a study of Tanzania,* (New York: 1975), pp. 66–70.

[49] One initially promising source on this issue regrettably could not be used owing to the existence of a confusing error which resulted in the inversion of at least some of the columns of exports and imports (R. Sau, 'Some aspects of foreign trade of India and China', *Economic and Political Weekly,* Special Number (August 1976)). Using biennial data from 1964–70 compiled by the Institute of Developing Economies, Tokyo, Sau constructed weighted and un-weighted price indices from 5-digit level commodity data for Chinese imports and exports by country. There are, of course, limitations to the particular measures (whether weighted or not) which he used: since they only provide a price index of commodity trade with a particular country relative to total Chinese trade in these commodities, they cannot take into account the extent to which that index differs from some 'true' world price index for the commodities concerned (assuming such an index can be constructed). However, his data in Table 3 show China *im*porting substantially from and *ex*porting inconsequentially to Hong Kong – an error which on careful inspection appears to apply not only to the entire table but also to the subsequent weighted price index table based on it.

[50] On this occasion when Western buyers were refusing to pay a reasonable price for Egyptian supplies, both China and the Soviet Union bought considerable quantities at a premium price (see further A. Hutchison, *China's African Revolution,* (London: 1975) Chapter 13.

[51] See for instance Y. Avsenev, L. Karshinov and I. Potyomkina, 'China's foreign trade', *Far Eastern Affairs* (1975), 4 pp. 34–5.

[52] Wu (1975), *op. cit., p.* 199.

[53] *Ibid.*

[54] Note that the aid-disbursement ratio was quite high for African countries during this period.

[55] Bartke (1975), *op. cit.*, p. 21.

[56] Tansky (1972), *op. cit.*, p. 371.

[57] Bartke (1975), *op. cit.*

[58] Horvath (1976), *op. cit.* Unfortunately, although he wrote later than Bartke, and although on occasion he obtains rather different estimates, he makes no attempt to explain such discrepancies.

[59] Fogarty (1975), *op. cit.*

[60] Thus a comprehensive composition of the total estimate is given whereas Horvath provides only rough project lines.

[61] All such agreements with African countries between 1961 and 1972 are reproduced in full in National Chengchi University, programme for African Studies, *Agreements on Technical Cooperation between the Republic of China and African States* (1974). In Africa it has been estimated that there is one Chinese technician for every $US 5000–$US 6000 of project aid disbursed (Fogarty, *op. cit.* p. 733).

[62] Since anything approximating to complete and comparable data for socialist LDCs is not available, these countries cannot be integrated into this part of the discussion.

[63] Horvath obtains slightly different rankings, primarily on account of the substantially lower estimate which he uses for Indonesia.

[64] Bartke (1975), *op. cit.*

[65] O. Cooper, Soviet economic aid to the Third World, in US Congress, Joint Economic Committee, *The Soviet economy in a new perspective*, (Washington: 1976).

[66] *Ibid.*

[67] Tansky, *op. cit.*, p. 378.

[68] China also extended $US 265 million to Romania in 1970, and $US 58 million to Hungary some years before that.

[69] Norway has in recent years offered some untied grants, and Sweden some untied interest-free loans.

[70] The Bank's lending rate was increased to 8·85 per cent for June 1976 and has subsequently been determined by a new formula whereby rates are revised at the end of each quarterly period and adjusted to the average weighted cost by amount and maturity of funds borrowed by the Bank during the preceding twelve months, plus 0·5 per cent. See *World Bank Annual Report* (1976).

[71] In December 1975, the Bank introduced the Intermediate Financing Facility (the 'Third Window') providing terms intermediate between ordinary and IDA loans (*ibid*).

[72] See P. Chaudhuri, Chapter 6 above.

[73] Cooper (1976), *op. cit.*

[74] Horvath (1976), *op. cit.*

[75] For instance, the Tanzam railway workers were on a two-year contract, paid at the rate of 180 shillings (about £10 a month), and were not allowed to bring their families with them (Hutchison, *op. cit.*, p. 217.)

[76] Bartke (1975), *op. cit.*

[77] The formulae concerned are given in full in Appendix 3.

[78] Horvath (1976), *op. cit.*

[79] Horvath's estimates of the adjusted and unadjusted grant ratios are made for the entire post-1957 period only.

[80] Fogarty (1975), *op. cit.* p. 734, see also Horvath (*op. cit.*) for slightly different estimates.

[81] Hsinhua News Agency reports provide plenty of examples of Chinese flexibility in ensuring the successful practical implementation of those sorts of projects. For instance (eschewing the more familiar examples from the construction of the Tanzam railway), during the construction of the Kisoundi Textile Mill in Congo (Brazzaville), Chinese workers found that the 4·2 million red bricks required were beyond the capacity of the local kiln. Consequently Chinese technical and engineering personnel built sheds and moulds to make the bricks themselves, and working along with Congolese workers, produced the supply needed. (*News from Hsinhua News Agency,* Brazzaville (24 August 1969), quoted in Hutchison (*op. cit.*), which records various similar examples).

[82] Cooper (1976), *op. cit.*

[83] Chang Kuo-sin, in *The Times,* Supplement on Hong Kong (29 September 1976).

[84] Hutchison (1975), *op. cit.,* pp. 201–2.

[85] King (1975), *op. cit.*

[86] Fogarty (1975), *op. cit.,* p. 733.

[87] This can easily be seen by examining the compound interest calculations. For instance, *ceteris paribus,* $2\frac{1}{2}$ per cent interest for 10 years on a loan as equivalent to a 30 per cent tying cost.

[88] Horvath (1975), chapter 5.

[89] Bienefeld, chapter 2, above Table 12.

[90] Wu (1975), *op. cit.* Chapter 6.

[91] *Ibid.,* chapter 4 (on Tanzania), Hutchison (1975), *op. cit.* chapter 13.

[92] Horvath (1975), *op. cit.* Table 2.4

[93] See for instance the criticisms of A. G. Frank, 'Long live transideological enterprise', *Economic and Political Weekly,* Annual Number (February 1977).

[94] See for instance T. Hayter, *Aid as imperialism* (London 1971).

[95] See section IV.3 above.

[96] See for instance N. Chandra, 'USSR and Third World: unequal distribution of gains', *Economic and Political Weekly,* Annual Number (February 1977) plus relevant references cited therein.

[97] *Ibid.*

[98] Chandra suggests that this may have arisen because lighter vehicles were exported to the West than to the Third World, but the magnitude of the price differentials are so substantial in some cases that this explanation can hardly be regarded as conclusive (especially trucks, where in 1973 the nominal unit price for the third world was nine times higher).

[99] No surprise would be expressed at food imports of this magnitude from, say, Shanghai's hinterland into greater Shanghai.

[100] No precise estimate can be obtained of total non-trade exchange earnings from Hong Kong, but it is probably around 20 per cent of China's total foreign exchange earnings.

[101] See for instance Wu (1975), *op. cit.* on the Tanzania case.

[102] Frank (1977), *op. cit.* p. 339.

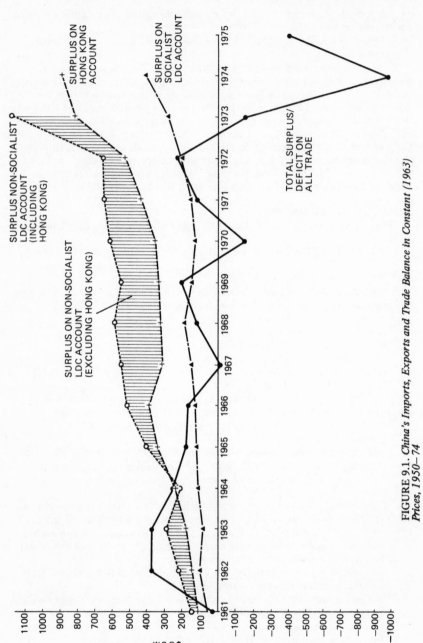

FIGURE 9.1. *China's Imports, Exports and Trade Balance in Constant (1963) Prices, 1950–74*

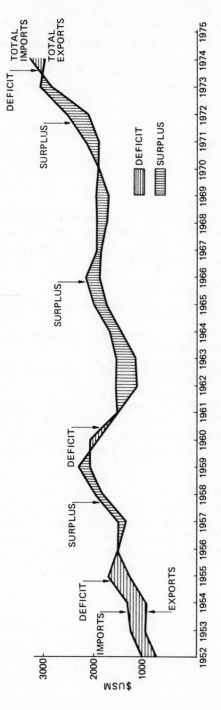

FIGURE 9.2. *China's Total Trade Surplus/Deficit, and Surpluses on LDC Subgroup Accounts (Current Prices)*

Appendix 1: A Brief Chronological Review of the Tanzam Railway*

1952 British Colonial Office survey on the question of linking the
Rhodesia railway and the East African railway found no engineering
objections.

1961 Independence of Tanzania.

1963 The 1952 report was reviewed by East African railways, but no action
was taken. The appeal by Tanzania and Zambia for World Bank financial support led to the despatch of the Sadove mission in December,
but there was great reluctance to involve the Bank in a full-scale feasibility study.

1964 Independence of Zambia.
In May, the Sadove mission advised in favour of improving the trunk
road and accompanying feeder road connections as an alternative to
the railway. Also, the separate UN/ECA/FAO mission led by Dudley
Seers advised against the rail link. Soviet, American and British sources
refused finance.

1965 UDI by S. Rhodesia (November).
Chinese offer to back the project made more concrete during President
Nyerere's visit to Peking in February, and consolidated during Chou
En-lai's visit to Tanzania in June. Tanzania accepted the Chinese offer,
while Zambia reserved her position.
The U.K. and Canada agreed to finance a feasibility study by the
Maxwell Stamp Consortium.
At the request of the Tanzanian government, a 12 man Chinese team
began work in August on a feasibility study of the railway.

1966 (Summer) The Maxwell Stamp survey reported that the railway was
feasible and would be more profitable than originally thought: the costs
per ton mile from Zambia through Tanzania would be less than through
to Mozambique and Angola or the South African ports. The estimated
total cost of $US300 million would be only $US45 million more expensive than the alternative of expanding capacity on existing routes. This
latter figure was not accepted by a joint African Development Bank —
IBRD review of the Stamp report, which put the additional cost of the
railway at $US170, on the ground that the cost of expanding existing
routes had been overestimated. Further engineering and economic studies

*This appendix draws very heavily on Wu (1975), *op. cit.*, chapter 6 —
much of which is reproduced almost verbatim in Bomani (1976), *op. cit.* Other
sources include M. Bailey, *Freedom railway*, London 1976, (and article of the
same title in *China Now*, 55, October 1975), R. Hall and H. Peyman, *The
Great Uhuru Railway*, London 1976 and 'Tanzam railway officially opened
to traffic', *Peking Review*, 30, 23 July, 1976.

were required before the Bank could make a decision (this refusal to accept the economic appraisal of the Stamp report was interpreted by Tanzania and Zambia as essentially being a preliminary to eventual refusal of the loan). The preliminary Chinese feasibility study reported favourably.

1967 Zambia formally accepted the Chinese offer of assistance following President Kaunda's visit to China in June.

On 5 September Chinese, Tanzanian and Zambian representatives signed the initial railway agreement in Peking. This focused mainly on technical matters, leaving the precise amount of China's financial contribution to be settled when all survey work was completed.

1968 The second round of negotiations on the railway took place in Dar es Salaam. Various technical principles were settled, an 800 mile route from Kidatu in Tanzania to Kapiri-Mposhi in Zambia was agreed, and three protocols relating to the form of loans, to technical personnel, and to survey and design work were signed. (A subsequent one covered loan accounting procedures.)

In view of the greatly increased costs of transporting Zambian freight on Rhodesian railways, the World Bank approved retroactive finance for part of the Tanzam road project on which construction had already started in 1967.

1969 The third round of railway negotiations took place in Lusaka in November, ending with a technical agreement and another series of protocols. In Tanzania the route was to be extended by 200 miles to Dar es Salaam. However, despite Zambian and Tanzanian hopes, no final agreement was concluded.

Announcement by Tanzania and Zambia that the local costs of building the railway would be financed by the sale of Chinese goods. This involved each country in a commitment to import $US24·06 million worth of goods for each of five years, which in turn meant that the Chinese share in imports would probably not exceed 5 per cent in Zambia and 10 per cent in Tanzania.

1970 Final agreement signed in Peking on 12 July entailing financial and technical protocols. The estimated total cost was $US 401 million, of which 17·5 per cent was for rolling stock and locomotives (as compared with the World Bank estimate of 5 per cent and the Maxwell Stamp estimate of 21 per cent). The Chinese loan, divided equally between Tanzania and Zambia, amounted to $US 401 million, and was interest-free and repayable over 30 years, commencing in 1983, either in convertible currencies or goods acceptable to China. $US240·6 million of this was to be matched by sales of Chinese commodities in accordance with the 1969 agreement.

Formal construction of the railway began in October.

1971 Dar es Salaam-Mlimba section completed in November.

1972 Workforce of over 50,000, including 13,000 Chinese engineers, technicians and supporting staff were engaged in its construction. Construction had started concurrently from three points in Tanzania, and was carried out in sections by means of mobile construction camps. Although the basic construction machinery for the rail link was Chinese, much supporting machinery — trucks, earth-moving equipment, etc — was European or Japanese.

1973   The most difficult section from Mlimba to Makambako was completed early in the year, and construction of the Zambian section began in August.

1975   In October the railway became operational one year ahead of schedule.

1976   On July 14, the railway was formally handed over after an official ceremony at Kapiri Mposhi station in Zambia. During the nine month trial operation period, it had carried 159,000 tons of Zambian copper and zinc, 130,000 tons of grain, fertiliser, steel and machinery, 100,000 tons of railway materials, 250,000 passengers, 20,000 luggage pieces, and shipments of engines, electricity generation equipment and sodium carbonate to Zaire. The Chinese gave Tanzania and Zambia a grant of 106 million yuan to cover the additional cost of the project above the initial estimate which had been incurred on account of inflation.

Appendix 2: China's Position on the Role of LDCs in the World Economy and on the Proposed New International Economic Order (May 1976)*

'International economic and trade affairs should be handled jointly by all countries of the world, instead of being controlled and monopolised by either of the superpowers or both. The developing countries enjoy permanent sovereignty over their own natural resources and have every right to exercise it and bring all foreign capital, particularly transnational corporations, under their control, supervision, administration or nationalisation. . . We support the righteous action of the developing countries in setting up and expanding raw material producing organisations and waging united struggle in order to safeguard state sovereignty and economic rights and interests; we support their reasonable proposition on an integrated programme for commodities and price indexations, and hope that the current session of the conference will reach positive decisions on the integrated programme for commodities. We are opposed to attempts to replace the integrated programme for commodities with individual commodity agreements or medium- and long-term contracts. We support the just demand of the Manila Programme of Action that an agreement should be reached . . . on a comprehensive strategy for manufactures and semi-manufactures [to] expand and diversify the export trade of the developing countries, reduce and eliminate tariff and non-tariff barriers and restrictive business practices, enable the developing countries to expand markets and secure renumerative prices, stabilise and increase

*Reported in full in *Peking Review* 21, 21 May, 1976, pp. 19–20.

export earnings . . . We support the just demand of the developing countries for convening a conference of major developed creditor and interested debtor countries to work out measures to solve the debt problems.

We maintain that transfer of technology to the developing countries must be practical, effective, cheap and convenient for use. All the unfair restrictions and obstacles to the transfer of technology from developed countries to developing countries must be eliminated. We support revision of the international patent system, the drafting of a legally binding code of conduct for the transfer of technology and the efforts to strengthen the technological capabilities of the developing countries.

We hold that the issue of reforming the international financial and monetary system should be tackled through consultations on equal footing among all countries. We stand for full and effective participation by the developing countries in the decision-making in international financial and monetary issues and in the reform of international financial institutions and their irrational rules and regulations. We support the reasonable demand of the developing countries for taking measures to adjust in a fair manner the international balance of payments deficit and to stabilise exchange rates.

We would like to express our deep sympathy with the least developed countries, landlocked and island developing countries for their difficult position. We are in favour of taking effective action in the fields of trade, aid, transport and communication, transfer of technology, etc., to implement special measures in favour of these countries, [and to] give special consideration to helping them expedite development.'

SOURCE: Speech by Chou Hua-min, Head of the Chinese Delegation, 4th
UNCTAD Session, Nairobi, on 11 May 1976.

Appendix 3: A Note on Horvath's Calculations of the Grant Equivalents of and Grant Ratios for Chinese Economic Aid Contracts

Various formulae have been derived to represent the grant equivalent (G — i.e. the difference between the face value of the loan (L) and the present value of repayments to be made) and the grant ratio (G/L), but the simplest variety in common use is probably the one used by Horvath,* i.e.

$$G/L = (1 - i/r) \frac{(1 - e^{-rm} - e^{-rt})}{(r(t - m)}$$

where

i = the interest rate to be paid on the loan,
r = the opportunity cost rate of discount expressed as a fraction,
m = the moratorium period during which capital repayments are not required,
t = the number of years to the maturity of the loan;

*Horvath (1976), *op. cit.*

and where it has been assumed that any interest rate charged during the
moratorium period equals that to be charged during the repayment period.
This formula can be developed to take account also of the effects of soft
currency repayment and of aid-tying by adding the appropriate terms as
follows:

$$G/L' = G/L + (1 - G/L)\cdot(1 - x_a/x_s) + \frac{p_w - p_d}{p_w}\,(y)$$

where

x_a = the actual exchange rate of the recipient country
x_s = the shadow exchange rate at which the donor would purchase the
       recipient country's currency
p_w = the world price of the goods to be bought with the loan
p_d = the domestic price of the goods to be bought with the loan
y = the percentage of the loan which is tied to purchases of donor products.

Despite what has often proved to be their initial deceptive attraction, use
of such formulae requires considerable care. Firstly, selection of a value
for r, the rate of opportunity cost is an extremely difficult matter in any
case: not only does its trend change over time in a fairly rapidly growing
poor country, but also it may be subject to significant year-to-year fluctuations which it would be misleading to ignore completely for some of the
questions which a measure of the grant element in foreign aid is used to
analyse. For instance, in the Chinese case there was obviously a major differential between the opportunity cost of capital used as aid in the mid-
1950s and the 'bad years' of 1961–2 as compared with during the 1970s.
This of course showed up in the changing terms on which Chinese aid was
offered, notably the increasing softness over time (t and m rising and
$i \rightarrow 0$). In other words, for the Chinese case at least, r has been closely interrelated with i, m and t. This in turn implies that even for comparisons between
beneficiaries of the grant element in the aid commitments, use of a constant
r for purposes of convenience will bias the outcome (the problems obviously
become very much more severe if the grant element in Chinese aid is being
compared with that of other countries). A second problem in the use of the
formula presented above arises from the difficulty in estimating the tying
component owing to the inadequate information about Chinese unit prices
and the frequent absence of such an item as a single 'world price' or of a
clearly identifiable 'price from the cheapest potential supplier'. Furthermore, some uniform percentage adjustment factor for tying would obviously
be inappropriate since the impact of tying varies according to the commodities purchased. A third problem arises in the estimation of any soft currency
repayment benefits as a result of the notorious difficulties in calculating
shadow foreign exchange rates.

The centrally important implication from all this is that sets of estimates
of the grant element in Chinese aid which are based on such heroic assump-

tions as a constant *r* and constant tying adjustment factor are biased, in addition to any across-the-board inaccuracies introduced by selection of percentages which are higher or lower than the true mean values. Unfortunately, Horvath's study — the only one which calculates such estimates for Chinese aid — does so precisely on the basis of such erroneous assumptions (using a constant opportunity cost rate of 10 per cent and a constant tying deduction of 10 per cent).

Index

Date Due